I0802236

E. J.

WAGGONER

To order additional copies of

E. J. WAGGONER, by Woodrow W. Whidden,

call **1-800-765-6955.**

Visit us at

www.reviewandherald.com

for information on other Review and Herald® products.

ADVENTIST PIONEER SERIES

George R. Knight, Consulting Editor

Published volumes:

James White: Innovator and Overcomer
by Gerald Wheeler

Joseph Bates: The Real Founder of Seventh-day Adventism
by George R. Knight

W. W. Prescott: Forgotten Giant of Adventism's Second Generation
by Gilbert Valentine

John Harvey Kellogg, M.D., Pioneering Health Reformer
by Richard W. Schwarz

Future volumes (partial list):

L. C. Schaefe
John Nevins Andrews
W. C. White
Ellen G. White
George I. Butler
Arthur G. Daniells
LeRoy E. Froom
Alonzo T. Jones
William Miller
F. D. Nichol

E. J. WAGGONER

From the Physician of Good News to the Agent of Division

WOODROW WHIDDEN

REVIEW AND HERALD® PUBLISHING ASSOCIATION
Since 1861 | www.reviewandherald.com

Copyright © 2008 by Review and Herald® Publishing Association

Published by Review and Herald® Publishing Association, Hagerstown, MD 21741-1119

All rights reserved. No portion of this book may be reproduced, stored in a retrieval system, or transmitted in any form or by any means (electronic, mechanical, photocopy, recording, scanning, or other), except for brief quotations in critical reviews or articles, without the prior written permission of the publisher.

Review and Herald® titles may be purchased in bulk for educational, business, fund-raising, or sales promotional use. For information, please e-mail SpecialMarkets@reviewandherald.com.

The Review and Herald® Publishing Association publishes biblically based materials for spiritual, physical, and mental growth and Christian discipleship.

The author assumes full responsibility for the accuracy of all facts and quotations as cited in this book.

Texts credited to NIV are from the *Holy Bible, New International Version.* Copyright © 1973, 1978, 1984, International Bible Society. Used by permission of Zondervan Bible Publishers.

Texts credited to NKJV are from the New King James Version. Copyright © 1979, 1980, 1982 by Thomas Nelson, Inc. Used by permission. All rights reserved.

Bible texts credited to RSV are from the Revised Standard Version of the Bible, copyright © 1946, 1952, 1971, by the Division of Christian Education of the National Council of the Churches of Christ in the U.S.A. Used by permission.

Texts credited to RV are from *The Holy Bible,* Revised Version, Oxford University Press, 1911.

This book was
Edited by Gerald Wheeler
Copyedited by James Cavil
Designed by Trent Truman
Typeset: 11/14 Berkeley Book

PRINTED IN U.S.A.
12 11 10 09 08 5 4 3 2 1

Library of Congress Cataloging-in-Publication Data
Whidden, Woodrow W. (Woodrow Wilson), 1944- .
E.J. Waggoner : from the physician of good news to agent of division / Woodrow Whidden.
p. cm.
"Published books of Ellet Joseph Waggoner"—P.
1. Waggoner, E. J. (Ellet Joseph) 2. Seventh-day Adventists—United States—Biography.
I. Title.
BX6193.W25W45 2008
286.7092—dc22
[B]
2007049812

ISBN 978-0-8280-1982-8

DEDICATION

To

JEAN DAVIS
an Adventist family historian from Battle Creek, Michigan, and

MARK PETERS
a great-great-grandson of E. J. Waggoner.

Without Jean's indefatigable sleuthing
in all sorts of nook and crannies
of the Waggoner family history,
this biography would have been greatly diminished.

Mark, an enthusiastic Waggoner family archivist,
has provided many photos
and a wealth of detail
in response to countless e-mail requests.

CONTENTS

PREFACE

IT IS WITH SOME FEAR AND TREPIDATION that I have undertaken the research and writing of a biography of E. J. Waggoner. No one who knows about Adventist history doubts his importance. Yet to attempt to define why he is significant immediately thrusts one into a historical and theological minefield in which every move must be made with the utmost care. Waggoner has always had his ardent admirers and detractors. If his earliest detractors could have had their way, they would have consigned him to oblivion. One individual, however, made it her business to give him great and sustained (though not unqualified) support from 1888 until 1904. And that person was the Adventist prophet Ellen G. White. Without her support I would most likely not be sitting here writing this biography (though, hopefully, I would be occupied with the central concerns that she affirmed in Waggoner's ministry).

With her staunch support, Waggoner, along with his longtime ministerial and editorial colleague, A.T. Jones, would forever become synonymous (as Jones and Waggoner) with the phrases "the glad tidings" of "righteousness by faith" (or "Christ and His righteousness") and the epochal "1888 Minneapolis General Conference Session." We could plausibly argue that these subjects (along with their associated issues) in Adventist history have stirred more interest and debate than any other.

Two key factors have contributed to the debate over the place of E. J. Waggoner in seeking to understand the historical and theological significance of the Minneapolis session and its controversial background and aftermath. While there have been a number of biographical sketches and numerous studies of his key themes by both his admirers and critics (especially on the issues of justification, sanctification, perfection, and the nature of Christ), there has been (1) no full-scale attempt to write a more detailed, comprehensive biography and (2) no in-depth study of all of Waggoner's major writings in their historical setting, including how the emphases of Jones and Waggoner compare to the writings of Ellen G.

White (the key authority who sought to legitimatize their basic theological thrusts).

Aside from numerous biographical sketches, the closest approximation of a biography was David P. McMahon's *Ellet Joseph Waggoner: The Myth and the Man* (Fallbrook, Calif.: Verdict Publications, 1979). His work, however, did little or nothing to add to our biographical knowledge of Waggoner. The main purpose of McMahon's effort was to critique Waggoner's understanding of justification by faith and its relationship to sanctification by faith from a scholastic Protestant, especially Reformed (Calvinistic) post-Reformation perspective.

While Waggoner has received sympathetic thematic theological treatment from such diverse figures as LeRoy Edwin Froom, Jack Sequeira, Robert J. Wieland, and Donald K. Short,* the two most detailed studies of his theology have come from Eric C. Webster and Clinton Wahlen.

Webster's *Crosscurrents in Adventist Christology* (New York: Peter Lang, 1984 [republished by Andrews University Press, 1992]) focused (somewhat critically) on Waggoner's Christology, while giving a fairly reliable (also critical) treatment of his understanding of salvation and closely related issues. The strength of Webster's work is that he did an extensive reading of Waggoner's major works (especially the vast numbers of periodical articles) and interacted with the key secondary interpreters on the nature of Christ and salvation.

Wahlen's unpublished Master of Divinity thesis, entitled "Selected Aspects of Ellet J. Waggoner's Eschatology and Their Relation to His Understanding of Righteousness by Faith, 1882-1895" (Andrews University, 1988) also exhibits an extensive reading of the primary publications (more sympathetic than Webster). As helpful as the two studies are, they are (by the nature of their subject matter and time delimitations) less than comprehensive in their attention to the totality of Waggoner's theological publications.

What this biography seeks to do is combine a serious attempt to write a comprehensive biography with a careful tracing of his key theological developments. In pursuit of these goals, I have taken the following steps:

Biographically, I have sought to gather as much detailed information on Waggoner as is possible. This task has proved to be daunting (in the frustrating sense) because of the fact that there exists relatively little biographical data of the kind that normally goes into a comprehensive biography. The reasons for this lack of data most likely result from the fact that Waggoner left relatively few letters and no diary or journal entries that anybody seems to be aware of. He was also very parsimonious in giving out personal references, both in his stenographically recorded lectures and sermons and in his published books, periodical articles, and editorials. I have sought to gather as much of these types of materials as I could find.

With the support of two research grants from Andrews University, I have made extensive searches into the files of the Ellen G. White Estate at the General Conference of Seventh-day Adventists headquarters in Silver Spring, Maryland, and their branch research centers at Berrien Springs, Michigan; Loma Linda, California; and Newbold College, Bracknell, Berkshire, England. Furthermore, I have benefited from the researches of Jean Davis of Battle Creek, Michigan; Mark Peters (a lineal descendant of Waggoner and ardent family historian); Paul Penno, Jr., of the Northern California Conference of Seventh-day Adventists; Glenda Insua of the Bentley Historical Library of the University of Michigan, Ann Arbor, Michigan; Stan Hickerson of Berrien Springs, Michigan; George Knight of Andrews University, Berrien Springs, Michigan; Michael Campbell, formerly of the Loma Linda University Library Heritage Room; Laurence Turner, faculty member at Newbold College; Roland Karlman of the Ellen G. White Research Center at Newbold College; Per Lisle of Newbold College; Brian P. Phillips of the Welsh Mission of the British Union Conference of Seventh-day Adventists; and Bert Haloviak of the Archives of the General Conference of Seventh-day Adventists.

In order to supplement the resources located with the help of the above researchers, I have also assiduously sought out biographical hints and details from my detailed reading of all that Waggoner ever published.

The above-mentioned, somewhat sketchy biographical materials are the most likely reason for the lack of a full-scale biography of Waggoner. Happily, however, such is not the case when it comes to his published works. His literary output was nothing short of astonishing (both in terms of sheer output and the variety of issues he addressed). While most of his works have been shelved in bound periodical volumes and out-of-print books at Adventist Research Centers (and thus not readily available to the interested reader), the advent of digital technology has made his writings much more readily available. Thanks to the tireless efforts of Paul Penno, Jr., all of Waggoner's periodical articles and *General Conference Bulletin* sermons, and many of his published books, are now available on a compact disk entitled "Unabridged Anthology of Ellet Joseph Waggoner (1855-1916)." I am the very grateful beneficiary of the persistent labors of Pastor Penno. His work has spared me (and many other Waggoner enthusiasts) untold hours, days, and weeks of reading from microfilm, microfiche, and brittle, dusty, and aging bound volumes (often composed of incomplete numbers).

Upon receipt of Penno's "Unabridged Anthology," I had its contents converted to print and have made it my business to read it in its entirety (approximately 10,000 pages). As I went through it I not only kept an eagle eye out for items of biographical interest, but also made extensive notations of Waggoner's expositions of important theological themes. I sought to inform myself from the primary documents on all of the major biblical/theological themes and issues that form the substance of Waggoner's thought.

Thus what follows in four sections, composed of 13 chapters, is a serious attempt to reconstruct the life and public ministry of Waggoner. But we cannot understand his life and ministry apart from his biblical and theological expositions. Were it not for his theological significance to the unfolding mission of the Seventh-day Adventist Church, Waggoner would be of little interest or significance. While his life does have some fascinating aspects, what mainly makes him a subject of vital interest are his theological contributions, especially to Adventism's understanding and proclamation of righteousness by faith and closely related issues. Each major section of this biography will end with a chapter devoted to the key theological developments as they unfolded in the four major eras of his life and ministry.

I must warn the reader that while there occurred many great moments and victories in the life and ministry of Waggoner, there were also some very painful failures. I have made solemn promises to his most devoted admirers (including his known living descendants) that I will forthrightly tell the whole story (with its ups and downs) and strive mightily to be empathetically positive, fair, and objective as I seek to present a balanced treatment of his life and work. Furthermore, I have attempted to trace and articulate his theological contributions as fairly and objectively as I can. While the reader will not always agree with my conclusions (I make no claims to total objectivity—who can?), I pray that my interpretations and critical interactions with Waggoner's thought will prove to be constructively informative and stimulating to my readers.

As already mentioned above, I have invested extensive time in seeking to read everything that Waggoner ever published. Additionally, I have sought to put all of my notations on the major themes of this thought into chronological sequence so that we can trace the development of his thinking over the entire trajectory of his career.

Though an able writer, Waggoner is not always easy to read or understand. I have, however, sought to make his thought accessible not only to the scholar but also to lay readers who have a vital interest in both Adventist history and the theological issues that Waggoner shaped.

I send forth this biography and interpretation of Waggoner's theological development with the prayer that my readers will be not only better informed and inspired to greater theological maturity, but also drawn closer to the Lord Jesus whom Waggoner so earnestly sought to exalt and serve.

In conclusion, I offer a special word of appreciation to Jack Stout and the Office of Scholarly Research at Andrews University for their generous support of my Research and to Aecio Cairus, the chair of my department at the Adventist International Institute of Advanced Studies in the Philippines, for graciously granting me extra writing time during the last stages of the manuscript preparation. And finally, a word of deep affection to my wife, Peggy Gibbs Whidden, who has willingly listened to a lot of discussion of Waggoner during the past five years.

—WOODROW W. WHIDDEN II
Silang, Cavite Province, the Philippines

*The latter two individuals have become known to late-twentieth- and early-twenty-first-century Adventism as Wieland and Short. They are, arguably, Waggoner's staunchest supporters since the arly 1950s.

FOREWORD

E. J. WAGGONER: *From the Physician of Good News to Agent of Division* is the fifth volume in an unprecedented series on Adventist biography. Thus far the series has seen biographies on James White, by Gerald Wheeler; W. W. Prescott, by Gilbert Valentine; John Harvey Kellogg, by Richard Schwarz; and my own work on Joseph Bates. Currently assigned volumes include full-length works on J. N. Andrews, Alonzo T. Jones, Uriah Smith, Dudley M. Canright, Ellen G. White, W. C. White, J. Edson White, Arthur G. Daniells, William Miller, George I. Butler, S. N. Haskell, and J. N. Loughborough. Each volume will focus on the individual's major contribution to the church and will be written by a person well-versed in his or her topic.

Ellet J. Waggoner is undoubtedly best known for his contribution to the righteousness by faith revival at the 1888 General Conference session held at Minneapolis, Minnesota. He and Alonzo T. Jones began a process that eventually gave a more visible place to faith and Christ's work in Adventist theology. Unfortunately, not all Adventist leaders stood behind Waggoner and his colleague. Foremost among their detractors were George I. Butler, president of the General Conference, and Uriah Smith, the denomination's executive secretary.

On the other side of the struggle stood such leading personalities as Ellen White and W. W. Prescott. Mrs. White stood shoulder to shoulder with the reformers in the late 1880s and the early 1890s. In various endorsements she would assert in no uncertain terms that "the Lord in His great mercy sent a most precious message to His people through Elders Waggoner and Jones. This message was to bring more prominently before the world the uplifted Savior, the sacrifice for the sins of the whole world. ... It invited the people to receive the righteousness of Christ."*

Waggoner was undoubtedly onto something important, but unfortunately for both him and the denomination his theology by the late nineties had drifted in a pantheistic direction and early in the twentieth century his personal life became complicated by his infatuation with a woman who was not his wife, his teaching of "spiritual affinity" (a belief that taught that people could have a different spouse in heaven than the one they had on earth), and a divorce. As a result Waggoner would spend his last years outside the denomination he had given so much effort to reform.

Whidden's treatment of this fascinating Seventh-day Adventist minister and theologian is Waggoner's first systematic biography. As such, it fills a much-needed gap in our understanding of Adventist history.

E. J. Waggoner: From the Physician of Good News to Agent of Division is not what might be called a "standard biography" that traces a person's life in some detail across the years. The sad fact is that the surviving records do not provide the kind of detail about the man that biographers find helpful. But the good news is that what is lacking in biographical details is compensated for by a relative feast of material on the course of his intellectual journey. Thus we might best think of Whidden's work as a "theological biography."

Whidden has made a major breakthrough in our understanding of Waggoner. Up to the present, students of Waggoner's life have had to choose between seeing some of the unfortunate events of his later life as some sort of aberration or hypothesizing that there was some theological connection between the ideas of the early and later Waggoner, but not being able to define just what that connection was. Whidden's most significant contribution is to demonstrate how Waggoner's mystical understanding of the atonement in his earlier years led him to his later theological conclusions.

We are indebted to Whidden for publishing the evidence that at last helps us understand one of the most important yet perplexing theologians in Adventist history. I trust that reading this book will be as fascinating and profitable for you as it was for me.

GEORGE R. KNIGHT,
Series Editor
Rogue River, Oregon
December 8, 2007

**Testimonies to Ministers* (Mountain View, Calif.; Pacific Press Pub. Assoc., 1923), pp. 91, 92.

E. J. Waggoner

SECTION ONE:
The Early Years

CHAPTER I

SERVANT OF THE VISION, CHILD OF THE MIDWEST, AND SON OF THE PIONEERS: 1855-1874

THE VISION

THE TURNING POINT of the Christian experience of the young adult Ellet J. Waggoner came on a "dismal, rainy afternoon" during a camp meeting held at Healdsburg, California, in October of 1882. While sitting on the edge of the main tent listening to a "servant of God" making a presentation on the grace of God, Waggoner suddenly found himself overtaken by a profoundly moving vision of the crucified Christ. His recollection breathes the rapture of vivid revelation and discovery:

"Suddenly a light shone about me, and the tent seemed illuminated, as though the sun were shining. I saw Christ crucified for me, and to me was revealed for the first time in my life the fact that God loved *me*, and that Christ gave Himself for me personally. It was all for me. If I could describe my feelings, they would not be understood by those who have not had a similar experience, and to such no explanation is necessary. . . .

"I knew that this light that came to me was a revelation direct from heaven; therefore I knew that in the Bible I should find the message of God's love for individual sinners, and I resolved that the rest of my life should be devoted to finding it there, and making it plain to others. The light that shone upon me that day from the cross of Christ has been my guide in all my Bible study; wherever I have turned in the Sacred Book, I have found Christ set forth as the power of God, to the salvation of individuals, and I have never found anything else."[1]

In the experience of many of God's prominent messengers throughout the history of the Christian church, there has come a defining spiritual breakthrough.

For the apostle Paul it was the "Damascus road" bolt of lightning.

For Augustine of Hippo it came in a garden in Milan during a profound moment of despair over his sinful life. Suddenly he heard the voice of a child from a neighboring house saying, "Take up and read." He immediately turned to a copy of the epistles of Paul that he had been reading and soon found his attention drawn to the words of Paul: "Not in rioting and drunkenness, not in chambering and wantonness, not in strife and envying. But put ye on the Lord Jesus Christ, and make not provision for the flesh, to fulfil the lusts thereof" (Rom. 13:13, 14). The incident would bring peace of mind and a deep conviction that he could overcome his sins which had hitherto so wretchedly bound him.[2]

For Martin Luther it was his alleged *turmerlebnis* (or "tower experience") that led to his key theological breakthrough on the primacy of justifying grace in the magisterial Protestant Reformation of the sixteenth century.[3]

For John Wesley it was his famous "Aldersgate experience," in which he felt his "heart strangely warmed" and that he did "trust in Christ, Christ alone for salvation, and an assurance was given" to him that Christ "had taken away *my* sins, even *mine*, and saved *me* from the law of sin and death."[4] After it he would go on to lead the great Methodist revival of the eighteenth century.

For E. J. Waggoner, his defining moment would point the way to his path-breaking contributions to the great righteousness by faith revival of late-nineteenth-century Adventism.

Waggoner would spend most of the next 20-plus years of his life making the message of God's love for "individual sinners" "plain to others." But if his life, message, and ministry are to be "plain" to us, we must drop back a few years and review his immediate family background, childhood, early education, and teen years.

SON OF THE MIDWEST[5]

Ellet Joseph Waggoner was the sixth of 10 children[6] born to Joseph H. Waggoner (1820-1889) and his wife, Maryetta Hall Waggoner (1823-1908). He entered the world on January 12, 1855, in Waukau, Winnebago County, Wisconsin.[7]

Ellet's father, Joseph H. Waggoner, was one of the more prominent and versatile figures of early Seventh-day Adventism. At various times he served the church as a writer/theologian, evangelist, editor, revivalist, periodical founder, health and dress reformer,[8] administrator, General Conference committee member, participant in the development of formal Seventh-day Adventist church organization, defender of religious liberty, and overseas missionary.[9]

Both of Ellet's parents were born in the northeastern sector of the United States[10] and as young adults subsequently migrated to the Midwest. Where and how they met is unknown, but their friendship led to marriage on April 30, 1845, in Portland, Whiteside County, Illinois. Soon after the marriage they went to Wisconsin, where Joseph found an opportunity to work in the publishing business.

During the following decade (1845-1855) the young family made numerous moves to various locations in Wisconsin. The best evidence we have for the time and location of these varied places appears in the birth records of the first six children: during the nine-year period from 1846 to 1855 the six births took place in five different towns (or villages): Prairie du Sac, Baraboo, Kingston, Packwaukee, and Waukau.[11]

While the record is a bit sketchy, it is a fair assumption that before his conversion to early Sabbatarian Adventism, Joseph's major occupation was editing political publications. His conversion to Adventism transpired in 1852 "after a period of independent study."[12] The account he wrote of it exhibits a bit of dramatic flair:

"I was a member of the Baptist Church when I first heard the third angel's message. I was a publisher and editor of a political paper. Although I knew I would have to go out of business and lose my standing in the Baptist Church, I decided to obey my conscience and accept the third angel's message. I also accepted the temperance message. Resolving 'that the Lord at His coming should not find me a slave to such a filthy habit, I threw my tobacco into the stove.'"[13]

Joseph lost little time in beginning to share his faith through public evangelism and writing for the church paper. Soon church leaders (especially James and Ellen White) recognized his abilities as an evangelist and writer and ordained him to gospel ministry (quite possibly sometime during his first year of church membership).

It was most likely because of Joseph's growing prominence in the rapidly forming Sabbatarian Adventist movement that the Waggoner family relocated from Wisconsin to eastern Michigan. Sometime during the late fall or early winter of 1855[14] the family settled into a humble home in the little town of Saline, Washtenaw County, Michigan. They stayed in Saline for approximately two years.

The three years from 1855 to 1858 were not easy ones, since they involved the tragic loss of two young children. Two-and-one-half-year-old son Ellis died in October of 1855, and the nearly 2-year-old daughter Ella passed away September 1, 1858. This woeful pattern would extend to September 11, 1864, when 4-year-old Ellsworth F. met an untimely death.

By the time Ellet was 10 he had already experienced the loss of two younger siblings. While such mortality rates were quite common in the nineteenth century, the commonality of it most likely would not have mitigated the effects on the sensitive Ellet. Thus by the year 1884 (with the death of the 36-year-old Christiana Waggoner Guyer), four of the original 10 siblings had perished, and the oldest brother, David, seems to have mysteriously vanished from his place in the family portrait.[15]

Furthermore, disease was an ever-present threat. A telling item concerning Joseph Waggoner's family appeared in the *Review and Herald* of November 1, 1864. It began by recalling the recent passing of the 4-year-old Ellsworth. The report then noted the disturbing news that "since then, four others of his children have been attacked with the prevailing fever of the season, and brought very low." We see the wretchedness of the situation further compounded with the revelation that though "some . . . had passed the crisis . . . [their] state . . . unremitting care and attention," compounded by "a scarcity of help," had so burdened the father with "watching" the "sick day and night" that he was "fast being reduced to utter prostration and disease himself."

Grinding poverty further worsened the lot of the family during this period of illness and loss (with its attendant grief). J. N. Loughborough gave the following description of the Waggoner family's living circumstances during the Saline years:

"Elder Waggoner had the use of a house and his wood free, the society there supplying most of the necessary provisions for the family. But he received very little money to expend for needed articles of clothing. . . . Elder Waggoner's boots were badly worn and his clothing threadbare."[16]

Most certainly they fed and clothed the young child, Ellet, but there wasn't much margin for financial and nutritional error in such circumstances.

The fortunes of the family, however, took an upswing with the move to Burlington, Calhoun County, Michigan, during the spring or summer of 1858. James White reported in *Review and Herald* of September 3, 1858, that the "brethren" had asked Joseph to visit "the Western field" (Iowa). White also reported that as Waggoner left for his tour through Iowa he was "worn down by incessant labors day and night, and entered upon his labors sick for want of rest and sleep. He remained feeble all summer. . . . He has preached too much, and in addition to this, had much of the labor and care of the Tent upon him, having no tentmaster."

On a more positive note, "friends of Brother Waggoner" pledged $125 for his new home in Burlington, which allowed Joseph to pay off the asking price.[17] Thus by 1858 the living circumstances of Joseph and his brood had grown much brighter.

They had a debt-free home, and Joseph drew a regular salary from the newly formed Michigan Conference, serving as the pastor of the Burlington church. The new Burlington home (still occupied as of 2007) was to be the Joseph Waggoner family base for much of the next 40 years.

THE CASE OF MARY(ETTA) WAGGONER

Certainly these were years of mixed blessings for the boy Ellet and his family because of family strife, most of it revolving around the somewhat dramatic and narcissistic personality of the mother.

Indications of the family challenges surface in a published confession by Mary(etta) that appeared in the *Review and Herald* of May 14, 1861. As this revealing communication will form an important backdrop to subsequent developments in the life of E. J. Waggoner (and his family), I cite it here in full:

"Dear Brethren: Although unworthy, permit me to address you. It is well known that I have been a thorn in my husband's flesh, and a reproach to the Lord's cause for years. I am now heartily sick of my past course. I am ashamed of the way I have treated those who wanted to be my friends. I have resolved to amend in the future.

"I have rejected counsel and grieved the Holy Spirit till God has taken it from me. I am now in the dark, and know not how to come to the light. I have not strength to return to the Lord. I want help. I regret that I have rejected the testimony given to me through vision. At times I have doubted, at other times disbelieved, and at other times *despised* the visions. Now I want to get in the place where I can thankfully receive reproof, whether it comes through vision, or any other way. Will you who have an interest at the throne of grace help me by your prayers and reproofs, that I may get in the place where God can bless me? I want to love God with all my heart, and serve him from a principle of love. I am now willing that my husband should labor in the message when and where duty calls. I have resolved to try to hold up his hands. Pray for me.

Yours praying for mercy.
Burlington, Mich.
Mary H.Waggoner"[18]

Two issues stand out in her cry for help:

First of all, it is quite possible that much of what caused Mary(etta) to be such a "thorn" in her "husband's flesh" resulted from his numerous and lengthy absences from home. Such grueling travels not only occasioned separation from spouse and family, but were very draining on Joseph. Thus not only were the lengthy separations bad enough, but when Joseph was home he was often prostrated with exhaustion and illness. Furthermore, the family's constant relocations within both Wisconsin and Michigan, the stresses of the daily care of six children,[19] the loss of two young children (1855 and 1858), threats from infectious diseases, and financial stringencies all added to the impact of the husband's absences.

One has to have some sympathy for the plight of Mary(etta) Waggoner. But tough as her plight was, she did not receive much sympathy from Ellen White.

Her public confession contains a second telling revelation that opened up some disturbing and intimate insights into her character. They were most obviously apparent in her acknowledged spurning of the Holy Spirit," which had been in "the testimony given [her] through vision." Her reaction included not just rejection, but outright disbelief that "at other times" caused her to "despise the visions." Clearly Mary(etta) here referred to the "counsel" of the Adventist prophet, Ellen White.

ELLEN WHITE AND THE JOSEPH WAGGONER FAMILY

Since Joseph's conversion to Sabbatarian Adventism in the early 1850s, a growing relationship had developed between James and Ellen White and Waggoner. The Whites had collaborated with him in sharing editorial duties at the Review and Herald publishing office as well as revival work, itinerant evangelism, the instituting of formal church organization, and various theological developments. Joseph Waggoner had been a strong support to the Whites during numerous debates over controversial issues. They also requested him to revise and edit a manuscript that eventually emerged as the 1888 edition of *Life Sketches of James and Ellen White*.[20]

The Whites had also manifested a significant degree of personal care for and interest in the Waggoner family.[21] Furthermore, Ellet Waggoner would develop a warm friendship with W. C. (Willie or Will) White, the young son of James and Ellen.[22] Thus it should come as no surprise that Ellen White would feel free to share her inspired letters of counsel with Joseph and Mary(etta) Waggoner.

What follows is one of the most painful passages in the life of Ellet and his family. I present it solely (1) to clarify the domestic dynamics (both the positive and the negative) that affected the maturation of the young Ellet Waggoner and (2) to show how such influences helped to shape later chapters in his life. Also I retrace them in order (3) to demonstrate the persistently redemptive nature of Ellen White's attempts not only to correct, but to heal personal lives (for time and eternity) and to restore ministries on the brink of irretrievable loss.

Were it not for Ellen White's letters of "counsel," the publicly published confessions of Mary(etta) Waggoner would have left posterity only guessing as to the details of her troubles and how they affected the development of her children. Aside from these two sources (the *Review and Herald* confession and the Ellen White letters of counsel and correction), we have little evidence of the family life of the Joseph Waggoner family and its most famous son.

ELLEN WHITE AND MARY(ETTA) WAGGONER: THE "SOBERING COUNSEL"

The first known communication of warning and correction appeared in a letter to J. H. Waggoner dated April 19, 1860.[23] The epistle opened with a rather general concern for the "messengers [that is, Adventist ministers] and their wives." But then Ellen White immediately began to address the "home troubles" of Joseph Waggoner. Such domestic "troubles" mainly had reference to Mary(etta), and the language of rebuke and correction is, to say the least, pointedly frank.

Mrs. White rebuked Waggoner for cursing "the churches" with his "wife, when she is in total darkness without a ray of light," and "such a body of darkness" was destroying her husband's "usefulness." Calling her a "shackle and clog," the very direct prophet then suggested to Joseph, in the light of Mary(etta)'s negative influence, that "it would be better for you to leave the gospel field entirely than . . . to carry with you death and a medium for Satan to work through."

Among other issues, Ellen White was deeply disturbed over the lack of parental discipline for the children, especially with reference to the case of Mary(etta)'s indulgent excuses for the behavior of the oldest child (David). Ellen White felt so strongly about the matter that she warned (and implicitly advised) Joseph Waggoner that he "will be accountable" for not putting the boy "under a guardian where he should have been taught industry and been under strict discipline."[24]

Mrs. White concluded by laying the lion's share of the blame for the distressing conditions on Mary(etta): "You [Joseph] have tried every means in your power to remove every cause of fretfulness from your wife. You have made every effort to please, but in vain. She is a medium for Satan to work through, to destroy your influence; and the influence of her continual fretfulness and finding fault is ruinous to your children."

Undoubtedly the deeply troubling contents of this letter were the "counsel" and "visions" of the "testimony" that Mary(etta) would refer to some months later in her published confession in the *Review and Herald*.

One could wish that both husband and wife would have followed the sobering counsel. Sadly enough, however, subsequent letters make it plain that they had not fully heeded the concerns of Ellen White.[25] The pattern of disobedient "neglect" by Mary(etta) would continue with marked consistency for most of the rest of her married life. Joseph would respond in a more irregular manner. First he would be slow to respond, then exhibit occasional, halting obedience, next a lengthy episode of striking neglect (especially in the early to mid-1880s), followed by a final stage of more reluctant, foot-dragging obedience.

The pattern of "neglect" in the 1860s, so evident in the attitudes of both Joseph and Mary(etta) Waggoner, would subsequently bear the fruit of more scandal, loss, and even starker revelations of the sinful tendencies of both spouses. Furthermore, the effects of all of this on their children (including the sensitive 5-year-old Ellet) must have been, at bare minimum, disconcerting.

ELLEN WHITE AND THE "SHOCKING" COUNSEL OF 1872

If the Ellen White letter of 1860 was sober and frank, the second letter of insight into Mary(etta)'s character and personality (approximately 12 years later) can only be described as shockingly frank. Written from Battle Creek on February 1, 1872, the letter provided one of the most painful portraits of domestic trauma to appear in all of Ellen White's personal testimonies sent to prominent Sabbatarian Adventist figures. Furthermore, we can characterize her counsel to Joseph as nothing short of radical.[26]

Ellen White opened with the direct statement that she "was shown [on] December 10, 1871, that you [Joseph] were not living in the light" and had "not been gaining strength for some time back." The initial issue concerned his self-reliant spirit, which displayed a marked and impulsive severity in dealing with others in his pastoral efforts involving "church difficulties." It then comes as no surprise that Mrs. White traced the source of his "perverted discernment and discrimination" to the "unsanctified *influence* of his *wife*." She then proceeded to describe Joseph as a "man of a peculiar temperament, which has been decidedly and unfavorably affected by connection with his wife" who "has deceived him," and played the hypocrite, "affecting *disease* and *pain* when it does not exist," selfishly drawing upon "Brother Waggoner and others wherever she is for care and *attention*."[27]

Then his longtime prophetic counselor once more rebuked Joseph, who had been harassed by Satan for not following "the *light* given years ago in putting out his *children* where the example and deceptive, lying *influence* of the *mother* would be counteracted by correct *discipline*." The children, "so long associated with the *mother*, who was a *medium of darkness*, have become imbued with her spirit, thoroughly educated in *deception* and falsehood and self-sufficiency." Such appalling influences on both Joseph and the children forced Ellen White to suggest the following counsel:

"Finally she was left to pursue her own course, following the promptings of her unconsecrated heart; then you could have been free from her and God designed that you should be free from her." Satan, however, "was not willing to let loose his hold on you through your wife." Quite obviously Ellen White is here describing adulterous behavior on the part of Mary(etta)[28] and that God's will was that Joseph not only take the children away from her influence, but that he also remove himself from her (strongly suggesting divorce). Mrs. White repeated this not-so-subtle suggestion a few lines later.

After describing Mary(etta)'s "affected *repentance*" (that "was not *genuine* any more than was Esau's") and the "*hypocrisy* and iniquity . . . in her heart," the no-nonsense prophet sternly laid out the radical path of duty: "The *law of God* and the *laws* of the land freed you from your *wife*, but this golden opportunity you let pass, and you voluntarily went back to your wife, fastening the *chains of bondage* upon yourself. When you went back to her . . . you displeased God and weakened your own soul."

Then followed a description of the terrible effects that Mary(etta)'s "whining, groaning, and drawing upon others for *sympathy* has" had on her husband: "You began to look to yourself, talk of yourself—of your weakness, your *infirmities*, your feebleness, your aches, your pains. In short, your *mind* was in danger of running in the same channel that your wife had so long been in." This last sentence would, ironically, prove to be prophetic for Joseph Waggoner in the 1880s: his being subject to imminent "danger" would evolve to his actually falling into "danger."[29]

ELLET'S SCHOOL YEARS IN NEW YORK

In the light of the radical counsels Ellen White gave Joseph in both the 1860 and 1872 letters (that is, to remove the children from the damaging influence of their mother), one begins to wonder if Joseph did finally heed the counsels of Ellen White and send the teenage (or younger) Ellet away to a safer environment in New York, where he lived with old family friends. This little-noted phase of the adolescent experience of E. J. Waggoner is shared in the recollections of Pearl Waggoner Howard:

"Burlington, Michigan, was my father's home in childhood—and remained the family home. Earliest teens (maybe earlier)[30] he attended school in Lockport, New York, while living in the fine Adventist home of

Brother Charles Lindsay at Burt (Niagara County)[31] and working his way on their large farm. The family thought a great deal of him and treated him as a son. He always considered it as a second real home."[32]

Further evidence for the speculation that Joseph Waggoner had finally decided to follow Ellen White's advice to remove his children from the influence of their mother is the discovery that Ellet's older sister Ruby (listed as "Rubia, Wagoner," "age 20") was also living in the same Niagara County, New York, neighborhood (Newfane Township) with the Harman (age 36) and Tamar "Lindsey" (sp.?) family (Harman was undoubtedly an older brother of Charles Lindsay).[33]

Could this just have been some coincidence? The evidence seems to suggest that these were definite, calculated moves on the part of Joseph to supply a safe haven for at least two of his children in the solidly "present truth"-oriented and loving families of Newfane Township, New York.

It is not certain how many years Ellet and Ruby lived in New York with the Charles and Harman Lindsay families, but we do know that they were both there at the time of the 1870 federal census.[34] What is clear, however, is that the interlude provided the setting for the building of strong attachments to the Lindsay family.

Ellet would often, along with his family (from the 1880s through the early years of the twentieth century), visit what Pearl Waggoner Howard referred to as the "farm."[35] The "farm," which later would become a haven of refuge from Ellet's highly demanding professional responsibilities (especially his numerous travels in the service of the church), was most likely the adolescent Ellet's haven of refuge from many a domestic storm that surely ravaged the Waggoner home throughout the 1860s and early 1870s.[36] And in the light of these insights, it does not seem too great a stretch to suggest that Joseph did consciously send Ellet and Ruby away to this much safer environment.

THE INFLUENCE OF MARY(ETTA) ON ELLET

When Ellen White describes the disconcerting and evil influence of Mary(etta) on both her children and husband, one could only hope that the young Ellet (who would be 17 in 1872) would emerge into later adolescence with any healthy degree of emotional stability and social sensibility. Sadly, he did not come through totally unscathed by such negative influences.

Writing three years later, Ellen White described Ellet,[37] now a 20-year-old college student and "lower *grade*" teacher (most likely teaching Sabbath school[38]) in somewhat unflattering terms:

"He is not disciplined with sobriety and I know he is unfitted for his *position*. He is altogether too *trifling*, and does not seem to know what it is to bear *responsibility* or burdens in spiritual things. The school of *younger pupils* should have a *teacher* with perfect *self-control* and *dignity*, with firm, commanding ways and good principles, one who can adapt himself to the situation."[39]

Not only do we have this interesting glimpse into the possible impact of the family "troubles" (mainly traced to Mary[etta]'s influence on her children, so evident in the Ellen White letter of 1872), but we also have some hints of Mary(etta)'s impact during the previous decade (1861–1871).

In a later narrative, written especially for children in the British *Present Truth* (1896), Ellet vividly recalled his childhood experience of accidentally killing a "bluebird" with a "rubber shooter."[40] With pitiful poignancy he described the wrenching aftermath:

"I was frightened when it came falling down at my feet, with a sad kind of little scream. I picked it up and tried to make it fly, or walk, but it would not; its pretty eyes were half shut, and it kept panting with its bill. It was a bluebird.

"I knew I never could keep it from mother; for when I have been doing anything dreadful, I always feel as if I was lost till I have told her. As I carried the poor bird through the garden, a drop of blood fell from its mouth, right on a great white lily that seemed looking up to ask me what I had been doing. Mother was standing near the back door; as I laid the bird on her hand, it stopped panting, and was still.

"Mother said, 'What is the matter?' But there was such a lump in my throat, I couldn't speak a word. Then she saw the shooter in my hand, and she said:—

"*'Did you kill that little bird?'*

"I tell you it scared me, the way she spoke. I never heard her speak in such an awful voice before.

"Then she said: 'You have stolen away its little life—it was all the life it had. The Lord loves His helpless little creatures; He gave them to us to make us happy, and He will never bless those who are cruel to them.'

"Then she put the little bird up to her cheek, and I saw her tears come. She took the shooter, and laid it on the kitchen fire, and then she said:—

"'You may go to your room.'

"I would rather have been whipped than to have to go there and just have to keep thinking. I thought of all the beautiful days of sunshine I had taken away from that poor little bird, and how it would never fly through the air, nor sing in the trees, nor see the flowers and the grass any more. And I wondered if it had a nest and little birds, and what would become of them."[41]

While the pathetic little vignette does not portray Mary(etta) as overly severe or dramatic, it does not reveal her extending much mercy to what was quite obviously a highly sensitive child. She assumed the worst, making no attempt to investigate the accidental nature of the incident. This certainly fits the marked propensity which the "unsanctified influence" of Mary(etta) inspired her husband "to deal with *severity*, when a mild course would be far better."[42]

But before we conclude the formative years of Ellet Joseph Waggoner's life, a brief review of the forces operating in them should prove helpful. They coalesced mainly around the strong parental influences of his prominent father and his troubled mother. Especially will the heritage bequeathed to him by his father prove pivotal in setting the stage for subsequent doctrinal, personality, and character episodes in the life and ministry of Ellet. Therefore, we can divide these key factors between those having to do with (1) Ellet's character development and (2) those that would shape his subsequent doctrinal/theological and ministerial developments.

THE SON OF THE PIONEERS: FACTORS IN CHARACTER DEVELOPMENT

The major factor that Mary(etta), but especially Joseph, would bequeath to Ellet had to do with their attitudes to the "counsels" of the "visions" of Ellen G. White. While Mary(etta) never seemed responsive to the "counsels" of Ellen White during the years from 1860 to 1874, Joseph's case during this period was more mixed. While he most certainly worked with both James and Ellen White (especially the latter) and greatly benefited from their support and guidance, he seemed to manifest a general pattern of neglect that alternated with some apparent spurts of obedience to Ellen White's counsel.

Ellet's early ministry, by comparison with the parents, was quite responsive to and supported by the ministry of Ellen White. Thus when we compare and contrast the role-modeling effects of the father Joseph in this early period with those of the son Ellet in his early adult ministry, what emerges is something like this: while the father was mainly neglectful, with brief periods of obedient response, Ellet was, in his early adult years, quite evenly responsive and obedient to the visions of Ellen White. Thus in his critical, formative years of ministry Ellet would transcend the patterns of his father (and mother). What would prove to be tragically ironic, however, was that the moral role-modeling of the father's last years would be replicated by the last years of the son, but with one exception. Both would receive very direct moral correction from Ellen White, and the father in the end would prove to be obedient. The son, however, would persistently neglect the moral counsels of the earnestly redemptive Ellen White. But these latter developments must await treatment in the final section of this story.

DOCTRINAL/THEOLOGICAL AND MINISTERIAL FACTORS

While J. H. Waggoner would make many interesting contributions to the theological and professional formation of his son Ellet, the following examples particularly stand out:

1. Joseph was an indefatigable writer, editor, and itinerant evangelist. Ellet would also subsequently write voluminously, serve as an editor of three important Adventist journals, and travel extensively as an evangelist, revivalist, and teacher.

2. As a theological force, Joseph would (a) pioneer the interpretive position on the "law in Galatians" as having primary reference to the moral law, not the ceremonial.[43] His son later adapted the basic outlines of this position, and it would become highly controversial in the run up to and aftermath of the fateful 1888 General Conference session (more on this later in chapters 4 to 8). (b) Ellet would also come to share important aspects of his father's basic non-Trinitarian views, which the

son would considerably modify, but never completely and explicitly repudiate.

3. The father's interest in health (he was the founder of the *Pacific Health Journal* [1885]) was most likely a factor in the son's choice to become a medical doctor and to contribute numerous editorials and articles on the subject of the relationship of physical health and healing to character formation and Christian service.

4. The father was an important player in the formation of Adventist Church organization in the 1860s and was a member of the three-person committee that suggested the name "Seventh-day Adventist" for the newly forming denomination. The son would always play a strong role in denominational organizational affairs. What would prove interesting, however, was that while the father's contribution helped to move the church in a strongly corporate direction, the son would advocate positions on church organization that tended to a highly individualistic, subjective, and centrifugal direction.

5. The elder Waggoner's concerns over the evil influence of spiritualism (he published *The Nature and Tendency of Modern Spiritualism* in 1857) appeared strongly in Ellet's numerous editorial comments and periodical articles on the subject.

6. The father had a keen interest in religious liberty issues and played an important role in the founding of the *American Sentinel* (the forerunner of today's *Liberty* magazine).[44] The son would become an editor of the *Sentinel* in the late 1880s and early 1890s and would make a major contribution to the fight against the efforts in Congress to declare the United States to be officially a "Christian nation" and to pass a national Sunday law (we will devote a portion of a later chapter to E. J. Waggoner's participation in these American battles and the subsequent struggles he would participate in in England, Norway, and Switzerland during the mid-1890s).

7. The father's work on "righteousness by faith" issues, especially in his book *The Atonement* (1868), a booklet entitled *Justification by Faith* (1882), and numerous periodical articles on the subject of justification[45] most certainly exerted a formative force on the very influential role that the thought of his son would subsequently play from the mid-1880s down to the present moment of Adventist history.

SUMMARY OF THE OVERALL TRAJECTORY OF FATHER AND SON

When it comes to matters of theology and ministry, both father and son labored closely with Ellen White on editorial matters, evangelistic programs, and advancing doctrinal clarity. Yet differences did exist between the two men. While the father, for the most part, worked responsively and cooperatively with Ellen White on all the previously listed seven doctrinal/theological and ministerial factors for his entire life (though imperfectly), Ellet would, toward the end of his career, increasingly neglect and ignore her counsels on most of the previous points of collaboration with and obedience to the counsels of Ellen White.[46]

Though the end of the story has its deeply disappointing notes, I would like to conclude this chapter on other, more positive points of the heritage he received from his father and the counsels of Ellen White.

Most certainly the work and thought of his Adventist pioneer father profoundly and positively influenced Ellet, especially in the following areas. Joseph passed on not only his interest in and emphasis upon such subjects as the right relationship between law and grace, but also a closely related concern for the subject of graced obedience. For both father and son the righteousness by faith discussions and debates orbited around sanctification by faith. These crucial factors, which found their source in the ministry of the father (outlined in this chapter), we will trace (with some detail) in the subsequent developments of the thought and career of the son. In fact, "Christ and His righteousness," and closely related issues, will become the major preoccupation of this volume as we move section by section through the life and thought of Ellet J. Waggoner. He was, in many important ways, the spiritual and theological son of the pioneer minister Joseph Waggoner, and of the pioneer prophet Ellen White.

---

[1] E. J. Waggoner, *The Everlasting Covenant* (London: International Tract Society, 1900), p. v.

[2] Williston Walker, *A History of the Christian Church,* rev. ed. (New York: Charles Scribner's Sons, 1959), p. 162.

[3] See Alister McGrath, *Iustitia Dei: A History of the Christian Doctrine of Justification, 2nd ed.* (Cambridge: Cambridge University Press, 1998), p. 196.

[4] Cited from Kenneth J. Collins, *A Real Christian: The Life of John Wesley* (Nashville: Abingdon Press, 1999), p. 62.

[5] What follows in this chapter traces the childhood and teen years of E. J. Waggoner. The

basic data (unless footnoted otherwise) I have largely drawn from (1) the family tree study of lay Adventist family historian Jean Davis (in the author's personal possession); (2) Pearl Waggoner Howard, "Biographical Sketch and Background" (Document File 236, Center for Adventist Research, Andrews University); and (3) Winona Fiebelkorn, *On the Road With Joseph Waggoner* (Bronson, Mich.: JC Printing, 1996).

[6] According to the family tree study of Jean Davis, the 10 Waggoner siblings were: David A., born March 7, 1846 (last known date for him is that he was attending school at Battle Creek in April of 1866; thereafter he seems to have mysteriously disappeared from the Waggoner family history); Christiana A., born October 10, 1848, died January 1, 1884; Ruby C., born March 16, 1850, died October 19, 1913; Maryetta (variations in spelling are Mary Etta or Maryette [according to Pearl Waggoner Howard]), born June 30, 1851, died March 3, 1920 (Pearl Waggoner Howard sets the date of her death as March 19, 1921; Jean Davis has provided compelling evidence that the March 3, 1920, date is correct—the obituary notices of the Battle Creek newspaper, the *Review and Herald,* and the *Lake Union Herald* all listed the date as March 3, 1920); Ellis E., born April 3, 1853 (Pearl Waggoner Howard sets the date of birth as April 8, 1853), died October 7, 1855; Ellet J., born March 2, 1855, died May 28, 1916; Ella Marie, born October 12, 1856, died September 1, 1858; Ellery Channing, born September 21, 1858, died June 25, 1941; Ellsworth F., born September 29, 1860, died September 11, 1864; and Alta A, born September 28, 1862, died January 9, 1949 (Pearl Waggoner Howard sets the year of death as 1949).

According to the research documentation for this biography, the only sibling who played any significant recorded role in the adult life of Ellet was the youngest child (and sister), Alta.

[7] Both Jean Davis and Pearl Waggoner Howard suggest this as the birthplace. Most previously published sketches have claimed that he was born in Baraboo, Wisconsin.

[8] See Fiebelkorn, pp. 25, 26.

[9] See Charles B. Hirsch, "J. H. Waggoner: Self-made Pioneer," *Adventist Review*, Aug. 24, 1989, and "Waggoner, Joseph Harvey," *Seventh-day Adventist Encyclopedia* (Washington, D.C.: Review and Herald Pub. Assn., 1996), vol. 11, p. 849.

[10] Joseph Waggoner was born on June 29, 1820, in Pittston, Luzerne County, Pennsylvania, and Marietta Hall on December 10, 1823, at Alexandria, Jefferson County, New York.

[11] Less than a year after their marriage the first child (David, March 7, 1846) was born in Prairie du Sac, Sauk County, Wisconsin; the second child (Christiana, October 10, 1848) arrived in nearby Baraboo, Sauk County, Wisconsin; Ruby C., the third child, came into the world (March 16, 1850) at Kingston, Green Lake County, Wisconsin; the fourth child, Maryetta (or Mary Etta, obviously named after her mother) arrived (June 30, 1851) in Baraboo, Sauk County, Wisconsin; child number five parted the womb (April 3, 1853) at Packwaukee, Marquette County, Wisconsin; and finally Ellet J. began his earthly sojourn (January 12, 1855) in Waukau, Winnebago County, Wisconsin.

[12] *Seventh-day Adventist Encyclopedia*, vol. 11, p. 849.

[13] In Fiebelkorn, p. 7.

[14] Fiebelkorn says that they left in the summer of 1850, but she must have meant 1855. The reason for suggesting that their move was during the late fall and early winter of 1855 is that the *Review and Herald* of January 3, 1856, gives the Post Office address of J. H. Waggoner as "Union District, Washtenew County, Michigan." Furthermore, the 2-year-old sibling toddler, Ellis E., died in Eureka, Winnebago County, Wisconsin, on October 7, 1855, and was buried at Packwaukee, Marquette County, Wisconsin (this information came to Jean Davis via E. J. Waggoner's nephew, Ellet J. Sanders—son of Maryette Waggoner Sanders and William Sanders).

[15] The fact is that we simply hear no more about David afterward. This strange disappearance has been confirmed by the recent recovery of the probate court proceedings that Ellery C. Waggoner initiated to settle the estate of his father, Joseph H. Waggoner. When Joseph Waggoner died, he left no last will and testament. Thus Ellery Waggoner had to give evidence as to whom the surviving family members were. The record lists David as a person whose whereabouts were "unknown" on January 2, 1913. It took Ellery Waggoner until October 10, 1921, to settle the estate. The author is indebted to the industrious research of Jean Davis of Battle Creek, Michigan, for the recovery of these interesting legal records, and photocopies are located in the Joseph Waggoner File at the Center for Adventist Research, James White Library, Andrews University, Berrien Springs, Michigan.

[16] In Fiebelkorn, p. 8.

[17] In *Review and Herald,* Sept. 3, 1858.

[18] Most certainly the middle initial stands for "Hall," Mary(etta)'s maiden name.

[19] The six surviving siblings ranged in age from the teenage David (15 years old) to two earliteen daughters, on down to the 6-year-old Ellet and 3-year-old Ellery.

[20] Arthur White, *Ellen G. White: The Lonely Years* (Hagerstown, Md.: Review and Herald Pub. Assn., 1984), p. 445.

[21] The degree of amicable cooperation between the Whites and Joseph Waggoner is immediately apparent in even the most casual tracing of the index listings for J. H. Waggoner in Arthur L. White's multivolume biography of Ellen G. White, especially the first two volumes: *Ellen G. White: The Early Years* (Hagerstown, Md.: Review and Herald Pub. Assn., 1985) and *Ellen G. White: The Progressive Years* (Hagerstown, Md.: Review and Herald Pub. Assn., 1986).

[22] The next chapter will briefly trace this friendship, which was clearly evident by their college age years in the mid-1870s. Ellet and Willie were almost identical in age.

[23] Letter 4, 1860.

[24] Some circumstantial evidence seems to justify this seemingly radical counsel. We have previously noted (note 15) that David Waggoner would totally drop out of the family picture by the time he was 20 years old, never to be heard from again (also see Pearl Waggoner Howard's "Biographical Sketch and Background," p. 1). The issue of parental discipline and the same radical counsel for the rest of the children would come up in subsequent "counsels" a decade later.

[25] As the very next paragraphs of this chapter make brutally clear, it would be "déjà vu all over again," with the pathetic qualification that things (not surprisingly) had gotten much worse!

[26] Letter 3, 1872 (italics supplied).

[27] If Ellen White is to be believed (and why should she not be?), we have here a classic exhibit of narcissistic indulgence of the first order.

[28] In letter 2, 1870 (dated Mar. 2, 1870), Ellen White rebukes her sister-in-law Mary Chase for gossiping about "Brother Waggoner's *private* matters." The expression "private matters" was Ellen White's euphemistic phraseology for Joseph's "wife's being *untrue* to him." (Italics supplied.)

[29] We will give further consideration to this sad episode in the final section of this Biography.

[30] If Howard's reports are correct here timewise, it could be that the deteriorating situation with his wife (her histrionics, severity, lack of discipline, adultery, etc.) led Joseph to take the initiative to separate the adolescent Ellet from such maternal influences.

[31] In the summer of 2006 the author was able to locate the Charles Lindsay farm and burial plot. The farm is situated at 1913 Coomer Road, just north of the junction of Old Coomer Road and Coomer Road, a spot just west of the village of Burt, Newfane Township,

New York. The Charles Lindsay burial plot is in the Harborview Cemetery on West Main Street, Olcott, New York. The present farmhouse owner shared with the author an early-twentieth-century picture of the house, and it does have every appearance of being a very "fine" home. The only out building that still survives is the stone smokehouse. The stone foundations of the two-story carriage house and other farm buildings are still visible. Some of the original interior woodwork of the farmhouse is well preserved, especially the staircase.

[32] Howard, p. 2.

[33] Information listed in the 1870 federal census. Jean Davis has done some very fascinating family history work and has noted complex ties between the Lindsay, Amadon, Lamson, and Gaskill families in nineteenth-century Adventist history. Most of these families were pioneer Seventh-day Adventists, with some even having ties to the Millerite movement and who then moved on to accept the "present truth" of the emerging "Sabbatarian, shut-door" Adventist descendants of the Millerites. They were the Millerites who eventually evolved into Seventh-day Adventism in the 1860s. The Amadons and the Lamsons would make noted contributions to the work of the Adventist Church in the latter part of the nineteenth and early twentieth centuries. As Jean Davis has perceptively observed, "Ellet and Ruby Waggoner were living in a very closely knit Adventist neighborhood in Newfane, Niagara County, New York, in 1870" (cited from an e-mail to the author dated Dec. 1, 2006).

[34] The federal census records for 1870 (dated July 14, 1870) lists "Ellet Waggoner" as located in "Newfane Town," Niagara County, New York. Newfane is the township containing the village of Burt. While the census records do not explicitly list him as being a part of the Charles Lindsay household, he is on the same census list with them. Furthermore, Pearl's recollection that he did farm work for the Lindsays is confirmed by the census taker, who classifies Ellet as a "farm laborer." At this time Charles Lindsay was 30 years of age, and he and his wife were the parents of two sons, Frank (age 3) and Harman (age 1).

[35] Sometime during the transitions of the Ellet Waggoner family from the United States to England in 1891 and 1892 Ellet's wife and children stayed at the Lindsay home. His wife, Jessie, would do some very strenuous nursing service for the seriously ill children of the Lindsay family.

[36] For documentation, see Howard, p. 5.

[37] She calls him "Elliot," which was a variation sometimes used by Ellen White for "Ellet." For instance, in letter 27, 1882 (written Apr. 20, 1882, from California to a "Brother Edwards") she reports that "Brother Waggoner [Joseph H.] is rather worn" and that "Elliott and his wife" are "not in the best of health."

[38] See the article entitled "Sabbath School" in the *Seventh-day Adventist Encyclopedia* for a brief history of the Sabbath school. This Adventist equivalent of the nineteenth-century evangelical Protestant "Sunday school" was already functioning in Battle Creek in the mid-1870s.

[39] Letter 40, 1875 (written from Battle Creek to Edson and Willie White). (Italics supplied.)

[40] Most likely the nineteenth-century version of what we today commonly call a slingshot.

[41] "A Lesson in Bird-Shooting," *Present Truth*, June 18, 1896.

[42] Letter 3, Feb. 1, 1872, to J. H. Waggoner.

[43] A position he laid out in his very first published book, entitled *The Law of God: Testimony of Both Testaments* (1854).

[44] *Seventh-day Adventist Encyclopedia*, vol. 11, p. 849, and vol. 10, pp. 922, 923. "Waggoner, Joseph Harvey" and "*Liberty*."

[45] "Justification by Faith." *Signs of the Times*, Nov. 25, 1886; "Justification and Salvation," *Signs of the Times*, Dec. 30, 1886.

[46] The final two sections of this biography will address more detailed attention to and documentation for these sad lapses.

CHAPTER II

COLLEGE, MEDICAL SCHOOL, PRACTICE, AND EARLY MINISTRY: 1875–1887

INTRODUCTION

THE SETTING WAS THE major assembly room of the newly founded Battle Creek College. The occasion was a well-attended monthly meeting of the college lyceum sponsored by Fide De Lectian, the young men's literary society. The atmosphere was electric with anticipation, as the main event would feature a debate between a team composed of Leroy T. Nicola and Drury Reavis,[1] with the opposition provided by O. A. Johnson and E. J. Waggoner.

Each young collegian was destined to prominence in denominational work, and all four were popular students with highly distinctive personalities. The contrast between Reavis and Waggoner was quite marked. Reavis was a colorful young man from the South who featured "a frontier style" and "Missouri drawl." He had a penchant for the flamboyant. The young E. J. Waggoner was, not surprisingly, pleasant, though possessed of a more serious and scholarly demeanor. The venerable Uriah Smith acted as the moderator, and George W. Caviness served as chair.

The topic to be "resolved" was "That the Ancients Were Superior to the Moderns in the Arts and Sciences." Johnson and Waggoner took the affirmative side, and Nicola and Reavis the negative perspective. The outcome proved interesting: Nicola and Reavis won, but only because "they decided to ham it up so that the audience would vote laughing."[2]

For the emerging Ellet Waggoner, this little snapshot into his college life was a telling harbinger of many public venues to come. The Battle Creek student years were to be a time of maturing that would prepare the way for a serious career in the ministry. Ironically enough, the thoughtful Waggoner would come to shun the venue of public face-to-face debate and would opt for the platform of positive proclamation—both by print and voice.[3]

THE COLLEGE YEARS

Aside from this event, the only other things known about his college years were the disappointing Sabbath school teaching experiences mentioned in the previous chapter, gleanings from a series of letters that he exchanged with W. C. White in the same year (1875), and the records of the courses he took while matriculating at Battle Creek College. While he mentioned the public debates, the main burden of his letters to Willie White involved his work at the sanitarium and his tutorials in anatomy and physiology conducted by Dr. J. H. Kellogg.

Ellet commenced his college experience during the inaugural 1874-1875 school year of the first Seventh-day Adventist experiment in higher education when he enrolled in the Collegiate Department. During the 1876-1877 school year he enrolled in the classical course, in which he took a course in "phonography."[4] Thus, in addition to the anatomy and physiology intensives that he had under the tutelage of John Harvey Kellogg, it appears he mostly followed a classical track. Quite possibly he took the anatomy tutorials as a more direct preparation for his medical school training, which began at Ann Arbor, Michigan.

MEDICAL SCHOOL

The evidence is quite clear that Ellet did go on to Ann Arbor and began his medical training at the University of Michigan. References to it appear in his letters to W. C. White during the late summer and fall of 1875 (from September until December), and the records of the University of Michigan Medical School alumni journal mention him.[5] The letters to "Will" reveal a warm, brotherly affection for and appreciation of the friendship of a childhood chum and are replete with the drudgery and stresses of student life. They also are full of interesting details of daily life in Battle Creek and Ann Arbor. Waggoner records trips to the woods to collect nuts, stories of typical college student antics, sporting contests between the medical and law students, and some interesting hubris expressed regarding the resignation of a Dr. Ginley from the staff of the

Health Institute at Battle Creek (the developing "Sanitarium"). The latter incident seemed to be in part blamed on Ellet, and the minutes of the operating committee of the institute independently chronicle Ginley's troubles (though their exact nature and Ellet's role in exposing them are not clear). We have no known sources to document how long the young medical student matriculated at Ann Arbor. But what we know for sure is that he did not finish his training there.

Unquestionably Ellet began his medical training at Ann Arbor, eventually completed his schooling, and went on to become a practicing physician.[6] What has proven more challenging, however, concerns the sorting out the evidence for (1) where he eventually finished medical school and (2) how long he practiced medicine. We turn first to the question of where he completed his medical training.

The sources give somewhat conflicting reports. Almost every biographical sketch has said that Ellet "graduated as a physician from Bellevue Medical College in New York City;"[7] yet Pearl Waggoner Howard consistently claimed (from 1956 to late 1961) that her father was "a graduate of Ann Arbor University, Michigan[8] and there received his diploma as Doctor of Medicine." As noted above, there was good reason for her to assume that he had graduated from the University of Michigan Medical School. She even recalled having a "graduation program, with the date and all the names of his class," but then had to acknowledge that she had "no idea where it can be now."[9] In a subsequent letter to L. E. Froom (dated November 18, 1960) she once more reaffirmed his alleged matriculation at "the Ann Arbor University, Michigan."[10]

In December of 1961, however, Pearl seems to have initiated some further research into the question of the place and dates of her father's medical school experience. Only this time she seemed more open to the Bellevue Hospital and Medical School option.[11] In just six weeks, however, her renewed efforts to clear up the matter were rewarded. Her investigations had led to contacts with the librarian of the New York University Medical Center, and on January 17, 1962, she received a letter from the librarian with some clarifying information:

"Your father was not a graduate of the Bellevue Hospital Medical College but received his degree from the Long Island College Hospital of Brooklyn, New York, in 1878.

"The Long Island College Hospital became the Long Island College of Medicine and later became the State University of New York, College of Medicine at New York City. . . . Incidentally, I did telephone their library and asked them to look through their school catalogs covering the years that your father was in school to see if anything was said concerning the possibility of taking an elective at Bellevue. They were able to verify the fact that your father did graduate from their school, but could give me no further information."[12]

Pearl then continued on to say that the librarian of the New York University Medical Center also suggested that it was "quite possible" that Ellet "did work at Bellevue Hospital during that time, or perhaps took the courses after his graduation." Finally, alluding to "information from Battle Creek," she then drew the "evident" conclusion that her "father did come in this category and [did] some work at Bellevue—which was connected with the Long Island College Hospital of Brooklyn, from which he received his degree."[13]

The data clearly suggests that Ellet did attend the Long Island Medical College and graduated in 1878 (with the possibility of staying on a while longer to take some more courses at Bellevue). But that does not fully answer the questions of when (and for how long?) and where he began his practice of medicine before turning his full-time attention to gospel ministry.

MEDICAL PRACTICE AND EARLY GOSPEL MINISTRY: 1878-1882

Early Medical Practice

The following facts form a framework to a somewhat incomplete picture of this period: Ellet did graduate from medical school in 1878 and became a full-time assistant editor to his father at the *Signs of the Times* in Oakland, California, during the spring of 1883.[14]

Furthermore, while the evidence is a bit sketchy, it does seem that Ellet returned to Battle Creek sometime in the summer of 1878 and began practicing medicine. Pearl Waggoner Howard claims that her "father did for some time . . . have a medical practice." As evidence, she cited a letter from her cousin Ellet Sanders who recalled that when he was about "seven or eight years old" Ellet pulled "a tooth for me" (most likely, the uncle Dr.

Ellet pulled a tooth out of nephew Ellet Sanders' jaw). Ellet Sanders then continued by recalling "his [Dr. Ellet] working with Dr. Green, who was a medical doctor and lived in the first house west of the Waggoner home."

Pearl then speculated that while cousin Ellet Sanders did not "state if that [house] was in Burlington or Battle Creek," it was most likely Battle Creek, since she positively knew that "both my parents had lived there."[15] The correspondence of Ellet Waggoner's father during this period supplements the recollections of Ellet Sanders and Pearl.

In a letter of July 29, 1878, written to W. C. White,[16] Joseph Waggoner bemoaned his circumstance of being "behind on Ellet's schooling," and he could not think of "taking either Ellery or Alta out of Battle Creek College." He then fretted that he had "counted on Ellet to help me along with them [obviously Ellery and Alta's college finances] as soon as he graduated and got into business."

While the picture is not entirely clear, it seems that Ellet had graduated from medical school and was already either practicing medicine or teaching (later in his letter Joseph argued that "Ellet better engage in teaching until the way opens further"). The conclusion that Ellet was either practicing medicine or teaching in Battle Creek receives further support by Joseph's wish (also expressed a bit later in the letter) that he would try to see Ellet "at the [upcoming summer] Michigan camp meeting."

The Joseph Waggoner letter, however, also speaks about Dr. Merritt G. Kellogg's desire to use Ellet's services at the newly founded Rural Health Retreat near St. Helena, California (the site had been selected in the summer of 1877 and construction had begun in January of 1878).[17] In reference to the possibility of Ellet's going to St. Helena, Joseph speculated that "it would take an advance of some means to get him to California, if he was needed there, which he is not at present." Joseph had tried to take a neutral position on whether Ellet should go to St. Helena.[18] Yet this was not to be the last of the matter.

In a later letter to W. C. White, dated February 5, 1879, Joseph said "they [Merritt Kellogg and staff] are pulling very hard for Ellet to come to St. Helena. I have not said a word to influence him either way. He says he loves to preach, and also loves the practice of medicine (or Hygienics)."[19] This last line gives a clue as to what was to come for Ellet Waggoner.

While the young physician was most likely practicing and teaching in Battle Creek soon after his graduation from medical school in New York City, he was already receiving urgent overtures from northern California to help out with the newly founded medical program at St. Helena. Yet he was clearly struggling with two dilemmas: the first was marriage, and the second arose out of persistent impressions that would radically change his vocational direction. The first "dilemma" would be settled in 1879, but the latter would not be resolved until sometime later in 1882 or early 1883.

And what was the latter dilemma? While the first related to love for a woman; the latter related to his love for both preaching and the practice of medicine.[20]

Marriage, Iowa Ministry, and the Move to California

During his year(s) as a student at Battle Creek College, Ellet had become acquainted with an attractive and talented 17-year-old girl from Iowa by the name of Jessie Fremont Moser.[21] While we have no record of correspondence between the two or references to their friendship by others, there must have been a courtship in flower from sometime during the college years, through the medical school years, and into the months of his early practice in Battle Creek. It led to their marriage on March 30, 1879, in Sigourney, Keokuk County, Iowa.[22]

At this stage of the narrative we are left with somewhat sketchy but helpful documentation as to where the newlyweds spent the next 15 months. Jessie's recollections of the work that occupied the young couple from the month of April to at least the early winter of 1879 appear in an October 17, 1923, letter to H. H. Cobban (in reference to her application for retirement support from the General Conference of Seventh-day Adventists): "Soon after [marriage], we went with Elder Ira J. Hankins and wife to conduct tent meetings in Birmingham and Farmington, Iowa. . . . We lived in a tent. I helped with the singing, visiting, and working for souls."[23]

After the months of evangelism with the Hankinses, the newlyweds returned briefly to Battle Creek sometime in the late winter or early spring of 1880. In a letter from James White in Battle Creek, to Ellen White, dated March 31, 1880, he revealed that Ellet and Jessie were in the city and were in the process of making the decision to go to California: "Dr. E. Waggoner and wife are here . . . The Doctor wants a job and looks to me for advice. I shall take them right in and set them to work for their board until the way opens for them elsewhere. The Doctor has a nice little wife, and I cannot see why they could not do well at the institution at St. Helena."[24] Thus it is quite clear that at least until March 31, 1880, Ellet and Jessie remained in Battle Creek.

The 1880 federal census contains the final piece of clear evidence that the contemplated move to northern California did take place. These records explicitly confirm that "Ellet J. Waggoner" resided with his wife "Jessie F." in "Saint Helena, Napa (county), California." Furthermore, the document lists Ellet as a "physician" and Jessie as "keeping house." The date this census was recorded was June 24, 1880. Thus it is abundantly evident that by June of 1880 the young couple were "keeping house" and practicing medicine on the West Coast at St. Helena.

Putting together the facts thus far presented paves the way for a plausible summary explanation of the locations of Ellet and Jessie from the latter months of 1878 to late June of 1880.

Most likely Ellet had begun practicing medicine or teaching (or a combination of both) upon his return to Michigan, soon after his graduation from medical school in the spring and summer of 1878. We know from the observations of his father that he was (1) being quite actively recruited to practice medicine at the newly founded Rural Health Retreat in northern California and that (2) Ellet was somewhat conflicted over whether he should practice medicine (which he and his father had spent considerable time, effort, and money to train for) or respond to a developing conviction that God had called him to preach.[25]

Furthermore, we know that he married Jessie F. Moser in Sigourney, Iowa, on March 30, 1879. Soon after the wedding Ellet and Jesse did a stint of ministry (mainly evangelism in the form of lecture series and revivals) in southeastern Iowa sometime during the period from the spring of 1879 until late 1879 or early 1880. They then returned to Battle Creek for a relatively short visit before making the long-contemplated move to California by June of 1880. Finally, we know that from June of 1880 until sometime late in 1882 Ellet would mainly pursue the practice of medicine at the Rural Health Retreat in St. Helena.

The events that ensued in the environs of St. Helena and Healdsburg, California, during those two years of medical practice formed the backdrop to Ellet's complete switch from medicine to full-time religious ministry and a steady rise to prominence in denominational service.

EARLY FULL-TIME MINISTRY: RISE TO DENOMINATIONAL PROMINENCE: 1883-1887

Ellet Waggoner's remarkable vision of Christ at the Healdsburg camp meeting in October of 1882 most certainly was the key turning point in his transition from a career in medicine to full-time gospel ministry.[26] While the transition would take a few months to a year, by the spring of 1883 he had begun assisting his father in editing the *Signs of the Times,* published at the Pacific Press in Oakland, California.[27]

During the transition he spent some months in ministry in northern California, including preaching tours with W. C. Grainger[28] and teaching at Healdsburg College. The teaching ministry at Healdsburg continued intermittently until at least 1886 (in addition to his unfolding editorial responsibilities at the Pacific Press).[29] The preaching tours became more numerous with his rise to prominence because of his editorial position at the *Signs of the Times.*

While the documentation is quite scarce, we have good evidence that during the years from 1883 to October of 1890 Ellet pastored the Oakland Seventh-day Adventist Church.[30] While the record is scant on his pastoral labors, they were most likely faithful and most certainly added extra burdens to an already-overworked man.

From the years of the mid-1880s until the fabled General Conference session of 1888, Ellet made numerous speaking and teaching appearances at camp meetings[31] and other conference convocations up and down the West Coast of the United States. He found great satisfaction in his ministry on the camp meeting circuit, and his very positive reports also reveal some important aspects of it.

In a published account of the California camp meeting (October 1886) he related that "the most encouraging feature was that almost from the first, individuals at the meetings in various parts of the camp would with tears of joy praise God for the blessings of sins forgiven. There was marked evidence throughout the meeting that the Spirit of the Lord was working."[32] Undoubtedly the Christ-centered messages that began to flow from his voice and pen in the aftermath of the October 1882 Healdsburg camp meeting vision were having their positive effects. Also, his Christ-centered emphasis included a stress on the forgiving grace of God—a note not receiving much emphasis from the law-centered focus of much Adventist preaching during this period.[33]

Evidence also suggests that his activities during the transition months (or years) from Healdsburg to Oakland included some less glamorous, more humble public work. Jessie later recalled that while she worked for $9 a week doing proofreading for the Pacific Press (claiming that it was "all we had to live on for awhile"), her husband would be out "canvassing for [the] 'Home Hand Book.'"[34]

Rise to Prominence in Church Assemblies

In addition to Ellet's demanding editorial duties, his itinerant speaking appointments, his selling books door to door, and his teaching at Healdsburg College and pastoral work in the Oakland church, these years witnessed the rise of both Ellet and Jessie to positions of influence in which they would play more prominent roles in important convocations and ministries of the growing Seventh-day Adventist organization.

The first major assembly that we have a record of his attendance at was the twenty-fifth annual session of the General Conference, which convened at Battle Creek on Thursday, November 18, 1886. The *Signs of the Times* reported that E. J. Waggoner had been appointed to serve on the "Resolutions Committee."[35] Not much else was reported publicly from this General Conference session, but we will come back to the 1886 and 1887 General Conference sessions in the next section of our story, because during those two sessions the debate over the "law in Galatians" would rise to fever pitch—a debate in which E. J. Waggoner played an important role. While his appointment to the Resolutions Committee does evidence his growing public presence in the assemblies of the Adventist Church, the appointment was only the tip of the iceberg of his involvement that would eventually catapult Ellet into the midst of important, path-breaking theological controversies.

The last General Conference session of this period was the twenty-sixth annual session that convened in Waggoner's hometown of Oakland.

It began at the Seventh-day Adventist church on the corner of Brush and Twelfth streets on November 13, 1887. Once again, Waggoner was a delegate[36] and served on the Resolutions Committee. The assignment would bring to his attention a number of important concerns that would come to occupy a great deal of the young editor's thought and time.

The first telling item of interest was the resolution that proclaimed "that we will, by the help of God, strive as never before to heed the injunction of the Scriptures, 'Be ye holy, for I am holy,' and so separate ourselves from all sin and impurity of heart and life, that the divine counsel may guide, and the divine power attend, all our efforts."[37]

Furthermore, the session's resolutions 4 and 9 came in for special consideration. They concerned the pressing issues of the rising crisis in matters relating to religious liberty. The delegates referred the two resolutions to a special committee of nine.

Waggoner then reported that the special committee had given consideration to "the whole subject broached" by these two resolutions in order to "frame a resolution defining our relation to the work of National Reform and to Sunday laws. The committee were also to plan for a daily class for instruction in National Reform principles and how to oppose them." The report went on to note that both A. T. Jones and E. J. Waggoner had been named to the "said committee,"[38] as a number of the "resolutions" considered and voted reflected concerns that were beginning to preoccupy these young preacher/editors.

Subsequent actions of the 1887 General Conference session also witnessed to the growing influence of not only Ellet, but also revealed that Jessie's talents had begun attracting attention. The delegates elected Ellet to the executive committee of the "International Sabbath School Association,"[39] and at a subsequent "very interesting meeting of the International Sabbath School Association" "Mrs. Jessie F. Waggoner gave an interesting talk upon the subject . . . 'Teachers and Teaching.'"[40]

One further action taken at a later meeting of the International Sabbath School Association was to change the constitution "so as to make unnecessary the election of a publishing committee, and to allow the election of a corresponding secretary."[41] The General Conference session of 1888 would elect Jessie the "corresponding secretary" of the International Sabbath School Association.[42]

One last voted action of the 1887 General Conference session (which further spotlighted the rising influence of E. J. Waggoner) was his appointment to membership on the newly formed "Book Committee, whose duty it shall be to labor for the improvement and wider circulation of our denominational literature." The composition of this important committee reflected the growing tensions over such issues as the law in Galatians and new interpretive positions on the book of Daniel. Other names listed on this committee were George I. Butler, Uriah Smith, and W. C. White—all of whom (along with Ellet) would emerge as major protagonists in subsequent developments that would prove explosive at and following the critical 1888 Minneapolis Conference session.

One final recorded indication of Ellet's growing recognition was his selection by the "California Conference Committee" to provide help for the upcoming "week of prayer." Not only was 1887 closing on a note of editorial, revival, theological, and denominational policy prominence for the young ministerial couple, but it was also apparent that Ellet was a rising star of spiritual influence.[43]

EARLY FULL-TIME MINISTRY: THE FAMILY MAN

The period of transition from medicine in St. Helena to a full-time religious ministry based in Oakland (fall of 1882 to spring of 1883) also witnessed some important family transitions. On November 26, 1882, Ellet and Jessie had the first of their three children, a girl they named Bessie. Most likely Bessie was born in St. Helena. The second child, Pearl, entered the world on February 27, 1885, in Oakland. According to Pearl, she was born at home (which she would later distinctly recall as being located at 1465 Castro Street). The last child was a son named Ernest Eugene who tragically passed away on May 20, 1889, at age "nine months and eight days."[44]

Pearl's recollections of life in the Waggoner household in Oakland were mostly pleasant. There was, however, one notable downside to their domestic circumstances, though it is not clear whether it was the home in St. Helena at the time of Bessie's birth, or the later home in Oakland. The family had an extremely smoky stove that Pearl firmly believed contributed to the lifelong visual complications of her sister Bessie (she had to wear "glasses from about the time she was six").[45]

Ellet's youngest daughter fondly remembered his "reading, singing, rocking us, etc., and helping us with verses." But there were also memories of more serious discussions that preoccupied the family circle—such as the persecutions of "Sabbathkeepers down in the southern states" and "earnest" discussions of the issues revolving around the mounting righteousness by faith revival. Pearl claimed that "small" though she was, she clearly recalled "much that was said about 'righteousness by faith'—and the scriptures quoted by my father. He was very much in earnest."[46] Quite obviously, Ellet's attention to such issues did not limit itself to the pages of his publications or to his public presentations. They became a part of everyday family life.

The family circle, however, had not only its rousing discussions of leading issues, but also its stresses. Not only was Ellet very busy in writing, editing, teaching at Healdsburg College, itinerant preaching, pastoring, and participating in the councils of the rapidly expanding Adventist Church, but Jessie was also quite busy with her proofreading, doing copy work for W. C. White,[47] involvement in the local Sabbath school, and numerous responsibilities with the California and International Sabbath school associations. The times for domestic tranquillity must have been very precious. But still another factor further complicated the situation.

While the Waggoner family seemed to enjoy quite good health, they did endure notable spates of illness (in addition to the sight problems of Bessie and the later untimely death of little Eugene). While Ellet had been teaching at Healdsburg in late 1885 and doing double duty at Oakland (because of the absence of many who had gone to meetings in Battle Creek), he apparently contracted a rather serious disease. A report appearing in the *Signs of the Times*, January 7, 1886, stated that "while there is general good health at the office, we are very sorry to find our efficient assistant 'E. J. W.' prostrated with 'brain fever.'[48] He has overworked in our absence, and was taken down the day we left Battle Creek, and is not able to sit up."[49]

Though Waggoner would recover from this bout with "brain fever," his proclivity to overwork would become an issue that would not only occasionally affect his health in the Oakland years, but continue for the balance of his public career in ways that would not always bear positive fruit. Overall, however, the reported bouts with disease for Ellet and Jessie would be relatively sporadic.

The extended family circle included two other notable components. The first consisted of both sets of grandparents. Though neither set lived directly with the family, they exerted an important social influence on Ellet's domestic scene. It is, however, very interesting that Pearl recalled almost nothing about Grandpa and Grandma Waggoner, but did express warm recollections of "my grandpa and grandma Moser" (Jessie's parents), who "lived just around the corner from the Press, in an upstairs apartment." She then added the revealing note that she knew the Mosers "much the best, of my grandparents."[50]

The reasons for the somewhat noticeable neglect of the paternal grandparents most certainly were hinted at in certain delicate issues involving the second significant family component—Ellet's youngest sister, Alta.[51] According to Pearl, "Aunt Alta" would live with Ellet and Jessie "from [her] earliest recollections," both in Oakland and in London, until sometime after her marriage in England.[52]

The issues related to the family stresses hinted at in Pearl's almost total lack of recollection of the paternal grandparents (Joseph and Maryetta Waggoner) would unfold in the counsel that Ellen White gave to Alta Waggoner regarding the nurture and care of her and Ellet's troubled and needy father.

In a rather sober and pointed letter sent to the 23-year-old Alta, Ellen White shed some revealing insights into the characters of both sister and brother. At the time the letter arrived from Ellen White (who wrote from Europe in April of 1886), Alta was living in Oakland and working at the Pacific Press. It is not totally clear from its context, or from other evidence, whether she resided at the Oakland home of her parents or with her brother Ellet and his family.[53] The context of the letter, however, suggests that she was most likely already with Ellet and his family, not with her parents.

What stands out in this letter were the ongoing negative effects in the young lives of Ellet and Alta by their self-absorbed mother and their father's indecisive reactions to the counsels that Ellen White had given him regarding Mary(etta)'s woeful attitudes and behavior. Joseph's neglect of, and halting obedience to, Mrs. White's counsels would contribute significantly to a harvest of woe for Joseph's own legacy and provide a foreboding harbinger of the later domestic distress of his most prominent son and daughter-in-law.

The central issue of Mrs. White's letter concerned her counsel that both Alta and Ellet should have made a serious effort to make "a pleasant *home*" for their "father"—the one who had "helped and planned and worked for" them.[54] She admonished them that they "should have in return" requited his "*love*, sympathy, and attention." And why was Ellen White so deeply concerned about their father's situation?

The answer was very direct—because "his life has been a disappointment, and you have not tried, as it was your duty, to make up for this lack."

When one ponders all of the Ellen White counsels to Joseph Waggoner (through many years), one receives the definite impression that she was very persistent in seeking to redeem the tragic domestic situation in which Waggoner had been so long ensnared, restore his denominational influence, and extend his ministry. And since we have little evidence that his wife had made any progress, Ellen White felt free to strongly suggest the duty and the responsibility of Alta and Ellet to alleviate his trying domestic circumstances.[55]

Most certainly two things were in play: (1) Mary(etta) was still living with Joseph, but had made little or no change that would bring any happiness to her husband, and (2) that Joseph was already deeply involved in a compromising social situation.[56]

In this apparently unrelieved atmosphere Ellen White's persistent efforts to mitigate Joseph Waggoner's sad circumstances seemed to have reached hand-wringing proportions. She told Alta that her father "needs the sympathy, the love, and the affection of his *children* which he has not had as he deserves."

What is interesting for our biographical purposes, however, was the way that she portrayed the "serious defects in" the "characters" of J. H. Waggoner's neglectful adult children. Mrs. White faulted Alta for being "selfish, thinking and planning" only for herself and being in a "state of supreme *self-love*" that produced "selfish plans," further compounded by a "peevish, irritable spirit." Ellet did not come in for as much rebuke as Alta, but he was clearly characterized as being "at fault" for his "neglect" of the plight of his needy and struggling father.[57]

What is sadly evident in this language of rebuke was the similarity of the character traits of Ellet and Alta to those of their mother—especially the narcissistic "neglect" (attributed to both children) and "supreme self-love," spiced with the unflattering description of a "peevish, irritable spirit" (more particularly applicable to Alta). Most certainly the years of Mary(etta)'s influence had borne hauntingly similar fruit in the lives of her adult children.

One further factor that sheds some light on the dynamics of the Waggoner family during the Oakland years was Ellen White's reaction to J. H. Waggoner's "treatment" of a certain individual conducting a rather "genuine" "revival at Healdsburg." The central issue seemed to have revolved around the suspected specter of "fanaticism." In a letter addressed to J. H. Waggoner, J. N. Loughborough, A. T. Jones, and E. J. Waggoner, the Adventist prophet acknowledged that while the threat of fanaticism was quite real, she strongly felt "there were deep movings of the Spirit of God" in the meetings under discussion.

What had apparently transpired was that Elder E. P. Daniels had been leading the revival, but had made some "mistake(s)" by not moving "wisely in all things" and as a result certain of the addressees of Mrs. White's letter had become overly critical of Daniels. Her pained reaction to their excessive negative reaction was quite pointed: "If Elder Daniels erred in some things, who of you dared to tell him to preach no more? Who of you dared to stop the work because in your finite judgment everything did not appear to meet your ideas?"[58]

She then became quite explicit in identifying the source of most of the overwrought criticism. "I wish you could see what a delicate, dangerous matter it is to meddle with the work of God unless you have light from heaven to guide you in your decisions. I have not the confidence in Elder J. H. Waggoner's judgment in these matters that you have." She then proceeded to elaborate on Waggoner's obvious character deficiencies during this period: "I know that he needs his soul as well as lips touched with live coals from off the altar, that shall refine and purify the uncleanness from his lips and soul."[59]

While the prophet seemed to be quite hard on the elder Waggoner, the current letter was very much in the same vein as many others that she had written to him during previous years. Furthermore, it was also part and parcel of her ongoing attempts to salvage his ministry at a time when his attitudes and behavior bordered on the scandalous.

What, however, proves quite interesting for our story were Ellen White's views on Ellet's role in the matter. Summing up J. H. Waggoner's sad state of mind and heart, she declared that she had "no confidence in Elder [J. H.} Waggoner's decisions or feelings." She then adds the further observation that "his son [Ellet] would naturally take his view of the case and seek to make his decisions appear true and righteous, because these decisions must be maintained."[60]

What should we make of these somewhat episodic, but repetitive criticisms that Ellen White directed to the young E. J. Waggoner?

First let's briefly review the litany of critiques. She had not expressed a very high opinion of his stability in the setting of the work he did in the Sabbath school at Battle Creek during his college years. One could chalk that up to youthful inexperience. But then came these latter two cases during the Oakland years: the sad neglect of the needs of his forlorn and failing father and then his unsanctified sympathy with his father's misguided criticisms of the Healdsburg revival. Furthermore, in 1886 and 1887 she will once again take him to task for failures in judgment in the unfolding debate over the "law in Galatians." We, however, must point out that on this latter issue, not only did Waggoner come in for criticism, but so did his opponents (more on the debate in the next section). Nonetheless, she did add the law in Galatians criticism of his judgment to her counsel to him. So how should we understand Ellen White's unflattering and critical observations?

Probably the best suggestion is that there was nothing very telling regarding future developments in Waggoner's life and ministry except the following two points:

1. Ellen White was always interested in the welfare of the Waggoner family. Both she and her husband had rather patiently and redemptively sought to give them whatever counsel they thought would bring appropriate reform. Such counsels would continue for Ellet for the rest of his ministry in the Adventist denomination. But the counsels of criticism would be sparse when compared to what his parents received. And they would become theologically and ethically pointed only quite late in his denominational service. It seems, however, that the second point is the most telling.

2. We must contrast this somewhat repetitive criticism of Ellet with

her hearty and sustained support that he would receive from her at the Minneapolis session and in the following 12-plus years. In other words, the issues involved in the later message of Waggoner were so important to Ellen White that she would not allow any possible lingering, negative predispositions to cause her to significantly hold back her support for the young revivalist/editor and his coworker, A. T. Jones. We will certainly want to assess this strong support. Suffice it to say that at this juncture it was not only a bit surprising but remarkable and sustained.

SUMMARY OF THE EARLY YEARS

During the years from 1874 to the end of 1887 the life of Ellet Waggoner gave every indication of being on the fast track to fulfillment. This span of 13 years began with college, ran on to medical school, flowed seamlessly into medical practice, some explorations of evangelistic ministry, marriage (and children), and then quite precipitately turned toward a role in ministry that would lead to a position of responsibility and influence that very few others had or ever would exercise in the Seventh-day Adventist Church. Most certainly these were years of preparation and significant accomplishment that proved to be promising anticipations of surprising and remarkable things to come.

When one reflects on the events of the 13 years between his college experience and his rise to a prominent place in the Adventist Church, it certainly has its singularly notable aspects. While undoubtedly the young Ellet Waggoner had "social location" advantages, most certainly other elements aided his rise to a position of key influence. While it did not hurt to be the son of a prominent Adventist pioneer, have close associations with the James and Ellen White family and other notables (such as Dr. John Harvey Kellogg), receive a college education and medical school training (opportunities granted to relatively few in the late nineteenth century), additional factors contributed to his noteworthy rise.

Most certainly they included a dedicated development of abundant native talent and spiritual gifts, penchants for hard work and multitasking, and the wise choice of a talented, dedicated wife. Yet these latter gifts also contained harbingers of sadness to come.

Abundant and extensive though Ellet's labors were during these years of ascendancy, they would also portend a pattern that would bear tragic fruit down the road. When one ponders his prodigious editorial labor, combined with teaching at Healdsburg College, numerous preaching tours up and down the West Coast, the growing committee assignments and pastoral duties in Oakland during the later years of the 1880s, one wonders how one man could have had the time and energy to spread himself so widely.

Yet these patterns would not change, and such prodigious multitasking would continue for the balance of Ellet Waggoner's public career in the Seventh-day Adventist Church. Sadly, the workload would eventually take its toll on the ministry and domestic life of this gifted young individual.

But who could anticipate such a tragic denouement during his seemingly providential rise to prominence? Yet these portents and their disappointing manifestations should not take away from what the Lord intended for this talented and dedicated young man and his immediate and extended family.

Thus when one takes seriously Ellet's life-changing, visionary experience with the exalted Christ at the 1882 Healdsburg camp meeting and the inspired messages of support that would come from the voice and pen of Ellen G. White, there has to be a providential element in the life of Ellet Joseph Waggoner.

Of course, to one degree or another, every believing Christian should have such providential privileges. But in Waggoner's case the opportunities that opened before him were most unusual. He (along with his newfound coeditor, A. T. Jones, and with the strong encouragement and support of Ellen White) would begin to proclaim "glad tidings" that sought to bring the three angels' messages to full theological maturity. Yet even that was not an end in and of itself! It had one main goal—to usher in the long-anticipated "loud cry" of end-time mission success for God's remnant people.

But before we turn to these exciting and controversial developments, which would directly lead up to and then flow forth from the great 1888 Minneapolis General Conference session and its subsequent revival of righteousness by faith, we need to turn our attention more directly to Waggoner's theological development during these early years.

In the next chapter we will begin to trace those ideas that would form the framework for and the heart of Waggoner's proclamation of the "glad tidings" of "Christ and His righteousness."

---

[1] See "Reavis, Drury Webster," Seventh-day Adventist Encyclopedia, vol. 11, p. 421.

[2] The incident appears in Meredith Jones Gray, *As We Set Forth: Battle Creek College and Emmanuel Missionary College,* Andrews Heritage (Berrien Springs, Mich.: Andrews University, 2002), vol. I, p. 21.

[3] In correspondence with W. C. White during the same year (letters from E. J. Waggoner to W. C. White, Apr. 1 and May 9, 1875 [Ellen G. White Estate letter files]), Ellet revealed a lively appreciation of the public debate format, both for young men and women.

[4] According to the *New Illustrated Webster's Dictionary of the English Language* (New York: PMC Pub. Co., Inc., 1992), p. 730: "Phonography is the art or science of writing by sound; especially, the art of representing words according to a system of sound elements that reduces their graphic reproduction to the simplest form: a style of shorthand which owes its principal development to Isaac Pitman, of Bath, England."

[5] Letters from E. J. Waggoner to W. C. White (located in the letter files of the Ellen G. White Estate, Center for Adventist Research, Andrews University) dated, respectively, May 9, July 8, and Sept. 15, 1875 (written from Battle Creek) and letters dated, respectively, Oct. 18, Nov. 13, and Dec. 11, 1875 (written from Ann Arbor). From at least the late spring through the late summer Ellet was in Battle Creek taking tutorials with John Harvey Kellogg and by October 18 he was in Ann Arbor taking chemistry and other premed or medical courses at the University of Michigan. He was in Ann Arbor until at least just before Christmas (last letter being dated Dec. 11, 1875).

[6] In a January 17, 1962, letter to L. E. Froom, Pearl Waggoner Howard cites the researches of the librarian (Gilbert J. Clausman) of the New York University Medical Center, who had written the following to her: "You may be interested in knowing that your father is listed in the following book . . . : *Medical and Surgical Register of the United States: Index to the Physicians of the United States,* 3rd edition, revised, 1893, published by R. L. Polk and Co., p. 111." (Froom Collection, PC 48: archives of the General Conference of Seventh-day Adventists).

[7] David P. McMahon, "Biographical Sketch," *Ellet Joseph Waggoner: The Myth and the Man*, chap. 2, p. 19.

[8] An obvious reference to the University of Michigan at Ann Arbor.

[9] Pearl W. Howard, "Biographic Sketch and Background," p. 3.

[10] Froom collection located in the archives of the General Conference of Seventh-day Adventists.

[11] Letter to Elder (L. E.) Froom, Dec. 1, 1961, in the Froom Collection, PC 48: archives of the General Conference of Seventh-day Adventists.

[12] Letter to L. E. Froom, dated Jan. 17, 1962, from the Froom Collection, PC 48: archives of the General Conference of Seventh-day Adventists.

[13] *Ibid.*

[14] Ellet's name first appears on the masthead of the *Signs of the Times* as "assistant" to his father on May 10, 1883.

[15] Howard, p. 3.

[16] Letter written July 29, 1878, to W. C. White from Springfield, Ohio. Document File

236a, located in the Ellen G. White Estate files, Center for Adventist Research, Andrews University.

[17] Merritt G. Kellogg was a founding contributor to help get the institution up and running. For more background on the beginnings and later development of the Rural Health Retreat and the St. Helena Sanitarium, see the article "St. Helena Hospital and Health Center" in the *Seventh-day Adventist Encyclopedia*, vol. 11, pp. 522, 523.

[18] Letter written from Springfield, Ohio, on July 29, 1878.

[19] Letter written by J. H. Waggoner to W. C. White, Feb. 5, 1879; found in Document File 236a, in the White Estate files of the Center for Adventist Research, Andrews University.

[20] *Ibid.*

[21] Jessie Fremont Moser was the daughter of Charles and Margaret (nee van Worsmer [sp.?]) Moser. Pearl Waggoner Howard claimed, in "Biographical Sketch and Background" (p. 2), that Jessie's parents "were Holland Dutch" (this ethnic note was handwritten in the "Sketch"). Pearl then reported that they "had accepted the truth in her [Jessie's] early childhood" and that Jessie "was baptized at age of nine." She then added that Jessie was "born in Vienna County, Ohio" and "grew up in Sigourney, Iowa." Winona Fiebelkorn supplements Pearl Waggoner Howard's narrative with the note that Jessie "was converted at a tent meeting when she was eight years old by Elders D. M. Canright and George I. Butler. Elder Butler baptized her the following summer at camp meeting." Pearl Waggoner Howard's recollections of her mother's conversion experience find support in what Jessie Moser Waggoner recorded in her "Sustentation Questionnaire" of 1923: "I was baptized when nine years of age by Elder G. I. Butler."

When others describe Jessie as "talented," they refer to her later prominence as the "corresponding secretary" of the International Sabbath School Association of the Adventist denomination, her editorial work, her subsequent lifelong involvement with Sabbath school work, her talents as musical composer, and her other work with young people. We will examine these developments later on in this and subsequent chapters.

[22] The only evidence so far for the date of their marriage appears in the public record of Jessie's divorce from Ellet filed on September 11, 1905, and finalized on December 31, 1905. Jean Davis did the research on the divorce records, and the legal records are recorded and located in "Library of Michigan, Microfilm F565: Summary of Returns Relative to Divorce [in Michigan]: Bay 1905 to Wayne 1906" ("Bay" and "Wayne" undoubtedly refer to Michigan counties, alphabetically arranged and listing the recorded divorces taking place from 1905 to 1906). The divorce was finalized in Calhoun County, Michigan, and listed as "record number: 179." We will deal in more detail with this tragic domestic disruption in the last section of this biography.

Sigourney, Keokuk County, Iowa, is located in the middle of the southeastern quadrant of the state, about halfway between the Iowa/Missouri line and Interstate 80.

[23] Jessie included a parenthetical recollection that she later met "a gentleman and lady" in Glendale, California, who "accepted the truth at those meetings." Cited from the H. H. Cobban letter in the file of Jessie Moser Waggoner's application for sustentation support.

Ira J. Hankins later confirmed that Ellet and Jessie had worked with him in Iowa. In a letter located in Jessie's sustentation file he wrote that "the beginning of Mrs. Jessie F. Moser's labours in connection with the organized work was in tent meetings in Birmingham, Iowa, in the summer of 1879. These meetings were conducted by Dr. E. J. Waggoner and I. J. Hankins, under the direction of the Iowa Conference. Dr. Waggoner's wife (formerly Miss Jessie F. Moser) was with us and assisted in the work" (letter from I. J. Hankins to P. E. Bordersen, Sept. 24, 1930).

Emmett K. Vande Vere, in his biography of George I. Butler, supplemented the recollections of Jessie Moser Waggoner and Ira Hankins. Referring to Butler's evangelism strategy while conference president in Iowa during the period from 1875 to 1880, he says that "lecture series, follow-up meetings, and revivals marked some 150 places in Iowa. Ministerial personnel numbered sixteen ordained and six licensed ministers. Names of men destined for wider recognition entered the lists: Louis R. Conradi, Arthur G. Daniells, Joseph H. Durland, Eugene W. Farnsworth, Ira J. Hankins, Leroy T. Nicola, Roscoe C. Porter, Henry Shultz, George B. Starr, and Ellet J. Waggoner."

[24] James White then adds a somewhat peppery little addendum, most likely targeting what he perceived to be the presumption of Ellet's father: "If Elder Waggoner [J. H. Waggoner] shall think favorably of his children going to California I suppose he has the same privilege that I have had in paying the fare of mine to the same point. But be it known to all men, and also women, that I take no responsibility in this case further than to dictate this letter."

[25] Joseph H. Waggoner to W. C. White, Feb. 5, 1879. Document File 236a, "Joseph H. Waggoner Miscellaneous."

[26] Ellet was not the only member of the family to engage in medical service at the Rural Health Retreat (the fledgling St. Helena Sanitarium and Hospital). Jessie recalled giving "treatments" and helping "the lady patients" (letter to "Brother Cobban," Oct. 23, 1924, in the sustentation file of the General Conference of Seventh-day Adventists).

[27] Ellet Waggoner's name first appeared on the masthead of the *Signs of the Times* as "assistant editor" to his father in the May 10, 1883, edition of the journal. A. T. Jones would join him as coassistant editor on May 7, 1885. The *Signs of the Times* of May 6, 1886, notified its readers that "E. J. Waggoner and A. T. Jones were elected editors" and their names first appeared one week later as coeditors on the masthead of the May 12, 1886, edition. Clearly the elder Waggoner was phasing out his work at the Pacific Press, and the younger Ellet Waggoner and A. T. Jones were in their ascendancy to prominence in the Adventist movement.

[28] Jessie Moser Waggoner recalls the preaching with Professor Grainger "in the northern part of the state" in her "sustentation fund application" (General Conference sustentation records folder of Jessie F. Moser).

[29] He was teaching at Healdsburg College as early as October 1, 1883, according to the reports of college president Sydney Brownsberger in the *Signs of the Times* (Sept. 27, 1883), and Ellet Waggoner's own reports in the December 6, 1883, *Signs of the Times* article entitled "Bible Study at Healdsburg College" and in "Healdsburg College Items" in the *Review and Herald* (Feb. 12, 1884). The Ellen White letter 42, Mar. 16, 1884, and letter 44, Mar. 27, 1884, also confirms his teaching. His lecture outlines for the classes at Healdsburg in 1883 and 1884 were published under the title *Bible Readings—No. 1. A Series of Readings Covering a Portion of the Ground Embraced in the Bible Course at Healdsburg College, 1883-84* (Oakland: Pacific Press Pub. Assn., n.d.). Once again, Waggoner was also most likely teaching at Healdsburg in the winter and spring of 1885, as there was very little copy from him published in the *Signs* during those months (*Signs of the Times*, Apr. 16, 1885; cf. *Signs of the Times*, Apr. 23, 1885). Furthermore, Sydney Brownsberger reported on Healdsburg College in the *Signs of the Times* (Sept. 3, 1885) that "Elder E. J. Waggoner is expected to come and remain during the spring term. The method of his instruction in the Bible Department, and the good results to the cause in this Conference from his past labors here, are well known." See also the work of Paul Penno, Jr., *Calvary at Sinai: The Law and the Covenants in Seventh-day Adventist History* (Vallejo, Calif., 2001), p. 33.

[30] "Waggoner Closes Pastorate in Oakland," *Signs of the Times*, Oct. 20, 1890.

[31] Waggoner made a tour of the Pacific Northwest camp meetings during the late spring of 1885. He preached and taught at a biblical institute held in conjunction with the Upper

Columbia camp meeting in Milton, Oregon, from May 24 to June 3, 1885 (*Signs of the Times*, Apr. 23, 1885, and June 25, 1885 [published report written from Portland, Oregon, on June 13, 1885]). He then spoke at a later "biblical institute" from June 14 to 24 held on the Portland campground of the Oregon Conference (notice had been given in *Signs of the Times* of June 4, 1885). Pearl Waggoner Howard recalls the report of her cousin Ellet that he "first heard him (EJW) speak at the camp meeting at Stockton, California, in August of 1885" (p. 3). For the year 1886 we find the following camp meeting reports in the *Signs of the Times*: "Wednesday, July 28, Elder J. N. Loughborough, Elder E. J. Waggoner, and Professor S. Brownsberger left San Francisco for Eureka, California, to attend the Humboldt campmeeting" (Aug. 5), then on to the "camp meeting in Santa Barbara County" (Sept. 9) and "the Woodland camp meeting" (Oct. 21) (quite possibly also referred to as the "California camp meeting" [Oct. 28]).

[32] *Signs of the Times*, Oct. 28, 1886.

[33] See the comments of Ellen White in manuscript 36, 1890, which appear in the compilation *Faith and Works* (Nashville: Southern Pub. Assn., 1979), pp. 15, 16, and 18: "The law of God has been so largely dwelt upon and has been presented to congregations, almost as destitute of the knowledge of Jesus Christ and His relation to the law as was the offering of Cain" (p. 18).

[34] Letter to H. B. Cobban, Oct. 23, 1924 (General Conference sustentation file). Undoubtedly the "Home Hand Book" that Jessie referred to was J. H. Kellogg's *The Home Hand-Book of Domestic Hygiene and Rational Medicine* (Battle Creek, Mich.: Good Health Pub. Co., 1881). The volume was most likely a colporteur staple, sold door to door as a "subscription" book.

[35] *Signs of the Times*, Dec. 2, 1886. An interesting footnote coming out of the 1886 Battle Creek General Conference session was the appointment of W.L.H. Baker and his wife, Josie, to serve on the staff of the newly founded missionary journal for Australia called the *Bible Echo*. Though Baker is a relatively minor figure in Seventh-day Adventist history, his name will later surface in conjunction with the notorious "Baker letter" that Ellen White would write to him in late 1895 or early 1896. This letter heavily influenced the subsequent twentieth- and twenty-first century Adventist debates over the meaning of the humanity of Christ (a subject quite central to E. J. Waggoner's theology). See Woodrow W. Whidden II, *Ellen White on the Humanity of Christ* (Hagerstown, Md.: Review and Herald Pub. Assn., 1997), pp. 59-66.

[36] *Signs of the Times*, Nov. 17, 1887, reported the list of delegates, which included "E. J. Waggoner."

[37] "General Conference Proceedings," *Signs of the Times,* Nov. 24, 1887.

[38] *Ibid.*

[39] *Ibid.*

[40] *Ibid.*, Dec. 1, 1887.

[41] *Ibid.*

[42] *Ibid.*, Nov. 9, 1888.

[43] *Ibid.*, Dec. 15, 1887.

[44] C. H. Jones (general manager of the Pacific Press Publishing Association) published the obituary notice for the infant Ernest Eugene Waggoner in *Signs of the Times*, June 3, 1889. In the next section of this biography we will return to this tragic death when we review a particularly painful litany of losses that Ellet Waggoner sustained during the first half of 1889.

[45] Howard, p. 3.

[46] *Ibid.*, p. 4.

[47] The copy work for W. C. White she recalled in her letter to "Brother Cobban" of

October 23, 1924: "I also did some copying for Elder W. C. White—copied some of his mother's writings" (letter located in the General Conference sustentation file of Jessie F. Moser).

[48] "Brain fever," according to American Adventist historian Gary Land (professor of history at Andrews University), was most likely late-nineteenth-century terminology describing either encephalitis or meningitis. Renowned American historian of medicine and science Ronald Numbers of the University of Wisconsin essentially agrees with Land's suggestion, though he does offer the caveat that it is hard to know for sure. Numbers also suggested that there is some evidence that in the American South at this time, the affliction of trichinosis (largely a result of eating improperly cooked pork) was also called "brain fever" (opinion expressed via e-mail on Oct. 4, 2006). It is hard, though, to imagine that the abstemious Waggoner was afflicted with trichinosis.

[49] *Signs of the Times* Jan. 7, 1886.

[50] *Howard.*, p. 3

[51] According to Jean Davis' family tree study, Alta N. Waggoner was born September 28, 1862, in Burlington, Michigan. She would subsequently marry Harry Armstrong in England and would pass away on January 9, 1949, in Glendale, California.

[52] Pearl Waggoner Howard to L. E. Froom, Nov. 18, 1960, p. 2, in the Froom Collection, archives of the General Conference of Seventh-day Adventists.

[53] As noted above, Pearl Waggoner Howard testified that Alta had lived with the family since her earliest remembrances. Since Pearl's birth was in early 1885, she most certainly would not have had conscious recollections from any earlier than 1887. See Howard (p. 2) and Document File 236a, "J. H. Waggoner Miscellaneous," E. G. White Research Center, Andrews University.

[54] We have abundant evidence for Joseph Waggoner's agonizing concerns for the financial support of his children in medical school (Ellet) and college (Ellery and Alta) in letters written to W. C. White on July 29, 1878; February 5 and June 11, 1879 (Document File 236a, "J. H. Waggoner Miscellaneous," Ellen G. White Estate files of the Center for Adventist Research at Andrews University). The Battle Creek College records indicate that Alta matriculated from 1877 until 1880, taking the teachers' course and that Ellery Waggoner matriculated during the four years between 1876 and 1881, and then took some work in the 1883-1884 school year, in the special course and the teachers' course (data taken from the Battle Creek College records, as researched by Jean Davis [with copies in the writer's personal possession]).

[55] Ellen G. White letter 21, Aug. 23, 1885, to Sister [Alta] Waggoner, Center for Adventist Research, James White Library, Andrews University.

[56] The details of the ticklish situation need not detain us at this juncture of the biography. We will return to these troubling circumstances later on in the story of E. J. Waggoner.

[57] Ellen G. White letter 21, Aug. 23, 1885, to Sister [Alta] Waggoner.

[58] Ellen White letter 76, 1886 (c. April), p. 1.

[59] *Ibid.*, p. 2.

[60] *Ibid.*, p. 3.

CHAPTER III

THE FORMATIVE THEOLOGICAL DEVELOPMENTS: 1875 TO OCTOBER 1888

INTRODUCTION

THIS CHAPTER IS THE FIRST OF FOUR (one chapter coming at the end of the each major section of the biography) that will specifically deal with the theological developments in the published and collected writings of E. J. Waggoner. Space does not permit a detailed treatment of all aspects of his theological and biblical expositions (he was simply too voluminous in his publications). Many aspects of his theology and ethics (both personal and social ethics) could productively occupy our attention. We, however, will concentrate on those themes that seemed to be not only the central focus of Waggoner's major presentations, but ones that have formed the major legacy he has bequeathed to subsequent theological trends in Seventh-day Adventist history. I do believe that the themes treated in the present chapter are the ones that all his interpreters acknowledge as the major subjects forming the core of his theology and his important legacy to Adventism.

These major themes orbit around his understanding of issues more directly related to his all-consuming passion—the subject of Christ and His righteousness. They comprised the heart of his understanding of the "glad tidings" of salvation by faith in the merits of Jesus. Maybe we could put it another way: the major developments always centered on his understanding of justifying, sanctifying, and perfecting grace. Closely related to these crucial subjects were his teachings on the meaning of the life and death of Christ, the covenants, the divine/human nature of the person of Christ, and the role of the last generation of the remnant people of God and how they would vindicate Him in the final actions of the pre-Advent investigate judgment. It is to these teachings that we will devote the largest share of attention.

Quite possibly we could sum up our focus this way: his themes that have proven most enduring and influential (and in some respects, controversial) are always those that express his understanding of the redeeming grace of God. Such expositions of grace did not, however, develop in some sort of doctrinal and theological vacuum. They had a definite historical and theological setting in which he quite self-consciously unfolded his stirring presentations on personal salvation. And that was a very traditional Seventh-day Adventist understanding of the primacy and fullness of biblical inspiration and authority and the great distinctive Adventist "present truth" doctrines.

As we have already established in chapter 1, Waggoner was very much the son of the Adventist pioneers and their doctrinal teaching. Without a doubt the young E. J. Waggoner firmly believed, ably presented, and defended (until at least 1894) such doctrines as the literal, visible, imminent return of Jesus followed by the millennial reign of the saints with Christ in heaven (rather than on the earth); the pre-Advent investigative judgment (with the traditional understanding of the "year for a day" prophetic chronology of the book of Daniel and the sanctuary imagery of the first five books of the Bible as well as Hebrews and Revelation); the eternal authority of the moral law of the Ten Commandments (including the binding claims of the seventh-day Sabbath of the fourth commandment); the unconscious state of the dead; strong opposition to the claims of spiritualism; the annihilationist understanding of hell (it will finally burn up or annihilate the rejecters of God's grace); the wholistic view of health and health reform (including a strong emphasis on total abstinence "temperance"); and the understanding that all of the "gifts of the Spirit" are available to the "remnant" church of God, including the "gift of prophecy."

The columns of the bound copies of the *Signs of the Times* and the British *Present Truth* (and other Seventh-day Adventist periodicals that reprinted his original articles) are replete with expositions that both proclaim and defend these great themes. In fact, just Waggoner's teachings and defense of the seventh-day Sabbath alone would provide the makings of an extensive research project. I do not know if he adds any distinctive developments to such "present truth" doctrines, but he was never very far away from their power to inspire his expositions of grace.

In a more focused way, the theme of the right relationship of law and grace always undergirded his presentation of Christ's redemptive person and power. Furthermore, his expositions of law and grace always carried with them a strong emphasis on the viability of graced obedience[1] and perfection.

Not surprisingly, such a stress on Christian obedience led Waggoner not only to give considerable time and attention to the doctrines of justifying, sanctifying, and perfecting grace, but also to Christian ethics. Before we turn our attention to his central themes of grace, salvation by faith,[2] and other closely related topics, it will prove helpful to offer a few observations regarding Waggoner's ethics.

ETHICS

First of all, he was just as tenacious to be truly biblical in his ethical teaching as he was in his general Christian and distinctly Adventist doctrinal interpretations. The heart of his ethical teachings was what we would today characterize as personal ethics. Here Waggoner was very conservative in his exposition of the law of God and the wider array of biblical commands and requirements. However, he did spend some space and time commenting on ethics that had broader social implications. Not only do his writings provide enough material for a book-length study of the Sabbath, but they offer plenty to ponder on the social issues of the day. Waggoner not only actively and extensively injected himself into the major religious liberty issues of the late nineteenth century (both in North American and in Europe), but he also had much to say about racial injustice[3] and the evils of war.[4]

While he did not hold out much hope for societal reform and had little patience for the social gospel types seeking to lead the broader Christian church to make such issues as social, racial, and economic reform the major, collective focus of its ministry,[5] he was a man with a deep burden to call social sin by its right name. For instance, it is not going too far to suggest that if Waggoner had lived in our time he would express strong support for the anti-war movement. He would probably not be in the streets carrying a placard, but he would be writing in opposition to war as a means of settling international grievances. It would not be stretching it too much to say that he was both a personal and a social pacifist. In matters of racial justice he was particularly critical of the way that the United States treated Chinese immigrants, especially Chinese mine workers and railroad builders. I am quite sure that in our time he would be most critical of the way that society and government deal with many immigrant groups.

Yet such things were not the central themes that occupied his fertile mind, his ready pen, and his moral passions. For Waggoner, the key to all societal reform was deep, inward personal reform of the heart and mind. The only way that the "public square" could become truly just was if the law of God was squarely enshrined in the heart of every child of God through faith in Christ, the gracious and redeeming lawgiver. The real passion of the ethics of E. J. Waggoner always focused on the hearts and minds of the "new covenant" believers. And it is to these unfolding themes and their development in his thought that we now turn our attention.

EARLY KEY DOCTRINAL DEVELOPMENTS: GODHEAD (TRINITY), ATONEMENT, AND THE NATURE OF CHRIST[6]

Godhead (Trinity)

During this early period of his ministry Waggoner had little if anything to say on the issue of the Trinity and the closely related issue of the deity of Christ. Important clarifying statements on such themes do not come until the year 1889 and later. It is most likely that he shared the emerging views on the nature of Christ's deity with other key pioneer Adventist thought leaders—who had been shifting from a classic Arian[7] to a more nuanced "semi-Arian"[8] understanding of Christ's divine nature.[9] The published records just do not tell us what Waggoner thought about such Trinitarian developments,

As to his understanding of the more technical aspects of the meaning of Christ's death and priestly intercession, Waggoner clearly taught that His death was a manifestation of His bearing the penalty for sin as our substitute. Our Lord bore the sins that were not His but ours.

"None can die except those in whom sin is found; our sins were laid on Christ, and accounted as His; and so, although personally He 'knew no sin,'[10] He was made to suffer the penalty of the law as a transgressor."[11]

God made Christ (the sinless one) to be *sin* for us. He was established in all things "like unto his brethren" (Heb. 2:17), and that means not simply as to His outward, physical frame, but that He bore sin, just as we do. The sins that he carried were not his own, but ours. He "knew no sin,"[12] yet "the Lord hath laid on him the iniquity of us all" (Isa. 53:6). Although the sins that he bore were ours, they were counted as His own, and so caused His death (verse 5).

This point needs to be clearly grasped at this stage of Waggoner's expositions of the atoning work of Christ. Through the years his position will change. But at this important juncture, before the famed 1888 General Conference session, Waggoner held a very traditional Protestant view that Christ bore the penalty of sin for us as our sacrificial substitute to satisfy the demands of the broken law. Furthermore, he most certainly considered that Christ's high-priestly intercessions in heaven had atoning significance.

The Humanity of Christ

Closely related to Waggoner's perspective on the atoning nature of Christ's death were his views on the nature of Christ's humanity. While they are not yet entirely clear, it does appear that Christ's human nature was sinful only in the sense that He bore the effects of sin. In other words, Waggoner regarded Him as sinful mainly in that He was bearing our sins. Yet Waggoner was already clearly coming to terms with the key passages in the New Testament that deal with the nature of Christ's humanity during the Incarnation.

In an important letter to G. I. Butler (subsequently published as *The Gospel in the Book of Galatians*),[13] he clearly equated Romans 1:3 (Christ "was made of the seed of David") with Hebrews 2:16, 17 ("made [in all things] like unto his brethren") and Romans 8:3 (made "in the likeness of sinful flesh"). Quite obviously Waggoner was teaching that Christ bore all of the weaknesses and passions of his sinful ancestors. He goes on to say that "if Christ had not been made *in all ways* like unto His brethren, then His sinless life would be no encouragement to us."[14] His understanding of Christ's humanity had, in some sense, clear post-Fall[15] aspects.

Yet, at this juncture, He seemed to accent the concept that the sinfulness of Christ was because of His being accounted a sinner, not that He was made to be such inherently. The tensions in Waggoner's thought were well expressed: "I do not know how the pure and holy Savior could ensure all the infirmities of humanity, which are the result of sin, and be reckoned as a sinner, and suffer the death of a sinner"[16] Just how much like sinful humanity the Savior was in Waggoner's thought at this point is not at all clear. Yet the implication seems to be that Christ was *affected* by sin, but was not deeply *infected* with it. He certainly was "accounted" as a sinner and most certainly that is the primary reason for His atoning death—our sins which He bore, not because of any sin in Him, either by condemnable nature, thought, or act.

The statements seeming to come closest to suggesting that Christ took human nature infected with the dark hues of human depravity (though Waggoner would never teach that Christ sinned by a thought or an act) went like this: "The spotless Son of God took upon himself the form of a servant of sin, and consented to be covered with the same *degradation*[17] into which man had plunged himself"[18] and that it was necessary "for Christ to assume the condition of those whom he would redeem. . . . Christ redeems none who occupy a position different from that which He took."[19]

Most certainly one could interpret the passages to mean that Christ bore the sinful tendencies and inclinations of the fallen race. During this pre-1888 period, however, such an interpretation can only be implied. But implications would become clear explications when his views on the inherently sinful nature of Christ would take a decided turn in the immediate aftermath of the 1888 Minneapolis session. Waggoner would, in early 1889, plainly declare that not only was the sin of all the race laid upon Him as our substitute, but that "the flesh which He assumed had all the weaknesses and sinful tendencies to which fallen human nature is subject."[20] We shall return to this important development for further elaboration in the next section of this biography.

SIN[21]

The early teachings of E. J. Waggoner on sin were fairly standard for the Arminian-influenced[22] Seventh-day Adventist view of the day. Most certainly Waggoner understood that the disobedience of Adam's original sin had drawn all humans into sin. Without the grace of Christ, the ultimate destiny of Adam and all of his posterity would be eternal death. Yet we cannot classify Waggoner's views in terms of the more classical perspective of "original sin." Waggoner felt that since no person should be blamed for what he or she did not personally do, there should be no automatic condemnation of Adam's posterity. Thus if sinful nature does not bring about condemnation, what does?

One of the key aspects of the traditional Arminian position, which Waggoner shared, was the teaching that God takes the redemptive initiative. He has to come seeking after sinful humans since they are dead in sin, as expressed in the classic doctrine of "prevenient grace."[23] God has placed in each person the gift of "enmity" toward Satan and sin, and if the person takes advantage of this most basic grace, there is no reason anyone should be lost—except through willful and persistent rejection of God's saving provisions inherent in the reconciling grace of Christ.

A major component in Waggoner's understanding of the gift of "enmity" was his strong emphasis on the classic "second use of the law." This teaching sees the law of God (especially the Ten Commandments) as an instrument of conviction of sin that will drive the responsive sinner to Christ for salvation from sin. Such an emphasis turned out to be a very controversial subject in the history of the Adventist interpretation of the "law in Galatians." Was the law in Galatians the moral or the ceremonial law? Waggoner felt very strongly that the primary reference to the law in Galatians was to the moral law. In his theology, only the moral law could bring a profound conviction of sin and thus lead sinners to Christ.[24]

We will deal with the issue of the lengthy and testy debate over the law in Galatians in more detail when we discuss the controversial run-up to the famed 1888 General Conference session in the next chapter. But for now it is important to understand that for Waggoner the moral law (the Ten Commandments) was the agency that God used to convict the sinner to seek Christ for salvation by faith.

For Waggoner, however, the key issue in defining sin was not so much that humans are born with sinful natures, but that the really damning sin is manifest when they willfully reject Christ's grace and deliberately indulge in thoughts and acts of sin. And thus, for Waggoner, the fundamental aspect of sin would always be the sins of thought and act resulting from spurning God's saving grace. It is in the tragic dimensions of rejecting God's offer of grace in which the real guilt of the human race finds its origin. It should come as no surprise, therefore, that Waggoner, along with many other Wesleyan/Arminians of his day, would put a great accent on graced obedience.

But of course, before there could be graced obedience (a high doctrine of sanctifying grace), there was the need to find a solution to the problem of the sins already committed by the sinful, but convicted and penitent, children of Adam. The justifying grace of God resolved this problem.

JUSTIFICATION BY FAITH[25]

It is this subject, in an intimate association with sanctification and perfection, that would become the most notable theme of Waggoner's ministry in the years of his great prominence following 1888.

In one sense, Waggoner's views on justification by faith[26] during the early years of his ministry are, for the most part, fairly standard for Seventh-day Adventists and other Arminian Protestants of the late nineteenth century. Yet even during the pre-1888 years his teaching had some seemingly distinctive aspects. Because of this, I would urge the reader to follow the discussion quite carefully. If we can get a handle on this aspect of Waggoner's teaching, it will greatly assist us in understanding the controversial nature of his work in his time and how it has influenced subsequent developments down to the present day.

What follows are the basic outlines of Waggoner's pre-1888 teaching on justification.

He clearly defined justification as God's forgiveness of the sinner's past transgressions. "Divine pardon is justification; God pardons the believer in Christ by imputing His righteousness 'for the remission of sins that are past.' The pardoned one is as though he had never sinned; where there was nothing but guilt before, God beholds nothing but righteousness—righteousness put there through His own wonderful love."[27]

Now we can understand this version of justification in the sense of an imputed, or reckoned, righteousness for the penitent sinner who has experienced the converting power of the Holy Spirit. God did not intend such a reckoned righteousness, however, as forgiveness for future sins of the individual sinner (certainly there was provision for such, but forgiveness was only for those who by faith claim the justifying merits of Christ).

Furthermore, Waggoner was careful to associate the experience of forgiveness and new legal standing in Christ closely with that of the new birth and regeneration. Christ does not justify anyone unless the Holy Spirit renews such individuals and gives them, through faith, the attitude of responsive love for Christ in the spirit of willing and loving obedience to all the known will of God. Again there is nothing unusual in his position, as we find it already outlined in the teachings of John Calvin, John Wesley, and Ellen White.

Yet Waggoner also went on to refer to the justified believer in the following, further sense of the word: "To such there is no condemnation. And why? Because in them sin has been condemned or destroyed. . . . When that is done, [the individual] is freed from condemnation, and not till then can the righteousness of the law be fulfilled or manifested in him."[28] Such an understanding raises a very pertinent question: In what sense was Waggoner claiming that justification includes God's work *in* the believer, in addition to God's work *for* them—that is, declaring them to be just? Was Waggoner here confusing the work of justification with that of sanctification?[29] These questions will most certainly be one of the key themes that will occupy us in our ongoing survey of Waggoner's theological developments in the succeeding phases of his public career.

While a thorough treatment of the previous question must await developments after 1888 (especially from 1893 onward), at this juncture I can offer a few observations for the sake of clarification. I do this for two reasons: (1) to offer a summary of early developments and (2) to anticipate interesting shifts in the 1890s.

First of all, Waggoner clearly understood that at the moment of justification by faith (forgiveness for past sins), the whole process of regeneration began, and that God justifies no one that He does not then go on to sanctify. Thus he clearly taught that conversion and regeneration usher in the Spirit of God to a place of supreme rulership in the new life of the believer. In this sense justification does provide the platform and the motivation for a life of Spirit-empowered obedience.[30]

Furthermore, the justified believer is made righteous in the sense of James' declaration that Abraham was justified by works. In other words,

James did not oppose Paul's emphasis on justification by imputation—accounting or reckoning as just—but was affirming the quality of the true faith that justifies. Such faith will always be a faith that works.[31] Quite obviously for Waggoner the justified sinner is "made righteous and just" in the sense that there will be "no works where there is no faith" (to state it negatively). We can also express the latter concept positively: faith "may be said to comprise all that is necessary for salvation, because works are included in faith; they follow it as surely as flowers follow the showers of spring."[32]

Yet in a unique way, for Waggoner there *seemed* to be the very real possibility that the justification of the believer is not just about the fruit of good works. He also appeared to suggest an additional work aspect of justification: it does, in reality, make the person righteous internally, and this internalized righteousness does also seem to form the meritorious basis of the sinner's acceptance with God. At the risk of being needlessly repetitive, I suggest some further clarification of Waggoner's "unusual" expression that justification "makes" the believer righteous.

I employ the word "unusual" here for the following reason: Waggoner's contention that justification not only declares a person to be legally just before God (for Christ's sake), but that such a declaration also somehow *"makes"* the believer righteousness has a bit of an odd ring to it. It seems to contrast with the traditional Protestant and Seventh-day Adventist terminology that normally associates *declaring* righteous with justification and *making* righteous with sanctification.

Furthermore, the traditional Protestant and Adventist understanding of both key terms is that they must never be separated in experience, but must always be carefully distinguished as to their theological purposes in the doctrine of salvation by grace from sin. Thus the provision for justifying grace is totally and wholly the meritorious work of grace accounted to, or reckoned to, the believer through faith in the provisions of Christ's atoning work. We must carefully distinguish the objective work of accounting righteous from sanctification. The latter is the subjective work of the Holy Spirit: through cooperation with the responsive faith of the converted believer, God actually and progressively transforms the characters of repentant, believing sinners.

What, then, did Waggoner intend to convey with this concept of justification that claims that justifying grace "makes" the justified believer "righteous"? Was he conflating justification and sanctification (as McMahon, Haloviak, and Hook strongly suggest, and Webster hints at), or was he intending to say that the experience of justification will always be inevitably followed with the fruit of obedience, which is the subjective working of God's grace in the truly justified believer (according to Wieland, Knight, and Wahlen)? It appears that the latter option is the more correct characterization of Waggoner's understanding of justifying grace.

For the pre-1888 era, the key to understanding Waggoner's concept of justification that "makes righteous" is his concept of the gift of a graced "*disposition*"[33] to do the right thing. Here is the essential antidote to any sort of abstract "legal fiction" view[34] of imputed or declarative righteousness.

This concept of "legal fiction" was the crucial concept that seemed to drive Waggoner's presentations on justification as they emphasized the subjective, transformative effects of the experience of justifying grace. What Waggoner seemed to want to indicate with all of this terminology was that the attitude of the truly justified believer now changes to one that not only thirsts for but also manifests the righteousness of law through faith. Thus the terminology of "*disposition*" best expressed what he was trying to convey, with his emphasis on justification "making" the believer righteous. Carefully ponder the following citation.

Referring to the experience of Abraham in receiving the *imputed* righteousness of Christ, Waggoner says "Abraham's faith could not have been imputed to him for righteousness but for the disposition to work. . . . This continued obedience is sanctification." Just three paragraphs later in the same article, he makes essentially the same point: "sanctification is but continued justification."[35] The believer is "made righteous" in the experience of justifying faith, not in the sense that he or she instantaneously became perfect, but rather from the perspective that they will normally manifest the "*disposition*" to do the will of God and grow in grace. Thus it is not that the newly justified believer is absolutely perfect in character in some instantaneous moment, but that the new child of God has all of the marks of a genuinely converted person.

In fact, the very same article that uses the language of "*disposition*" also contains one of the clearest statements of the lack of absolute perfection on the part of the genuine believer in all the writings of Waggoner! He was explicit about the need for the "continual imputation of Christ's righteousness to make up for our deficiencies." What follows is the fuller context of this important statement: "In our best efforts there is so much imperfection that, but for the continual imputation of Christ's righteousness to make up for our deficiencies, we should be lost. The best that we alone can do is bad. . . . The redeemed saint will have no cause for boasting over the lost sinner. True, the law, when applied to their lives, reports perfection in the one case, and only sin in the other; but the saint cannot boast, for without Christ he would have been nothing. If Christ had not put His own righteousness upon him, he would be in as hopeless a condition as the sinner."[36]

A summary, though a bit repetitious, is in order so that the reader will clearly grasp Waggoner's concept of dispositions. It is this simple word, disposition, that best expresses the concept that justifying grace is no "legal fiction" fig leaf meant to cover the excusing or harboring of sinful attitudes and actions on the part of the professed believer. And in this important terminology, Waggoner very much shared the collective Adventist fear of what they sensed to be the pervasive attitudes of many Christians who were doing away with the law of God and manufacturing "cheap grace" attitudes of excusing, in the name of grace, the most blatant transgression of the holy law of God. This argument against antinomian attitudes was always undergirding and driving the Adventist expositions of law and saving grace.

Needless to say, we will with great care keep in mind these questions in succeeding sections of this biography. It is this important sector of theological and practical understanding that will prove to be one of the most challenging, persistent, yet controversial themes in the expositions of Waggoner for the balance of his public career.

Before we leave the topic of justification, two other issues merit careful attention. They involve (1) the concept of "universal legal justification" and (2) the final justification of believers in the pre-Advent judgment, or the Most Holy Place phase of Christ's justifying intercession. The latter issue is closely related to the state and status of the justified ones during the time between the close of probation and the second coming of Christ and their final deliverance from the presence of sin at glorification.

"UNIVERSAL LEGAL JUSTIFICATION"

A number of notable twentieth- and twenty-first-century interpreters of Waggoner have claimed that he taught a doctrine of "universal legal justification."[37] The position holds that God pardons the sinner prior to any conscious belief in Christ. In fact, its advocates claim that this understanding is one of Waggoner's unique contributions to Christian thought, and has been a leading bone of contention between them and other Waggoner interpreters. Thus a clear distinction is made between being universally, legally justified at the death of Christ and experientially justified at the moment of belief, or the conscious appropriation of the merits or justifying benefits of Christ's atoning work.

The simple fact is this: if this was Waggoner's pre-1888 understanding, he did not emphasize it. I am aware of only one statement that comes even close to suggesting such a distinction between a universal legal justification of all humanity and the experiential appropriation of the merits of Christ during the conversion experience of the repentant believer:

"It may be said that God does not actually forgive men until they repent. This is true; but He desired that they shall receive His pardon, and therefore, so far as He is concerned, He has pardoned them. All that is lacking is for them to accept the pardon which He offers them; if they will not, He is clear, and the responsibility of their ruin rests upon themselves."[38] What should we make of this interesting passage?

First of all, it is instructive that Waggoner here affirmed the truth that "God does not actually forgive men until they repent." He explicitly said that "this is true." Yet, positively, what he seemed to want to communicate was not some version of "universal legal justification," but the deep "desires" of God "that they shall receive His pardon." Thus, in the mind of God "He has pardoned them."

Quite possibly, we find the most positive interpretation of the statement through the illustration of anyone who has ever been deeply hurt by another and the offended party finally comes to not hold the offense against him or her. A change of attitude can occur even if the offender does not repent before the one offended develops an attitude of forgiveness and loss of grievance. Most likely the reader has experienced something similar. Maybe an example from my own experience can depict this very practical point of forgiveness and reconciliation.

I once unintentionally grieved one of my students. On further reflection, I came to a clear conviction that I had acted wrongly, and went to the person to ask for forgiveness. The offended person graciously responded to me that they had gotten over it a long time ago and had already forgiven me. In this case I am sure that my acknowledgment of the offense was gratifying to my long-suffering student; yet *I* was the key beneficiary of the confession!

And thus it must be with God. In one sense, He has forgiven us long ago, but this is not the biblical understanding of justification by faith. Normally, only an act of genuinely trusting faith can effectually appropriate the justifying merits of Christ.[39] This is not just Waggoner's consensus position, but also the overall emphasis of both Ellen White and the Bible.

Furthermore, Waggoner was explicit that justification is a personal, not a corporate or collective, matter. Commenting on Galatians 3, he plainly declared that "there can be no Christian experience, no faith, no justification, no righteousness that is not an individual matter. People are saved as individuals, and not as nations."[40] Could words be plainer?

There is at least one more key point that Waggoner himself made about the issue of justification by faith. What follows is a strongly expressed concept by which Waggoner seemed effectively to preclude any possibility of universal legal justification. Ponder carefully the following statement that speaks explicitly to the experience of being "justified by faith."

"It must not be forgotten that we are now speaking only of the sins that are *past*. It is impossible that *remission* of sins could have reference to anything else, for that which does not exist cannot be taken away; and to justify a man for sins not yet committed, in other words, to grant indulgence for sins, would throw contempt on the law, and bring in anarchy and ruin. And no sins are remitted except of those who believe in Jesus. If any are Christ's, they are Abraham's seed (Gal. 3:29), and therefore, with him, their faith is imputed unto them for righteousness (James 2:23)."[41]

Thus, for Waggoner, justification can deal only with sins of the past, since sins not yet committed cannot be remitted. He then goes on to equate such a concept with an "indulgence for sins." Little wonder that he then concluded that "no sins are remitted except of those who believe in Jesus." It just seems that if we impute the doctrine of "universal legal justification" to E. J. Waggoner, we would have Waggoner militating against Waggoner.

Another curious factor that this theology generates is the inability of its advocates to demonstrate any unique, saving effects that such a teaching seeks to impart that have not already been laid out by those who have, before Waggoner or Ellen White, advocated the Arminian doctrine of "prevenient grace" mentioned earlier in this chapter.

During many exchanges with the sincere champions of the "universal legal justification" interpretation, its advocates repeatedly struggle to articulate the difference between their claims and the Wesleyan/Ellen White doctrine that saving grace has been and is still being freely offered to all and that the initiative is God's, not that of sinful humans. It will prove instructive to restate briefly the central issue that all are striving to get at and to do it in the context of the claims of those who strongly impute the doctrine of universal, legal justification to Waggoner.

The core idea is that, in Christ, God has made full, legally *sufficient provision* for the salvation of the entire human race and has persistently taken the initiative to bring redemption to everyone. But this fully *sufficient provision* for justification, and God's sovereign, powerful, and persistent initiative to bring it to every lost sinner, will prove only to be *redemptively efficient* for those who appropriate the justifying merits of Christ by faith alone.

The advocates of the "universal legal justification" interpretation of Waggoner (and the Bible) readily admit that all legally justified sinners will ultimately be lost if they refuse to exercise faith. For this reason we must conclude that the teaching has generated a futile exchange that we can best characterize as a classic example of "a strife about words." It ignores (1) the most obvious teachings of Waggoner (in terms of what he actually presented in his early ministry) and (2) the theological implications of such a concept. Thus I would respectfully suggest that the whole disagreement is a historical, theological, and practical nonstarter for all Bible-believing thinkers who claim the following: God's universal and free-grace initiative offers the gift of salvation to all through the means of faith, and faith alone, in the justifying merits of Christ, and that without such faith, there is no such thing as justification.

Now, historically this doctrine, in the life and teachings of Waggoner, might find some footing as one of his teachings in his later ministry (and we will track this carefully); but in the pre-1888 and early post-1888 years, the support for it is slim to nonexistent. In fact, we could justifiably classify the evidence against this alleged teaching of "universal legal justification" during the early years of Waggoner's writings and the larger context of his Protestant theological background (especially the Wesleyan tradition) as an outright rejection of this well-meant but misplaced concept.

MOST HOLY PLACE FINAL JUSTIFICATION AND ETERNAL JUSTIFICATION

Waggoner's classic expression of this concept goes like this: "The sin is not blotted out as soon as it is pardoned. If it were, God could not deal with us as the king did with his servant. The merit of Christ's blood is set down opposite the sins of the one who is forgiven, and if it remains there until 'the times of refreshing shall come from the presence of the Lord' (Acts 3:19), they will be blotted out. But if the forgiven one shows by his actions that he is unworthy of the grace of Christ, and attempts by his evil course to make Christ the minister of sin, then the favor is withdrawn, and he stands face to face with his sin, the same as though he had never been forgiven."[42]

This concept arises out of the whole idea of the pre-Advent investigative judgment teaching. While the moment of forgiveness in the experience of initial justification immediately frees the penitent sinner from condemnation, the sins of the saints will not be finally blotted out until probation closes. For the living saints, at the time when probation ceases, it means that they are sealed in the sense that they are so settled into their relationship with God that He can declare that "he that is righteous, let him be righteous still" (Rev. 22:11).

This teaching has been a flash point for Seventh-day Adventist debates (internal and external) over how perfect the saints must be in order to stand faithful during the "time of Jacob's trouble" between the close of probation and Christ's second coming.[43] Whether the state of being "righteous still" is because they are now irrevocably declared as just as a result of the persistence of their faith or that they have been instantaneously perfected so that Jesus no longer needs to legally declare them perfect (since they are now actually sinlessly perfect) is hotly debated. Whatever the position, it is clear for Waggoner that these saints have experienced the "times of refreshing" called the latter rain of the Holy Spirit and that they are irrevocably justified.

This whole idea is very close to the one Ellen White expressed in her *Great Controversy* statement: God's people, after the close of probation, will have to "stand in the sight of a holy God without a mediator" (p. 425).[44] The question for both Waggoner and Ellen White is: Does this mean that Christ is no longer mediating in the sense that He is no longer declaring the sealed ones just, since they are now sinlessly perfect, or is it that He is no longer interceding to draw people from sin to salvation by faith? For Waggoner it seems that Jesus is mediating sustaining grace to keep the saints from falling into sin, but is no longer mediating justifying grace for any sort of unavoidable deficiencies.[45] Paul Penno, Jr., expresses it this way: "The final blotting out of sins is justification by faith or forgiveness retained by the believer. This is the sanctuary message of the final atonement by Christ in the most holy."[46]

Thus the period between the close of probation,[47] when Jesus ceases His mediation, and that of the Second Coming is the time for the initial, irrevocable gift of justification. And this permanent gift is one key explanation for their endurance during the "time of trouble," that is, the interval of crisis between the close of probation and the Second Advent. Then it is at the second coming of Christ that the sealed are now once and for all removed from the context of sin and are finally glorified. Glorification is the beginning of the eternal retention of justification.

Most assuredly, the glorified saints will no longer need the constant intercession of Christ. But they will be saved eternally on the lasting basis of the eternal effects of Christ's gift of forgiveness. It will be the foundation of everlasting life, and the justified believer will no longer be subject to external temptation and the possibility of death.

We will critique Waggoner on the concept of living without a mediator during the time between probation's close and the appearing of Christ at His second coming in later chapters. But the above concepts seem to form the gist of his teachings on the "final atonement" and the saints' eternal retention of the effects of justifying faith.

The preceding discussion has sought to encapsulate the key ideas of Waggoner on justification. But before we leave the issue of justification, we must raise one more point regarding its larger contours in Waggoner's overall theology. The reader needs to be alerted to the fact that Waggoner's understanding of justification and sanctification is closely bound up with his views on the covenants. We can never isolate the subjects of justification, sanctification, and perfection from his teachings from that context. But before we introduce his early views on the somewhat complex subject of the covenants, we need to clarify his understanding of transforming grace—the inevitable accompaniment of converting and justifying grace.

SANCTIFICATION, PERFECTION, AND FINAL GENERATION VINDICATION

Waggoner's pre-1888 teaching on sanctification and perfection was very much what one would expect from a Ten Commandment-defending Seventh-day Adventist writer. Furthermore, it exhibited nothing exceptional when compared with the thought of Ellen White.

He understood sanctification to be an ongoing process of character transformation that would eventuate in character perfection. The Holy Spirit ministers it in the converted soul. Waggoner strongly opposed the "holiness now" teaching of the American Holiness movement that emphasized instantaneous sanctification as a definite "second work" of grace in the soul.

In contrast to justification (complete the moment that the convicted sinner believes), sanctification is a "gradual" or "progressive" work.[48] Waggoner clearly taught that there would be imperfections left in the character of the growing sinner that would necessitate the justifying merits of Christ for the responsive, but yet imperfect believer.

He observed that "great changes are not made instantaneously. Even though men are converted, they need instruction, since they are then but babes in the truth; and this fact shows that old habits of thought and practice cannot at once be entirely forgotten. We do not mean to intimate that the converted man has any license to sin, or any excuse for it; but pardon for sins is not sanctification; the one who has been pardoned is not perfect, but is to 'go on to perfection'; and he still needs an advocate with the Father, that his imperfections may still be pardoned and overcome."[49]

The passage is one of the finest pre-1888 Minneapolis General Conference session expressions of the dynamic, supplementary interrelationship between the experience of justifying and sanctifying grace. As his teaching unfolds, we will constantly be on the alert for such balance. But let's be very clear on one issue: sanctification had a very definite goal for Waggoner—it was to "go on to perfection." And this most certainly will become abundantly apparent in the great, optimistic emphasis in his teachings on transforming grace. His preoccupation with it will manifest itself in a great flood of statements as the years of Waggoner's ministry unfold after the Minneapolis meeting in late 1888.

We need to note carefully the optimism of grace in Waggoner's teaching on Christian perfection. The work results not from human power, but from divine power. Waggoner was quite pronounced in his declaration that "it is not a question of whether we can overcome, but whether we will overcome."[50] Through divine power, the transformed believer will be enabled "to overcome all his faults, to endure all his trials,"[51]and he forcefully and soberly affirmed it with the direct declaration that "no one can enter heaven with the least taint of it [sin] about him. Christ is our pattern."[52] Waggoner's early understanding of perfection focused on perfection of character, not perfection of nature. And for him character perfection means basically that Christians obey the perfect law of God. He was clear that we will not be finally "saved" until glorification. But we can be delivered from the power of known, willful sin this side of glorification.

Furthermore, he understood perfection to have a dynamic aspect, often employing the following expressions; "not a gift suddenly bestowed"; "a constant work"; a "state of righteousness"; and a "progressive" work or process.

Clinton Wahlen has pointed out that Waggoner's understanding of perfection could lead to elitist attitudes. But he hastens to suggest that the early Waggoner would draw attention to two factors that would militate against any sense of superiority on the part of the perfected, First, Christian growth never has any stopping place. But the key point that prevents elitism, even in those most advanced in holiness, he describes in the following words: "The nearer one gets to God, the greater will seem the contrast between God and himself. If it were not so, there would come a time when he would cease to say 'Worthy is the lamb that was slain,' and would ascribe worthiness to himself. That time can never come."[53] Later he observed that "the more he [the believer] beholds Christ, the more will he feel his own nothingness in comparison; this will beget humility; humility will beget trustfulness; and trustfulness will bring strength."[54]

We can conclude this brief description of Waggoner's teaching on perfection with one of his best summary statements on the issue: Commenting on Ephesians 5:27 (describing a "glorious church, not having spot or wrinkle . . . ; but that it should be holy and without blemish"), Waggoner says that "surely if one abides *in Christ,* and if the word of truth by which he was turned away from sin still remains in him, it will continue to have the same effect that it had at first, and will keep him from sin. This does not mean that the individual will necessarily be perfect in knowledge, nor that he will be in a position where there is nothing more to gain; but it does mean that so far as he has knowledge of the law of God he will walk in it. He will be one of the 'undefiled in the way.' Psalm 119:1. Such an one will never boast of his goodness."[55]

Once more we must emphasize that Waggoner understood perfection to be the overcoming of all known sin in the life and that the key attitude of the overcomer would always be one of humility. Such humility would arise from the knowledge that all praise was due to the Lord of the marvelous transformations, and that each individual had a lot more work to be done in his or her life.

Along with his teaching on justification, we will continue to trace carefully any developments in Waggoner's teachings on sanctifying and perfecting grace. The two closely related concepts of justifying and transforming (sanctifying and perfecting) grace will always be closely related and deeply intertwined in Waggoner's expositions on personal salvation from sin—its guilt, power, and presence.

Now, regarding the subject of what some have come to refer to as the perfection of the "final generation" of God's people (which will bring vindication to God), nothing really like it appears in the pre-1888 writings of Waggoner. The theme will begin to receive attention in the early 1890s, but will come to prominent emphasis and full elaboration only in the later

1890s and the early years of the first decade of the twentieth century.

COVENANTS

In the earlier discussion on justification we attempted to suggest the complexity of Waggoner's covenant thought and that it is intricately related to his teaching on justification and sanctification. The general outlines of his covenant thought are as follows.[56]

Waggoner strongly emphasized that in the "old covenant" (1) God's people made well-intentioned promises to keep His law, but that it was impossible for them to obey it in their own strength since they had already broken it and had thus become sinful by nature;[57] (2) that it contained "no provision for forgiveness of sins" and that "it was ratified by the blood of beasts, which could never take away sin."[58] Most certainly sins could be forgiven, but this could be done only through "the promised sacrifice of Christ, and not because of anything in the old covenant."[59]

But what the old covenant could not do, the provisions of the new covenant could. And here was the key point in all of Waggoner's complex arguments about the covenants: the new covenant not only provided the promised cleansing from sin "by securing the remission of past sins (Rom. 3:24, 25)," but also enabled "us to walk in harmony with the law. Gal. 2:20; Eph. 2:10; Heb. 13:20, 21."[60] It was not that the new and old covenants disagreed over the demand for perfect obedience. They did not. Both required obedience. But the new covenant's requirement rested on better promises.

Please carefully note Waggoner's emphasis on the interrelatedness of both forgiveness and obedience: "There is the forgiveness of sins, and the blotting out of transgressions. More than this, the law is to be written in the hearts of the people, and that means that they will be enabled to keep it perfectly. See Ps. 40:8. This work is done by Christ. Through Him pardon is secured, and He enables us to be made the righteousness of God."[61]

Thus Waggoner was extremely clear that forgiveness and subjective moral transformation were the work of Christ in His ministry in the true sanctuary in heaven: "Christ is the minister of the new covenant (Heb. 8:1, 2) and is now performing the ministration in the true sanctuary in heaven. Heb. 9:24."[62]

Waggoner, however, would go on to make a further distinction regarding the fruit of Christ's internal work in the heart: The "letter" of the new covenant can be just as deadly as the human obedience of the old covenant: "Holding the mere letter of the new covenant—the performance of the gospel ordinances while not receiving Christ in the heart—is really a rejection of Christ. . . . If the ministration which could not cleanse from sin was glorious, the ministration of the Spirit, which gives freedom from sin, must be more glorious."[63]

Once again, we need to stress that for Waggoner the key differences between the old and the new covenants are that the old provided neither forgiveness of sins nor the writing of the law on the heart of the believer. But the new covenant did. The following statement sums it all up: "This covenant [the new] makes it possible to arrive at perfection, for that is what is meant by the writing of the law in the heart. Forgiveness of sins is an instantaneous work, but the writing of the law in the heart is a progressive work, the work of a lifetime. When the law is full written in the heart, then the individual is indeed sanctified; he is like Christ (Ps. 40:8), and is ready for translation."[64]

Thus Waggoner's interpretation of the covenants pulls together the various strands of his understanding of personal salvation. While it certainly puts a strong emphasis on the forgiveness of sins, the ultimate focus is on the work of the High Priest in the heavenly sanctuary, who comes to dwell in the hearts of believers.

Furthermore, Christ's centrally important role is to write the law of God upon the hearts of converted believers. When He has perfectly done so in them, Christ will then come to claim them as His own. Thus one can see how Waggoner has pulled together the various issues of redeeming grace (forgiveness, sanctification, perfecting grace, the person of Christ as mediating high priest in heaven); but above all else, the accent ultimately focuses on the Christ who lives in the heart and brings it to perfection through writing the law on the heart. And this will prepare the way for "translation" at the Second Coming (glorifying grace).

The final aspect of Waggoner's covenant thinking was his strong antidispensational view that God granted salvation on the same basis for everyone during all of His dispensations—by grace, through faith in His promises. For Waggoner there was no such thing as salvation by the law in the Old Testament times and salvation by grace during the New Testament period after the cross. Salvation is always by grace, through faith in the redemptive accomplishments, promises, and empowerment of Christ, not through the works or promises of any sinful human being.

SUMMARY

We will follow all of these theological developments carefully over next 15-plus years of Waggoner's career. The basic foundation has been put in place. The key question is: How does Waggoner go on to clarify the interdynamic relationship between forgiveness (justification by faith—the objective, accounting work of Christ) and character transformation (sanctification—the subjective work of Christ in the soul, leading to translation perfection)? Every aspect of his theology ultimately feeds into or off of this important question.

---

[1] "Graced obedience" means Christian obedience to the law of God that results from (1) gratefulness to God for the forgiveness and acceptance of the merits of His justifying grace and (2) God's imparting of divine power to the responsive and cooperating believer in order that the actual doing of God's will may be manifested in righteous attitudes and acts.

[2] "Salvation by faith" means to be saved from the guilt and power of sin by actually trusting or depending on the work of Christ for us to forgive us and to transform us into His likeness, both during the sanctification process that is the work of a lifetime and glorification that finally purges all sin from our human natures at the second coming of Christ.

[3] A good example of his running battle against racism appears in his comments on the back page of the *Signs of the Times*, May 18, 1888: "A church founded on caste may gain names, but it cannot gain souls. In Christ Jesus there is neither Jew nor Greek, there is neither bond or free, there is neither male nor female, but all are one."

[4] For a good sampling of his anti-war and pacifist ethics, see *Present Truth*, Apr. 19, 1894, p. 1, and "The Editor's Private Corner: Foundation Principles," *Present Truth*, Nov. 21, 1901.

[5] On his very apolitical stance for the church, see "The True Relation of the Church to the State," *Present Truth*, Jan. 2, 1896.

[6] For an understanding of Waggoner on these key issues, I have not only drawn on my own reading of Waggoner, but have greatly profited from the expositions of Eric C. Webster, *Crosscurrents in Adventist Christology*.

[7] Arianism refers to the position that basically subscribes to the teaching of Arius of Alexandria, a fourth-century A.D. thinker and writer who denied the eternal preexistence of Jesus Christ. "There was a time when Jesus was not" was Arius' classic declaration. In other words, Arius and his followers held that Christ did not exist before the Father brought Him into existence. Arius taught that God the Father created the Son as some sort of semideity. Arians have also consistently denied the personhood of the Holy Spirit.

[8] Semi-Arianism refers to the teaching that while the Father and the Son are not coeternal Persons, they do, however, share divinity in that the Son was "begotten" by the

Father in the following sense: Jesus was generated out of the divine nature of the Father in some sort of "amoebic split" in the Godhead. Thus while there was a time that Jesus, as a separate and identifiable person, did not exist, the divine nature of Jesus was alleged to have been derived from that of the Father.

[9] In an earlier published comment on Waggoner's theology I made the unfortunate observation that Waggoner taught "that Christ was a created god." Such a description would make Waggoner a classic Arian. But that was not the case. The statement appeared in my volume *Ellen White on Salvation* (Hagerstown, Md.: Review and Herald Pub. Assn., 1995), p. 90. I deeply regret this misstatement. The better characterization of Waggoner's understanding of the deity of Christ is to say that he was "semi-Arian," a position that will become explicit in the years 1889 and 1890. During the 1888-1892 period Waggoner will clearly enunciate a "semi-Arian" position and never explicitly repudiate it during the balance of his career.

[10] Here is an obvious quotation from 2 Corinthians 5:21, and Waggoner is using it to mean that Christ was "accounted" as a sinner, not so much made sinful in His human nature. We will carefully follow his developing understanding of this often cited and variously interpreted passage as our tracing of Waggoner's understanding of the humanity of Christ and salvation unfolds.

[11] E. J. Waggoner, "Under the Law," *Signs of the Times*, Sept. 18, 1884.

[12] Once again, we have a clear quotation from the key passage 2 Corinthians 5:21. How was it that Christ "knew no sin"? The answer to this question will become a key interpretive issue for Waggoner's developing understanding of Christ's humanity and the atonement.

[13] The original letter was written February 10, 1887, and published as a booklet in Oakland, California, by Pacific Press in 1888.

[14] *The Gospel in the Book of Galatians* (Oakland, Calif.: Pacific Press Pub. Assn.,1888), p. 61.

[15] "Post-Fall" is normally used in discussions on the nature of Christ to refer to those aspects of Jesus' nature that were somehow "affected by" or "infected" with human sinfulness. The "pre-Fall" advocates normally acknowledge that somehow Christ was affected by sin in some way, but do not believe that He was "infected" with sin—at least in the sense that He had taken inherent or natural sinful propensities, inclinations, tendencies, or bents to actually sin. Both the "pre-Fall" and the "post-Fall" advocates teach that Christ did not exhibit actual acts of sin—either in thought or action. Ellen White often used the expressions "inherited tendencies" (what all persons receive from their ancestors) and "cultivated tendencies" (what an individual acquires as character development unfolds) to sin.

[16] *The Gospel in the Book of Galatians*, pp. 60-62.

[17] *Ibid.* (Italics supplied.)

[18] E. J. Waggoner, "Under the Law," *Signs of the Times*, May 13, 1886.

[19] *Ibid.*

[20] E. J. Waggoner, "God Manifest in the Flesh," *Signs of the Times*, Jan. 21, 1889.

[21] Again, the following is the fruit of not only my own study of Waggoner—but I am indebted to the excellent synopsis of Waggoner's views on sin during this period give by Clinton Wahlen, "Selected Aspects of Ellet. J. Waggoner's Eschatology and Their Relation to His Understanding of Righteousness by Faith, 1882-1895" (M.Div. thesis, Andrews University, 1988), pp. 10-13.

[22] An Arminian is any Christian thinker who subscribes to the basic views of the late sixteenth-century Dutch Reformed writer and theologian Jacobus Arminius. Generally speaking, Arminians oppose the extreme deterministic views of Calvinism in regard to the doctrine of irresistible election. They generally hold that God gives the gift of graced free will to those responding to His saving initiatives through the work of Christ and the Holy Spirit.

[23] *Prevenient* comes from the Latin prefix "*pre,*" which means "before" and the Latin *venio,* which means "to come." Thus it refers to the grace that God sends before sinners even realize that He is working for them in their state of deadly heedlessness. God takes the initiative to awaken those who are "dead in trespasses and sins" (Eph. 2:1).

[24] This interpretation of the "law in Galatians" would begin in earnest with a 10-part series of articles in the *Signs of the Times* that ran from June 19 until September 18, 1884. The series would be the opening salvo in a four-year battle between Waggoner and the old guard leadership, headed by the General Conference president, G. I. Butler, and the editor of the *Review and Herald*, Uriah Smith. The conflict would culminate in major showdowns at the 1886 and 1888 General Conference sessions (with numerous subsequent skirmishes).

[25] Again, I am the beneficiary of the insights of Clinton Wahlen and Eric C. Webster. Also I have gleaned yet further clarification from the following: Robert Wieland, especially *The 1888 Message: An Introduction,* revised and enlarged (Paris, Ohio: Glad Tidings Publishers, 1997); George R. Knight, *A User-friendly Guide to the 1888 Message* (Hagerstown, Md.: Review and Herald Pub. Assn., 1998); Bert Haloviak, "From Righteousness to Holy Flesh: Judgment at Minneapolis" (unpublished manuscript; copies located at the archives of the General Conference of Seventh-day Adventists, Silver Spring, Md., and the Center for Adventist Research, James White Library, Andrews University, Berrien Springs, Mich.; privately copied and given to the author in the late 1980s); David P. McMahon, *Ellet Joseph Waggoner: the Myth and the Man;* and Milton Hook, "The Message of E. J. Waggoner," in Arthur J. Ferch, ed., *Towards Righteousness by Faith: 1888 in Retrospect* (Wahroonga, New South Wales, Australia: South Pacific Division of Seventh-day Adventists, 1989), pp. 25-49. While the challenging and conflicting interpretations of these writers have informed and stimulated my thinking, the following interpretive positions ultimately arise out of my own reading of Waggoner's primary publications on justification by faith.

[26] Justification by faith refers to the work of Christ to forgive sins and to grant a new legal standing of righteousness to the repentant, believing sinner. Two classic views exist on the subject. The objective view sees this as accomplished by Christ legally imputing, accounting, or reckoning the believer to be sinless for Christ's sake (even though the person is not yet sinlessly perfect in either character or nature). The subjective view regards Christ as somehow actually making the believer sinless through some sort of infusion or sowing of righteousness because he or she has actually been made righteous in character or nature or both. Both the objective and the subjective concepts hold that it is accomplished by faith through the grace of God.

[27] E. J. Waggoner, "The Lord's Prayer," *Signs of the Times*, May 5, 1887.

[28] E. J. Waggoner, "The Condemnation of Sin," *Signs of the Times*, Oct. 12, 1888.

[29] The key words "sanctification" and "sanctify" refer to what God does in the believer subjectively to bring about actual transformation of character from a life of sinfulness to one of obedient conformity to the law of God and the character and likeness of Christ. It involves all that grace does to change believers to be good and perfect in Christ.

[30] See Waggoner's "Salvation—Present and Future," *Signs of the Times*, May 25, 1888; "Comments on Galatians 3. No. 9," *Signs of the Times*, Sept. 2, 1886; and "A Lesson on Forgiveness," *Signs of the Times*, Feb. 3, 1888.

[31] For Waggoner on the justification of Abraham as taught by James, see his "Notes," *Signs of the Times*, Mar. 23, 1888: Abraham's "work was the outcome of his faith; it was the evidence of perfected faith. If it had not been for Abraham's faith, he never would have performed that work. . . . So faith is necessarily first. There cannot be works that will justify, without underlying faith." Furthermore, Waggoner said that "forgiveness must pre-

cede a righteous life," and that "no man can be righteous before his sins are forgiven" ("Forgiveness Real, Not Pretended," *Signs of the Times*, Aug. 3, 1888).

[32] E. J. Waggoner, "Faith and Works," *Signs of the Times*, June 23, 1887.

[33] Waggoner used the term *disposition(s)* to refer to the basic attitude of the professed believer, not more directly to the attendant actions of sinless perfection or totally reckless neglect of the will of God (and Christian believers have claimed both in the name of grace).

[34] "Legal fiction" is an expression often employed by the advocates of subjective justification to censure those who support the objective or legal aspects of justification by faith alone. In other words, the former argue that justification must be actually effective to make a person righteous in character or nature (or both) before God can declare such as righteous. If not, then we are dealing only with a "legal fiction," declaring a person righteous when they are not in actual attitude or character. Roman Catholics and perfectionistic Seventh-day Adventists often make this "legal fiction" charge against Protestants who advocate a strong doctrine of justification by faith alone.

[35] E. J. Waggoner, "Justification and Sanctification," *Signs of the Times*, Apr. 1, 1886, and later republished in the same journal of Nov. 30, 1891 (Italics supplied.)

[36] *Ibid.*

[37] They include Robert J. Wieland and Donald K. Short, their leading colleagues in the 1888 Study Committee movement, and their well-known fellow traveler, Jack Sequeira. For ready documentation, see Wieland's *The 1888 Message: An Introduction*, chap. 8, especially pp. 95 to 104, and Sequeira's *Beyond Belief* (Boise, Idaho: Pacific Press Pub. Assn., 1993), especially chap. 3, pp. 29 to 37.

[38] "The Lord's Prayer. Forgive Us Our Debts," *Signs of the Times*, May 5, 1887. The author must confess that he missed this statement in his personal reading of Waggoner's primary published writings and that Paul Penno, Jr., brought it to his attention.

[39] I invoke the qualifier "normally" here in order to recognize two key issues: (1) the salvation of infants and little children who have not yet come to accountability; and (2) the cases of non-Christians who have not been formally evangelized, but who will be redeemed. While these issues certainly allow for the possibility of salvation, they do not deny the overall biblical emphasis that salvation is by grace, through consciously trusting in the saving merits of Christ.

[40] Waggoner, *The Gospel in Galatians*, p. 45.

[41] "Justified by Faith," *Signs of the Times*, Nov. 23, 1891.

[42] E. J. Waggoner, "A Lesson on Forgiveness," *Signs of the Times*, Feb. 3, 1888.

[43] For a ready summary of the Adventist teaching on this issue, see Ellen G. White, *The Great Controversy Between Christ and Satan* (Mountain View, Calif.: Pacific Press Pub. Assn., 1911), pp. 603-652. For further Ellen White comment on the issues that involve the "time of Jacob's trouble," see also the compilation entitled *Last Day Events* (Nampa, Idaho: Pacific Press Pub. Assn., 1992), pp. 143-252.

[44] For a more extended treatment of this issue, see Woodrow Whidden II, *Ellen White on Salvation*, pp. 131-142.

[45] I could find no pre-1888 documentation for this concept, but it is quite clear in the following: "We think that because there will be no mediator then, that we stand in our own strength. There will come a time when there will be no mediator; but those who stand at that time will not stand in their own strength, but in the power of Christ that will keep us at that time; because we will be without sin, we shall need no mediator, but we shall need a Savior every moment" (E. J. Waggoner, "Bible Study: Letter to the Romans—No. 16," *General Conference Daily Bulletin*, Mar. 25, 1891, p. 242).

[46] Views shared with the author in a personal e-mail entitled "Observations on Justification."

[47] "Close of probation" is an expression that refers to the period that follows the end of Christ's pre-Advent investigative judgment in heaven and the second coming of Christ. Adventists also commonly understand it to be the period of the great "time of Jacob's trouble" and the pouring out of the seven last plagues of the book of Revelation.

[48] E. J. Waggoner, "Holiness of the Angels," *Signs of the Times*, Feb. 10, 1887.

[49] E. J. Waggoner, "Surroundings of the Early Church," *Signs of the Times*, Aug. 31, 1888.

[50] E. J. Waggoner, "Living Beneath Our Privileges," *Signs of the Times*, Jan. 11, 1883.

[51] E. J. Waggoner, "Notes on the International Lesson [2 Samuel 5:1-12]," *Signs of the Times*, June 19, 1884.

[52] E. J. Waggoner, *The Honor Due to God* (Oakland: Pacific Press Pub. Assn., 1884), p. 48.

[53] Wahlen, pp. 31, 32. This key statement and previous ones in quotation marks are drawn from E. J. Waggoner, "Practical Thoughts on Psalm 63," *Signs of the Times*, July 1, 1886.

[54] E. J. Waggoner, "Born of God," *Signs of the Times*, June 16, 1887.

[55] *Ibid.*

[56] Probably the best summary survey of the essentials of Waggoner's covenant thought is found in Ellen G. White's *Patriarchs and Prophets* (Mountain View, Calif.: Pacific Press Pub. Assn., 1890), pp. 363-373. As George Knight has aptly observed: "Ellen White and Waggoner were in essential harmony on the covenants. Her treatment of the two covenants, penned in the late 1880s [in *Patriarchs and Prophets*] provides a nice summary of their very similar view on the topic" (*A User-friendly Guide to the 1888 Message*, p. 98). For a more detailed, historical treatment of the development of Waggoner's teaching on the covenants in the setting of the late nineteenth-century Seventh-day Adventist debates about the issue, see Paul E. Penno, Jr., *Calvary at Sinai*.

[57] E. J. Waggoner, "Under the Law (Concluded)," *Signs of the Times*, June 3, 1886.

[58] E. J. Waggoner, "God's Covenant With Israel," *Signs of the Times*, June 22, 1888.

[59] E. J. Waggoner, "Exposition of 2 Cor. 3:7-11," *Signs of the Times*, June 2, 1887.

[60] *Ibid.* Compare the following from the above-cited article, "God's Covenant With Israel:" "It [the new covenant] provided forgiveness for transgression of the law concerning which the covenant was made, and also help to keep the law."

[61] E. J. Waggoner, "Under the Law (Concluded)," *Signs of the Times*, June 3, 1886.

[62] E. J. Waggoner, "Exposition of 2 Cor. 3:7-11," *Signs of the Times*, June 2, 1887.

[63] *Ibid.*

[64] E. J. Waggoner, "Bondage and Freedom," *Signs of the Times*, Sept. 3, 1885.

SECTION TWO
1888, Minneapolis General Conference Session, Its Background and Aftermath: 1888–1892

Chapter IV

THE RUN-UP TO MINNEAPOLIS: THE IMPENDING CRISIS

AS I HAVE PONDERED how to best introduce the reader to the path-breaking and tumultuous events of the year1888 and its controversial Minneapolis General Conference session, one image keeps coming to mind. It is not so much an image of the preaching of either E. J. Waggoner or A. T. Jones, who would play such leading roles in the revival of interest in the subject of righteousness by faith. Rather the visual sensation that seems better to encapsulate the importance of this meeting is a somewhat imaginary glimpse of the Adventist prophet, Ellen White.

This remarkable woman was moved at Minneapolis to become the leading advocate for Jones and Waggoner and the basic thrust of their vital message. My inspiration for this image comes from what amounts to an afternote, or PS, to a letter that Ellen White wrote to her terminally ill daughter-in-law, Mary K. White,[1] on the last day (November 4, 1888) of the trying conference (which Ellen White characterized as an "incomprehensible tug of war").

After reviewing her and her son Willie's contributions to important events and decisions of the meetings, Ellen White shared the following vignette: "I have one nice warm pair of stockings knit for Willie and I have the second pair almost done." She then concluded with the telling revelation that "just as I was folding this letter this great blotch [of ink] came to make it look badly."[2]

In my reflections on the significance of this storied General Conference session of 1888, it seems that the essence of the meeting centers on the reactions and responses of Ellen White to the deeply troubling spiritual and theological situation that had developed among the ministerial leadership of the Seventh-day Adventist Church. We will certainly go into more detail regarding the background to this most controversial of all General Conference sessions, its key issues, and its conflicted aftermath. But before we explore those aspects, we need to clarify what Ellen White understood to be the heart of the meaning of Minneapolis, especially the 12 public presentations (including nine lectures) of E. J. Waggoner.

While she was not totally clear on all of the details, she picked up on one central theme and then proceeded to voice her very strong support for it. "When I stated before my brethren that I had heard for the first time the views of Elder E. J. Waggoner, some did not believe me. I stated that I had heard precious truths uttered that I could respond to with all my heart." And what were those "precious truths"? She was very forthright: "The righteousness of Christ and the entire sacrifice made in behalf of man."

While Ellen White went on to remind her readers that the crucial subjects had "been imprinted indelibly" on her "mind by the Spirit of God" and had been "presented in the testimonies again and again," she was adamant that the talks given by Waggoner (and Jones, to a lesser extent) were a restatement of a vital truth that was "the message for this time." But she was not finished with her explanation for her controverted and heartfelt support for the message(s) of the two young men.

She strongly suggested that "the third angel's message is the proclamation of the commandments of God and the faith of Jesus Christ. The commandments of God have been proclaimed, but the faith of Jesus has not been proclaimed by Seventh-day Adventists as of equal importance, the law and the gospel going hand in hand."

Then she proceeded to get more specific as to what the "faith of Jesus" was: "[The faith of Jesus] is talked of, but not understood. What constitutes the faith of Jesus that belongs to the third angel's message? Jesus becoming our sin-bearer that He might become our sin-pardoning Savior. He was treated as we deserve to be treated. He came to our world and took our sins that we might take His righteousness. Faith in the ability of Christ to save amply and fully and entirely is the faith of Jesus."[3]

In another closely related reflection on the meaning of E. J. Waggoner's presentations at the Minneapolis meetings, she made it clear that he had placed "the righteousness of Christ in the law" and that this powerful combination is a potent recipe for revealing "God in His true character and . . . the law as holy, just, and good, glorious indeed when seen in its true character."[4]

Now at this juncture, some readers are probably muttering to themselves, "What has all of this to do with Willie's stockings and a blot of ink on a letter to a daughter-in-law who was about to perish from TB?"

The whole thing about the stockings, the blot of ink, and a dying loved one presents marvelous symbolism for the meaning of the messages of E. J. Waggoner, A. T. Jones, Ellen White, and the historic moment referred to as "Minneapolis and 1888."

The stockings reference kindled a vision of the embattled, struggling Ellen White sitting in her rooming house accommodations knitting away on Willie's stockings, all the while reflecting on the Christ-centered messages being presented by Waggoner. As her thoughts deepened they must have elicited intensely felt amens from her soul-burdened heart. And what was the burden of her heart? The sad spiritual state of the ministerial and administrative leadership of the church and the deadening effect such a condition was having on the rank and file and their collective mission to the world. Thus the blot on the letter to her beloved daughter-in-law Mary was a rapt symbol of the bitter opposition to this message boiling over from the wrought-up emotions of leading administrative and editorial ministers of the embattled Seventh-day Adventist Church.

Furthermore, the forebodings of the imminent death of Mary Kelsey White reflected a doomed and dying world desperately needing the message that Waggoner, Jones, and Ellen White sought to give to it through the proclamation of a Christocentric renovation of the mighty third angel's message of Revelation 14.

Now, the thought of Ellen White belting out heartfelt amens while knitting socks for Willie might be a bit far-fetched (the fruit of my somewhat dramatic imagination), but the rest of it is pure fact: Ellen White did give the young men and their message strong endorsement(s), and she would soon join them in a concerted campaign to take the message of Christ and His righteousness to the rank and file of the Sabbatarian Adventist movement. Furthermore, the opposition of so many of the leading ministers of Seventh-day Adventism during the late 1880s became one of the foul blots on the record of the movement (and the opposition was amazingly persistent, even in the face of the strong support coming from the acknowledged, prophetically inspired "messenger to the remnant").

And finally, Ellen White firmly believed that this message of the uplifted Christ and the reaffirmed authority of the law of God was the heart of the last message that God intended to bring to the attention of a dying world, a planet fast hurtling toward its imminent and irreversible destiny on the great day of the Lord.

As we sit here in the first decade of the twenty-first century, the question comes to all students of Adventist history: what truly was this message and why was it so controversial? While we have given some hints regarding its serious content and implications from the reactions of Ellen White, we will deal with the first part of our question through further sustained attention as this biography unfolds.

But for now we need to turn our attention to the controverted background of events leading up to this most fabled of all Seventh-day Adventist General Conference sessions. Why were the leading ministers so suspicious and bitterly persistent in their resistance not only to Jones and Waggoner, but even to the respected and authoritative Ellen White?

THE CRISIS BACKGROUND OF MINNEAPOLIS

Seven major things contributed to the poisoned atmosphere that enveloped the General Conference session of 1888.[5] While other issues spun off from the following seven key background factors, the following dynamics provide the essential backdrop for the tensions that boiled over at Minneapolis and its complex and troublesome aftermath.

Briefly stated, the seven factors were:

1. The multiplication of Sunday laws in the United States during the 1880s.

2. Controversy over the interpretation of the 10 horns of Daniel 7 (mainly originating in a tense debate between A. T. Jones and Uriah Smith, the venerable longtime editor of the *Review and Herald*).

3. A lingering, unfortunate public debate between E. J. Waggoner and leading Adventist ministers led by G. I. Butler (the incumbent president of the General Conference) regarding the identity of the law in Galatians and the controversial General Conference session of 1886. At the latter

session Butler made a strong effort to head off the influence of the teachings of Jones and Waggoner on the horns of Daniel 7 and the law in Galatians.

4. The personalities of the key protagonists: E. J. Waggoner, A. T. Jones, and their leading denominational opponents, especially G. I. Butler and Uriah Smith.

5. The low spiritual and moral tone of the Adventist ministry (including at least six notorious scandals during the mid- to late 1880s).

6. Tensions over calls for reorganization, especially the diffusion of decision-making power away from the power brokers at the administrative center in Battle Creek.

7. And finally, the rumors of a "California conspiracy," which suggested that Willie and Ellen White were involved in a sinister plot with Jones and Waggoner to insinuate their views on the "ten horns" and the "law in Galatians" into the doctrinal structure of Adventism.

Together the seven controversial issues set the table for the insidious tug-of-war that would ensue at Minneapolis. We will elaborate them one by one in this chapter before we address the events and dynamics of the conference itself and its preceding ministerial institute in the following chapter.

1. The Sunday Laws of the 1880s

During this decade Sunday legislation and the zealous prosecution (persecution) of those who had allegedly broke them spread across the United States. The issues related to Sunday laws and Seventh-day Adventists came to an initial flashpoint during 1882 in California. Not only were Sunday laws a major political topic during the local elections of that year, but political arguments morphed into actual enforcement with the arrest of none other than W. C. ("Willie") White. Officials charged him with operating the Pacific Press in Oakland, California, on Sunday.[6] While this agitation soon died down with the repeal of California's Sunday law, national agitation for such legislation continued to grow.

The campaign became so intense that the Seventh-day Adventist Church felt led to found a periodical especially to address religious liberty issues. Initially named the *Sabbath Sentinel* (founded in 1884), it would become the *American Sentinel* and *Sentinel of Christian Liberty* (in 1886 and afterward). For a number of years E. J. Waggoner and A. T. Jones would edit the latter publication. In addition to their editorial duties at the *Signs of the Times* and their itinerant revivalism after 1888, both became known for their articulate and vocal opposition to Sunday legislation and other issues related to the Sabbath and separation of church and state.[7]

When things had settled down in California, the focus on religious liberty shifted to Arkansas in 1885. Arkansas Sunday laws had been on the books since 1883, including an exemption for Sabbathkeepers. But in 1885 the state repealed the exemptions, and from 1885 to 1887 prosecuted 21 cases of Sunday desecration, with all but two involving Sabbathkeepers (with the two non-Sabbathkeepers being released without bail and the dismissal of their cases). The Seventh-day Adventists, however, incurred heavy penalties.

What proved ironic was that Arkansas had revoked the exemptions in order to target Jewish saloon operators, yet the authorities had not arrested a single saloonkeeper, and many of the witnesses and informers against the arrested Adventists had also been working on Sunday themselves. That the courts would bring severe penalties only on Seventh-day Adventists was a clear travesty of justice and caused much alarm among Adventists nationally. Yet such incidents did not restrict themselves to Arkansas. By the late 1880s the Sunday law prosecutions had shifted to Tennessee, with some Seventh-day Adventists (including ministers) even serving time on prison chain gangs.

During 1887, however, the issue began to take on an ominously national character. That year both the Prohibition Party and the highly influential national Women's Christian Temperance Union began supporting the National Reform Association's campaign for Sunday laws. The stated rationale was to promote American morality. In the same year the energetic and excitable Wilber Crafts (whom we will meet later on in our story) formed the American Sabbath Union for the purposes of promoting Sunday laws.

As if all of this mostly Protestant inspired activity was not enough, one can imagine the eschatological foreboding and excitement among Seventh-day Adventists when the renowned Cardinal James Gibbons (of the influential Baltimore Archdiocese of the Roman Catholic Church) united his influence with the Protestants in support of national Sunday legislation.

The push for such laws reached its climax on May 21, 1888, when New Hampshire senator H. W. Blair introduced a Senate bill to promote national Sunday observance, calling it "the Lord's Day" and a "day of religious worship." Four days later he submitted a proposed constitutional amendment that would Christianize the American public school system.

Most certainly all of this did not escape the lively eschatological and apocalyptic consciousness of Seventh-day Adventist students of Bible prophecy, especially the long-looked-for fulfillment of Revelation 13 and its promised "mark of the beast" persecutions. Such an atmosphere makes it easy to understand how new interpretations of the great antichrist prophecies of the Bible (especially Daniel 7, with its Roman fourth beast and 10 threatening horns, all of which show up later in Revelation 13) and the identity of the law of Galatians could stir the emotions of Adventist ministerial leadership. In such a crisis it did not appear to be a wise moment to be making adjustments to longstanding interpretations that appeared to be essential to a correct understanding of the imminently impending crisis. Thus one can appreciate the intensity of the next two background issues that made the 1888 General Conference session so sensitive and suspicious of the initiatives of Jones and Waggoner.

2. Controversy Over the 10 Horns of Daniel 7

This conflict primarily occurred between A. T. Jones (already a rising star in Adventism because of his editorial position at the Pacific Press) and Uriah Smith and centered on the interpretation of the 10 horns of Daniel 7. Though Waggoner never played any significant role in this debate, he found himself touched by it because of his close association with Jones, who had become his associate editor at the *Signs of the Times* in 1884. The issue, plus their joint advocacy of a differing interpretation of the law in Galatians, would trigger friction between the two young editors and the Battle Creek leadership of Uriah Smith, George I. Butler, and their numerous allies.

The entire "horns" controversy began innocently enough, even amicably. The young A. T. Jones had quickly developed quite a reputation as a historical researcher, especially in relationship to the historical fulfillment of important Bible prophecies. Thus it seemed natural that the delegates of the 1884 General Conference session should ask him to "write a series of articles gathered from history on points that showed the fulfillment of prophecy."[8] The venerable Uriah Smith, the veteran and acknowledged champion of Adventist prophetic interpretation,[9] had initially expressed his support for Jones in undertaking a more thorough treatment of the 10 horn kingdoms of Daniel 7.

But the friendly commencement of the new study initiative became strained as Jones began to unfold his new interpretation of the 10 horns in early 1885—conclusions that not so subtly suggested that Smith's long-established and published list was incorrect.

Jones' research had led him to conclude that the Alemanni, not the Huns, better fit the identity of the tenth horn of Daniel 7. Initially he sent his conclusions to Smith for review. He requested that the *Review and Herald* editor present firm support for his interpretation of the horns, and review the evidence that Jones shared with him. Smith did not reply to the first request and pleaded that he had no time to examine Jones's material. The result was that Jones went ahead and published his findings in the *Signs of the Times* and sent copies to Smith in October of 1886. The reception of Jones's articles aroused the heretofore-unresponsive Smith to an irate counterattack.

Smith's reply went to the core of the issue that Jones's new interpretation raised: he basically argued that if the Huns are not one of the 10, then "we are yet ten percent short on the fulfillment of Daniel 2 and 7," and such an admission would raise questions about the whole Seventh-day Adventist prophetic scheme. Quickly Smith suggested that "if our preachers, after presenting the ten kingdoms as they have for the past forty years, should now change upon a point which has been considered so well established, that it has never excited a dissenting voice," then "thousands would . . . say, 'Oh! now you find that you are mistaken on what you have considered one of your clearest points; and so if we give you time enough, you will probably come to acknowledge finally that you are mistaken on everything.' Thus the tendency would be to unsettle minds upon all points, [and] create confusion."[10]

Jones's reply to him was to the effect that the "real battle" for the "truth" had only just begun, as Seventh-day Adventists, up to this point, had gained little notice. But now that the Sunday law crisis had arisen, it was a sure thing that Adventist beliefs in the looming end-time crisis would "become the principal subject of discussion in this whole nation," and such prominence would array the believers before the "high in the land." Then "every point is going to be analyzed and challenged by the scholarship and dignity of judges, statesmen, and the greatest in the land. . . . Then it will be that our views will have to be examined by men who are acquainted with all the avenues of history, and will have to pass the challenges that all these men can put upon the truth."

He forcefully concluded that "when we shall have to run down these lines through the history to show that we are right in our statement of the third angel's message, we shall then to these men have to present some better reason for our faith than that 'it has been preached for forty years' or that Bishop Chandler said so." Only reliable historical evidence would suffice in the face of such challenges. Jones pointedly concluded with the not-so-subtle suggestion that Uriah Smith should clear up the errors in his *Thoughts on Daniel,* which "every well-informed person knows" are "not true."[11]

In response, Smith accused Jones of "ransacking history" to prove him wrong. Such a reply revealed the venerable editor's reliance on the authority of a 40-year tradition rather than dealing with a factual refutation of Jones's new interpretation. Characteristically Jones was not impressed with such an appeal and again challenged Smith to come up with facts and not to rely on traditional authority, "third-rate names," and commentators whose authority one could not substitute for the testimony of "standard historians." He concluded his pointed reply by writing that if Smith had "any reliable authority at all to show the kingdoms of the Huns" as the fulfillment of the prophecy, Jones would be glad to publish his findings in the *Signs of the Times.*[12]

It is absolutely essential, from our contemporary perspective, to note clearly that both contestants in this interpretive joust had framed their replies in the setting of the looming Sunday law crisis. The Adventist prophetic interpretation of the Sunday law threat was a central plank in its platform to vindicate its concepts of both the Sabbath and its historicist principles of prophetic interpretation (especially of Daniel 7-12 and Revelation 12-14). Since they regarded the church as on the verge of the great apocalyptic finale, we can understand that they considered it critically important to be historically and interpretively right.

From Smith's perspective it was hardly a propitious moment to be tinkering with the church's long-held position. For Jones, though, the impending crisis demanded that the Adventist position be right according to the facts, not right according to what he perceived to be a hoary and unsupported tradition. Thus to Jones the issue was truth, and if that called for a shift in interpretations, so be it. Better to be right late in the contest than be seen as standing around pleading a tradition that had no factual confirmation.

The debate did not restrict itself to the private exchanges between Jones and Smith. Jones's publication of his findings practically guaranteed that the issue would go public. Not surprisingly, it did come up for consideration at the 1886 General Conference in Battle Creek, but its major impact would surface at Minneapolis.

By the time of the eve of the Minneapolis session, General Conference president G. I. Butler would be utterly convinced that Jones was bent only on stirring up new interpretations that went "contrary to the long-established faith of our people taken forty years ago."[13] Quite obviously, Butler shared Smith's perspective and was also relying on the authority of long-held, traditional consensus, utterly convinced that a change in interpretive positions at such a decisive moment was dangerously counterproductive.

In the face of such heated controversy, it is a bit surprising that W. C. White was able to get a renewed discussion of the issue onto the agenda of the ministerial institute immediately preceding the formal session of the October/November 1888 General Conference.

Once more, to no one's surprise, the ensuing discussion became quite heated. The debate generated such intensity that even during the breaks between the sessions of the 1888 ministerial institute the various partisans reportedly became so wrought up that when meeting one another (possibly even on the streets) they would confront each other with the question "Are you a Hun or an Alemanni?"[14] One can only imagine the puzzled looks that must have crossed the faces of non-Adventist pedestrians who happened to be passing by during such exchanges!

We see a further glimpse of the situation in a comment by a conference delegate from Minnesota (Lewis Johnson).[15] When asked about the "horns" of Daniel 7, he allegedly replied that he wished "there were no horns." Johnson went on to recall that "when someone asked Mrs. White what she thought about the horns," he claimed that she "cryptically" replied that "there are too many horns."[16]

That the issue of the "horns" of Daniel 7 became a dynamic flashpoint at the Minneapolis meetings should come as no surprise to any informed student of Adventist history. Yet, if the debate over the 10 horns was "intense," the crisis over the issue of the identity of the law in Galatians "was literally explosive."[17]

3. Debate About the Law in Galatians

It was one thing to be making adjustments in matters of history and prophetic interpretation, but to be seen as making changes to long-held positions on the Adventist theology of the law was more than the leadership at Battle Creek could tolerate.

To get some perspective on this issue, we need to review the history of the debate and seek to understand why this particular controversy had become so intense for Seventh-day Adventists in the 1880s.

As we have already mentioned in the previous chapter, Waggoner and Jones had both been writing in *Signs of the Times* and teaching at Healdsburg College, since at least 1884, that the law in Galatians, which leads to Christ, had primary reference to the moral law, not the Mosaic, or ceremonial, law. Such a position, however, went against a strong current of a long-established teaching tradition in Adventism.

It is important to understand that Adventist ministers and evangelists had for some time felt the need to fight a battle on two highly important fronts. The first had to do with the defense of the seventh-day Sabbath of the fourth commandment. Not only did such a position stir up Sundaykeeping Protestant (and to some extent Catholic) opposition, but they had to face a strong current of evangelical teaching that claimed that the death of Christ had done away with the law. This was especially true of those evangelicals influenced by the Restorationist[18] preachers, or Christianites, a movement spawned earlier in the nineteenth-century revivalism of Thomas and Alexander Campbell and Barton W. Stone (the founders of the modern-day Church of Christ [so-called non-Instrumental, because of its refusal to use musical instruments in worship services] and the Disciples of Christ—often simply called the Christian Church).

While such groups shared some key perspectives with a number of the founders of the Seventh-day Adventist movement (especially James White and Captain Joseph Bates, both of whom had been New England "Christianite" ministers [associated with the now-defunct Christian Connexion movement] before turning to Millerism and subsequently to Sabbatarian Adventism), the anti-law (technically referred to as antinomianism—from the Greek *anti* [against] and *nomos* [law]) and strong anti-Old Testament dispensationalism of the heirs of the Campbells and Stone presented a powerful challenge to the Adventist proclamation of the Sabbath, the eternal authority of the law, and their doctrine of the pre-Advent investigative judgment based on the standard of the Ten Commandments.

To counter the Seventh-day Adventist teachings on the law and the Sabbath, many of the opponents of Adventist teaching had gone to Galatians, especially chapter 3 and its "added law" of verses 19-25, to prove that the law spoken of there was the Ten Commandments, which New Testament believers were no longer "under" (they understood verse 25 to mean that believers were no longer required to obey this "added law").

In response to such interpretive challenges, which seemingly struck right at the heart of the messages of Sabbatarian Adventism's distinctive "present truth" doctrines, Seventh-day Adventist writers and evangelists had come up with what they felt was an effective interpretation of the law in Galatians to counteract the anti-law/anti-Sabbatarian arguments of their evangelical opponents.

It involved an interpretation that the law in Galatians (especially the "added law" of Galatians 3) referred to the typical offerings of the ceremonial law that Christ had made of none effect through His great antitypical sacrifice at Calvary. Thus the law in Galatians was not the moral law, but the temporary ceremonial requirements of the first five books of the Old Testament (the Pentateuch).

Not surprisingly, it just so happened that three of the great developers of this polemical interpretation were Uriah Smith, G. I. Butler, and Adventism's leading public evangelist and debater/defender of the moral law, Dudley M. Canright.[19] But the concept was not original to them. The ceremonial law idea had had an interesting history in early Seventh-day Adventism.

A debate about the law in Galatians had taken place during the late 1850s. In it Joseph Waggoner, E. J. Waggoner's father, had assumed a leading role in arguing that the law was the moral law, not the ceremonial. He had even published a book entitled *The Law of God: An Examination of the Testimony of Both Testaments* (1854). Initially it had seemed that J. N. Andrews, James White, and Ellen White had agreed with the elder Waggoner on the issue. But because of a strong protest from church members in New England, led by Stephen Pierce of Vermont, these venerable founders swung over to the "ceremonial law" position in interpreting the law in Galatians.

Furthermore, reports circulated that Ellen White had had a vision during the late 1850s on the matter, and it had shown her that the ceremonial law interpretation was the right one (a claim especially alleged by G. I. Butler and Uriah Smith). Eventually James White had Joseph Waggoner's book removed from the market. And thus the matter had stood until the elder Waggoner's son resurfaced the issue in 1884, renewing the contentious debate.

As the internal debate between E. J. Waggoner and his influential opponents in Battle Creek heated up between 1884 and 1886, General Conference president G. I. Butler took the lead in squelching what he deemed to be a breach in doctrinal solidarity. For Butler and his followers, their interpretation of the law in Galatians had risen to the level of a "pillar" of "present truth."

In fact, Uriah Smith, who stood shoulder to shoulder with Butler on the issue, had felt so strongly about the matter that he claimed that if the church changed its position, "they may count me out." His convictions (feelings) ran so deep on the question that he could claim that if the traditional position had been wrong for more than 30 years, then "Seventh-day Adventism has been developed and built upon error." The implications, in his mind (and Butler's), were so grave that he could even declare that if the denomination adopted the ten-commandment view of the law in Galatians it would "overthrow the Testimonies and the Sabbath."[20]

Thus it was abundantly apparent that in the minds of such defenders of long-established "present truth," the whole platform of doctrinal Adventism and its prophetically destined role seemed to be at serious risk. For these proponents of the Adventist faith, it was an epic struggle of titanic proportions. The "dragons" of antinomianism and the minions of anti-Sabbatarianism were at the gates of the "kingdom," and even the fortress of the Testimonies (the seemingly authoritative biblical interpretations of Ellen White) appeared to be in danger of falling to the enemy.

For E. J. Waggoner, however, in a vein of thought similar to that of Jones's response to Uriah Smith during the "horns" debate, it was more important to be right than simply to cling to a faulty interpretation. "As we approach the end [of time] all the forces of the enemy will be concentrated" upon the Adventist interpretations of the law and thus "every point in our argument will have to be subjected to the test of the most rigid criticism." He continued by telling Butler that "you will say that it will be a humiliating thing to modify our position on so vital a point . . . in the face of the enemy. But if a general has a faulty position, I submit that it is better to correct it . . . than to run the risk of defeat because of his faulty position."

Humiliation was not the key issue to Waggoner. Rather, the core of the conflict had to do with a willingness to make modifications for the sake of the truth. Such a change in position "would simply be an acknowledgment that" Adventists "are better informed to day than they were yesterday."[21]

Once more, we should carefully note that these debates occurred in the shadow of the Sunday law crisis that had enveloped the Adventist Church, and both sides felt that the stakes were terribly high (for the "pioneers," the better metaphor could have been that the "stakes had been driven into the most fundamental of theological grounds").

The whole litany of the different phases of this debate that unfolded from early 1886 and onward are too complex to explore in any great detail.[22] But for our purposes here, we need to observe the main strategies Butler proceeded to invoke in his attempts to rein in Waggoner and his allies.

The embattled General Conference president's first line of strategy was to seek to enlist the support of Ellen White on his side. He hoped that since she had settled the earlier debate in the mid- to late 1850s (at least according to his recollection), she should conveniently step in once more and quickly resolve this one. But, much to his frustration and even surprise, the prophet proved to be quite unresponsive to his appeals and suggestions.

So he then turned to his second tactic, which was to publish a "brief comment on the Epistle to the Galatians" regarding the law. His "brief comment" emerged as an 85-page book entitled *The Law in the Book of Galatians* (1886). It was, in fact, not just a "brief comment," but a thoroughgoing polemical attack on Waggoner's interpretation. In addition to the release of Butler's book, he had D. M. Canright's *Two Laws* (first published in 1876) revised and reprinted in 1886, with the section on the law in Galatians expanded fourfold, from a mere six to 24 pages.

Butler's third tactic was to use the 1886 General Conference session to seek to put Waggoner and Jones and their "false teachings" in their place and get the seemingly derailed church back on the right track of theological and evangelistic mission.

In pursuit of his goals, Butler saw to it that each delegate received a copy of his newly minted polemic, *The Law in the Book of Galatians*, and then proceeded to organize a special theological committee to settle both the issues of the 10 horns and the law in Galatians.

The committee consisted of nine members, including the major protagonists (Uriah Smith, Butler himself, E. J. Waggoner, and D. M. Canright). To no one's surprise, they had "an argument of several hours" and split five to four over the key issues. Such a thin margin of victory was most certainly not a resounding vindication of the beleaguered president's efforts. Thus Butler found his hopes to achieve some sort of creedal decision on the issues frustrated. Rather than take the issue to the main floor of the conference (and "have a big public fight over it"), Butler wisely worked to achieve some sort of compromise.

The result was that the desperate leader was able to get a resolution passed that, in effect, sought to legislate that "doctrinal views not held by a fair majority of our people" should not be taught in Adventist schools or printed in church publications unless they had passed the examination and approval of "leading brethren of experience."[23]

The collective result of all three approaches, including the latter compromise resolution, was to create a situation that was a classic stalemate that satisfied neither side. The simmering war would continue and the showdown simply got put off to a later date. Both Butler and Ellen White would look back on the 1886 General Conference as that "terrible conference" (of course, for differing reasons).

What seemed to really trouble Ellen White was that she felt that "Jesus was grieved and bruised in the person of His saints" in the terrible manifestations of "harshness" and "disrespect, and the want of sympathetic love in brother toward brother." As George Knight has sagaciously observed, the "dynamics of Minneapolis were already in place."[24]

Ellen White would dish out rebukes to both sides in the conflict, as she was particularly grieved that both parties were carrying on such divisive debates in a public manner that made a needless spectacle of the interpretive fractures in the Advent movement. But she would eventually go on to hold that since the debate had spilled over into the public venue with Butler's publication of his polemical *Law in the Book of Galatians*, fairness would demand that Waggoner receive a chance to reply. And this he was allowed to do in two ways: the publication of his lengthy 1887 letter to Butler entitled *The Gospel in the Book of Galatians,* and an opportunity to air his views at Minneapolis publicly. The letter, turned booklet, was ultimately published in 1888 and was distributed to the delegates at the Minneapolis General Conference session.

While issues of public divisiveness and of fairness weighed heavily on the mind of Ellen White, the main aspect that pained her was the aforementioned "harsh" way that church leaders dealt with one another. She would repeatedly stress that they needed to settle the whole debate through a Christlike, respectful discussion. But she had one more principle that she placed increasing stress upon: the whole thing should undergo a testing on the anvil of patient Bible study and should not be decided by any vision from her or the invoking of any long-held, seemingly settled traditional interpretation. This issue was not a "pillar" of the faith.

Thus Butler's hope that Ellen White would effectually end the discussion with a visionary stand was dashed. She was never able to recall clearly or to confirm whether she had had a decisive vision in the 1850s. In fact, although she carefully searched to see if she had any record of such a testimony, she was unable to locate any such written record.

We cannot stress too much that, for Ellen White, the following principles were paramount: (1) leaders should cease their harsh and "pharisaic" ways; (2) the issue was not as serious as either side claimed that it was; and (3) the truth of the matter should be decided by good, old-fashioned Adventist Bible study. But it was to be the type of study that featured reverent, humble, and prayerful discussions and exchanges, carried on in a Christlike spirit of sincere searching and deep respect for the honest opinions held by both sides. To her seemingly endless dismay, however, she would also be largely frustrated in her hopes, and Minneapolis would be the final major battle in the conflict. It too would turn out to be another "terrible conference"—what Ellen White would characterize as "a most laborious meeting" and the "most incomprehensible tug of war we have ever had among our people."[25]

While Ellen White would eventually affirm the essential truth on the law in Galatians that Waggoner and Jones had championed, she never felt that the actual interpretive question was at the core of the issue. In fact, she never accepted Smith and Butler's not-so-subtle suggestion that if she did not side with them it would make of none effect her prophetic authority (based, of course, on their allegation that she had settled the issue in the 1850s with a visionary revelation).

Ellen White was not about to be bullied in such a way. She had bigger spiritual and theological irons to shape as her prophetic fires warmed to the larger issues facing the Seventh-day Adventist Church! From her unflappable perspective, if there was any truth in the interpretations of either side, it was to be understood as a vehicle to come to grips with larger issues that she perceived as of more fundamental and serious import. What she kept persistently focusing on was that leaders (1) must act in a Christlike way, (2) be open to Bible truth, and (above all) (3) become much more Christ- and grace-centered in their expositions of Bible truth, especially those contained in the great three angels' messages of Revelation 14.

Later we will return to the theological significance of the law in Galatians debate and carefully seek to understand how this issue eventually played out in what E. J. Waggoner and A. T. Jones sought to proclaim and what Ellen White would so strongly and affirmatively endorse. But for now we need to understand clearly that the collective effect that the rancorous and drawn-out debate over the law in Galatians had was the major storm center around which all other factors played out. And the net result was the pall of a terribly tense and confrontational atmosphere hanging over Minneapolis in late October and early November of 1888.

Yet still other factors contributed to the controversial mix that was Minneapolis and its smoldering aftermath. They derived mainly from the personalities involved, especially the stubborn administrative style of G. I. Butler.

4. The Personalities of the Key Participants[26]

While the controversy involved a number of personalities, the four key ones were E. J. Waggoner, A. T. Jones,[27] Uriah Smith,[28] and George I. Butler.[29]

Ellen White had rebuked Waggoner in 1887, pointing out his need for humility and meekness during the law in Galatians exchanges with Butler, and he had subsequently manifested a meek and humble spirit.[30] Aside from Ellen White's occasional rebukes during this period of controversy over the law in Galatians, the only other sour note regarding Waggoner's public demeanor came from his old childhood friend and college-years correspondent, W. C. ("Willie") White.

Willie White would later recall (in 1930, 42 years after the session) that "the pomposity and egotism" of Jones and Waggoner "seemed out of place in such young men" at the Minneapolis gathering.[31] His is the harshest assessment recorded. Yet one gets the distinct impression that most of his recollection involved A. T. Jones, not Waggoner.

Ellen White's observations regarding Waggoner's conduct, stated publicly at the Minneapolis session itself, seems to better reflect his overall demeanor and conduct. In a highly affirmative manner she told the deeply divided delegates the following: "Dr. Waggoner has spoken to us in a straight-forward manner. . . . Dr. Waggoner . . . has presented his views in a plain, straight-forward manner, as a Christian should."[32]

Thus, despite her earlier, somewhat unflattering observations and Willie's suggestions of "pomposity and egotism," the main impression was that the young editor/revivalist had kept his cool, acted the part of an astute thinker and preacher, and acquitted himself as a "Christian" gentleman at Minneapolis. While some reportedly heckled him for his short stature, we have no record that he made any retaliatory retorts or exhibited any of his possibly unflattering personality traits as a decisive feature in his public presentations.

While Jones was more fiery and cocksure by nature than the more studious Waggoner and had been the recipient of unflattering recollections by W. C. White and some public rebukes by Ellen White (most notably, for some caustic remarks directed at Uriah Smith at Minneapolis), he had also, for the most part, conducted himself with considerable restraint in the face of some tough opposition.

His much more forceful personality was to be both a great asset and liability in the subsequent years of his prominent and varied career in Adventism. But with the exception of some of the above-mentioned W. C. White memories and the Ellen White cautions and counsels, his personal conduct at Minneapolis did not appear to play a decisive role in the session. While Jones did make presentations at the pre-session ministerial institute on the horns of Daniel 7 and one copresentation with Waggoner during the main conference, Waggoner was the main public presenter of their shared ideas on "Christ and His righteousness" issues.

Uriah Smith, although capable of an irate response from time to time, was generally a man of a calm and considered spirit. Yet an opinionated and stubborn streak in him made him a tough individual in dialogue.

The master of a smooth and clear writing style, he had developed a long history of producing classic expressions of Seventh-day Adventist doctrinal truth and was the denomination's acknowledged authority on prophetic interpretation. The longtime editor of the *Review and Herald* (by 1888 he had been editor for 25 years) and long-serving secretary of the General Conference of Seventh-day Adventists (he had served as secretary for all but a few years since 1863), he was a man who commanded immense respect and venerable authority.

Smith's problem was not that he lost his cool in quick and cutting retort—he just had a hard time changing his mind. While not as pronounced as Butler in his self-understanding of his accrued authority in matters of doctrinal and biblical interpretation, he seemed to have a pretty high view of his expositions and defenses of "present truth." "Smith viewed himself as a guardian of denominational orthodoxy."[33]

His stated editorial philosophy quite clearly revealed the authoritative sense he had of his role in the Advent movement. "Having by long study, and years of observation in the work, become settled on certain principles, I am not prepared to flop over at the suggestion of every novice."[34] And when he had made up his mind, he could be adamant in his opposition to and rejection of the urgent counsels of Ellen White. Smith's resistance to the emphases of Ellen White, Jones, and Waggoner in the aftermath of the Minneapolis session would bring much anguish and many stiff "testimonies" from her voice and pen.

Probably the most formidable personality of this leading cast of Minneapolis characters was George I. Butler, the incumbent president of the General Conference. Because of illness, most likely a result of being so worked up about the numerous controverted doctrinal issues of the period, the seeming lack of support from Ellen White, the care of a failing and frail wife, and the heavy burdens of office, he was not even present at Minneapolis. But his strong role in the controversies that led up to and fed into the conference, as well as his numerous letters before, during, and after the conference, most certainly made his presence felt.

Similar to Uriah Smith, Butler had also developed a lengthy résumé of distinguished service. Through the years he had worked in the capacities of pastor, evangelist, writer, and local and General Conference administrator. He had served ably in Iowa and had completed two long terms as president of the General Conference (1871 to 1874 and 1880 to 1888).

Butler's most striking personality trait was that he had confessed to having "too much iron in my nature." Realizing that he had been too belligerent in his dealings with the law in Galatians issue, he had confided to Ellen White that he wanted "to be like Jesus—wise, patient, kind, tenderhearted, frank," with a "love of justice and fairness to all." No wonder that he could express sorrow for a significant amount of "human nature left in me" and that "I have great struggles with the old man." He desired that the old nature "die. WHOLLY DIE."[35]

It comes as no surprise that someone possessing such a firm and pronounced character and extensive experience in the cause of God would have some very decided views of his own authority. He firmly held that by virtue of his experience and office (as president) he was obligated to rule from the top and that it endowed him with "clearer views than others." Such inherent powers not only involved practical administrative authority, but also made him the major arbitrator and protector of theological orthodoxy.[36]

5. The Low Spiritual and Moral Tone of the Adventist Ministry

The period of the mid- to late 1880s seemed to witness a rash of moral falls involving well-known Adventist ministers. It is probably futile to suggest any one definitive reason for such an unfortunate phenomenon. Yet the key factor most likely had to do with a low spiritual tone that involved a lack of Christ-centered spirituality. This tragic deficit always seems to engender a spirit of pharisaism. And legalistic pharisaism always begets a strangely superficial, perfectionistic tendency that seems especially vulnerable to sexual and financial irresponsibility.

The reader might question such a suggestion until one recalls the course of a number of the Pharisees that Jesus encountered. Such individuals could engage in a fair bit of judgmentalism, all in the name of moral responsibility, and at the same time take sexual advantage of the vulnerability of the objects of their censure. When anything cheapens the expensiveness of grace in the mind of believers, it seems inevitable that they will regard sin lightly. And without a spirituality deeply affected by the infinite cost to the Godhead in the sacrifice of Christ for the sin of the world, there exists no limit to the depths that even professing Christians can fall. When there is a heartfelt appreciation of God's expensive love, it will create a powerful revulsion against any attitude or act that brings open shame upon the Lord and His church.

The identity of the various fallen ministers is ultimately beside the point of this biography. Yet two other factors related to this sad history seem relevant.

The first one is that the leaders at Battle Creek seemed almost blind to the bankrupt nature of their understanding of sin and salvation. While some may challenge our analysis of this theology and its fruits, the second factor that impacted the crisis "spirit of Minneapolis" is much easier to understand: all of these tragic moral lapses had greatly burdened the spirit of George Butler. Only a pastor or church administrator who has had to suffer through the pastoral and administrative consequences of such public scandals can appreciate the complex, delicate, yet always wrenching nature of such situations. And G. I. Butler was no exception. And the burden of it all became one more factor contributing to his failing physical, mental, and spiritual condition.

The whole circumstance had become so troubling that Ellen White had to declare that "a sick man's mind has had a controlling power over the General Conference Committee, and the ministers have been the shadow and echo of Elder Butler about as long as it is healthy and good for the cause. Envy, evil surmisings, [and] jealousies have been working like leaven until the whole lump [has] seemed to be leavened."[37] Quite obviously the stresses of leadership had taken its toll on the failing and flailing leader.

6. Tensions About Calls for Reorganization

Most likely the tensions evident in these early requests for reorganization, especially the diffusion of decision-making power, came mainly as a result of the authoritarian style of such administrators as Butler. Already in 1885 Ellen White had sensed that too much power had become concentrated into too few hands. That year she had written to Butler personally and to Butler and S. N. Haskell jointly about their desire to insinuate themselves into too many matters.

To Butler she wrote that "God does not require you to take such a course that the workers in New York or anywhere else shall not feel at liberty to make advance movements unless they consult you, and ask what your judgment of the matter is before they advance. . . . The workers would have to rely upon one man's brain and one man's judgment, and the result would be that men would be left to inefficiency because of their inactivity."[38] In the same communication she clearly connected the issue of church employees learning to have freedoms "very much out of the common order of things" so that the work could go "forward under the direction of the angel who joins the third angel." Furthermore, she felt that such freedom should include "simple means" that will "bring about and perfect His work of righteousness."[39]

Clearly the issue of the diffusion of power was bound up with the spread of the message of Christ's righteousness over the world. It is small wonder that Ellen White would soon write jointly to both Butler and S. N. Haskell that "God has not given to special ones all the brain power there is in the world." She then proceeded to direct them to "take your hands off the work" and spoke of the danger of "one man's mind and one man's plan" being "followed without question." In this same context she spoke about the "mingling" of various "elements of mind and character" that would allow a "view [of] matters from an entirely different" perspective. The results would thus be a means of more fully perceiving both practical and doctrinal truth.[40]

It is quite remarkable that Ellen White would later write to Butler at the time of the 1888 General Conference session with special reference to his role in the "terrible conference" of 1886. She believed that one of the contributing factors to the failures of the 1886 conference was a lack of the "energy of Christ" because those attending it looked to the minds of leaders and not to the Bible for direction. The desire to rule over others in every detail she deemed to be a spirit of pharisaism that had to a large degree taken possession of "those who occupy important positions in the work of God." The point was clear that everyone, not just the authoritarian leaders, needed one another to make wise decisions that would tend to further the work of Christ on earth.[41]

While extensive organizational reform would not occur until 1901, the issue was already crying out for attention, and the authoritarian attitudes of such figures as Butler and Smith, and even the earlier failures of J. N. Andrews and J. N. Loughborough in Europe, made evident the necessity for reform. Undoubtedly Butler especially felt the heat in the run-up to and during the General Conference session of 1888.

7. The California Conspiracy

In early 1888 W. C. White began to communicate with G. I. Butler about the possibility of a ministerial institute to precede the General Conference session scheduled for the late fall. He suggested a few topics that the proposed institute might deal with. Butler replied that the agenda should include the 10 horns and the issue of the law in Galatians for further consideration.

By early August the extremely busy Butler had forgotten his suggestions. He had suddenly grown cool to the idea of such topics. W. C. White appealed to the now-reluctant administrator that such a discussion would be healthy, especially if the divided leaders could "sit down together in a kind and Christian spirit and patiently hear each other present their views."[42]

In the end Butler did reluctantly agree to the institute and the inclusion of the controverted points. While it is not entirely clear as to why

Butler had begun to distance himaelf from his earlier suggestion that the 10 horns and the law in Galatians should be on the agenda for the proposed ministerial institute, events and communications taking place behind the scenes would effectually throw the final potion of controverted poison into a hot pot of soupy events that would soon be cooking at Minneapolis.

What had transpired was that a number of the California Conference delegates to the upcoming General Conference session felt the need to caucus at a retreat held on June 25 and 26 at a location called "Camp Necessity" near Oakland. A few of the leading players who would figure in the Minneapolis meetings gathered to discuss the law in Galatians and other topics related to that subject. The participants included W. C. White, A. T. Jones, E. J. Waggoner, C. H. Jones (the manager of the Pacific Press), and an assortment of other unnamed individuals. We have no documentary evidence that Ellen White was present.

W. C. White reported that they spent a day discussing Butler's booklet *The Law in Galatians*. During it Waggoner shared some of the ideas contained in his letter/manuscript reply to Butler. Waggoner went on to seek the counsel of those gathered at Camp Necessity as to whether he should publish his manuscript for the purpose of placing it in the hands of the delegates at the upcoming session. The group encouraged him to do so, and he thus had it printed as *The Gospel in the Book of Galatians*.

According to the later accounts of a number of the participants, those present had no deep conspiratorial reason for the gathering. But that was not how some subsequently represented it to George Butler. By the time of the California camp meeting in September of 1888 a bitter spirit clearly manifested itself toward Waggoner and Jones.

Apparently W. M. Healey started the hostility. As a California Conference minister and evangelist, Healey had gotten wind of the Camp Necessity study retreat and had sent a letter filled with ominous suggestions to Butler. In his ill-fated missive he seemed to give the impression that the participants "were secretly working up a scheme," suggesting that what some came to call the "California conspiracy" sought to overthrow the church's position on the law in Galatians.

As the conspiracy rumor spread, it alleged that not only had there been the secret Camp Necessity meeting, but that Ellen White was deeply involved in supporting the whole plot. For her part Ellen White repeatedly denied any involvement with the participants or any alleged conspiracy. However, she did strongly support an open and fair discussion of the 10 horns and the explosive issue of the law in Galatians. She felt that it was not only a matter of fairness that Jones and Waggoner be able to respond, but that the issue should be decided on the basis of good, sound Bible study.

While Healey did acknowledge writing to Butler, he never admitted to suggesting any sort of conspiracy. Ellen White had a far different view of the matter, though, and severely rebuked Healey for his actions and the malevolent spin he put on the gathering of the West Coast delegates.

While we cannot confirm the total truth of Healey's claims, the fact is that Butler had had his mind once again stirred up about the issue of the law in Galatians. The Healey letter to Butler further poisoned the atmosphere of Minneapolis.

In late September Butler wrote a long accusatory letter to Ellen White that she received on October 1, just days before the Minneapolis meeting. He angrily alleged all sorts of ill treatment at her hands and those of her son, Willie. Also he sent off telegrams to the delegates warning them to "stand by the old landmarks" at the approaching session.

George Knight has given an incisive summary of the California conspiracy. "Healey's letter found fertile ground in Butler's emotionally exhausted mind. He had been smarting for 18 months" from the letters that Ellen White had sent him rebuking him for his wrong attitudes to Jones and Waggoner and their views. With the Healey letter "suddenly it all came together for him. Now he could see why W. C and Ellen White had urged that he place the 10 horns and the law in Galatians on the Minneapolis agenda. Certainly here was a conspiracy of the first magnitude and a threat to the denomination's traditional beliefs."[43]

SUMMARY

So now we have the key background factors that greatly contributed to the crisis atmosphere of the Minneapolis General Conference session and its ministerial institute. At the core of the whole situation were the deep forebodings of the "pioneer" leaders at Battle Creek and their felt need to defend the faith of the third angel's message. Yet this deep sense of preservation met head-on with the rising Christ-centered emphases emanating from the young West Coast ministers and the deeply aroused prophetic spirit of Seventh-day Adventism's preeminent voice—Ellen G. White.

The atmosphere was charged with the potential for terrible strife. And yet, from the perspective of Ellen White, A. T. Jones, and E. J. Waggoner, the positive stakes were even higher. Their vision was one of radical renewal: they envisaged a movement of reform that would sweep the strife aside and be profoundly energized by the revelation of the righteousness of Christ that would suffuse the third angel's message with the latter-rain power of the Holy Spirit.

In comparison with the fears and prejudices of the entrenched leadership and their cohorts, the striking imagination of the young editor/revivalists and the embattled, yet far-seeing prophet would take on an inviting transcendence. This is certainly the stuff that the decisive, providential moments of history always seem to be endowed with. A failure to embrace the new vision could portend disaster while the beckonings of the uplifted Savior, the soon-coming King, could open the way for the ultimate triumph of the people of God. The alternatives could not be more stark and yet more filled with joyous possibilities. The judgment at Minneapolis was at the gates.

---

[1] Mary was dying of the dreaded consumption, the nineteenth-century term for tuberculosis (TB). Mary had contracted the infection while residing (with her husband and mother-in-law) at the Adventist publishing house in Basle, Switzerland, during the middle years of the 1880s. For more background on Mary's failing health and death, see Arthur L. White, *Ellen G. White: The Lonely Years*, pp. 372, 373, 377, 461.

[2] Ellen White letter 82, Nov. 4, 1888, in Ellen G. White, *The Ellen G. White 1888 Materials* (Washington, D. C.: Ellen G. White Estate, 1987), vol. 1, p. 185.

[3] Ellen G. White manuscript 24, 1888 , *The Ellen G. White 1888 Materials,* vol. 1, p. 217.

[4] *Ibid.*, p. 215.

[5] What follows is a digest of the historical background material given by George Knight in his *User-friendly Guide to the 1888 Message* (pp. 30-49) and Bert Haloviak in his unpublished manuscript, "From Righteousness to Holy Flesh: Judgment at Minneapolis" (chapter 4, "Doomsday Context: The Eschatological Setting").

[6] It was in this situation that E. J. Waggoner contributed some of his earliest articles to the *Signs of the Times*, even before he had become a full-time staff member. Also it launched his career as a religious liberty campaigner.

[7] In subsequent chapters we will further elaborate E. J. Waggoner's involvements in the fight for religious liberty, both in North American and Europe.

[8] Quoted in Knight, p. 34.

[9] His *Thoughts on Daniel and Revelation* had already become the standard authority in matters of prophetic interpretation and would become a classic for subsequent generations of Adventist readers and students of Bible prophecy (even to the point that some considered it to be inspired).

[10] Uriah Smith to A. T. Jones, Nov. 8, 1886; cited in Knight, pp. 34, 35.

[11] Jones to Smith, Dec. 3, 1886; in Knight, p. 35..

[12] Jones to Smith, Dec.27, 1886; in Knight, pp. 35, 36.

[13] G. I. Butler to Ellen G. White, Oct. 1, 1888; in Knight, p. 36.

[14] L. E. Froom, *Movement of Destiny* (Washington, D.C.: Review and Herald Pub. Assn., 1971), p. 245.

[15] For a complete list of all the delegates to the conference, along with photos of 77 of them (including Johnson), see Beverly Herbrandson Koester, "Faces at Minneapolis: Delegates at the 1888 Conference," *Adventist Heritage* 13, no. 1 (winter 1988): 12-21.

[16] In Froom.

[17] Knight, p. 36.

[18] Restorationism refers to an early-nineteenth-century movement teaching that the purity of the teaching and practices of the Christian church of the first century should be "restored" to their contemporary church. It had an understanding of history that viewed the Christian church as having descended into a terrible abyss of apostasy at the end of the first and the beginning of the second centuries A.D. (now commonly referred to as C.E.—"Common Era") and had only gradually been pulling itself out of this spiritual pit since the days of the sixteenth-century Reformation. Now, in the nineteenth century, it was time to complete the process of "restoration." The movement strongly advocated the principle of the "Bible and the Bible alone as our only creed" and featured a very strong New Testament dispensationalism that greatly downgraded the authority of the Old Testament and anything that smacked of Judaism. For more on this movement, see the *Encyclopedia of the American Religious Experience* (New York: Charles Scribner's Sons, 1988), Vol. II, pp. 845-858; Richard T. Hughes, "Christian Primitivism as Perfectionism: From Anabaptists to Pentecostals," in Stanley M. Burgess, ed., *Reaching Beyond: Chapters in the History of Perfectionism* (Peabody, Mass.: Hendrickson Publishers, 1986), pp. 213-255; and Woodrow W. Whidden's article "Restorationism," in the forthcoming *Ellen G. White Encyclopedia* (Hagerstown, Md.: Review and Herald Pub. Assn.).

[19] Knight gives some background on Canright, his understanding of the law, and his apostasy (pp. 41-43); Paul Penno also devotes chapter number 7 of *Calvary at Sinai* ("The Case of D. M. Canright," pp. 71-75), which gives some theological analysis of Canright's apostasy. To my knowledge, there has been only one book-length treatment of the life of Dudley M. Canright. Written by his former secretary, Carrie Johnson, it is entitled *I Was Canright's Secretary* (Washington, D.C.: Review and Herald Pub. Assn., 1971).

[20] Knight, p. 39.

[21] *Ibid.*, pp. 39, 40, and cited from E. J. Waggoner's *Gospel in the Book of Galatians*, p. 70.

[22] Knight gives the best, most succinct review of the whole story (pp. 36-46).

[23] *Ibid.*, p. 41: the above quotes are taken from a letter by Butler written to Ellen White, Dec. 16, 1886. The *Review* of Dec. 14, 1886, reported the resolution passage.

[24] *Ibid.*, pp. 41, 42.

[25] Expressions cited from Ellen White's letter to her daughter-in-law, Mary Kelsey White, Nov. 4, 1888, the very same letter with which we introduced this chapter.

[26] Once more, the succinct character portraits presented by George Knight and Bert Haloviak are the source of most of what follows.

[27] The only book-length biography of A. T. Jones is George Knight's *From 1888 to*

Apostasy: The Case of A. T. Jones (Hagerstown, Md.: Review and Herald Pub. Assn., 1987).

[28] The definitive biography of Uriah Smith is Eugene F. Durand, *Yours in the Blessed Hope: Uriah Smith* (Washington, D.C.: Review and Herald Pub. Assn., 1980).

[29] The only book-length biography of George Butler is Emmett K. Vande Vere, *Rugged Heart: the Story of George I. Butler* (Nashville: Southern Pub. Assn., 1979).

[30] Knight, *From 1888 to Apostasy*, p. 26, and *User-friendly Guide*, p. 44.

[31] W. C. White to Taylor G. Bunch, Dec. 30, 1930; cited in Knight, *From 1888 to Apostasy*, p. 33.

[32] Cited from an address given at Minneapolis, in the *Ellen G. White 1888 Materials*, vol. 1, p. 163.

[33] Knight, *User-friendly Guide*, p. 27.

[34] *Ibid.*, pp. 27, 28.

[35] *Ibid.*, p. 26.

[36] *Ibid.*, p. 27.

[37] Quotation taken from the same letter to Mary Kelsey White excerpted in the introduction of this chapter: Ellen White letter 82, Nov. 4, 1888, cited in *The Ellen G. White 1888 Materials*, p. 182.

[38] Letter 5, 1885, dated Oct. 1, 1885, and cited in Haloviak, chapter 2. See also Ellen G. White, *Testimonies to Ministers*, pp. 297-300.

[39] *Ibid.*

[40] Letter 12, 1885, Oct. 28, 1885. See Ellen G. White, *Testimonies to Ministers*, pp. 301-304.

[41] Ellen G. White letter 21, 1888. See *The Ellen G. White 1888 Materials*, vol. 1, pp. 92, 93.

[42] In Knight, *User-friendly Guide*, pp. 46, 47.

[43] *Ibid.*, pp. 48, 49.

CHAPTER V

THE 1888 MINNEAPOLIS CONFERENCE SESSION: THE CRISIS UNFOLDS

ON TUESDAY, OCTOBER 23, 1888, the Minneapolis General Conference session had reached a decisive turning point in the mind of Ellen G. White. During the previous two days E. J. Waggoner had delivered his eighth and ninth lectures. The eighth had been devoted to the subject of the two covenants, and their relation to the law; the ninth had involved a "discussion" of the controverted issue of the "law and Galatians, or justification by faith."[1]

With these two final "lectures"[2] devoted to the most controversial issues on the agenda, a key moment of potential confrontation had now arisen in the ebb and flow of the conference. Not only had Waggoner set the salvation agenda, but this was the day that the forces of Butler, led by the team of Uriah Smith, R. M. Kilgore,[3] and J. H. Morrison,[4] received scheduled time to begin their rebuttals in support of the traditional position on the law and related "righteousness by faith"[5] issues.

Though those in charge of the session had appointed J. H. Morrison the main spokesperson, it was sometime during this day that R. M. Kilgore made a strong effort to shut down the whole discussion totally.[6] The attempt would prove to be the culmination of a whole series of negative reactions to the presentations of E. J. Waggoner and Ellen G. White.

Such hostile responses were what Ellen White had collectively labeled as a "spirit which burdened" her since it was "so unlike the spirit of Jesus."[7] Others referred to it as the "spirit of Minneapolis." Ellen White listed the following sad aspects:[8] (1) sarcasm and jesting, calling Waggoner "Sister White's pet"; (2) constant carping criticism; (3) envy, evil surmising, hatred, and jealousy; (4) "sharp, hard feelings" and attitudes; (5) being "intoxicated with a spirit of resistance" to the impressions of the Holy Spirit; (6) inflammatory language employed about those advocating differing or opposing views; (7) a spirit of contention and doctrinal debate rather than respectful dialogue; and (8) attitudes that led to "playing upon words" and "quibbling upon words" in doctrinal discussions. Knight succinctly summed it up: such a "spirit" was "uncourteous, ungentlemanly, and not Christlike."[9]

Our list is one of persistent provocation, yet Waggoner and Ellen White had, up to this point, patiently held their peace. Kilgore's maneuver, however, had finally prompted the long-suffering "messenger to the remnant" to deliver a "testimony" of strong public rebuke.

R. T. Nash has provided a firsthand account of Kilgore's appeal and Ellen White's firm, pointed reply. Kilgore stated that "Elder George I. Butler is detained at Battle Creek on account of his sick wife and cannot be here until later on. I would like to move that we stop this discussion on the subject of 'righteousness by faith' until the president of the General Conference can be present."

W. C. White supplemented the recollections of Nash with the report that Kilgore had argued that it was unfair for Waggoner to have the opportunity to present his case, because if Waggoner had been sick, it was claimed, it would have been unfair for Butler to be able to present his case. Kilgore charged that the whole thing was "cowardly."

His clincher, however, was that the point at issue had been settled years ago when Ellen White gave a testimony about the law in Galatians and had told J. H. Waggoner that he was wrong to teach that it was the moral law. The argument had long been one of the centerpiece planks in Butler's ceremonial law platform, and apparently Kilgore now directly intended to force Ellen White's hand to maintain her prophetic integrity. But his not-so-subtle challenge to her inspired counsels on the matter did not intimidate her. It was at this point that the emboldened prophet could no longer hold neither her peace nor her seat.

Nash continued his report: "Mrs. E. G. White, who had been seated on the platform, arose to her feet and . . . said: 'Brethren, this is the Lord's work; does the Lord want His work to wait for Elder Butler? The Lord wants His work to go forward and not wait for any man.'" Nash added the simple comment that "there was no reply to what she said." The stunned gathering sat in deafening silence.

Though Ellen White had stopped Kilgore's special pleadings, she was not finished. The next day (Wednesday, October 24), during the early-morning devotional hour, the forthright and galvanized prophet got even more direct in her remarks.

"Had Brother Kilgore been walking closely with God he never would have walked onto the ground as he did yesterday and made the statement he did in regard to the investigation that is going on. That is, they must not bring in any new light or present any new argument notwithstanding they have been constantly handling the Word of God for years. . . . And then to take the position that because Elder Butler was not here that that subject should not be taken up. I know this is not of God."

Having disposed of the argument that her alleged previous "testimony" in the late 1850s had shut down any further need for doctrinal clarification and advance in understanding, she then turned her prophetic laser beam toward the "conspiracy" rumors and allegations.

"Well, one says, 'Your prayers and your talk run in the channel with Dr. Waggoner.' I want to tell you, my brethren, that I have not taken any position; I have had no talk with the doctor nor with anyone [else] on this subject, and am not prepared to take a position yet. . . . If Elder Waggoner's views were wrong, what business has anyone to get up and say what they did here yesterday? If we have the truth it will stand. These truths that we have been handling for years—must Elder Butler come and tell us what they are?"

She then pointedly concluded with a direct address to Kilgore: "Elder Kilgore, I was grieved more than I can express to you when I heard you make that remark, because I have lost confidence in you."[10]

What had transpired had more than fulfilled the foreboding, tersely stated sentiments of Ellen White on the eve of the commencement of the ministerial institute—"We are in for it."[11]

I have often tried to imagine what it would have been like to be on the receiving end of such a dramatic public rebuke. It is a sobering thought, to say the least! Yet once again the question comes to every (re)searcher for the truth of Minneapolis: what was it that was really at stake for Ellen White in her persistent, open, even stubbornly held conviction that the message of E. J. Waggoner and A. T. Jones be given a fair, honest public hearing? This question is really the fulcrum upon which the message of Minneapolis turns.

But before we seek to identify more especially what the message of the Minneapolis revival was, we need to try to grasp what the theological and spiritual condition of the Seventh-day Adventist Church of the 1880s was. If we can get a clearer conception of the prevalent ideas of Adventist spirituality and its understanding of the dynamics of saving grace, we should be able to make some real progress in more accurately reconstructing what E. J. Waggoner presented at the Minneapolis meetings.

ADVENTIST SPIRITUALITY AND ITS DEFECTIVE VIEWS ON SAVING GRACE

When we employ the terms *spirituality* and *defective views* in this context, we do not so much use them in reference to the clearly acknowledged "pharisaism" that Ellen White had so strongly sought to neutralize. Rather, we seek to explore the general attitudes to doctrinal truth, the person of Christ, and the church's implicit understanding of how a person is reconciled to God.

It seems that Jones, Waggoner, and Ellen White had almost intuitively sensed that something was amiss in the church. It was not so much that it was lurching toward yielding to some temptation to jettison its distinctive "pillars." Rather it needed to be more Christ-centered in its expositions of "truth," "present truth" included. We could explore many factors, but the matter of being Christ-centered seemed to be the overriding concern of both Waggoner and Ellen White.

For Ellet Waggoner it obviously stemmed from his compelling vision of the crucified Christ at the Healdsburg camp meeting some six years earlier. Years of Bible study, writing/editing, preaching, pastoral care, and revivalism had strengthened the vision's spiritual and doctrinal clarity.

For Ellen White the sense of a palpable lack of Christ-centeredness had become more obvious during the last years of James White's life. They both had keenly sensed its absence, and it was at the bedside of her dying husband in 1881 that Ellen White had made solemn vows to rededicate her energies and influence to a more concerted effort to bring a new element of the love of Christ into the work of God.[12]

Another factor that had played perverse havoc in the Seventh-day Adventism of the time, and especially among its leading evangelists, was the spirit of what Ellen White called "theoretical" and "argumentative" "discourses." Such an attitude stood in sharp contrast to what she would often refer to as "meat in due season," or matters of "practical godliness."[13]

It seems that one of the main contributing factors to the growing spiritual dryness was the understanding that if a preacher could just intellectually convince people of the "truth," the very weight of doctrinal or theoretical truth would have some sort of automatic transforming effect on others. This is what Ellen White meant when she spoke of carelessly "handling the truth."

Adventists had certainly presented a lot of good, clear doctrine, especially when it came to the logical reasons to believe the unique teachings of "present truth." But unless such truth brought a greater and clearer focus on the atoning and reconciling work of Christ, it was the proverbial "sounding brass" and "a tinkling cymbal" (1 Cor. 13:1). Such a scholastic "spirit" lacked the power to engender the deep stirrings of the Holy Spirit. It was actually more conducive to the rude rumblings of "Christless sermons" that were more law-centered than Christ or cross-centered.

Another factor that had spawned such a Christless, dry, and scholastic tone involved the sharp thrusts that Adventist ministers often made against their real or imagined opponents. The spirit had very naturally grown out of the prevalent evangelistic technique of entering a targeted town or village and opening up public meetings by challenging some leading evangelical Protestant minister to a debate.

Adventists had largely drawn their debating (maybe we should say "baiting") technique from the Campbellite or Christianite heritage of Adventism. But it was not a very helpful way to gain solid converts. And it is not at all surprising that individuals in the habit of making sharp thrusts at their non-Adventist opponents would also turn the same weapons of theological warfare on their own fellow Sabbatarian Adventists who happened to disagree with them.

Again, the underlying assumption seemed to be that the intellectual and rational grasp of truth was the supreme thing to get across to one's evangelistic audience. The Whites especially sensed that if the church did not lead people to the loving and saving person of Christ, the doctrinal "truth" did not have much potential to truly convert and soften sin-hardened lives.

Now, clarity of truth is one thing. But clarity that does not engender a warm heart appreciation of God's reconciling love will never bring about the kind of "Christly clarity" that convinces one that the real core truth of all essential doctrinal understanding is that of God's great merciful love. And the sad reality that many were discovering was that if the "message" had no deep love implicit in it, it had little saving substance.

But this scholastic and rationalistic attitude to solid doctrinal truth was not the only falsehood wafting about in the Adventist world. Some highly defective views had negatively infected Adventism's theology of salvation. The deadening "spirit of Minneapolis" involved not only a lack of piety and Christ-centered focus but also a deficiency in doctrinal understanding. The situation at Minneapolis resulted not only from woefully inadequate piety, but counterproductive theological ideas and emphases.

Trying to pin down the outlines of the salvation theology of the Battle Creek "pioneer," or "traditionalist" opponents of Waggoner and Ellen White is not easy. Maybe it is best to begin with what both the "pioneers" (Smith, Butler, and their allies) and the "progressives," or "reformers" (Jones, Waggoner, W. C. White, and their supporters),[14] held in common.

As already suggested, all sides shared a deep concern about the preservation of the authority of the Ten Commandments, the Sabbath of the fourth commandment, and the importance of obedience to divine law in the life of genuine faith. Adventism had not suffered many temptations to indulge in "cheap grace" attitudes that would make of none effect the holy law of God and a life of obedient discipleship. Most certainly, both the pioneer and progressive wings of Seventh-day Adventism sought to fulfill the vision of Revelation 12:17 and 14:12, which portrays a people who "keep the commandments of God" (found in both verses in the KJV). But what the pioneers had seemingly not properly accented were the phrases referring to the "testimony of Jesus" (Rev. 12:17) and "the faith of Jesus" (Rev. 14:12).[15]

Furthermore, both groups claimed to believe in justification by faith.[16] It was around this issue that the divergences between them began to become more subtly manifest. While the progressives talked a lot about a living, working obedient faith that trusted the forgiving and transforming grace of the indwelling Jesus, the pioneers seemed to hint that one comes to Jesus through obedience rather than obedience being the fruit of a genuinely trusting faith. Both parties agreed that justifying grace dealt with the sins of the preconversion experience of the believer. In other words, both acknowledged that there was forgiveness for the past sins of the penitent, trusting believer.

The underlying issue in all these debates, however, seemed to be most apparent when the issue evolved to the question of how a justified, forgiven believer would stay justified after the initial forgiveness of the sins of the past, pre-conversion life.

The strong impression given by the pioneers was that the saints just gritted their teeth, recalled the sound doctrinal truth taught by the argumentative evangelists, sought inspiration from the example of Jesus and the dictates of the law, bucked up their spiritual courage, and muddled through by some sort of "pull yourself up by your own bootstraps" type of no-nonsense obedience to God's holy Ten Commandment law.

By contrast, for the Waggoner and White (both Ellen and her son Willie) progressives, obedience was one of the sure results of being in a faith relationship with Jesus. The indwelling Christ would surely bring forth the fruit of Spirit-created obedience. While Waggoner could be somewhat confusing in the way that he often seemed to conflate justifying with sanctifying grace, he was very clear on two things as he came to Minneapolis: (1) no one ever achieved justification through any internal, subjective righteousness that generated justifying merit (before or after conversion) and (2) a genuine faith in Jesus would be a working one that would manifest the fruit of obedience to all God's commandments.

Thus for Waggoner and his associates, the key word was "faith" in the forgiving and indwelling Christ. For the pioneers and their partisans, the key words were "law" and "obedience," and one could sum up their motto as "Obey and Live." The not-so-subtle suggestion was that maintaining "justification after conversion was a matter of 'justification by works.'"[17]

Furthermore, Waggoner suggested two types of obedience to the law. The first was an "old covenant" works obedience not based on the promises of God. It focused on the efforts of the old, fallen nature. Paul would negatively characterize it with a variety of expressions: "deeds of the law" (Rom. 3:20); "works of the law" (Gal. 3:2, 5); "not of works" "of yourselves" (Eph. 2:9, 8); and "mine own righteousness, which is of the law" (Phil. 3:9). This, Waggoner strongly suggested, was the implicit teaching of the traditional Adventist pioneers. But works resulting from genuine "faith" in Christ were designated as "the righteousness which is of God by faith" (verse 9).

As one seeks to sort through the original writings of each party, the distinct impression emerges that the pioneers possessed only a superficial understanding of the claims of the law and lacked a deep understanding of human depravity. They assumed that if one just worked hard, kept the law, and manifested an obvious conformity to the outward letter of the law, one could be deemed as blessed with obedient works.

Here most likely is what caused such dissension over the law in the Galatians issue. Waggoner held that the only law that could effectually strike a deep note of the conviction of sin in the depraved heart of the sinner and drive that person to Christ for forgiveness and transforming grace was the moral law. Thus he saw the law primarily as the agency to convict of sin, not an instrument possessing any inherent power to aid one in overcoming sin. Such "works of the law" obedience offered no real victory that would result in gaining eternal life and provide a sufficient preparation for the Day of the Lord. Thus, in Waggoner's view, such teachers and believers were trusting "their own works, and did not submit to the righteousness of God."[18]

Once more, we can aptly sum up the issue with these key words: for the traditionalist pioneers it was "obedience," while for the reforming progressives it was "faith." We will try to sort this out in more detail when we seek to sum up the theological developments of the 1888-1892 period in this section of the biography. But for now, these basic outlines of the opposing emphases and positions on salvation will suffice to set the context for the presentations of Waggoner and the responses of his opponents at Minneapolis.

We will also do our best to capture the basic substance of the subjects and key themes that Waggoner actually made at Minneapolis. But before we turn to that task, we need to give some background on the personal and public circumstances of Ellet and Jessie Waggoner at Minneapolis and the agenda of the meeting in which they would play such an important role.

THE WAGGONERS' ARRIVAL AT MINNEAPOLIS

While numerous interesting and important events happened at the conference, we will not spend a lot of time on many of the details of the meetings—unless such details more directly involve the work of E. J. Waggoner and those who either engaged with or arrayed against him.[19] This is not primarily a history of the 1888 General Conference session and its events, but the story of Ellet Waggoner and his associates, their participation in the meetings, and how the developments of this important conference shaped his subsequent influence on the thought and mission of the Seventh-day Adventist Church.

Ellet and Jessie had begun their six-day train journey from Oakland, California, on September 27 and had arrived in Battle Creek on Tuesday night, October 2. Surviving documents mention nothing about their preschool daughters Bessie (6 years old) and Pearl (3 years old), nor their infant son, Eugene. It is thus reasonable to assume that the couple had left them in the care of Jessie's parents or Ellet's sister Alta.

After spending a few pleasant and restful days in Battle Creek (lodging at the Sanitarium), they left for Minneapolis on the night of October 8 in the company of "a party of Michigan delegates." They reached Minneapolis on Wednesday morning, October 10, just in time for the opening of the ministerial institute beginning that same day.[20]

While the documentary record reveals few details about the personal circumstances of the Waggoners at Minneapolis, it does mention their public roles and involvements. Ellet was an official delegate from the California Conference and Jessie was there to assist in the business of the International Sabbath School Association.[21] At the meetings she presented lectures on effective Sabbath school teaching and was elected the international "corresponding secretary" of that organization during its business sessions.[22] Jessie and Ellet were also part of a "model Sabbath school" demonstration on "Sabbath morning, Oct. 27." Jessie conducted the intermediate division (juniors and teens). After 44 classes (from all of the divisions) had met to study the lesson, "Dr. E. J. Waggoner, of 'Pacific Press,' conducted the general review exercise in the senior division." The upbeat report concluded with the observation that "great interest was manifested by all."[23]

During the same meetings of the Sabbath School Association, Ellet served on both the nominating and resolutions committees and was elected to the Pacific Press executive committee. Furthermore, he served on the General Conference session's "Committee on Resolutions"[24] and received another committee assignment during the session: appointment to a committee of three with the mandate "to confer with the committee on Sabbath school lessons in reference to health and temperance lessons."[25]

As one combs through the *Signs of the Times*, *Review and Herald*, and *General Conference Bulletin* records, the name of E. J. Waggoner not only pops up in committee reports dealing with different assignments, but often appears as reading "resolutions," making motions, and offering comments on the varied issues the church felt called to deal with.

Quite likely, the reason we do not find much mentioned about the personal circumstances of the Waggoners during the conference is that they obviously did not have much time of their own. It was to be a very busy conference for them both, not just for the high-profile Ellet. But while Jessie was busy, Ellet would carry the heavier burdens of the delicate theological presentations and play a major role in the deliberations on religious liberty.

THE CONFERENCE VENUE, AGENDA, AND IMPORTANT ISSUES

The ministerial institute began on October 10 and ran for the next six days until the formal opening of the General Conference business sessions on the morning of October 17. The official General Conference session would then run until Sunday, November 4. We should note, however, that while the official business items were restricted to the General Conference session proper, the discussions and reactions having to do with the "theological issues flowed from the institute into the regular session as if they were one meeting."[26]

Both the ministerial institute and the General Conference business sessions took place in the newly constructed Minneapolis Seventh-day Adventist Church, located at the corner of Lake Street and Fourth Avenue South. The ministerial institute convened in the basement and the General Conference sessions in the main sanctuary.[27]

In his "Editorial Correspondence" notes Waggoner shared some details of the ministerial institute schedule, along with a listing of the issues it would deal with. Under more practical items was the subject of "instruction in regard to the church and church officers." Waggoner would make the first two of his total of 12 known formal public presentations (including his nine theological lectures, to be detailed shortly) on the subject of the duties and responsibilities of church officers. Beyond these more practical concerns, he cited the projected subjects for the Bible study hour of the ministerial institute and the session to follow: they included the "ten kingdoms" (of Daniel 7), "the establishment of the Papacy . . . , the proposed National Reform government; and the law and the gospel in their various relations, coming under the general head of justification by faith."

He then went on to note that the latter subjects had "aroused a deep interest" and that the discussion of the topics, which began during the ministerial institute, had continued "during the Conference" proper for "one hour a day."[28] Uriah Smith's report in the *Review and Herald* gave a similar proposed list of subjects. He, however, added the topics of "the divinity of Christ," "how far we should go in trying to use the wisdom of the serpent, and predestination."[29]

The proposed subjects for Bible study were quite numerous, but the intensity of the debate over three of them (the 10 horns, National Reform and Sunday laws, and the law and gospel as related to justification by faith) prevented any significant discussion on the other topics.[30]

So the stage was set, and the drama was about to unfold. While Jones and Uriah Smith would take the center stage in the discussions about the 10 horns, Waggoner did make a significant, strategic contribution. According to a report in the Minneapolis *Tribune* of October 18, some friends of Uriah Smith (led by G. B. Starr) sought to force a vote on the 10-horns issue, seeking to declare Smith's "Huns" interpretation the official teaching of the church. Waggoner managed to block the move by arguing that no vote should take place until after a thorough investigation of the matter. After this maneuver, a *de facto* stalemate seemed to prevail, and no further action occurred to elevate the "ten horns" issue to some creedal status.[31]

Furthermore, both Jones and Waggoner would make significant contributions at Minneapolis to the discussions and considerations regarding Sunday laws and the National Reform proposals then looming in

Congress. We find no note of controversy recorded between Jones and Waggoner and the rest of the delegates on the church-state issues. And the participation of the young West Coast editors in the church's response to the Sunday law crisis was one of the two or three major, mostly positive highlights of their individual and combined careers (more on this in the next chapter).

Waggoner, however, would become the main individual (with Jones's moral and occasional public support) in the presentations and intense discussions regarding "the law and the gospel" and "justification by faith." It is to these public presentations of Waggoner that we now turn our attention.

WAGGONER'S NINE PUBLIC LECTURES

In my early ministry I had developed a deep interest in the subject of salvation and its related themes. I can recall voraciously reading such books as L. E. Froom's *Movement of Destiny*, A. G. Daniells' *Christ Our Righteousness,*[32] and Robert Wieland and Donald K. Short's original edition of their controversial 1950 book entitled *1888 Re-Examined.*[33] An admirer of the authors had lent me the latter volume, and I can still recall the excited anticipation that I experienced as I sought to get to the bottom of the issues of Minneapolis and its related themes. It did not take me long, however, to discover that the actual presentations made by Waggoner at Minneapolis were enveloped in much mystery and controversy. For many years I sought to resolve the claims and counterclaims made by the researchers who have shared my own fascination with the subject. And this is probably one of the reasons that I accepted the invitation to write this biography.

But personal searches and curiosities aside, the facts are that we really don't know, in exact detail, what Waggoner presented at this legendary conference. The reason is simple: no known stenographic copies of his lectures were recorded.

The encouraging news is that we are much clearer today on the basic contours of his major lectures given at Minneapolis than we were in the days of A. G. Daniells, L. E. Froom, the early years of Wieland and Short, and numerous other industrious researchers from the early 1900s up through the late 1970s.

The major sources then available were the *General Conference Bulletin*, reports given in the *Review and Herald* and the *Signs of the Times*, the sermons of Ellen White, and the incoming and outgoing letters in the files of Ellen G. White Estate and the General Conference Archives.[34]

In the 1980s, however, two important sources surfaced that have shed additional light on what Waggoner actually presented in his lectures. They were (1) the diary of R. Dewitt Hottel, a delegate from Virginia (his diary record contains a day-by-day report of topics covered) and (2) two notebooks of W. C. White in which he recorded some sketchy notations of comments made by Waggoner and the texts that he used in his lectures.

So what was it that Waggoner presented? To date, the best studies on the question of Waggoner's content at Minneapolis are those of Paul Penno, Jr., George Knight, and Clinton Wahlen. The most thorough study is Wahlen's.

Wahlen's interpretive method is really quite simple. Using all of the above-mentioned documents, especially the Hottel diary, the W. C. White notebooks, and the notations in the denominational periodicals and local newspapers, he pieced together the basic subjects and the key themes that Waggoner presented and was able to identify the particular day of the conference of each lecture. Having identified the topics, some of the texts Waggoner used, a few scattered details from W. C. White, the comments of Ellen G. White, and notes from Uriah Smith in the 1888 *General Conference Bulletin* and the *Review and Herald*, Wahlen (and to a lesser extent, Knight and Penno[35]) proceeded to draw on the key publications of Waggoner on the listed topics, themes, and Bible texts that Waggoner had written in the six years before 1888. In other words, Wahlen's key assumption is that what Waggoner presented at Minneapolis was the condensed substance of what he had been preaching on law and gospel themes for the previous six years.

In support of his assumption, he claims that "Waggoner's soteriology [theology of salvation] and eschatology [theology of closing events] show that his fundamental concepts underwent little change during the period from 1882 to 1888. . . . Armed with [Waggoner's key writings of the previous six years], we can now begin to reconstruct Waggoner's lectures."[36]

It is the most sensible approach that can be taken, and very much parallels my own conclusions. In the broad sense, what we have already presented in chapter 3 of this biography (especially on the themes of law, faith, justification, and sanctification) contains the substance of Waggoner's message at Minneapolis. And the topics, texts, and some details of more specific themes gleaned from the documents directly contemporary to Minneapolis can lead us to the appropriate writings of the previous six years to attempt to flesh out (with some degree of speculation) the theological details of his lectures.

Thus what follows was the gist of the Waggoner's lectures, synthesized from my own study and what I have drawn from the previously mentioned researchers, especially Wahlen.

WAGGONER'S MINNEAPOLIS LECTURES

First of all, we will list the specific days (and times, if available) of his lectures and what the topic(s) were, and then seek to give the substantive gist of each presentation. After that we will offer some observations on Waggoner's overall presentation strategy in the content and sequence of these important lectures.

Lecture one occurred on October 15, during the next to the last day of the ministerial institute. The topic was "Hope in Christ." Waggoner began by emphasizing the "hope" of the believer in the face of the powerful demands of the law.

Lecture two also took place on October 15, most likely immediately following the first one. Its theme focused on how God's law is not contrary to His plan of salvation, but is the absolutely necessary agency to effect the conviction of sin and to drive the sinner to Christ. As George Knight has suggested, "one of Waggoner's most important contributions to Adventist theology" is that *"he had built a bridge between law and gospel by making explicit the gospel function of the ten-commandment law (i.e., to lead individuals to Christ for forgiveness and justification)."*[37]

Lecture three: lectures three, four, and five occurred on October 16 and 17. Thus it is not entirely clear what Waggoner presented on which of the two days. Lecture three, however, must have taken place on October 16, and commenced Waggoner's attempt to draw forth the logical conclusion to the first two lectures—"that a man is justified by faith without the deeds of the law" (Rom. 3:28).

Thus lectures three, four, and five were pivotal in his presentation of the gospel. In them he revealed the inevitable conclusion to the stated demands of the moral law—that justice must be perfectly satisfied. And that comes only through justification by faith in Christ. Waggoner, however, quickly added that works were necessary for the perfecting of saving faith (in the spirit of James 2:17 and 22). Through the latter theme Waggoner sought to show the profound, inseparable relationship between law and grace, faith and works.

The date for lecture four is not absolutely clear, except it took place on either October 16 or 17. The key point was that since sin has seized and imprisoned sinners, the only way of escape is through Christ. Quite clearly Waggoner was here expounding the theme that the only solution to the conviction that the moral law shackles us with is through the grace of Christ.

Lecture five, delivered on October 17, was obviously a continuation of what he had begun in lectures three and four. The *General Conference Bulletin* of October 19, 1888, says that on the first day of the General Conference session itself "at 2:30 p.m. Elder E. J. Waggoner discussed the question of the law of God and its relation to the Gospel of Christ. The discussion was based principally on the Epistle to the Romans." Waggoner went on to identify the "two opposite conditions of bondage to sin and freedom through Christ with the two 'marriages' depicted in Rom. 7:1-6."[38]

Lecture six took place on October 18. Uriah Smith reported all that we know about it in the *General Conference Bulletin* of October 19, 1888. The issue gave reports for activities of both October 17 and 18. Regarding Waggoner's lecture on October 18, Smith reported that "at 9:00 a.m. Elder E. J. Waggoner gave another lesson on the law and gospel. . . . The first and second chapters of Galatians, in connection with Acts 15, were partially presented by him to show that the same harmony existed there as elsewhere; that the key to the book was 'justification by faith in Christ,' with the emphasis on the latter word; that liberty in Christ was always freedom from sin, and that separation from Christ to some other means of justification always brought bondage. He stated incidentally that 'the law of Moses' and 'the law of God' were not distinctive terms as applied to the ceremonial and moral laws, and cited Num. 15:22-24, and Luke 2:23-24, as proof. He closed at 10:15 by asking those present to compare

Acts 15:7—11, with Rom. 2:20-25. Appeals were made by Brother Waggoner and Sister White to the brethren, old and young, to seek God, put away all spirit and prejudice and opposition, and strive to come into the unity of faith in the bonds of brotherly love." It is thus clear that lecture six was a continuation of the themes of salvation by faith in Galatians that he had been exploring in his previous lectures from Romans.

Lecture seven, delivered on October 19, continued Waggoner's comparison of Acts 15 with Galatians. At this juncture he then clearly made the point that the need for justification is only because of the convicting effects of the moral law. Obviously Waggoner had sought to make justification by faith the primary emphasis, and not the debate over the law in Galatians. Only after his attempt to clarify the moral law's role in justification by faith did he specifically turn to the debate on the "law in Galatians"—the main issue that had cast such a shadow of controversy over the Minneapolis session.

Lecture eight: Wahlen and Penno both suggest that Waggoner presented his eighth lecture on Sunday, October 21, and lecture nine on Monday, October 22. As to what Waggoner included in either lecture, W. C. White says nothing, and the only source that reported on them were the local newspapers. Lecture eight's focus: "Two Covenants, and Their Relation to the Law."[39] Here is a theme that contained key undergirding principles for Waggoner's whole positive presentation on justification by faith and the righteousness of Christ.[40]

Lecture nine: given on Monday, October 22, the local newspapers reported that it was "a discussion of law and Galatians, or justification by faith."[41] It seems that the last two lectures sought to pull together the major salvation themes and their relationship to the law in Galatians.

Wahlen has plausibly argued that in lecture nine Waggoner had broached a discussion of perfection. He draws his conclusion from the fact that J. H. Morrison, in one of his subsequent "rebuttal" presentations, had made critical remarks about what he deemed to be an extreme view of the subject. Apparently Morrison tried to smear Waggoner with the not-so-subtle suggestion that he was teaching the "popular Doctrine [that] says Two leaps carry a man from sin to perfection." It was a bold attempt to associate Waggoner with the "instantaneous sanctification" teachings of the American Holiness movement. Seventh-day Adventists had pretty roundly condemned the Holiness movement and thus would not regard such an association as any sort of compliment. Morrison attempted to demonstrate that the perfection Waggoner allegedly taught was not something that believers can gain in this earthly life. Then Morrison concluded by saying: "I believe in a certain kind of perfection. Perfect submission to the will of God."[42]

WAGGONER'S OVERALL LECTURE STRATEGY

Waggoner redemptively conceived his lectures to lead the church in a new direction of grace, rather than the traditional law obedience emphasis. Instead of directly tackling the law in Galatians issue, he immediately pointed to the need for hope in the grace of God and sought to show its profound links to the convicting work of the moral law. Of the nine lectures, the first six dealt mainly with law and gospel in the setting of Paul's portrayal of the gospel in Romans. Only after he had laid out the gospel intent of the classic "second use of the law" (as an instrument to convict of sin) in Romans did he turn more directly to the gospel of grace as unfolded in Galatians. He had thus sought to sidetrack discussion of the divisive issues attached to the debate over the law in Galatians and instead to focus on issues having to do with how God leads convicted believers to Christ for personal salvation from sin—both its guilt and its power.

And not only had Waggoner manifested practical wisdom in trying to direct his opponents onto more fruitful and positive grounds—he had also gained the enthusiastic endorsement of Ellen White. She forthrightly told the assembled delegates at Minneapolis that she saw "the beauty of truth in the presentation of the righteousness of Christ in relation to the law as the doctor has placed it before us." Then she added that what he had presented "harmonizes perfectly with the light which God has been pleased to give me during all the years of my experience."[43]

WHAT WAS THE MINNEAPOLIS MESSAGE OF 1888?

So here we have an overview of what appeared to be the key substance of the themes and the overall strategy of Waggoner's presentations at the Minneapolis General Conference session. How then shall we sum up the "Message of Minneapolis" that Ellen White so strongly endorsed? Please ponder the following.

Just as Ellen White has probably given the best summary of the enduring substance of Waggoner on the covenants (in her *Patriarchs and Prophets* chapter entitled "The Law and the Covenants," pp. 363-373), so she has provided the best overview of Waggoner's contributions at Minneapolis in a letter written to O. A. Olsen in 1895. This important condensation of the positive presentations of Waggoner appears in the compilation *Testimonies to Ministers and Gospel Workers* (pp. 91-98). We will cite the most important portions at some length.

"The Lord in His great mercy sent a most precious message to His people through Elders Waggoner and Jones. This message was to bring more prominently before the world the uplifted Savior, the sacrifice for the sins of the whole world. It presented justification through faith in the Surety; it invited the people to receive the righteousness of Christ, which is made manifest in obedience to all the commandments of God. Many had lost sight of Jesus. They needed to have their eyes directed to His divine person, His merits, and His changeless love for the human family. All power is given into His hands, that He may dispense rich gifts unto men, imparting the priceless gift of His own righteousness to the helpless human agent. This is the message that God commanded to be given to the world. It is the third angel's message, which is to be proclaimed with a loud voice, and attended with the outpouring of His Spirit in a large measure.

"The uplifted Savior is to appear in His efficacious work as the Lamb slain, sitting upon the throne, to dispense the priceless covenant blessings, the benefits He died to purchase for every soul who should believe on Him. . . . Christ is pleading for the church in the heavenly courts above, pleading for those for whom He paid the redemption price of His own lifeblood. Centuries, ages, can never diminish the efficacy of this atoning sacrifice. The message of the gospel of His grace was to be given to the church in clear and distinct lines, that the world should no longer say that Seventh-day Adventists talk the law, the law, but do not teach or believe Christ."[44]

So here we have the explicit, positive appraisal of Ellen White concerning the numerous themes that she highlighted in Waggoner's message preached at Minneapolis in 1888. Among the most prominent were (1) the uplifting of Christ as Savior (not just lawgiver); (2) justification by faith in Jesus; (3) the connection between the righteousness of Christ and obedience to God's commandments; (4) the need for Adventists to focus on Jesus; (5) that Christ's righteousness, or "righteousness by faith," has an intimate relationship to the third angel's message of Revelation 14:9-12; (6) that Jesus has special "covenant blessings" for His children; (7) that Adventists had been emphasizing the law but neglecting Jesus and the importance of faith in His sacrifice; and (8) that God had raised up Jones and Waggoner to redirect the gaze of Adventists to Jesus, to faith in His sacrifice and merits.

Now what has happened is that many of Waggoner's twentieth- and twenty-first-century supporters have wanted to add a number of other themes to this list of what Ellen White explicitly stated as the substance of his message. Both they, and those who have differed with them, have all sought for support in the writings of Ellen White to either affirm or deny the extent of her convergences with Waggoner (and Jones). The issues that have proved to be the hot-buttons of controversy are justification by faith alone, perfection, the human nature of Christ, the covenants, and the role of the final generation of saints in the vindication of God. We will not dodge these issues and will address them at length when we shall later review and assess the major theological developments in Waggoner's thought, not only during this 1888-1892 period, but also for the balance of his life.

SUMMARY

The Minneapolis crisis had reached its zenith. As the meetings ended, Ellen White's outlook was both pessimistic and optimistic. The spirit of resistance to the emphases of Waggoner's stirring presentations had saddened her. But she was not about to allow her pessimism to carry the day. If a significant number of the leading ministers and administrators would not seize the moment of God's opening providence, she would lend her support for a major campaign to take the message of Minneapolis to both the ministry and the laity of the Seventh-day Adventist Church.

E. J. Waggoner and A. T. Jones would respond with zeal to this challenge and would join the undaunted Ellen White in one of the great revival efforts in the history of Sabbatarian Adventism. The coming campaign would continue from November of 1888 until at least the time when Ellen White left for Australia in 1891 and Waggoner moved to England in 1892. Their efforts included extensive travels around the Midwest, the South, and the East to meet camp meeting appointments, Weeks of Spiritual Emphasis at many Adventist institutions, local church revivals, and two lengthy ministerial institutes at Battle Creek (for further instruction in the unfolding light of justifying faith in Christ as the sinner's only hope), as well as teaching Bible courses at Battle Creek College. Waggoner, Jones, and Ellen White would release a torrent of publications in support of the new emphasis on Christ and His righteousness. These years would prove to be the high tide of Waggoner's influence in North American Adventism.

The impact of his work on righteousness by faith issues would spread through his pen, voice, and continued participation in the councils of the church. It would also include some major triumphs and disappointments in the area of religious liberty activities. But these same years would also witness cruel personal losses that would send the young minister through some periods of fiery refining. It is to these halcyon yet transitional years that we now turn our attention.

---

[1] The only source for these lecture topics came from the local newspaper reports. We will review all nine lectures in this chapter.

[2] Two careful researchers on 1888 (Paul Penno, Jr., and Clinton Wahlen) have held that Waggoner gave nine lectures on the law and gospel, the law in Galatians, and other issues related to justification, and the righteousness of Christ. All researchers agree that he made at least three other presentations—two lectures during the ministerial institute on church officers and their duties, and the Sabbath sermon at the worship service on the next to the last day of the conference (Nov. 3), with the last day being Sunday, November 4. During an additional session Jones and Waggoner simply stood up and read numerous selections of Scripture without any comment. On the last day Waggoner engaged in a question-and-answer session right after the conference formally concluded. Some evidence indicates that he made further lecture presentations after his ninth lecture on October 22. The *General Conference Bulletin*, vol. 2, no. 7 (Oct. 26, 1888), reports that on October 25 E. J. Waggoner brought to a close "a series of instructive lectures . . . given on 'justification by faith'" (cited in *Manuscripts and Memories of Minneapolis 1888* [Boise, Idaho: Pacific Press Pub. Assn., 1988], p. 382). No known document either confirms or refutes this *Bulletin* report of October 25. But these questions do not negate the evidence that the exchanges between R. M. Kilgore and Ellen White (described below) took place on October 23 and 24.

[3] Delegate by virtue of his position in the General Conference.

[4] President of the Iowa Conference and a delegate.

[5] This expression came directly from the lips of R. M. Kilgore (see below regarding

Kilgore's public attempt to suppress the ongoing discussion) and is positive evidence that the debate about the "law in Galatians" and the "covenants" involved salvific issues.

[6] The following paragraphs largely draw from P. Penno, *Calvary at Sinai,* pp. 108—110.

[7] Ellen White manuscript 24, 1888, cited in G. Knight, *User-friendly Guide*, p. 62.

[8] Knight, *User-friendly Guide,* p. 63.

[9] *Ibid.* Cited by Knight from his earlier book *Angry Saints* (Hagerstown, Md.: Review and Herald Pub. Assn., 1989), pp. 81, 82.

[10] The entire text of Mrs. White's morning devotional message appears in A. V. Olson, *Through Crisis to Victory 1888-1901* (Washington, D.C.: Review and Herald Pub. Assn., 1966), pp. 290-293 (rereleased as *Thirteen Crisis Years, 1888-1901* [Washington, D.C.: Review and Herald Pub. Assn., 1981]). The texts of all of the Ellen White devotional messages given at Minneapolis are located in *The Ellen G. White 1888 Materials.*.

[11] Ellen White to Mary K. White, Oct. 9, 1888, cited in Knight, *User-friendly Guide*, p. 49.

[12] I have traced this shift in the focus of the Whites in *Ellen White on Salvation* (Hagerstown, Md.: Review and Herald Pub. Assn., 1995), pp. 23-31, and in an article entitled "The 'Way of Life' Engravings: Harbingers of Minneapolis?" *Ministry,* October 1992, pp. 9-11.

[13] We see this emphasis laid out most clearly in Ellen White's testimony recorded in the chapter "Preaching Christ" in the book *Gospel Workers* (Washington, D.C.: Review and Herald Pub. Assn., 1915), pp. 156ff.

[14] Bert Haloviak coined the words "pioneers" and "progressives," and George Knight the terms "traditionalists" and "reformers."

[15] George Knight, in his recent biography of Captain Joseph Bates (*Joseph Bates: The Real Founder of Seventh-day Adventism* [Hagerstown, Md.: Review and Herald Pub. Assn., 2004], pp. 83-88), has argued that two basic approaches to salvation emerged in early Seventh-day Adventism. Of the three original founders (James White, Ellen G. White, and Joseph Bates), the Whites were the founders of the progressive reform calling for a salvation by faith in Christ emphasis, while Bates seemed to be the main advocate of the "obedience to the law and the Sabbath" emphasis. Although not meaning to demean the absolutely essential contributions of Bates on so many levels, Knight has made a rather strong case about the ultimate legalism of Joseph Bates. Thus the "progressive," or "reform," emphasis became more and more apparent in the thinking of the Whites and those whom they supported, while the traditional pioneer emphasis most apparent in the salvation thought of Joseph Bates seemed to be permeating the thinking of Smith, Butler, and their followers.

[16] Once more, I am indebted to the insights of Knight (*User-friendly Guide*, pp. 86-91) for most of what follows in the discussion of the distinctions between the salvation views of the opposing camps.

[17] *Ibid.*, p. 87.

[18] In Knight, *User-friendly Guide,* p. 88.

[19] One interesting detail involved the presence of a certain "crank on religion" who sought to thrust himself into the meetings on November 1, 2, and 4. The individual proclaimed that Jesus had already come. Ellen White summarily disposed of such demented nonsense by reminding the delegates that Adventists had already had enough of such fanaticism during the early days after the Great Disappointment in 1844. Sad to say, such individuals turn up at every General Conference session.

[20] These travel notes, obviously written by E. J. Waggoner himself, appear in the column entitled "Editorial Correspondence" in *Signs of the Times*, Nov. 2, 1888 (see *Manuscripts and Memories*, p. 413).

[21] The back page of the *Signs of the Times*, Oct. 5, 1888, gives the following report: "Thursday, September 27, Elder E. J. Waggoner started East, to attend the meeting of the General Conference, soon to be held in Minneapolis. Brother Waggoner was accompanied by his wife, who goes especially in the interests of the Sabbath-school work. . . . They will probably be absent about six weeks." The records do not refer to the children. Normally, articles would mention children traveling to church meetings with prominent parents.

[22] *General Conference Bulletin*, Oct. 24, 1888 (in *Manuscripts and Memories*, pp. 374, 375). This *Bulletin* report gave a rather detailed summary of the major points presented in Jessie's "informal talk on 'How to study the Lesson.'" The report stated that she "would not attempt to lay down any set of rules that would apply to all cases, but the following is how to study the lesson, in a nutshell:

RpErAaDy]
SpTrUaDyY] ALL THE WEEK.
TpHrIaNyK]

"'Read, study, think' are all necessary, but the most important is prayer. We should mix prayer through all our reading and studying and thinking, during the entire week." Then there followed 12 important elaborations in paragraph form filling up a half-page column in the *Bulletin*. Ellet was not the only master teacher in the family! Jessie would continue in Sabbath school activities for the rest of her life. She was also the author of many Sabbath school songs, some of which have become Adventist classics. The most well known is her Sabbath song entitled "The Seventh Is For Jesus" ("One, two, three, four, five, six for us [repeated three times], but the seventh is for Jesus"). (For more on Jessie's Sabbath school interests, see appendix B.)

[23] *General Conference Bulletin*, Oct. 29, 1888 (in *Manuscripts and Memories*, p. 386). The reader is probably wondering what the "general review exercise" was. A traditional practice for Seventh-day Adventist Sabbath schools that still survived in the 1950s (when the author was a youngster), it consisted of a general review of the major points of the senior Sabbath school lesson for the week just concluded. The "review" was always the last item on the Sabbath school agenda, just before adjournment and the transition to the church worship services.

[24] "Editorial Correspondence," *Signs of the Times*, Nov. 2, 1888.

[25] *General Conference Bulletin*, Nov. 2, 1888 (*Manuscripts and Memories*, p. 398). The *Bulletin* listed Waggoner as "E. W. Waggoner" (most certainly a typo), and the other two members of this special committee were C. C. Lewis and W. H. Wakeham.

[26] Knight, *User-friendly Guide*, p. 52; see also *General Conference Bulletin*, Oct. 19, 1888. Copies of the *Bulletin* are readily accessible in the compilation *Manuscripts and Memories*, pp. 358, 359.

[27] The original church still stands on the same location to this day, though somewhat modified in appearance.

[28] "Editorial Correspondence," *Signs of the Times*, Nov. 2, 1888.

[29] Uriah Smith, in *Review and Herald*, Oct. 16, 1888.

[30] "Editorial Correspondence," *Signs of the Times*, Nov. 2, 1888.

[31] Knight, *User-friendly Guide*, p. 54.

[32] Washington, D.C.: Ministerial Association of Seventh-day Adventists, 1926.

[33] *1888 Re-Examined* (Baker, Oreg.: Adventist Forum Association, 1950). This volume was revised and updated by the original authors in 1987 with the new subtitle "1888-1988—The Story of a Century of Confrontation Between God and His People" (Leominster, Mass.: Eusey Press, 1987).

[34] For the more isolated minister and lay researchers, the releases of the White Estate on the topic of 1888 and the wonders of digital technology have made the most important documents more readily available. The most significant were (1) the 1987 publication of the four volumes entitled *The Ellen G. White 1888 Materials,* containing Ellen White's letters, manuscripts, and copies of the sermons she preached at Minneapolis; and (2) the 1988 release of *Manuscripts and Memories of Minneapolis*, containing selected letters of various participants in the conference, copies of the denominational and newspaper reports of the meetings, the 1888 *General Conference Bulletin*, various relevant periodical articles, the Hottel diary, and the two W. C. White notebooks. The latter document does contain a wealth of the most important documents, but is not an exhaustive collection. Thus both the professional scholar and the lay researcher have most of the main documents related to Waggoner's presentations at their fingertips.

[35] Penno says: "All credible firsthand evidence indicated that Waggoner presented justification by faith in the context of the covenants and the law in Galatians, Romans, and Hebrews. Though the actual lectures of Waggoner were not recorded, eyewitnesses, such as W. C. White, newspaper accounts, and the *Daily Bulletin*, took notes and accounts which strengthen this conclusion. In addition, articles and pamphlets that Waggoner published *just prior* to the Minneapolis conference indicated that this was the message he brought to the Seventh-day Adventist church" (*Calvary at Sinai*, p. 114).

[36] Clinton Wahlen, "What Did E. J. Waggoner Say at Minneapolis?" *Adventist Heritage* 13, no. 1 (Winter 1988): 27, 28. The article drew from Wahlen's M.Div. theisis, "Selected Aspects of Ellet J. Waggoner's Eschtology and Their Relation to His Understanding of Righteousness by Faith, 1882-1895," pp. 83-98.

[37] Knight, *User-friendly Guide*, p. 55.

[38] Wahlen, "What Did E. J. Waggoner Say?" p. 33.

[39] *Manuscripts and Memories*, p. 582.

[40] The substance of which we have previously laid out in chapter 3 of this biography.

[41] *Manuscripts and Memories*, p. 557.

[42] Wahlen, "What Did E. J. Waggoner Say?" p. 34.

[43] Ellen White manuscript 15, 1888, in *The Ellen G. White 1888 Materials*, vol. 1, p. 164.

[44] Pp. 91, 92.

CHAPTER VI

THE AFTERMATH OF MINNEAPOLIS: THE SEASON OF THE UPLIFTED CHRIST: 1888, 1889

INTRODUCTION

THE SITE WAS WILLIAMSPORT, PENNSYLVANIA, and the event was the Pennsylvania camp meeting of the late spring of 1889. E. J. Waggoner had come to it to bring spiritual renewal for the people of God gathering in the verdant Allegheny Mountains of central Pennsylvania. But a tragic crisis of stunning and unexpected proportions would overwhelm it. Before we consider the Pennsylvania tragedy, however, we need to provide some context of Waggoner's life during this period.

On May 17 he had departed from Oakland on what was to be the initial major itinerary of his involvement in the great "righteousness by faith" revivals of late-nineteenth-century Adventism. He, along with Ellen White and A. T. Jones, had begun to emerge as the dominant figures in a concerted effort to change the spiritual and theological tone of the church. It would involve intense attempts to make Christ and His righteousness the all-consuming passion of the mission of the Seventh-day Adventist Church (both corporately and individually).

After brief stops in Chicago and Battle Creek, Waggoner traveled on to Williamsport, arriving on May 28. Here he joined A. T. Jones for the Pennsylvania Conference ministerial ("workers") meeting that had already been in session for the better part of a week. The ministerial gathering was the prelude to the Pennsylvania camp meeting scheduled to begin Tuesday, June 4, and run through June 10 on the same grounds.[1]

But events suddenly altered everything! In the midst of the workers' meeting one of the great, storied disasters of American history literally burst forth on the afternoon of May 31—the infamous Johnstown Flood. Waggoner's personal report vividly described the "terrible story . . . from Pennsylvania."

"The news seemed almost too horrible to be true, but later dispatches have confirmed the matter, and the details are simply heart-rending. Near Johnstown, Pennsylvania . . . lies a large artificial reservoir, the largest in America, extending over thousands of acres, and formed by an immense dam [measuring] over 100 feet high . . . [and] something like 1,000 feet wide. The extraordinary rains of the two days preceding resulted in so increasing the volume of all the streams emptying into the reservoir that the dam could no longer withstand the pressure, and in the afternoon of May 31 the entire structure gave way, allowing the raging mass of water to sweep unchecked downward through the narrow valley, carrying death and destruction in its mad onward course to the towns and cities miles away."

The deluge swept away numerous small towns and villages before it finally hit "the beautiful city of Johnstown, with its busy thousands, all unthinking of the terrible fate so soon to befall them."

Waggoner's compelling narrative laid out "the terrible fate" in its appallingly dramatic dimensions:

"Here alone it is estimated that 1,500 people lost their lives, 1,000 houses were swept away in a twinkling [of an eye], and as the great mass of floating debris lodged against the massive railroad viaduct at the lower end of the city, a second dam was thus formed and in a few minutes the water was 35 feet deep all over the plain covered but a moment before with human habitations. Two heavily loaded passenger trains, which had been delayed by the rains, were washed away, and many passengers [lost]. To add to the horror, the mass of buildings crowded against the viaduct to the height of 50 feet caught fire, and it is estimated that at least 500 persons perished in the flames. The whole occurrence simply beggars description, and the loss of life has been terrible. Incredible as it may seem, it is stated that the whole number of lives lost by the calamity is not less than 8,000, while some fear that even a higher figure will be reached. The loss of property will be many million dollars."[2]

Then Waggoner went on to report that, aside from the towns that were directly in the path of the flood, Williamsport "was the greatest loser."[3] Thus the gathered Adventist ministers and the church members arriving for the soon-to-open camp meeting were not immune to the effects of the catastrophe.

Though initially delayed, the camp meeting did proceed, but with a much smaller attendance than anticipated. Ellen White had come to join forces with Jones and Waggoner. She had also experienced some of the trauma of the larger storm that had caused the flood. The torrential rains that had enveloped her journey and precipitated the Johnstown Flood made her trip from Elmira, New York, down to Williamsport one of the most harrowing and dangerous of her life.[4] Though burdened from the fatigue of the trip and suffering from the effects of a sprained foot (that had put her on crutches), the indomitable Ellen White spoke 13 times at the very sodden and sobering camp meeting.

As one could well imagine, the apocalyptic setting made the participants especially attentive to the presentations of White, Waggoner, and Jones. We have no record of how many talks Waggoner gave, but he did report that many at the ministerial meeting "expressed themselves as already having received light on the subject of the righteousness of God and how it may become ours through faith in Christ." Most certainly these were the themes that this dynamic revival trio presented at the ensuing camp meeting (undoubtedly, with many obligatory comments about the capricious nature of life and the urgent implications for eternity).

THE YEAR AFTER MINNEAPOLIS

In a steady, ostensibly providential emergence to prominence (though buffeted with controversy), the young editor/revivalist had come out of Minneapolis as one of the most pivotal personalities in Adventist history. During the preceding six years he had worked hard in many facets of ministry, had written extensively in defense of the faith, and had proven persistent in his attempts to reshape the Adventist proclamation into a more gracious, Christ-centered vision and tone.

Furthermore, he and Jones had received steady, even unparalleled support from Ellen White. His and his family's prospects seemed as bright as any in the Adventist ministry, and the church he served had been on the receiving end of the early tidings of a most precious message that clearly testified that the Adventist body of believers was the "only object on earth on which" Christ "bestows His supreme regard."[5]

Yet such bright personal prospects would suddenly find themselves enveloped in wrenching personal loss, tragedy, and ongoing opposition from the entrenched Battle Creek leadership. It was almost as if the Johnstown Flood provided a vivid metaphor for the events and forces already beginning to break over the life and ministry of this rising star in the Adventist firmament of ministerial luminaries. The momentous year of 1889 would severely test Waggoner's spiritual and emotional mettle.

THE MONTHS OF LULL AND LOSS

The Waggoners had retraced their travel route back to Battle Creek fairly soon after the conclusion of the Minneapolis meetings. The *Review and Herald* reported that on November 8 a follow-up meeting to the General Conference session in Minneapolis convened to tie down a few loose ends. The report of the session tells of E. J. Waggoner speaking about appropriate nomenclature for the General Conference Association.[6] Thus we know for sure that he was there, but how soon it was that he and Jessie would return to Oakland is not clear. The original notice of their departure and travel plans that had appeared in the *Signs of the Times* of October 5 had suggested that the entire trip (beginning on September 27) would last "about six weeks."[7] Thus it is reasonable to assume that with young children beckoning, especially considering the delicate health of their infant son, Eugene, the Waggoners were most likely back in Oakland by the end of November.

The next four-plus months proved to be the "lull" time before the "storm(s)." After the return to Oakland, Waggoner became preoccupied with writing, editorial duties, pastoring, and the usual load of correspondence. But mid-April brought tidings that would begin the opening of the floodgates of tragedy for Waggoner and his family.

On April 17 a cable from Europe contained the "sad news" of the sudden death of Ellet's venerable father, J. H. Waggoner.[8] A subsequent notice from J. N. Loughborough suggested that "the cause of Brother Waggoner's death was declared to be aneurism, and his sufferings are supposed to have been of short duration."[9]

All of this must have been small comfort for Ellet and Alta in Oakland. He told the readers of the *Signs of the Times* that the "cause has lost a faithful worker, and we have lost a most kind and loving parent."[10]

Most certainly J. H. Waggoner, as a parent, had had a strong influence on his children. It must have been especially true of the sensitive Ellet, who, of all the siblings, had turned out to be the child that most closely replicated his prominent father. While Joseph Waggoner had often been slow in following the counsel of the Lord regarding the care and nurture of his children, the record reveals a man who was especially solicitous for the welfare of his four youngest—Ruby, Ellet, Ellery, and Alta.

Yet this blow was just the beginning. Just three days after setting out for the East on May 17 and just one month after receiving the untimely notice of his father's death, Ellet would encounter another cruel blow. From Oakland came the lamentable news of the death of his 9-month-old infant son, Ernest Eugene Waggoner, on May 20.[11] Ellet, who had been the grieving son, suddenly found himself thrust into the role of a grieving father!

Waggoner could be quite stoic (or maybe just trusting and calm in his faith) in the face of such losses. Or it could be that he had grown somewhat toughened to such news through his previous experiences of the deaths of childhood siblings. As in many things, his inner feelings were not always apparent. But he must have acutely felt the loss of his son so soon after the death of his father.[12] Though he did not record his own feelings, his daughter Pearl did, and her sentiments most likely reflected those of the rest of the sorrowing family.

Pearl vividly recalled the day of Eugene's funeral. "I remember how badly I felt to see him buried; but I also remember trying to comfort my mother—at our first meal after [the] funeral—by reassuring her that Jesus was going to come and would 'go down into that hole and bring Baby Ernest up and give [him] to us again.' I knew the 'blessed hope' at an early age."[13] Most certainly the main consolation for the grieving father traveling in the East would have been sentiments very similar to those of his daughter Pearl, the older sister who must have often heard the same thoughts from the lips of her father in family worship and from the pulpit of the Oakland church.

We can only imagine the thoughts that must have crossed the mind of the lonely, itinerant revivalist after two such blows when he encountered the devastating flood during the days following his arrival at the site of the Pennsylvania workers' gathering and conference camp meeting.

"When is this string of loss and tragedy going to end?" he must have asked himself.

Yet we find no record of any note of despair. The preoccupations of the urgent work at hand—lecturing, preaching, writing articles and reports for the *Signs*, and the numerous consultations that must have transpired with A. T. Jones and Ellen White about the great revival unfolding in their collective ministry—must have offered some solace.

THE REVIVAL MEETINGS OF 1889

The post-Minneapolis era got off to a rather rough start. Though the messengers of the new Christ-centered perspective had received the ringing endorsements of Ellen White, the entrenched leaders at Battle Creek were not yet convinced. The "spirit of Minneapolis" was alive and well, and the struggle would continue for a considerable time following the General Conference session of 1888.

Soon after the Minneapolis meetings[14] A. T. Jones, Ellen White, and E. J. Waggoner returned to Battle Creek and immediately began to face the very basic challenge of reaching the general church membership. The first issue concerned a battle over a proposal that Jones assist Uriah Smith in teaching Bible at Battle Creek College. Though the appointment had been suggested in April of 1888, the board of trustees, under Smith's obvious influence, had refused to act on it. In November the issue came up once again, but this time the board, with some reluctance, accepted it. But it required a lengthy meeting during which the board extracted assurances from Jones that he "would not knowingly teach any opinions contrary to those which the Board desired to be taught."[15]

In effect, Jones had caved in to the essence of the creedal statement that the Battle Creek leadership had sought to impose on the church at Minneapolis—the same thing that Ellen White had strongly and successfully opposed. Yet the promise would soon be moot after the college president, W. W. Prescott (1855-1944),[16] became a fervent convert to the new salvation by faith perspective and a firm ally and follower of Jones and Waggoner.

The next battle in the campaign involved access to the local churches. The opposition was so bold in Battle Creek that the local elders, under the direction of Uriah Smith and led by W. W. Prescott (who was also the educational director of the General Conference),[17] questioned Ellen White as to what subject(s) she intended to speak on, fearful that she would present some "Minneapolis ideas." In fact, the temerity of Prescott and company was so pronounced that the Smith-influenced locals had even launched their inquiry on the very Sabbath morning that she was scheduled to speak. She forcefully responded to her inquisitors that they should leave the choice of topics to "the Lord and Sister White." Then she confronted them with the suggestion that they invite A. T. Jones to speak at the Tabernacle. They responded that they would have to get the approval of Uriah Smith. To no one's surprise, Smith refused.

But because of the rising prominence of Jones in the fight against the dangerous church-state legislation (including the national Sunday law) pending in Congress, it was not easy to keep him from the pulpit of the Battle Creek church. Jones's speaking sparked a revival in the church. What was intended to last for a week, beginning in December, continued for the better part of a month. Under the leadership of Jones, Ellen White, and J. O. Corliss, the revival spread to the college and the sanitarium. Its main subjects were justification by faith and the hot topic of the "religious amendment" and the fulfillment of Bible prophecy.

In the wake of the Battle Creek revival in December of 1888 and early 1889, Ellen White felt that a "measure of victory" had been gained. But that was only after what amounted to ecclesiastical trench warfare in which they had to "fight for every inch of ground." Ellen White was in full battle mode and called for a spiritual revolution in the churches that would manifest the "fruits unto righteousness . . . in our daily life."[18] For the most part, the challenge of access had been settled in favor of the new emphasis and its key spokespersons—Ellen White, Jones, and Waggoner.

The rest of the year 1889 would witness a widespread advance in behalf of the ringing theme of "justification by faith in the righteousness of Christ." In quick succession, during the winter and spring, Ellen White and Jones took the message across the Midwest and the Eastern seaboard of the United States, including a Week of Prayer in mid-January at South Lancaster Academy (today's Atlantic Union College) in South Lancaster, Massachusetts, a two-week-long convocation in Chicago in April, and the Ottawa, Kansas, camp meeting in mid-May.[19] In late May Waggoner would come on board the revival train crisscrossing the land.

As previously noted, Waggoner had spent the better part of five months in Oakland. In mid-May he had departed the city on his way to join the revival campaign in Williamsport, Pennsylvania. After a brief stopover in Chicago he had gone on to Battle Creek. Here he paused to spend a few days with his recently widowed mother, who had promptly returned to Burlington, Michigan, after the death of her husband in Europe. Then it was that after these days of travel and tending to family concerns he finally ventured on to the ill-fated events of Williamsport, Pennsylvania, and joined forces with A. T. Jones and Ellen White.

From Williamsport the White/Jones/Waggoner team took their gospel caravan via train to the New York camp meeting in Rome, New York (June 11-18). Once more, the pattern of the reports was most encouraging.

S. H. Lane announced that the messengers of Minneapolis "ably presented the wonderful themes of justification by faith, the righteousness of God, and the consecration to God and His cause which our work demands at the present time. . . . As these themes were presented, light, joy, happiness, and peace of soul seemed to take possession of the meeting, and filled each heart with joy and gladness which were expressed by the flowing tear and heartfelt expressions of praise to God."[20] An earlier report from R. F. Cottrell struck pretty much the same tone:

"The preaching presented the faith of Jesus in its simplicity and perfect efficacy, by which alone we can be justified from sins that are past; and the warning of the coming test upon the commandments of God was faithfully set before us." The results were that "union and harmony prevailed in the meeting," and "several of the youth started in the service of the Lord" and others "who had been on the background began anew."[21]

After the Rome, New York, camp meeting our narrative takes a bit of a surprising change of direction and pace—-Waggoner would take a study break!

THE HEBREW SCHOLAR

One of the little known facets of Waggoner's life was his interest in biblical Hebrew. His youngest daughter, Pearl, reminisced late in her life about his "studying and reading Hebrew aloud."[22] An interesting and instructive note in the *Signs* reported that in the midst of his strenuous, protracted travels during 1889, Waggoner found time to study Hebrew with one of America's most well-known biblical scholars, William Rainey Harper (1856-1906).[23]

Harper was a "liberal" Baptist Old Testament scholar who became one of the most renowned American academic personalities of the late-nineteenth and early-twentieth centuries. Harper tutored at Denison University (1876) and then became an instructor in Semitic languages at Baptist Union Theological Seminary, Morgan Park, Illinois, in 1879. During those years he developed a correspondence course in Hebrew that had generated a national enrollment of some 3,000 students.

In 1886 he began teaching ancient Near Eastern languages and literature at Yale University, where he became nationally known as a teacher, lecturer, and editor. He would remain at Yale until 1892, when he received the invitation to be the founding president of the University of Chicago. Oil baron John D. Rockefeller had richly endowed the school, and it would quickly become one of America's major comprehensive research universities.[24]

Harper not only had a correspondence course in Hebrew, but was also active in the Chautauqua movement (serving for some years as the president of its college of liberal arts). The reason for his involvement in the movement was that by 1875 the study of Hebrew had been introduced at Chautauqua and "this augured the development of a fairly complete offering of liberal arts and biblical subjects. However, the immediate result was the establishment of a school of biblical languages under the leadership of William Rainey Harper."[25]

The above facts help to explain the previously mentioned notices regarding the travels of Waggoner in the *Signs* of May 27, 1889. After highlighting the Pennsylvania and New York camp meeting appointments, the back page report said that "Brother Waggoner" will spend "some time with Prof. Wm. R. Harper, at Philadephia [from "June 18 to July 3 at (the) Protestant Episcopal Divinity School"] and Chautauqua [from "July 5 to August 15 at Chautauqua, New York"], for the purpose of completing a course of study in Hebrew which he has been pursuing for several years."

Although we have no direct documentary evidence that Waggoner took such a course (no family heirlooms, such as correspondence lessons, diplomas, textbooks, etc.),[26] undoubtedly Waggoner was one of the 3,000 students who had been enrolled in Professor Harper's correspondence course in Hebrew. What must have transpired in Philadelphia and at Chautauqua was that Waggoner had attended what we would today call "intensive" classes in the study of Hebrew. For the scholarly Waggoner, this must have been a welcome respite from the woeful losses of the previous months, the intense travels, and the revival meetings that had preoccupied him since the middle of May.

THE FINAL MONTHS OF 1889

Good evidence suggests that Jessie must have joined him in either the East or the Midwest sometime during August and that they then traveled and ministered together until the middle of October. It was during these two months that Ellet and Jessie made some extensive tours under the auspices of the International Sabbath School Association and the General Conference camp meeting committee, traveling to Michigan, Illinois, Indiana, and Nashville, Tennessee.[27] The appearances in Nashville took place in late September.[28] The next venue that we have any known record of attendance was the 1889 General Conference session in Battle Creek. It lasted from October 18 until November 5.[29]

THE GENERAL CONFERENCE SESSION OF 1889

Both Ellet and Jessie would play varied roles in the Battle Creek General Conference session. In fact, with the exception of Ellet's very limited public presentations (a discourse entitled "Why We Oppose Religious Legislation," given on Thursday evening, October 24), their committee involvements were very similar to those at Minneapolis the year before. While A. T. Jones and Uriah Smith gave a number of public presentations and sermons, Waggoner, attending as a delegate at large, mostly served as a committee member[30] and active participant in floor discussions at the various business sessions of the main conference and the submeetings of such organizations as the International Religious Liberty Association, the International Sabbath School Association, and the International Tract Society.

His nominated/elected appointments included the General Conference "Book Committee" and both the "editorial" and "executive" committees of the National Religious Liberty Association. The session also elected him to serve on a committee with the assignment to prepare a

"Bible-Reading" on the first-day offering mentioned in 1 Corinthians.

In some respects, Jessie's public role as the incumbent "Corresponding Secretary" of the International Sabbath School Association proved more interesting than Ellet's public involvements.

Her corresponding secretary's annual report contained some touching explanations for her inability to fulfill adequately her elected role as corresponding secretary: "For the greater part of the past year it has been utterly impossible for me to perform the duties of a corresponding secretary; and what I have done has been accomplished under many difficulties. . . . The spirit has indeed been willing, but the flesh weak."[31] Quite obviously, the litany of tragedies and losses, compounded by months of separation from her itinerant husband, had taken their toll on the dedicated, normally reliable, and always creative Jessie.[32]

If, however, the Sabbath school delegates were unimpressed with her explanations, it certainly was not reflected in their actions—they reelected her as corresponding secretary and appointed her to be an "examiner" (proofreader?) for the English Sabbath school lessons and to write the special camp meeting lessons for the primary division for the year 1890. The highlight of her public presentations was an address given to the Sabbath School Association entitled "Small but Great," published in the *Bulletin*.[33]

One other interesting sidelight on the many responsibilities of Jessie Waggoner came from a diary entry of Ellen White's for October 26. In it Mrs. White tells of a conversation "with E. J. Waggoner's wife in regard to the management of Christmas for the best good of the youth."[34] Undoubtedly Jessie had received a request to develop some sort of Sabbath school or Week of Prayer program for Christmas in the interest of the youth and she was seeking counsel from Ellen White.[35] It is just one more indication of Jessie's growing reputation as a creative writer and curriculum/program developer.

On the whole, this General Conference, though providing a much less conspicuous role for Ellet than the previous year, had to be more gratifying than the trying circumstances of the crisis-laden gathering at Minneapolis. Ellen White was quite pleased with the overall spirit of the session: "We are having most excellent meetings. The spirit that was in the meeting at Minneapolis is not here. All moves off in harmony."[36]

Although the lingering effects of the "spirit of Minneapolis" would continue to generate some distress during the coming months and years, it was the period of the greatest public impact for Ellet and Jessie Waggoner. While they had endured loss, lengthy separation, and strangely persistent opposition, they had valiantly carried on in the face of not only their personal trials, but also in their important roles in the public councils of their beloved church.

THE BRIEF RETURN TO THE WEST COAST

Ellet and Jessie Waggoner did not return to Oakland until December 6, being delayed by their attendance at the "ministerial and biblical institute for Portland, Oregon.[37] Ellet's stay in Oakland, however, would last only a few days, as he would soon turn around on December 20, 1889, and head back to Battle Creek for a stint of teaching Hebrew and theology at the college and the first of two major ministerial institutes that ran from October 31,[38] 1889,[39] until March 25, 1890. He would not get back to Oakland until late March of 1890.[40]

Our brief review of the trials, travels, and triumphs of a very full year of strenuous revival programs gives us some sense of these important events in the life of E. J. Waggoner and the history of the Seventh-day Adventist Church. The pace, especially from May to December of 1889, while varied, had been challenging, even hectic at times. Waggoner sought to bring the church to a deeper experience with God through faith in the righteousness of Christ. The fruits seemed be those of a genuine, expanding revival. We are not finished with all of the important facets of the righteousness by faith revivals, but first we need to give some attention to another fascinating, yet vital aspect of Waggoner's public personae.

The renewal under way in the proclamation of the uplifted Christ, the study of Hebrew, and participation in the councils of the General Conference session of 1889 were not Waggoner's only preoccupations during the fateful year of 1889. He and A. T. Jones played pivotal roles in the battle over Sunday laws and the issue of separation of church and state in the United States.

THE RELIGIOUS LIBERTY CAMPAIGN

One of the interesting developments of the 1888 Minneapolis General Conference session was the recommendation of the Committee on the

Distribution of Labor that A. T. Jones spend the bulk of his time visiting "suitable places to reach the masses of the people, and present the subject of religious liberty."[41] It would effectively end his responsibilities as the coeditor of the *Signs of the Times*. He would largely devote the next few years to religious liberty problems and the revival of justification by faith and related issues.

As we have already seen, both Waggoner and Jones had labored in the righteousness by faith revival (often together and with Ellen White); but Waggoner had also been consistently connected with the fight for religious liberty. Though Jones would take the leading role in appearances before congressional and state assembly committees and numerous lectures, Waggoner was often in the thick of the battle (though more in the role of editor, writer, and supporting ideologue for Jones).

It was not something new for Waggoner, having been involved in religious liberty advocacy since the early 1880s and contributing numerous articles to the *Signs* and the *American Sentinel* on the subject before becoming an editor of the *Sentinel*. During the first year of the publication of the latter journal (1886) he and Jones effectively acted as assistant editors to J. H. Waggoner, the founding editor.[42] But with the departure of Joseph Waggoner for Europe in late 1886 and early 1887, Jones and Waggoner became the editors of the journal in June of 1887. They would remain together as editors until May 15, 1890, when the masthead would list Jones as the sole editor. Once more, we must emphasize that in the great religious liberty campaign running from the late fall of 1888 to 1895 (with special intensity in 1889 and 1890), A. T. Jones was the major public figure.[43]

In the main, their efforts in this area would be one of the outstanding positive contributions that both Jones and Waggoner would make to the Adventist Church during the late nineteenth century. Jones especially attained national attention for his appearances in Congress and contacts with leading public figures (even meeting with the president of the United States, seeking his veto of Sunday legislation).

Yet their activities, while mostly upbeat and effective, did have their down sides.

The problematics of their religious liberty writing and much celebrated opposition campaigns against Sunday laws and advocacy for the maintenance of a strict division between church and state arose from their fervent ideological approach to the issues. By the word "ideological" I refer to their rigorous logic on any number of issues having to do with their more radical separation of church and state convictions.

Jones especially became noted for his opposition not only to Sunday laws, but also the proposed constitutional amendment to make America a "Christian nation." Furthermore, he also rejected a litany of other church-state involvements and exchanges. For example, he resisted the idea of Christians being official "citizens" of any country. Briefly stated, his basic rationale was that since they were "Christian citizens" of God's kingdom, political involvement at any level (except, of course, for fighting for religious liberty) was not worthy of their heavenly citizenship. In addition, he opposed required Bible readings and prayers in the public schools; churches receiving property and other tax exemptions; and the receipt of any aid from the state to support church institutions (such as land grants given to Adventists in southern Africa during the 1890s).

But the issue that Jones and Waggoner both fervently held in common was their interpretation of the fourth commandment. They believed that it was just as much a responsibility of Sabbathkeepers to work six days as it was to refrain from labor on the seventh day, the biblical Sabbath. In other words, if a person was in any way seen to be in conformity with any Sunday law (even though actual Sabbath desecration was not required), that individual was in disobedience to God and in danger of the "mark of the beast." Thus it was only logical for Jones and Waggoner to advocate strongly that Adventists should go right ahead and work when Sunday laws forbade them to do so.[44]

While we could debate the merits or demerits of Jones and Waggoner's more rigid, ideological approach to church-state issues at some length, they faced one major and immediate problem: the more pragmatic approach of their chief supporter and comrade in arms in the "Christ our righteousness by faith" revival—the Adventist prophet, Ellen G. White. Although she profoundly opposed Sunday laws and was leery of church-state complicity, she was always less ideological and more pragmatic than Jones and Waggoner on any number of separation of church and state issues.

In addition to differences based on philosophical/ideological grounds, we find also the simple fact of a definite divergence of approach when it came to the basic tactics of dealing with opponents. For Jones, and at least by editorial complicity for Waggoner, it involved aggressive confrontation of Sunday law advocates. But Ellen White was not happy with such abrasive measures. Her counsels to Jones on church-state issues and tactics would be the initial cause of his ultimate alienation from her and her counsels. But what was it in 1889 that gave Ellen White and other leading Adventists such pause for concern?

Jones was never one to back down from a challenge. The most notorious manifestation of his and Waggoner's confrontational approach arose in the case of Wilbur Crafts. A little background will prove helpful.

In December of 1888 the General Conference Committee organized a Press Committee that would soon evolve into the National Religious Liberty Association during July of 1889 and the International Religious Liberty Association during 1893. Closely associated with the group was the *American Sentinel* and its editors, Jones and Waggoner.

One of the key accomplishments of this alliance was to spearhead a national petition campaign to obtain signatures of those against Sunday laws. By October of 1889 the campaign had secured nearly 500,000 names in opposition to the proposed national Sunday bills of 1888 and 1889 that Senator Henry Blair of New Hampshire had introduced into Congress.

As one might well surmise, the man who was in the forefront of this campaign was the ever intrepid A. T. Jones, ably supported by E. J. Waggoner. One of the interesting side effects of such aggressive activity was to goad the equally combative Wilbur Crafts, the secretary of the National Reform Association, into action. Crafts challenged the nation's 26 million Sundaykeepers not to let themselves be outdone by 25,000 Seventh-day Adventists. The result was a vigorous, even brutal, confrontation between Jones and Crafts.

The struggle became particularly intense during the spring and summer of 1889. In the July 1889 numbers of the *American Sentinel* Jones accused Crafts of being dishonest, an unrepentant liar, not too far removed from a dishonest politician, and contemptible of minority groups. Jones capped his litany of insults with the claim that Crafts' National Reform Association was nothing but the Protestant front for the "American Papacy."

Crafts in turn described Adventists as "a little 'insignificant set of hair-brained, woolly-headed fanatics.'" He then claimed that Adventist opposition to Sunday laws put them "in with liquor dealers," who also warred against Sunday laws. Jones returned this insulting association back on Crafts by claiming that he was a fine one to be delivering such a low blow when he was teamed up with the Catholics, who had no reservations about saloonkeeping.[45]

The tactics employed by Jones and Waggoner to counteract Crafts' pro-Sunday law campaign further aggravated the exchanges. For example, they would secure his travel itinerary and flood each destination with religious liberty publications before he arrived. Thus everywhere Crafts went he encountered a firewall of opposition. Furthermore, Jones made it his business to go around the country, camping "on Crafts' trail."

The climax to the whole battle swirled around a proposed debate between the two antagonists scheduled for June 12 to 14 in Chicago. But the blood between the two antagonists had become so bad in June (during Crafts' speaking tour in Colorado) that they canceled the debate. But debate or no debate, Crafts finally exploded on June 28 by filing a public affidavit against both Jones and Waggoner, as editors of the *Sentinel*, for "wholesale slander and falsehood, for which they might properly be called to answer either in civil or church courts."

Thankfully, the matter never got into the civil courts. Instead, Crafts sent a copy of the "affidavit" to Dr. John Harvey Kellogg to pass on to the local congregation (Oakland, California) in which Jones and Waggoner were members.

In August Crafts was in California and once more encountered the same tactics that had dogged him elsewhere. Only this time Jones showed up at his meetings in San Francisco and personally invited Crafts to attend his and Waggoner's church trial in Oakland. Crafts hinted that he might come to present his charges, but never showed up. To no one's surprise, the congregation found the editors not guilty. A General Conference examining team came to the same conclusion.

While the Crafts affair did not go any further legally, both the local church and the General Conference examining committees did have some firm counsel for Jones and Waggoner. They blamed the editors of the *Sentinel* for "unnecessary sharpness," "harshness of expression and tone," and unnecessarily explicit personal attacks on Crafts. Such a response from their own camp must have come as disconcerting news to the two young editors, revivalists, and religious liberty campaigners.

It does appear, from the evidence, that the lion's share of the blame fell on Jones, not Waggoner. But others apparently saw him as at least complicit in the approach. It could be that Waggoner may have cautioned his friend, but we have no explicit evidence. While such behavior was not characteristic of Waggoner, sadly enough, Jones would never seem to overcome his proclivity for aggressiveness. Even the counsels of his old friends and supporters, W. C. White and Ellen G. White, were ultimately of no avail in reining in the pugilistic side of Jones's character.[46]

SUMMARY

While Waggoner experienced many successes during the year following Minneapolis and its conflicted General Conference session, the year 1889 also witnessed some real losses and deep disappointments. Most certainly the tragic back-to-back deaths of his father and infant son were the most woeful. But the persistent resistance to the "most precious message" of the uplifted Christ, who brings peace, victory in grace, and hope for the future, had to be hardest to absorb. The rebukes arising out of the Wilbur Crafts fiasco also were certainly a source of embarrassment.

Yet Waggoner had a growing sense of solid and persistent support from the one person in Adventism that counted the most—Ellen G. White. And with her endorsement and the blessings of God's Spirit in his ministry, the best was yet to come. We now must turn our attention to the ongoing Christ our righteousness revival that continued to unfold in the ministerial institutes of 1889-1890 and 1890-1891 and the wonderful responses of the upbeat General Conference session of 1891. They would be the high points of the final years of ministry in the United States before his departure to new challenges in England and Europe.

---

[1] "Editorial Correspondence," *Signs of the Times*, June 24, 1889.

[2] *Signs of the Times*, June 10, 1889, p. 16.

[3] "Editorial Correspondence," *Signs of the Times*, June 24, 1889.

[4] A brief account of her perilous journey appears in Arthur L. White's *Ellen G. White: The Lonely Years*, pp. 429-431.

[5] E. G. White, *Testimonies to Ministers*, p. 15.

[6] *Review and Herald*, Nov. 20, 1888 (in *Manuscripts and Memories*, p. 412).

[7] *Signs of the Times*, Oct. 5, 1888, p. 16.

[8] "J. H. Waggoner: Death Notice," *Signs of the Times*, Apr. 22, 1889. J. H. Waggoner had departed from the West Coast sometime in 1886 and initially returned to Michigan. After a relatively brief stay at Battle Creek and his home in Burlington, he then moved on to Europe in August of 1887, where he worked for two years in connection with the publishing house at Basel, editing the French edition of the *Signs of the Times* (the previous facts were listed in J. N. Loughborough's published memorial to J. H. Waggoner, *Signs of the Times*, May 20, 1889). We will give further attention to the circumstances of the Joseph and Mary(etta) Waggoner's transition from the West Coast of the United States to Europe in the last section of this biography.

[9] "Elder J. H. Waggoner," *Signs of the Times*, May 20, 1889.

[10] "J. H. Waggoner: Death Notice," *Signs of the Times*, Apr. 22, 1889.

[11] The death notice of Ernest Eugene Waggoner appeared in the *Signs of the Times*, June 3, 1889.

[12] We do not know when or how he received the news, but he most certainly would have received notice by the time he reached Chicago on May 22.

[13] "Biographical Sketch and Background," Document File 236, Ellen G. White Research Center, James White Library, Andrews University, Berrien Springs, Mich., pp. 3, 4.

[14] What follows is a digest of the narrative of Knight, *From 1888 to Apostasy*, pp. 46-48.

[15] In Knight, *From 1888 to Apostasy*, p. 47.

[16] *Seventh-day Adventist Encyclopedia*, vol. 11, p. 380. Gilbert Valentine has authored two extensive treatments of the life and thought of Prescott. The first was *The Shaping of Adventism: The Case of W. W. Prescott* (Berrien Springs, Mich.: Andrews University Press, 1992). The second is a revised edition of *The Shaping of Adventism*, entitled *W. W. Prescott: Forgotten Giant of Adventism's Second Generation* (Hagerstown, Md.: Review and Herald Pub. Assn., 2005). This latest, revised edition is a part of the same series of Adventist biographies as the present volume.

[17] Valentine, *The Shaping of Adventism*, p. 56.

[18] Ellen G. White letter 22, 1889, in *The Ellen G. White 1888 Materials*, p. 241.

[19] A. L. White, *Ellen G. White: The Lonely Years*, pp. 424-430; A. V. Olson, *Through Crisis to Victory*, pp. 59, 60; and Knight, *From 1888 to Apostasy*, pp. 48-56.

[20] "The New York Camp Meeting," *Signs of the Times*, July 15, 1889.

[21] "The New York Camp Meeting," *Signs of the Times*, July 8, 1889.

[22] "Biographical Sketch and Background," p. 4.

[23] For a brief overview of Harper's life and work, see T. H. Olbricht, "Harper, William Rainey (1856-1906)," Daniel G. Reid, coordinating ed., *Dictionary of Christianity in America* (Downers Grove, Ill.: Inter-Varsity Press, 1990), pp. 509, 510.

[24] *Ibid*. The biographical facts are gleaned from the above-mentioned dictionary article.

[25] C. Gregg Singer, "Chautauqua Movement," ed. J. D. Douglas, *New Twentieth-Century Encyclopedia of Religious Knowledge*, 2nd ed. (Grand Rapids: Baker Book House, 1991), p. 168. The Chautauqua movement was essentially the summer retreat version of the aging, permanent Methodist camp meeting venues. These great retreat sites became gatherings for not only religious pursuits (lectures, sermons, prayer meetings, and religious musical presentations), but also all sorts of cultural, artistic, and educational lessons and lectures—including studies in biblical languages. Some of them offered college credit.

The Chautauqua campground in extreme western New York, located on the southwestern shore of Lake Chautauqua, just west of Jamestown, New York, provided the name and home of the movement. Other notable sites that offered (and still do to this day) similar fare are Lake Side, Ohio (facing Lake Erie, north of Sandusky Bay, just across from the famed American amusement park Cedar Point) and Ocean Grove, New Jersey (just to name two of many institutes still functioning at traditional Methodist camp meeting sites).

[26] In fact, Pearl Waggoner Howard explicitly mentioned, in a letter to L. E. Froom, the following: "Two large boxes of books that we left stored in London, expecting later to return there, simply dropped out of sight—including *important volumes, from my father's library*, most of our youthful personal books (my sister's and mine), and some *diplomas and important papers*" (in Pearl Waggoner Howard to L. E. Froom, Oct. 30, 1956, PC 48: Howard, General Conference of Seventh-day Adventists Archives, Silver Spring, Md.; italics supplied).

[27] *General Conference Bulletin*, Oct. 21, 1889. We find further evidence for these travels in the "General Conference Committee Minutes" of July 8, 1889, which listed the camp meeting assignments for the late summer and early fall. The committee asked E. J. Waggoner to visit the camp meetings in southwest and eastern Michigan, Illinois (with Ellen G. White), and Indiana. They were the same locations mentioned in the International Sabbath School Association president's report, at which Jessie had made appearances.

[28] P. Penno, *Calvary at Sinai*, p. 121.

[29] This General Conference session would be the last annual session ever held. The delegates voted that it would henceforth convene every other year, with the next scheduled session set for 1891 (*Signs of the Times*, Nov. 25, 1889, p. 16).

[30] Ellet was a member of the resolutions, judiciary, and the Sunday persecutions committees. In addition to being a conference delegate, he was also a delegate to the business sessions of the International Tract Society.

[31] *General Conference Bulletin*, Oct. 21, 1889, p. 19.

[32] Yet one is astonished at what she did list as her accomplishments: she had written "seventy letters, about twenty articles for the *Sabbath School Worker*, given twelve or thirteen public talks on the Sabbath school work, had charge of four camp meeting Sabbath school divisions, three divisions in campmeeting Teachers' Meetings, about thirty-six children's meetings at the camp meetings, and given considerable private instruction in connection with the camp meetings and a few small schools which I happened to visit" (*ibid.*).

[33] *General Conference Bulletin*, Nov. 4, 1889, pp. 133-138.

[34] Ellen G. White manuscript 22, 1889, in *The Ellen G. White 1888 Materials*, vol. 1, p. 463.

[35] According to the article "Christmas" in the *Seventh-day Adventist Encyclopedia*, vol. 10, pp. 350, 351, special attention had been given in the years from 1888 to 1890 to integrate the Week of Prayer reading with the Christmas season and "Christmas programs" had been sent out to the churches.

[36] Ellen G. White manuscript 10, 1889, published in *Selected Messages* (Washington, D.C.: Review and Herald Pub. Assn., 1958), book 1, pp. 361, 362.

[37] *Signs of the Times*," Nov. 11, 1889, p. 16, and Dec. 16, 1889, p. 16.

[38] Or Nov. 5, 1889, depending on which report you believe. We will return to a more detailed consideration of the two major ministerial institutes of 1890 and 1891 (1890 in the present chapter and 1891 in the next).

[39] *Signs of the Times*, Dec. 30, 1889.

[40] *Ibid.*, "Announcement," Mar. 31, 1890.

[41] "S. D. Adventist General Conference," *Review and Herald*, Nov. 6, 1888. One other action of related interest in this same committee report was the recommendation "that M. C. Wilcox, of New York, go to the *Signs* Office, to assist in editing the *Signs of the Times*" (*Manuscripts and Memories*, p. 407). M. C. Wilcox would effectively take Jones's position and would play a progressively more prominent role in editorial duties at the Pacific Press. It was the beginnings of transition for both Jones and Waggoner to the revival and religious liberty trail. Wilcox would become editor in 1891, with the departure of Waggoner.

See "*Signs of the Times* (Nampa, Idaho),"*Seventh-day Adventist Encyclopedia*, vol. 11, pp. 607-609.

[42] It is interesting as one leafs through the copies of the *American Sentinel* from its beginning in January of 1886 until May of 1887 that it lists no one person as either editor, coeditor, assistant editor, or so forth. Only in the June 1887 number do Jones and Waggoner appear as editors. After the departure of E. J. Waggoner in May of 1890, Jones would be the editor from May 15, 1890, until 1894; from 1894 until 1896 he would share the position with C. P. Bollman, and then would return as sole editor from 1896 to 1897. For a brief sketch of the history of this journal, see "*Sentinel of Christian Liberty,*" *Seventh-day Adventist Encyclopedia*, vol. 11, p. 571.

[43] Once more we are in the debt of George Knight, who has given a well-documented and stirring history in his A. T. Jones biography, *From 1888 to Apostasy*, especially chapters 6 (pp. 75-88) and 9 (pp. 117-131).

[44] We will see how this plays out in the next section of this biography when Waggoner will rigidly apply his Sabbath interpretation against the Sunday laws he would encounter in London.

[45] See Knight, *From 1888 to Apostasy*, pp. 78-80.

[46] See Knight, *From 1888 to Apostasy,* pp. 80-83.

CHAPTER VII

THE "HIGH TIME"—TO LEAVE: 1890-1892

INTRODUCTION

ONE OF THE TRULY DELIGHTFUL little snapshots into the life of the Waggoner family is a recollection daughter Pearl had of the family train trip from Oakland to Battle Creek in mid-October of 1890. Her father was slated to teach at the second major ministerial institute that was already under way, and would participate in the 1891 Battle Creek General Conference session.

During the weeklong train trip Pearl and her sister, Bessie, had made friends with another little girl (about their same age) who had wandered into their coach from an adjoining one. The little girls had a wonderful time playing together and sharing with one another.

Pearl, ever the little church girl and up-front witness, proceeded to share with her newfound friend "all about our church in Oakland, incidentally mentioning A. T. Jones and Sister White." When the little girl, obviously in some puzzlement, asked her who A. T. Jones and Sister White were, Pearl blurted out with indignant astonishment, "You don't know Brother Jones and Sister White! Why, where do you live?" In her account Pearl added the wonderfully childlike observation that she "really thought everyone should know *them*."[1]

One can only imagine the startled but bemused wonderment that must have been evident on the expression of Pearl's little fellow traveler. As for Pearl, she had very definite ideas about who the really important people were in her understanding!

Childish though her recollections were, they do represent a certain reality of the life and times of E. J. Waggoner. They were truly the "high times" of Ellet's prominence in the Adventist "universe." If you were Adventists during these years, you had to know about E. J. Waggoner, A. T. Jones, and Ellen G. White. Particularly for Waggoner, the next two years would witness the pinnacle of his public fame and influence in North America. And furthermore, they were also years of transition that would prove to be the staging time to new venues of labor on a broader, international stage.

But before we turn our attention to those dawning European developments, we need to complete our narrative of the final two years of Waggoner's full-time American ministry in the last decade of the nineteenth century. The most important events in these years involved the two major General Conference ministerial institutes and the 1891 General Conference session.

THE MINISTERIAL INSTITUTES OF 1889-1890

In addition to General Conference sessions, local church and conference-wide revivals and workers' meetings, camp meetings, and institutional gatherings (such as at the Battle Creek Sanitarium and South Lancaster Academy), the revival team of E. J. Waggoner, A. T. Jones, and Ellen White also found important opportunities to present the new Christ-centered emphases at two ministerial institutes held in Battle Creek between late 1889 and early 1891.[2]

BACKGROUND AND RATIONALE FOR THE INSTITUTES

The new General Conference administration of O. A. Olsen desired to bring healing and unity to the deep fractures that had opened up between the self-appointed defenders of the traditional views of the law and the "progressive" advocates of the more Christ-centered, justification by faith emphasis. In pursuit of such a healing strategy, the organizers of the ministerial institutes sought to have representation from both camps on the teaching team. The faculty for the institutes included Uriah Smith, W. W. Prescott, Prof. McKee, W. A. Colcord, A. T. Jones, and E. J. Waggoner.[3] Smith, Prescott, and Waggoner were the most prominent presenters, with Waggoner being the star attraction.[4] Though they did witness some conflict, on balance, the fact is that the schools did break down a lot of prejudice and seemed to be a key factor in clarifying the contested issues. But we should not conceal the sobering fact that controversy would persist for some years.

Yet the leadership also had another important aim in developing these important institutes—the raising of ministerial educational levels.

With the support of O. A. Olsen, W. W. Prescott (with the backing of W. C. White) served as the key mastermind behind the ministerial institutes. Prescott had for some time been nurturing a growing concern over the marked academic deficiencies of the majority of Adventist ministers. Most of them had what we could only call a basic "proof text" knowledge of the Bible. Thus denominational leadership was certainly justified in its desire to raise the educational quality so that Adventist clergy would have a broader "general understanding of the Bible" and greater theological adeptness in its use and application.

Furthermore, the organizers of the institutes undoubtedly believed that the superficial biblical knowledge of the Adventist ministry had greatly contributed to the crisis of 1888. Not surprisingly, church leadership appointed Prescott the "principal" of the institutes.[5]

FIRST MAJOR MINISTERIAL INSTITUTE, 1889-1890

The first institute, or "ministers' Bible school," lasted from November 5, 1889, until March 25, 1890.[6] Some 50 students attended this initial Adventist attempt to do "seminary."[7] The second institute had more than 130 students during the fall of 1890 and the winter of 1891. In terms of any clarification of the issues confronted at Minneapolis and its aftermath, the first institute was the most important.

As mentioned in the previous chapter, Waggoner had left Oakland on December 20, 1889, for Battle Creek with the specific mission(s) to teach Hebrew and theology in the college and serve as one of the instructors at the first major ministerial institute, which had already been in session for almost two months.[8] He most likely arrived sometime between Christmas and New Year's Day.

Waggoner began his work rather quietly by teaching a course on the book of Isaiah. But in early January he made a unilateral decision to present the biblical covenants. It was an incendiary maneuver guaranteed to further stoke the ongoing fires of controversy over the issue. The outlines of the ensuing controversy are as follows.[9]

THE COVENANTS CONTROVERSY OF 1890

A growing unanimity among scholars who have taken a careful look at the controverted theological issues of Minneapolis and its smoldering aftermath holds that the most inflammatory issues involved the law in Galatians and the covenants.[10]

It is thus not surprising that Waggoner's decision to switch from teaching the Old Testament book of Isaiah to the subject of the covenants in early January of 1890 greatly disturbed Dan T. Jones, the newly elected secretary of the General Conference.[11] In the temporary absence of Prescott, Dan Jones acted as institute principal and sought to dissuade Waggoner from teaching on the covenants—at least until Prescott returned. Jones's two-hour conversation with him on a January Friday failed to dissuade Waggoner. The latter insisted to Jones that he had already made his plans to begin his covenants presentations on the following Monday, and a change at this late date would prove disconcerting.

On Sabbath morning Dan Jones sought Ellen White's counsel, and she suggested the formation of a committee to investigate both sides before any public presentation on Monday. When Dan Jones subsequently approached Waggoner, the latter was still quite resistant to the idea of changing his plan, but did agree to meet with the committee. After alerting Uriah Smith as to what was afoot, Jones gathered the investigative committee on Sunday evening at 7:00 p.m.

The committee consisted of Dan Jones (chair), Uriah Smith, R. C. Porter, an individual named McCoy, W. C. White, J. Edson White (the other surviving son of Ellen White), E. B. Miller, and E. J. Waggoner. As one would expect, the committee divided on the advisability of Waggoner proceeding with his presentations. Facing a procedural impasse, the committee then asked Dan Jones to lead a discussion of the points at issue in the debate.

Jones felt that the best way to proceed was to quote from Waggoner's Sabbath school lessons on the subject that were in current use that very quarter. He then cited the following: "Let the student note that the terms of the old covenant were really all on the part of the people." To no one's surprise, Jones indicated that he could not agree with this point, and both Smith and Porter sided with him.

To support his rejection of Waggoner's viewpoint, Smith cited

Deuteronomy 26:17-19. The *Review and Herald* editor contended that the passage did clearly refer to the old covenant and that God had made the promises to Israel on the condition of their obedience. From his perspective, they were clearly promises offered to Israel, and the blessings of the old covenant would be theirs if they were obedient. So Smith could argue that the terms of the covenant were not just with the people, but also rested on God's promises to Israel. While Waggoner did not directly respond to Smith's point in the committee discussion, his overall emphasis was that the nation of Israel was a sinful people and thus doomed to failure since the first, or old, covenant contained no promises of divine pardon or aid.

Now, if all of this seems a bit strained to the reader, the point is well taken. But we must try to see what both sides were getting at. It all ultimately appears to come down to the following distinctions.

For Smith the key covenant idea was "obey God and His law, and the covenant blessings are yours." But for Waggoner the issue was that the covenant given at Sinai lacked divine promises of forgiveness for sins and divine aid to overcome sinful tendencies. Such promises appear only in the new covenant, the everlasting covenant whose blessings were not restricted to any dispensation in time. The everlasting covenant was always a covenant of grace and grace alone.

Thus the covenant issue had come full circle to the very basic, practical question of how a sinful human being is saved. Is it by human-generated obedience based on human promises to God, or does it rest on the promises of God for the forgiveness of sin(s) and grace (power) to overcome persistent character defects?

Now, while the covenant question does involve other closely related issues, the above seemed to be the heart of the issue for Waggoner and Smith.

The rest of the committee discussion covered issues relating to how Waggoner's current Sabbath school lessons on the covenants got into print in the first place. Waggoner astonished the group with his reported declaration that all (including those present at the meeting) must have agreed with him on the covenants because of two reasons: (1) a number of those present had approved a new "reading" that he had prepared on the subject for a recently released, revised edition of the book *Bible Readings* (being members of the Book Committee) and (2) that Smith had signed off on the then-current Sabbath school lessons on the covenants authored by Waggoner.

Most certainly Waggoner's assumptions were quite remarkable in the light of all the arguments previously printed by the Review and Herald publishing house in support of Smith's traditional position. Though Waggoner's claim was technically true, Smith was most certainly not persuaded by such arguments. To editorially or administratively sign off on a project was one thing—to be in full harmony with it quite another! The committee discussion reached no clear-cut conclusion.

Furthermore, Dan Jones still remained of the opinion that Waggoner should not teach on the subject. He held his position on the grounds that the faculty and managing board did not agree with Waggoner's views. Waggoner responded that he had come to the school with the understanding that he could "teach his own views." Further, he intimated that he really had not wanted to teach at it in the first place, but had finally agreed to do so when assured that he could present what he felt led to.

The upshot of the opposition of Dan Jones and the Sunday evening committee discussion was that on Monday Waggoner handed Jones a letter of resignation for the class on the covenants. It put Dan Jones into a quandary as to how to present it to the students eagerly anticipating Waggoner's course on such a contested issue. Jones sought to come up with an acceptable explanation as to why Smith, not Waggoner, would be teaching in the allotted time slot.

Finally Jones claimed that Waggoner was overworked and needed rest and thus the institute had asked Smith to take up the slack and teach on the sanctuary question. While there might have been some plausibility to Dan Jones's explanation, Waggoner had effectively thrown sand into those less-than-honest gears by immediately communicating to the students the real reason for the class's cancellation. He stated that "there have been objections made to my teaching the covenant question in this school and Brother Dan Jones will explain to you the change that has been made."

Waggoner's preemptive strike had effectively foiled Jones's ruse. Jones could speak only the truth to the expectant students—"that it had been thought best to postpone the presentation of the covenant question for the present time at least, and that Bro. Smith would take up the sanctuary question."

The issue did not pass quietly, and a number of students registered their dismay and disappointment regarding Waggoner's departure from the classroom.

Ellen White was also upset with Dan Jones's less-than-transparent dealings with Waggoner. She again stressed her persistent theme that there must be open and fair discussion of the divisive issues: "Do not keep up a criticism and objections, in an underhanded way. . . . If the ideas presented before the ministerial institute are erroneous, come to the front like men and present candidly your Bible evidence why you cannot see the point as they do." Then she clearly admonished Dan Jones and his cohorts to stop "resisting the light or views and ideas presented by men whom I know to be agents whom the Lord is using."[12]

Clearly Ellen White was not very happy with Jones's attempts to cut off discussion. The administrative tide, however, was about to turn in Waggoner's favor.

In mid-February W. W. Prescott, the principal of the institute, and O. A. Olsen, president of the General Conference, returned to Battle Creek and soon decided that Waggoner would receive time to present his views on the covenant issue. On Sunday, February 16, the same day that Uriah Smith began to "outline" his views, Waggoner was "allowed the floor to present his views." In all, Waggoner gave six presentations. R. C. Porter also presented one and a half lectures in support of the traditional view. Smith would continue his formal presentation on February 19. An open and frank airing of the differences had finally come to pass.

What should we make of the whole exchange? First of all, Ellen White was coming to greater clarity and conviction on the issue of the covenants.

Ellen White Openly Sides with Waggoner

It is in this context that Ellen White gave one of her most crucial statements of support for the ministry and teachings of Waggoner and Jones. Before the ministers of the institute, on February 7, 1890, she laid out her coalescing convictions: "I believe without a doubt that God has given precious truth at the right time to Brother Jones and Brother Waggoner. Do I place them as infallible? Do I say that they will not make a statement or have an idea that cannot be questioned or that cannot be error? Do I say so? No, I do not say any such thing. Nor do I say that of any man in the world. But I do say God has sent light, and do be careful how you treat it."[13]

While Dan T. Jones and Uriah Smith must have rankled at her words, a growing number did not. It was only a harbinger of more pronounced changes to come—not just in the institute itself, but also in Ellen White's open and avowed support for Waggoner's covenant position.

During the last days of the institute she forthrightly affirmed the essential outlines of his covenant teachings. In fact, she not only supported his concepts but also directed unmistakable rebukes toward the entrenched opposition.

On March 8 Ellen White publicly made a clear reference to Uriah Smith: "Do not hang on to Brother Smith. In the name of God, I tell you, he is not in the light. He has not been in the light since he was at Minneapolis."[14] But she was not through with him that day. In the evening she spoke to him (and his compatriots) the following pointed words:

"Yourself, Brother Dan Jones, Brother Porter and others are spending your investigative powers for naught to produce a position on the covenants to vary from the position that Brother Waggoner has presented. Had you received the true light which shineth, you would not have imitated or gone over the same manner of interpretation and misconstruing the Scriptures as did the Jews. . . . The covenant question is a clear question and would be received by every candid, unprejudiced mind, but I was brought where the Lord gave me an insight into this matter. You have turned from plain light because you were afraid that the law question in Galatians would have to be accepted. As to the law in Galatians, I have no burden and never have."[15]

Having twice addressed Smith on the same day, she also (in the same sermon that she declared Uriah Smith as not being "in the light") addressed further remarks to his supporter, R. C. Porter: "Brother Porter, . . . you are not in the light. Do not be surprised if I, when you are in the darkness, refuse to have an interview with . . . you."[16]

On the very next day, March 9, in a letter to Willie White and his wife, Ellen White laid it all on the line: "I have no brakes to put on now. I stand in perfect freedom, calling light, light, and darkness, darkness. I told them yesterday that the position of the covenants I believed as presented in my volume I[17] [*Patriarchs and Prophets*]. If that was Dr. Waggoner's position then he had the truth. We hope in God."[18]

If her public and letter communications were not clear enough, on March 10, in another letter to Willie and his wife, she went on to say that "since I made the statement last Sabbath that the view of the covenants as it had been taught by Brother Waggoner was truth, it seems that great relief has come to many minds." [19]

The Significance of the Covenants

Ellen White had arrived at a forthright, even blunt, clarity. What then is the crux of the covenant doctrine in the larger scheme of the debates swirling within Adventism during the aftermath of 1888?

In all probability, Paul Penno, Jr., has summed up the situation about as well as it can be done: "There was agreement on the objectives of both covenants according to Dan Jones. The sticking point was on how it was accomplished. More than likely, Waggoner's opponents would have said that the first covenant depended on obedience plus God's help. The second covenant also depended on obedience, but it was Christ's obedience in the sinner's stead. God's covenant promised forgiveness of sins and divine aid."[20]

Certainly, from our contemporary perspective, we could debate the detailed exegesis and interpretation of the key scriptural references undergirding the covenants doctrine. But we need have no doubt that Ellen White clearly affirmed the essence of Waggoner's theological direction on the question of the covenants (and later on she would also support the core of his position on the law in Galatians).

Furthermore, Waggoner had also strongly argued that there was *real forgiveness*, not just *"figurative" forgiveness,* for the Israelite believers of Old Testament times. Just because the ceremonial law was "figurative," it did not mean that the forgiveness it pointed to (as a blessed benefit of the death of Christ) was figurative. Waggoner most emphatically sought to shut out any sort of dispensational suggestion that the basis of salvation was different in Old Testament times than it was during the New Testament period. It was the same salvation from the guilt and the power of sin in both dispensations, and it came through the promises of the everlasting covenant, the new covenant, that Christ ratified by His death. Such a position reflected Waggoner's oft-repeated contention that the Lord of the Bible was not an inconsistent God, saving people only figuratively in the Old Testament and in reality in the New Testament era.

The Irreducible "Bottom Line"

So what was the bottom line for Waggoner and Ellen White on such a complex subject? The real point at issue was that Christ always has justifying grace that is really and truly available, no matter where one lives in the stream of earthly time after the Fall. And for those justified by faith, there is also available the power of divine grace to write the law of God on the fleshly tables of the heart. In other words, the life of the believer has victory over both the guilt and the power of sin.

And here was the key to the overarching issue of the theology of E. J. Waggoner that Ellen White so strongly endorsed: would it be Christ who was uplifted as the complete Savior from sin, or would the emphasis be placed on the law, human obedience, and the promises of a weak and sinful people who were doomed to failure outside of the eternal covenant of grace, the second or new covenant?

CLARIFICATION ON THE CALIFORNIA CONSPIRACY

While the church gained significant clarification on the issues of the covenant (though no real breakthrough to consensus with Smith and Dan Jones), the major healing accomplishment of the latter part of the 1889/1890 ministerial institute involved clearing the air on the "California conspiracy."

Until March of 1890 Smith, Butler, Dan Jones, and many others had continued to hold on to the "California conspiracy" suspicions that had so riled Butler in the weeks before the Minneapolis meetings. Still wary, they continued to detect some sort of conspiratorial master plan to inflict the new theological perspective upon the church. Smith was convinced that the combined work of A. T. Jones, E. J. Waggoner, and Ellen White was unmistakable evidence of a malevolent conspiracy. What had proved most disconcerting was the obvious conclusion that they could no longer trust Ellen White, because she was now under the unholy influence of the young West Coast upstarts. The pioneer stalwarts of Battle Creek did not dare to throw her totally overboard, but their finely parsed rationale for their pick-and-choose attitude on the authoritative reliability of Ellen White was that her opinions were merely her own and "are no better than our opinions, unless it is something she has seen in vision."[21]

It was during this early March setting and its tense discussions on the covenants that Ellen White and W. W. Prescott decided to make a concerted effort to clear the air on the conspiracy rumors.[22] She sensed that the tide was beginning to turn and that the time had come to lance this festering boil.

On March 13 she called a special meeting of the leading ministers so that she and Waggoner could tell their side of the story. A few days later A. T. Jones arrived to take part in the discussions. After a number of days of candid exchange, the explanations seemed to bring satisfaction to Dan T. Jones. Others would soon follow him in accepting the position of Ellen White, A. T. Jones, and Waggoner. It proved to be an important turning point in the tensions that had enveloped post-Minneapolis Adventism.

But no one should entertain any illusions that Smith had changed his mind on the contested theology or that he had experienced a marked change of heart. In actual fact, it was not until the very end of 1890 and the beginning of 1891 that Uriah Smith would actually deal with the issue of his persistent opposition to Ellen White and her associates in the revival.[23] Uriah Smith was not a person to change his mind or feelings quickly.

While his slow shift of attitude did bring some significant relief to the contentious atmosphere of Adventism in the spring of 1891 and afterward, once more we need to remind ourselves that Smith never altered his viewpoint on the covenants and the law in Galatians.[24] Furthermore, both Smith and Dan Jones would continue to drag their feet in the interest of the unfolding revival led by Ellen White, A. T. Jones, and E. J. Waggoner. And Smith's intransigence and resistance to change further evidenced itself later in the year 1890.

THE CHAUTAUQUA MEETING OF W. W. PRESCOTT

In mid-1890, following on the heels of the developments of the ministers' Bible school, W. W. Prescott sought to open up a chance for another dialogue between the key contestants, especially Smith and Waggoner. He sensed that some more face-to-face exchanges might foster further understanding, friendship, and harmony.

In pursuit of such noble goals, Prescott began to plan a consultation between "leading teachers of theology" at the Chautauqua retreat and conference center in New York. While he received the enthusiastic support of church leaders, he did not get much of a response from either Smith or Waggoner. W. C. White had urged Waggoner to attend, but even the appeals of his longtime friend and persistent supporter would not move Ellet to go to the shores of Lake Chautauqua and make peace with Smith.[25] Even though 18 scholars eventually showed up at Chautauqua, both of the key figures in the theological conflict "stubbornly refused the invitation and found excuses for not participating."[26]

Uriah Smith was clearly not following the leading of God in this and a number of other attitudes and actions that had steadily emerged as his post-Minneapolis pattern. Waggoner, however, is more difficult to gage in the matter of the Chautauqua dialogues. Most likely the best face that we can put on it is that he had simply given in to despair in making any further progress with the stubborn Smith and had concluded that he would no longer waste his valuable time in making overtures to the *Review* editor.

While both would continue to play prominent roles in the church during the next decade, they just never managed to see eye to eye on these theological issues.

THE LAST YEARS IN THE STATES: SPRING OF 1890 TO EARLY 1892

When the ministerial institute of 1889/1890 drew to a close on March 25, 1890, Waggoner's stateside ministry would begin to conclude. While he would continue editing, writing, making revival appearances, and sharing in the councils of the church, his major American public contributions were beginning to point to new spheres of ministry. But a number of interesting developments do merit some detailed tracing in regard to his final two years of service in the United States.

He spent the weeks following the close of the ministerial institute on March 25, 1890, in travel to Fresno for the California camp meeting. Ellen White apparently suggested that he accompany her to Texas on the way back to California, but we have no record that he did so. The Fresno camp meeting took place during the first two weeks of April, and by April 19 Waggoner had returned to Oakland. He had been expected back by the time of the last Sabbath in March to celebrate the quarterly services (Communion) of the Oakland church. But his ministry at the Fresno camp meeting caused the congregation to postpone the celebration of the Lord's Supper until April 19.[27]

At the Fresno camp meeting Waggoner's preaching "was mainly directed to the imparting of instruction in church duties, the responsibilities of church members, their relation to one another, etc., and to unfolding the simple principles of the gospel."[28] The subjects have a familiar ring to them since they were the very themes that Waggoner had presented at the ministerial council and business session Bible study hours in Minneapolis. Apparently Waggoner had developed quite a reputation as an instructor on the practical side of church life, in addition to his rising reputation as an exponent of "the simple principles of the gospel."

On the Sabbath following his return from Battle Creek and the Fresno camp meeting, the Oakland church did celebrate the quarterly meeting, and Waggoner "gave an instructive, earnest, and appropriate discourse in the morning on the Lord's death and resurrection, and what they should be to us in our daily life, and in the afternoon the ordinances were celebrated, a larger number taking part than ever before." Also reported was the "blessed sight" of "many young people showing their faith in Christ."[29]

The fellowship of the Oakland congregation must have been a welcome solace to its pastor after an absence of almost four months and the trying circumstances of the ministerial institute in Battle Creek. The occasion would be one of the last quarterly services that Waggoner would share with the congregation that he had pastored for "some years."

What Waggoner did between May and mid-October of 1890 is mostly unknown. The most likely assumption is that he spent the time in his pastoral, editing, and writing responsibilities.[30] Yet the minutes of the General Conference committee reveal an interesting assignment. The leadership of the church had become concerned about the neglect of Seventh-day Adventists in the major encyclopedias of the day (both religious and general). Furthermore, if they did get mentioned, Adventists deemed the treatment to be distorted. So the church leadership took an action to put Waggoner on a standing committee whose specific assignment was to "furnish information to publishers" of the "leading Encyclopedias" of that era.[31]

One other interesting little vignette in the life of Waggoner has to do with the vivid recollections of his daughter Pearl: she and her sister were privileged to go with their father as "part of a group on [a] trial trip of [the] ship *Pitcairn*." The denomination used the legendary schooner to transport missionaries across the Pacific Ocean from 1890 to 1900. The 1889 General Conference session had voted its construction, and it must have been a stirring experience to be a part of the sea trials of the storied vessel.

It is somewhat ironic that the name originally chosen for this vessel was *Glad Tidings*; "but on further consideration the Foreign Mission Board settled on the name *Pitcairn*," chosen because of the famous South Pacific island whose legendary inhabitants (descended from the infamous mutineers of Captain Bligh's ship, the *Bounty*) had recently converted to Seventh-day Adventist Christianity.[32] This little voyage proved to be a harbinger of many transoceanic travels in the coming years of Waggoner's international ministry.

Already the sense of transition seemed to be in the air during the fall of 1890 as Waggoner would close out his pastorate of the Oakland church on October 11, 1890.[33] His final official Sabbath as pastor was just two days before he and his family would leave for Battle Creek "to take a prominent part in teaching in the ministers' school . . . this winter."[34]

It was not, however, just pastoral responsibilities that seemed to be winding down, but also his editorial duties at the Pacific Press. The previous two years had seen very lengthy absences from Oakland and the staff of the *Signs* and the administration of the Pacific Press seemed to sense that the end of his more than seven years of service was imminent.

In a somewhat plaintive tone of exceeding "regret," the publishing house author noted that they would "lose his help from this office; in fact, we know not how we could get along without him if it were not for the assurance that our work was God's work, and that he will supply 'all our needs.' Brother Waggoner will still write for the SIGNS."[35]

On October 13, 1890, Waggoner and his family, along with numerous other prominent church employees, left Oakland by train for Battle Creek.[36]

The major reason for this trip was to attend (1) the second of the two major ministerial institutes that would start on October 31 and run to February 28, 1891, and (2) the General Conference session to commence on March 5, 1891, soon after the ministerial institute ended.[37] But for the

Waggoner family, the trip would be the actual beginning of the end of their residence in Oakland. While they would return for one more visit, their home for most of the next two years would basically be Battle Creek, with extended stays in western New York. But before we trace the personal pilgrimage of the Waggoner family, we will first deal with important developments in the public ministry of Ellet at the second ministerial institute and the 1891 General Conference session.

THE SECOND MINISTERS' INSTITUTE[38]

This second major ministers' institute (or the ministers' school) began on Friday, October 31, at 9:00 a.m. in Battle Creek and continued for 16 weeks, until February 27, 1891.[39]

This important institute had four important factors associated with it. The first had to do with Waggoner's teaching role. The second was the growing convergence of the views of W. W. Prescott and E. J. Waggoner on the law in Galatians. The third was the persistent and stubborn opposition of G. I. Butler to the new perspective on the law in Galatians, as well as the new emphasis on justification by faith. And the fourth dealt with the experience of Uriah Smith in "falling on the rock," but not being entirely broken.

WAGGONER'S TEACHING ROLE[40]

One of the early factors in the second institute was the fact that Dan Jones served on the managing board of the institute.[41] While he had gotten over his belief in the "California Conspiracy" rumors, he had not fully abandoned his opposition to Waggoner's viewpoints on the law in Galatians and the covenants. Thus it was not surprising that he had expressed concerns about allowing Waggoner to teach the book of Galatians.[42] In the face of Jones's reservations, W. W. Prescott, once more serving as the principal of the institute, arranged to handle the disputed subject. But what Prescott began, Waggoner finished. Prescott covered only the first three chapters of Galatians, and somehow, Dan Jones notwithstanding, Waggoner dealt with the rest of the book and then promptly proceeded to an exposition of the book of Romans.[43] It was in his teaching role that Waggoner would make his most lasting contribution to the 1890-1891 ministers' institute.

PRESCOTT'S GROWING THEOLOGICAL CONVERGENCE

The evidence for Prescott's growing agreement with Waggoner is twofold: (1) the very fact that Prescott allowed him to finish his work on Galatians evidences his confidence, even in the face of the stated reservations of Dan T. Jones. Furthermore, (2) the record reveals that Prescott taught Waggoner's view on "the seed" in Galatians "in the minutest detail."[44]

G. I. BUTLER'S ONGOING REACTIONS AND OPPOSITION

The evolving agreement between Waggoner and Prescott was so marked that when G. I. Butler, from far away in his self-imposed Florida exile, received credible intelligence on this development, he gave the following, enraged outburst: "Great Scott, has it come to this that such things are to be indoctrinated into the minds of our young people!" It, along with other evidence, clearly reveals that the convalescing Butler was not the least bit repentant in his persistent opposition to the theology of Waggoner and his supporters. Ellen White had continued to labor for the former General Conference president through numerous letters. But during 1890 she had become even more straightforward in her characterizations of Butler and company's positions on the law in Galatians and the covenants.

She compared their attitudes to those of the Jews who persistently entertained "ideas and customs and practices" that enabled them to reject Christ. In fact, she characterized such attitudes and their undergirding "ideas" as "idols." Once more she let it be known that the "law in Galatians" was not a "vital question and never has been" and that she had no "anxiety" about how that discussion over its interpretation would play itself out. But she did express a strong "anxiety that our leading brethren" would continue to use this issue as an excuse to resist "light and the manifest testimonies of the Spirit of God, and reject everything to idolize their own supposed ideas and pet theories."

Then she finished her remarkable testimony of support for Waggoner and his allies with the statement that she was "forced" to conclude that the attitude of her fellow church leaders and "the spirit evidenced" had caused her to draw back from them in horror—she could only cry out to God for deliverance "from your ideas of the law in Galatians, if the receiving of these ideas would make me so unchristian in my spirit, words, and works as many who ought to know better have been. . . . I am warned again and again of what will be the result of this warfare" that has been so "persistently maintained against the truth."[45]

Not surprisingly, Butler's attitude greatly mirrored the thought of Uriah Smith. But in Smith's case there would soon be some positive change in the final days of 1890 and the first three weeks of 1891.

URIAH SMITH "FALLS ON THE ROCK" AND IS PARTIALLY "BROKEN"

Probably the most positive development during the period of the second ministers' institute was the partial softening of the attitude of Uriah Smith. The whole process had begun during the December 1890 Week of Prayer, when W. W. Prescott had read to the Battle Creek church, on Sabbath, December 17, 1890, a strong testimony by Ellen White (not present, but soon to return to Battle Creek from Washington, D.C.) that had been published as a *Review Extra*.[46]

As Gilbert Valentine has so picturesquely expressed it, the eloquent and charismatic W. W. Prescott was "a nineteenth-century equivalent of a public address system on account of his vocal powers." But with stentorian voice, or sometimes with no voice at all, the deeply penitent Prescott responded strongly to Ellen White's powerful rebukes of those who had "cast contempt" on the message of Minneapolis. She even called the stubborn opposition to the all-consuming theme of Christ's righteousness as "dangerous." In fact, for Ellen White everything was "dangerous" that stood in the way of this subject, which she regarded as destined to "swallow up" all other topics.[47]

Prescott had been so deeply moved in his penitence that he had difficulty restraining his emotions, often losing his powerful voice. He expressed the deepest repentance, openly confessed to Jones and Waggoner, and then went into the congregation to take the elderly Uriah Smith by the arm and escort him to the rostrum.

While Uriah Smith responded to the leading of Prescott, it was only with the most obvious foot-dragging. With the utmost reluctance he could, at first, only croak out that "the matter comes home to me; it means me." At least it was a slight harbinger of things to come. But he had by no means fallen (to use the biblical expression) "on the rock" of deep, heart-breaking repentance. While Smith's initial movements were glacially slow, the Lord and Ellen White were not yet finished dealing with him.

During the next few days and in deep "agony" of soul, the long-suffering prophet prepared a letter for the reluctant denominational patriarch. Trying to be careful, she had withheld the letter for a few days. Finally her patience began to bear fruit.

The following week Smith came to visit her, requesting a meeting with a few select individuals. It was before this meeting that she finally gave Smith the letter penned a few days earlier. Its contents could not have been more direct: "the feelings cherished by yourself and Elder Butler were not only despising the message, but the messengers. . . . You write that you have said that you would have [no] controversy with Sister White. Better, far better, [to] have had this controversy openly than under cover, for this controversy has been and there has not been harmony between us since the Minneapolis meeting. You have been extremely stubborn."[48]

Finally the protracted struggle ended the next day, Wednesday, January 7. Smith read Ellen White's letter before the select few who had gathered, and "with tears, made a full and free confession of the wrong course he had pursued."[49] Then, taking her hand, he addressed her in deep contrition, begging her forgiveness "for all the trouble and distress" that he had caused her and assuring her that this would be the "last time" he would create for her such agony of soul: "I will not repeat the history of the past three years."[50] It was then that Ellen White penned in her diary those famous words: "He had fallen on the Rock and was broken. I cannot describe to you my joy."[51]

On the following Sabbath (January 10) the penitent Smith once more confessed his wrong attitudes that went back to Minneapolis, admitting that he and others had, in their boardinghouses, "made light of the truth and of those who advocated the truth."[52] He would even repeat this same basic confession on January 20, in the presence of the full assembly of the ministers' institute.

While Ellen White would continue to record some personal reflections in her diary about the long-lasting effects of habitually resisting light, especially for the likes of Smith and his cohort, she was ever the redemptive optimist. Thus she must have felt deeply gratified by Smith's stirring and positive presentation "The Spirit of Prophecy and Our Relation to it," made on the second Sabbath of the soon-following 1891 General Conference session.[53] After more than two years of resistance and the most underhanded, subtle whittling away at her authority and credibility, a positive note of admiration for the gift of prophecy was like rain on an arid desert of withering denial.

The results of Smith's confession had a more immediate impact on Ellet Waggoner. On January 12 he communicated, in a personal interview with Ellen White, how much better things were going during the current institute when compared to the sad experiences of the previous Bible school.[54] Life was certainly much more bearable without the machinations of the Battle Creek clique and their constant undercurrent of opposition.

While we cannot doubt Smith's sincere repentance for his attitudes, there still remained a troubling negativity toward Jones, Waggoner, and their allies. If individuals do not ultimately become convinced of the truth that they have opposed, it is hard for genuine penitence to take deep root in the soul. While Ellen White did voice her "respect" for Smith and that "confidence in him is restored," she also sensed that things were not completely resolved.

On the twenty-second of January she recorded a more qualified assessment of Smith and his repentance: "There is a nominal assent to the truth but its deep spiritual meaning is not understood. We have for years been waging a war with spiritual idolatry."[55] Persistent resistance can leave a strong stain on the character and attitudes. And such was the sad case of Uriah Smith and his coterie.

One interesting little glimpse into Smith's lingering negativity surfaced two years later in the aftermath of the Anna Rice affair.[56] In 1893 and 1894 both A. T. Jones and W. W. Prescott, along with the likes of E. W. Farnsworth and J. H. Durland, had rushed to affirm Miss Rice's claims to the gift of visions and prophecy. But a firm statement from Ellen White had taken the wind out of the sails of this unwise rush to accept the young woman's alleged prophetic gift.

The net effect of the embarrassing episode was a deeply discouraged W. W. Prescott. His public embarrassment was so intense that the General Conference president had tried to console him. Olsen was fully aware that the anti-Jones/Waggoner forces were gloating over the whole affair.

It wasn't long before word came that Uriah Smith had expressed his opinion of Prescott and Jones's blundering judgment with a rather vivid metaphor—that Mrs. White had given them a good "whack on the snout."[57] Satisfaction about the church avoiding danger was one thing, but finding pleasure in the failures of others was quite another.

In spite of some who took devilish delight in "whacks on the snout," the ministers' institute of 1890 and 1891 had been highly positive. Ellen White would mostly share the upbeat assessment of Waggoner. She reported to church employees on the West Coast the following stirring report: "The ministerial institute was a season of close searching of the Scriptures. The doors of hearts were not barred with iron, lest rays of light should penetrate the darkened chambers of the mind, and the sanctifying power should cleanse and refine the soul temple. Right in the midst of their study, during the past winter, there have been times where there was not a question with the class but that the Comforter, the Holy Spirit of God, was doing its work."[58] It was a powerful affirmation of the efforts of the teaching staff and the sincere desire of the students to get things right with God.

And furthermore, the positive accomplishments of those months of study and penitence would flow relatively smoothly into the last major churchwide public appearance of Waggoner on the North American scene before his permanent transfer to England and Europe.

THE 1891 GENERAL CONFERENCE SESSION

Beginning on March 5 the interesting session would run until the twenty-fifth of the same month. But before we examine the major events of Ellet's public participation, we need to explore his personal circumstances and those of Jessie and the girls further.

As already noted, Waggoner's family made the trip with him for the second Battle Creek ministers' institute and the following General Conference session. Undoubtedly he and his family must have considered it a great privilege to be able to be together. His numerous travels during the previous two years had caused many lengthy separations. But their much-anticipated time together turned into a virtual nightmare. While the record does not reveal exactly where the Waggoner family resided, they soon had to lodge separately.

Pearl reveals that in "early February of 1891" (during the ministers' institute) her father "had to move over to [the] college entirely, as the rest of us were quarantined for scarlet fever." She had to celebrate her sixth birthday bedridden with the fever. But Jessie appears to have been the family member hit the hardest: "Mother had [an] extra hard time."[59] Mercifully, both Pearl and Jessie made a slow but steady recovery. Their isolation must have also been difficult for the already overburdened Ellet to bear in the trying circumstances of the just-completed ministers' institute and the major involvement he would bear at the 1891 General Conference session.

The bout with scarlet fever provides a plausible explanation for the apparent absence of Jessie from the proceedings of the International Sabbath School Association meetings that took place at the 1891 session. Delegates to the meetings learned that she had resigned as corresponding secretary sometime since the 1889 General Conference session (because of "other duties"). In fact, those "other duties" laid on her by the Sabbath School Association had turned out to be quite significant.

Not only had the 1889 business meeting asked her to assume additional editorial responsibilities and to develop other Sabbath school curricula items, but the association president's report revealed that she had been appointed coeditor of the *Sabbath School Worker*. The journal, founded in 1885, had originally been a quarterly publication, but in February of 1890 it had become a monthly.[60] Undoubtedly it was a responsibility that must have consumed much of her time and energy. Furthermore, Jessie was one of the early editors of the long-enduring children's paper called *Our Little Friend*.[61] The more one learns about her versatility and penchant for creative multitasking the more one wonders how the woman had any time for family and friends.

Yet in spite of the personal woes of his family, for Ellet the 1891 General Conference session was one of the genuine high points of his public career. Not only did he once more serve as an at-large delegate and ably fulfill numerous committee assignments,[62] but the leadership had also asked him to be the major speaker at the session's "Bible study hour." In fact, his presentations created "so much interest . . . on the part of the Battle Creek church, the students at the college, the helpers at the sanitarium, and [the] hands in the Review office, that the time [of the Bible study hour] was changed" from the less-accessible 9:00 a.m. time slot "to 7:00 p.m., in order to accommodate all."[63]

The Bible study series had actually commenced on March 1 when W. W. Prescott spoke on the subject of biblical inspiration. On Friday, March 6, however, Waggoner took over the time and began a series of 16 lectures on the biblical book of Romans. They continued daily (except on Fridays) from March 8 through 24.

The well-received series[64] must have contained the essence of what he had been presenting in the classes on Galatians and Romans during the just-completed ministers' institute. In fact, O. A. Olsen, in his presidential address of March 5, publicly stated that Waggoner's studies on Romans were to be seen as an extension of the highly successful ministers institute. Thus, in a very important sense they were an effective continuation of his efforts in the previous months of the Bible school for ministers.[65]

Furthermore, Ellen White was greatly pleased about the overall tone of the session. "We have had a deeply interesting conference. . . . The Lord has been in our midst, and we have seen of His salvation." She would go on to enthuse that she had "never attended a General Conference where there was manifested as much of the Spirit of the Lord in the study of His Word, as on this occasion."[66] In Letter 3, 1891, Ellen White offered much the same observations on the General Conference session as she had on the preceding ministers' institute. It also gave a ringing endorsement of the Bible teaching of Ellet J. Waggoner, who had, along with the steady guidance of Ellen White, provided the major highlights of one of the most successful General Conference sessions in the history of Seventh-day Adventism.[67]

While a number of important public appointments still awaited him in the States, this General Conference session was the final major public appearance before the commencement of his British and European years. But before we turn our attention to that narrative, we must deal with a few remaining biographical details for the last part of 1891 and the early months of 1892.

THE FINAL MONTHS OF MINISTRY IN THE STATES

While the life and ministry of E. J. Waggoner had numerous dramatic incidents, some of the more decisive ones took place in seemingly prosaic, somewhat functionary committee meetings.

Two such fateful sessions took place, one in late 1890 and the other on February 5, 1891, just before the March 1891 General Conference session. Since we know only one aspect about the first meeting, we will concentrate on the February 5, 1891, gathering.

The February 5, 1891, meeting was of the Foreign Mission Board. Those listed as present included General Conference president Olsen, Eldridge, Miller, Chadwick, Edwards, White (most likely W. C.), W. W. Prescott, and "Dr. Waggoner by invitation." One of the major items on the agendas of both the February and March meetings had to do with the success of the Ministers' Institutes. The positive developments of the Institutes had inspired the leadership of the church to multiply their number and extend their reach to include the fledgling Adventist mission in Europe. In light of this expanding vision, W. W. Prescott was asked to "state the plans of the Committee on District Conventions."

Prescott proceeded to report that the committee was prepared to recommend "the holding of a ministerial institute in each General Conference district, and also, during the summer vacation, a convention for Bible study, especially for those teachers who are to conduct the Bible work in our schools and for those ministers who may be chosen to teach in the district institute. This convention could best be held from the middle of July to the middle [of] August, and since he was convicted that Dr. Waggoner should be present, he desired the board to plan our European work for Dr. Waggoner accordingly."

The minutes of Foreign Mission Board then concluded with the revealing observation that "it seemed to be the mind of the members present that Dr. Waggoner should return from Europe in time to attend the summer Institute."[68] Quite obviously the references to the planned trip to Europe by Waggoner indicate that the Foreign Mission Board had voted it some time in late1890.[69] The General Conference in session on March 25, 1891, subsequently ratified the combined recommendations for the projected European teaching tour. "Elders O. A. Olsen and E. J. Waggoner [are] to visit Europe and hold biblical institutes in England and Scandinavia."[70]

In just a little more than three weeks E. J. Waggoner would arrive in London to begin numerous engagements with camp meetings and institutes in England; Copenhagen, Denmark; Christiania, Norway; and Basel, Switzerland.[71]

But before departing for Europe, Ellet made an important side trip. Even though Jessie and Pearl had partially recovered from their scarlet fever, Jessie was still weak from her "extra hard" and "prolonged" bout with the nineteenth-century scourge. Once more Ellet's thoughts turned to his old friends, the Lindsay family at Burt, New Fane Township, in western New York. Pearl reports that her "father took us all to the old Lindsay farm" so that she and her mother "could fully regain strength" while her father conducted "various meetings" and assisted "in camp-meetings in Europe."

One of the interesting ironies of her stay with the Lindsay family was that the recuperating Jessie found herself pressed into action to nurse back to health two of the ailing Lindsay children.[72]

The Foreign Mission Board committee and General Conference actions of late 1890 and early 1891 signaled the beginnings of a process that would radically alter the directions of the life of E. J. Waggoner and his family for the next 12 years. While the actions did not assign him exclusively to work in Europe, they were definitely harbingers of a more permanent appointment that would soon unfold. While this initial trip to Europe lasted only a few months, by late May of 1892 Waggoner and his family would be in London for a stint of ministry that would last until late September of 1903.

As already mentioned, the mid-October 1890 departure of the Waggoner family from Oakland had been noted with some sense of finality in the pages of the *Signs of the Times*. In actual fact, the premonitions of the staff at the *Signs* were correct. The departure was, for all practical purposes, the end of his residence on the West Coast. With the news of Waggoner's appointment by the Foreign Mission Board to spend extensive time in Europe and the upcoming district institutes in North America, the management of the Pacific Press concluded that the proverbial handwriting was on the wall for Waggoner's service at the *Signs*. Thus it only seemed inevitable that the *Signs of the Times* of May 4, 1891, would be the last number in which Waggoner's name would appear on the masthead as editor.[73] The May 11, 1891, issue would list M. C. Wilcox as the sole editor and E. J. Waggoner as a "special contributor."

When Ellet returned to the States "at the end of the summer" he "spent a few days at the [Lindsay] farm" with the family before their return to Battle Creek where they resided until sometime in early 1892. While at the farm Ellet had a wonderful time sharing the stories of his travels and the many blessings experienced in Europe.

Pearl particularly recalled "what he told us about [his] experiences in Scandinavia. He studied Danish on the ship on the way over . . . and after [his] first sermon with [an] interpreter" he "began his own preaching, in Danish." Pearl went on to share that later on she personally received reports from the Danes as to how well her father did and noted the "many warm and permanent friends" that he made.[74] The subsequent records of Ellet's many trips to Denmark, which would continue intermittently until near the end of his life, certainly testify to the very positive impact he had during his initial trip to Europe—especially in Scandinavia.

Quite likely the reports of the successes of his 1891 spring and summer tour of Europe must have surfaced at the General Conference, and the idea of offering Waggoner a permanent appointment in England received serious consideration. Thus it seemed only a matter of time before the General Conference would assign him as the editor of the British *Present Truth*. And the appointment did come sometime in early 1892.[75]

Waggoner spent the late months of 1891 and the early months of 1892 largely in extensive travels and teaching. In a rare preserved personal letter, written from Des Moines, Iowa, on April 1, 1892, to his old friend and colleague Professor Sydney Brownsberger (from Healdsburg College days),[76] Waggoner noted the extensive travels of the previous months since his return from Europe. He listed camp meetings in Michigan, other meetings in Illinois, a ministerial institute in Georgia, a few days at home in Chicago,[77] and another institute in Lancaster, Massachusetts. Then followed two months of teaching in the Bible school in Chicago and institutes in Kansas and Healdsburg, California. Jessie and the girls had joined Ellet in Kansas and made the trip with him back to California for the Healdsburg institute in early 1892.[78]

One of the more revealing notes in the Brownsberger letter is the forthrightness with which Ellet described his health and outlook on change. He shared with his friend that things had looked a little shaky for him in the fall of 1891, but gave the cheering news that since then he had "kept up remarkably well."

A telling feature of his little health update is a glimpse into the intensity of his work schedule during those grueling itineraries. He reported averaging two presentations a day "all the time" and "sometimes" speaking for more than "five hours a day." Although he acknowledged that the Lord had given him "special help" in such circumstances, he did look forward to a lighter schedule in England, where he would not "have to work so hard for a while" since the *Present Truth* was published only every other week.

One of the constant features of his professional life would be intemperance in work. The same syndrome seems to have afflicted Jessie. We will follow this characteristic carefully through the British years, as it will come to play an important role in some of the sad reverses that will envelope the hardworking couple. The anticipation that the workload would be lighter in Britain was only a wishful pipe dream for the seemingly perpetual-motion Ellet Waggoner.

Anticipation of the challenges that lay ahead must have filled Waggoner's mind as he prepared to leave for Europe. But he must also have reflected on the momentous events that he had experienced during the past 10 years since his glorious vision of the uplifted Christ at the Healdsburg camp meeting of 1882.

Soon after the close of the California institute he left his wife and children in Oakland and headed to Iowa. He noted that "Jessie wanted to be with her mother as much as possible before we leave the country." His wife would arrive from California in Des Moines on April 15. They then would leave Iowa to "start on our journey east," with projected stopovers in Chicago and Battle Creek.

The stay in Battle Creek allowed them to pack their household goods stored there and "spend a few days providing for my mother's wants before I leave." After the Battle Creek interlude, Ellet, along with his family and sister Alta, once again spent "a few days at [the Lindsay] farm" before proceeding on to New York City and the departure for England on May 11, 1892, aboard the transatlantic liner *Teutonic*.[79]

SUMMARY

The time for new vistas was at hand. Waggoner would exchange the highs and lows of the post-Minneapolis era in the States for bracing challenges in England and on the European continent. The three and a half years since the epic 1888 General Conference session had been filled with loss, grief, lengthy separations from family, and challenges from the entrenched forces in Battle Creek. But he had helped in establishing the denomination's rising emphasis on the uplifted Christ—the channel of both justifying and transforming grace that constantly emanates from the covenant-keeping God.

While Waggoner would return for numerous General Conference meetings in the coming decade (1897, 1899, 1901, and 1903) and his writings (both books and articles) would continue to come off Adventist presses and appear in periodicals in North America, Australia, and South Africa, his major focus would now be on Britain and Western Europe.

While the pending mission appeared full of both bright prospects and daunting challenges, Waggoner could, on the voyage to England, indulge some moments of grateful reflection. He must have sent up many praises to God for the blessings of strong support from Ellen White, O. A. Olsen, W. W. Prescott, and his longtime "blood brother in 'the blood of the everlasting covenant,'" A. T. Jones (and numerous others).

He and Jones could both rejoice that God had bolstered them not only with strength and backing but also with unparalleled access to the major venues of education and spiritual revival. They had already been pivotal agents in the beginnings of the loud cry and its expectation that soon the latter-rain power of the Holy Spirit would be manifest. The past years had been filled with accomplishments that few other men in Adventist history could, or ever would, experience.

Ellen White had already gone to Australia the previous year. Now that Waggoner was headed to Europe, Jones would become the main agent for continued revival in the States. Though divided by great distances, the three would continue to unfold, in their respective ministries, the remarkably grace-laden vision of Minneapolis. Our next major quest will be to see what the European years (1892-1903) had in store for the gospel vision of E. J. Waggoner.

But before we turn our attention to it, we need to review the theological developments of the first three and a half years of the post-Minneapolis period. What were the key themes of this exciting period and how did they mesh with the theology of Waggoner's key partners in the revival, especially the thought of Ellen White?

[1] Pearl Waggoner Howard, in "Biographical Sketch and Background," Document File 23b.

[2] Already the ministerial Bible schools, or institutes, had commenced in the winter of 1889. Even before O. A. Olsen arrived from Scandinavia to take up his presidential responsibilities in early May, "a ministers' and workers' institute provided for at the 1889 General Conference session had been held in Battle Creek." The meeting convened in the college building from January 17 to March 28. This gathering was mainly for "those engaged in public labor, and younger ministers were urged to attend." About 50 responded to the announcement for "the institute" that "emphasized that 'Elder A. T. Jones will take a leading part in the instruction' [*Review and Herald*, Jan. 1, 1889]" (A. V. Olson, *Through Crisis to Victory*, p. 66). While the series would last until 1896, the churchwide institutes of late 1889, early 1890, and late 1890/early 1891 in Battle Creek were the most important for the revival story we are tracing (see G. Valentine, *The Shaping of Adventism*, p. 51).

[3] P. Penno, *Calvary at Sinai*, p. 130.

[4] Valentine, *The Shaping of Adventism*, p. 50.

[5] G. Knight, *From 1888 to Apostasy*, p. 50. This paragraph and the three preceding are mainly a digest of Knight's handy review of the background of the Ministerial Institutes, supplemented by Valentine, *The Shaping of Adventism*, pp. 49-52.

[6] Knight and Penno give differing starting dates: Knight suggests November 5 (*From 1888 to Apostasy*, p. 50) and Penno says it began on October 31 (*Calvary at Sinai*, p. 130). Penno was most likely drawing from Valentine, *The Shaping of Adventism*, p. 50.

[7] Knight presents the 50 figure, while Valentine claims that "a surprising 157 ministerial students were attracted to this first formal 'seminary' program." Prescott designed the program to last 20 weeks and modeled the course of study on William Rainey Harper's "Chautauqua plan." The curriculum was very similar to what Prescott had experienced at Dartmouth, featuring "Christian Evidences, Church History, Greek, Hebrew, Church Government, Logic, Civics, Biblical Studies, and Bible Doctrines" (Valentine, *The Shaping of Adventism*, p. 50).

[8] *Signs of the Times*, Dec. 30, 1889, p. 16.

[9] The following narrative derives primarily from the able researches of Valentine and Penno.

[10] In chapter 3 we have already examined the basic issues involved in these controversies. The following seeks to shed further light on this somewhat elusive aspect.

[11] No relation to A. T. Jones, either genetically or theologically.

[12] Ellen White to Brethren Ballenger and L. Smith, Jan. 17, 1890, in *The Ellen G. White 1888 Materials*, vol. 2, pp. 528, 529.

[13] Ellen G. White manuscript 56, 1890, in *The Ellen G. White 1888 Materials*, vol. 2, p. 566.

[14] Ellen G. White manuscript 4, 1890, in *The Ellen G. White 1888 Materials*, vol. 2, p. 596.

[15] Ellen G. White manuscript 59, 1890, in *The Ellen G. White 1888 Materials*, vol. 2, p. 604.

[16] Ellen G. White manuscript 4, 1890, in *The Ellen G. White 1888 Materials*, vol. 2, 595.

[17] "Volume I" is an obvious reference to the first of five volumes in Ellen White's most beloved and influential set of books called the Conflict of the Ages Series.

[18] Ellen G. White letter 82, 1890, in *The Ellen G. White 1888 Materials*, vol. 2, p. 617.

[19] Ellen G. White letter 30, 1890, in *The Ellen G. White 1888 Materials*, vol. 2, p. 623.

[20] Penno, *Calvary at Sinai*, p. 136.

[21] Knight, *From 1888 to Apostasy*, p. 51. The quoted phrase is not from George Knight, but was Ellen White's own expression that she invoked to sum up the rationale of Smith,

Butler, Dan T. Jones, and others who had so persistently and perniciously opposed her and Waggoner. See her letter 83, Mar. 13, 1890, to W. C. White and wife, in *The Ellen G. White 1888 Materials*, vol. 2, p. 627.

[22] Knight gives the impression that the initiative was mainly Ellen White's. Valentine suggests that Prescott had sponsored the meetings and that Ellen White joined them in an effort to clear the air once and for all (Knight, *From 1888 to Apostasy*, pp. 51, 52, and Valentine, *The Shaping of Adventism*, p. 51).

[23] For Ellen White's perspective on Smith's "falling on the rock" in public repentance and confession in late 1890 or early 1891, see the various letter and diary entries in *The Ellen G. White 1888 Materials*, vol. 2, pp. 787-801; 839-853; 861-864; 871- 876.

[24] Valentine, *The Shaping of Adventism*, p. 58: "The editor's confession related strictly to his attitude to Mrs. White, not to the theological issue. Just a year before his death, Smith stated that he had never changed his view on the law in Galatians."

[25] If we wanted to play on the Native American associations with the name Chautauqua, we could say that Prescott wanted to smoke the Adventist peace pipe, though I recognize that it is an awkward metaphor to use for abstemious Adventist clergy.

[26] For further background and details on this ill-fated effort, see Valentine, *The Shaping of Adventism*, p. 57.

[27] *Signs of the Times*, Mar. 31, 1890, p. 16..

[28] "The Fresno Camp Meeting," *Signs of the Times*, Apr. 28, 1890.

[29] *Signs of the Times*, Apr. 28, 1890, p. 16.

[30] An interesting brief report on the vitality of the Oakland Seventh-day Adventist Church appeared in the *Signs of the Times*, Jan. 20, 1890: the membership was expanding, mainly because of transfers, and the listed number was 408.

[31] "General Conference Committee Minutes," July 27, 1890. See online at adventistarchives.org.

[32] For more on the story and details of this vessel, see the article "*Pitcairn*" in the *Seventh-day Adventist Encyclopedia*, vol. 11, p. 354.

[33] *Signs of the Times*, Oct. 20, 1890, p. 16.

[34] An obvious reference to the second major ministerial institute of 1890 and early 1891.

[35] *Signs of the Times*, Oct. 13, 1890, p. 16.

[36] This was the train trip referred to in the introduction to this chapter.

[37] *Signs of the Times*, Oct. 13, 1890, p. 16, and Olson, p. 67.

[38] Once more, I am indebted to the careful researches of Paul Penno, Jr., for much of the following material on the second ministers' institute (shared with the author in personal correspondence and the pages of *Calvary at Sinai*).

[39] O. A. Olsen, "The Opening of the Ministers' School," *Review and Herald*, Nov. 4, 1890; Ellen White manuscript 21, 1891, "Christ Our Righteousness," in *The Ellen G. White 1888 Materials*, vol. 2, pp. 890-899.

[40] The General Conference Committee Minutes of July 25, 1890, recorded the action of the appointment of Uriah Smith, A. T. Jones, and E. J. Waggoner as "teachers" for the fall ministers' school (adventistarchives.org).

[41] "Bible School for Ministers, Battle Creek, Michigan, Announcement for 1890-91," p. 2.

[42] D. T. Jones to R. C. Porter, Oct. 23, 1890, p. 21: Box 60, Letter Book 4, General Conference Archives; E. W. Farnsworth, "Ministerial Institute in District No. 3," *Review and Herald*, Dec. 22, 1891.

[43] "Bible School 1890-91," p. 6.

[44] George I. Butler to Dan Jones, Feb. 6, 1891. Paul Penno, Jr., shared the contents of

the letter with the author but did not cite its archival location. Most likely it is located at the General Conference Archives or in the letter files of the Ellen G. White Estate.

[45] Ellen G. White manuscript 55, 1890, "Peril in Trusting in the Wisdom of Men," *The Ellen G. White 1888 Materials*, vol. 2, pp. 840-842.

[46] Ellen G. White, "Be Zealous and Repent," *Review and Herald Extra*, Dec. 23, 1890. See Ellen G. White, *Manuscript Releases* (Silver Spring, Md.: Ellen G. White Estate, 1990), vol. 2, p. 55.

[47] Valentine, *The Shaping of Adventism*, p. 57.

[48] Ellen G. White to U. Smith, Jan. 6, 1891; in *The Ellen G. White 1888 Materials*, vol. 2, p 846.

[49] Ellen G. White manuscript 40, 1891, "Diary Entries," in *The Ellen G. White 1888 Materials,* vol. 2, p. 873.

[50] *The Ellen G. White 1888 Materials,* vol. 2, p. 863.

[51] *Ibid.*

[52] Ellen G. White manuscript 40, 1891, *The Ellen G. White 1888 Materials,* vol. 2, p. 875.

[53] For more on his presentation, see *General Conference Bulletin*, 1891, pp. 146, and A. L. White, *The Lonely Years*, pp. 483-485.

[54] Ellen White manuscript 40, 1891, *The Ellen G. White 1888 Materials*, vol. 2, p. 876.

[55] *Ibid.*, pp. 885, 887.

[56] For a fuller account of the Anna Rice fiasco, see Valentine, *The Shaping of Adventism*, pp. 63, 64 and Knight, *From 1888 to Apostasy*, pp. 104-116.

[57] Valentine, *The Shaping of Adventism*, p. 64.

[58] Ellen White letter 3, 1891, cited in A. L. White, *The Lonely Years*, p. 476.

[59] Pearl Waggoner Howard, "Biographical Sketch."

[60] *General Conference Bulletin*, Mar. 8, 1891. Jessie's coeditor was Mrs. C. H. Jones, the wife of the head of the Pacific Press Publishing Association. See also the article entitled "Sabbath School," *Seventh-day Adventist Encyclopedia*, vol. 11, pp. 508-510.

[61] Her editorial involvements in 1890 with *Our Little Friend* appear in her application for greater sustention support (the old term for the Adventist retirement fund) in 1931.

[62] *General Conference Bulletin,* Mar 6, 1891, pp. 3, 10, 11, 15, and Mar. 24, 1891, pp. 218, 220. Waggoner served on the Committee on Resolutions, was a delegate to the International Tract Society's meeting, and was elected to serve on the Tract Society's Committee on New Books. Other elected appointments included the General Conference Book Committee and to the Executive Committee of the International Sabbath School Association.

[63] *General Conference Bulletin*, Mar. 6, 1891; see also A. L. White, *The Lonely Years*, p. 477.

[64] Each lecture was an hour long, and all were published in the *General Conference Bulletin.*

[65] *Ibid.*, Mar. 6, 1891, pp. 4, 15; Mar. 8, 1891, p. 33.

[66] Letter 3, 1891, in A. L. White, *The Lonely Years*, p. 489.

[67] For a more sober assessment of this General Conference session, see Olson's chapter 12, "The Minnespolis Spirit at the 1891 Session," pp. 131-142.

[68] "Records of the Foreign Mission Board of the Seventh-day Adventists," pp. 70, 71.

[69] O. A. Olsen to Brother Ericson, Dec. 28, 1890.

[70] *General Conference Bulletin*, Mar. 26, 1891, p. 249.

[71] O. A. Olsen to S. N. Haskell, June 22, 1891, Christiana, Norway, and O. A. Olsen to W. C. White, July 12, 1891, Basel, Switzerland.

[72] Pearl Waggoner Howard, "Biographical Sketch."

[73] Waggoner's name would once again appear as editor on the masthead of the *Signs of*

the Times later on during the 1890s, but he never really edited the paper again. It was really more of a corresponding editor's role.

[74] Paul Waggoner Howard, "Biographical Sketch."

[75] The author has looked in vain for any recorded action by the General Conference Committee to assign Waggoner permanently to England and Europe. It could well be that the action was simply lost or that the official call came either through the General Conference Mission Board or from the executive committee of the International Tract Society (the publisher of the British *Present Truth*). See D. McMahon, *The Myth and the Man*, p. 21, and Penno, *Calvary at Sinai*, p. 195.

[76] A copy of the letter is in the personal possession of the author. My guess is that the original is located either at the White Estate offices in Silver Spring, Maryland, Berrien Springs, Michigan, or Loma Linda, California, or at the General Conference Archives in Silver Spring. I cannot even recall who gave it to me or where I located it in the process of my research.

[77] Pearl does recall spending the "winter in Chicago [or early part of it] where my father in conjunction with Eld. Geo. B. Starr conducted a Bible Institute." This memory seems to place this institute during the winter of 1890/1891, but it seems more likely that it took place during the early winter of 1892. Pearl sometimes, despite a fairly accurate recollection of things, got her times and places a bit mixed up.

[78] We find a close parallel between Ellet's litany of camp meetings and district ministerial institutes during those final American months and the recommendations for his work by the General Conference committee for the same period. See "General Conference Committee Minutes" for the meetings of July 27, July 30, and August 19 of 1891. The reminiscences of Pearl Waggoner Howard ("Biographical Sketch") partially supplement the itinerary.

[79] Pearl Waggoner Howard, "Biographical Sketch," and the Brownsberger letter of Apr. 1, 1892.

CHAPTER VIII

THEOLOGICAL EMPHASES AND DIRECTIONS: 1888-1892

INTRODUCTION

THE ATMOSPHERE WAS THICK with theology during the years following the legendary Minneapolis General Conference session of 1888. And at the center of the debates over the relationship between "present truth"[1] Adventism and the subject of "Christ and His righteousness" was Ellet Joseph Waggoner.

Put in the larger context of Seventh-day Adventist theological development(s), it was the period that Sabbatarian Adventism was seeking to settle the question of "what was Christian" about the Adventist message for the world. Such a thought might seem a bit strange to those not intimately familiar with nineteenth-century Adventist history, but the denomination had spent most of the latter half of the century in clarifying what was "Adventist" about Adventism. Until then most members had tacitly assumed that the "Christian" aspect of Adventism, or the "third angel's message," was that it was pure, restored biblical truth of the most relevant nature.[2]

The problem, however, that began to manifest itself in a more conscious way during the late 1870s was that while pure biblical truth, especially of the proof-text variety, was OK, it was not sufficient. If believers didn't know much about Jesus, the "truth" had lost its appealing "savor" (or even its Savior). Yes, they had patiently quarried the precious truths of the "present truth pillars" from the Bible like the cherished marble of the hills of Vermont. Furthermore, they had done much to give Seventh-day Adventism its distinctive self-understanding. It was a "truth movement" destined to prepare the world for the coming of Christ. But the whole process had veered strangely onto a troubling sidetrack, because it had not properly seated Jesus as the driving engineer of the gospel train known as Sabbatarian Adventism.

It had begun to be quite apparent to James and Ellen White that something was missing—and that "something" was none other than a focus on the love of God as revealed in the person and atoning work of Jesus, who is the very embodiment of the "truth of all truths." And thus it was that the deeply concerned Ellen White had begun a campaign to restore Jesus as the great centerpiece of "the present truth"—the Jesus who is "the way, the truth, and the life."

As she began her campaign to refocus on Jesus and His love, she encountered a disconcerting problem—-she found few other conductors and firemen on the "present truth" train who shared her deeply felt burden to be proclaimers of her Christ-centered message. The sad truth was that for most of the next decade she had to carry on the "Jesus campaign" by herself.

In view of the resistance of the self-satisfied Battle Creek leadership, Ellen White could have simply caved in. But she would manifest a determined persistence in her vision and convictions that the church had to chart a new direction that would keep the issue in focus. In the meantime, she stayed alert for the appearance of the best individuals that she could find to join her in the "Jesus as Savior" emphasis. And in due time her patience received its reward.

Around 1887 she found some interesting allies who were surprisingly near at hand. The first was her own son, W. C. White. But Willie would soon discover support for his mother's effort in the persons of his old childhood chum, Ellet Waggoner, and Ellet's newfound brother in the "gospel army"— A. T. Jones. It was basically in this young trio that Ellen White finally identified the nucleus that would become her "team Minneapolis." And their game plan was to bring a new element into the mission of the Seventh-day Adventist Church.

The key question that now confronts us is: What were the essential doctrinal factors that became the framework of their strategy and the new "Christ and His righteousness" emphasis that had so captivated their collective imagination?

As we attempt to answer this vital question, we will first seek to review the key components of E. J. Waggoner's unfolding theology. It was his teaching that initially provided the core of what Ellen White called the beginnings of the proclamation of the loud-cry[3] message. She deemed it to be the last message that the Seventh-day Adventist Church would proclaim to a world fast hurtling toward its date with eternal destiny.

We will pursue our answers in essentially the same way that we did in chapter 3 at the end of the first section. But we will do so now with an increased focus on the issues that mainly orbited around how Christ reconciles lost sinners to Himself. The central concern of those participating in the Minneapolis emphasis was salvation, not ethics. Ethics were certainly of interest, but the key concern of their minds and energies was Jesus and His great salvation plan. To put it simply, Ellen White and the others sought to help the church renew its love for Jesus and to understand more clearly how He saves lost sinners.

What follows are the major themes that developed during the critical period from late 1888 up to mid-1892. After we lay out the key points and their undergirding components, we will then begin to seek an answer to the question as to what the "Minneapolis message" truly was and—just as important—some preliminary suggestions as to what it was not. In order to do this, we will need to listen patiently not only to the writings of E. J. Waggoner but also to the insights and affirmations of the main person who had been most responsible for putting him and A. T. Jones on the Adventist map—Ellen G. White.

If Ellen White had not supported him, there would have most likely been no prominence and influence for Waggoner and his message. The Battle Creek leadership would have never even given him a hearing, much less a podium, at their major church gatherings and in their influential publishing venues. We simply cannot understand the "Minneapolis message" apart from the authoritative insights and correctives of Adventism's main thought leader, Ellen G. White. The "lift up Jesus" crusade had been her brainchild.

Once more, let's refocus the issue at hand by asking ourselves a simple question: who has the most authority to identify a message—the one who credits the "messengers," or those who have received the endorsement? Our question has two aspects. First, what did Waggoner teach? But equally important, we also need to determine what it was that he presented that possessed lasting value. We can determine that final aspect only through close testing on the anvil of truth.

And for Seventh-day Adventists and the issues of 1888, that has to do *initially* with the insights of Ellen White and then *ultimately* the Bible (with both rightly interpreted). So what theological concepts have withstood the test of Ellen White and biblical authentication? We shall begin with some very basic Christian doctrines and then move on to the central issues of salvation by grace through faith alone.

THE GODHEAD (TRINITY) AND THE NATURE OF CHRIST

As mentioned earlier in chapter 3, Waggoner had not fully fleshed out his views on either issue in the pre-1888 period.

While he did give hints of moving toward the essential outlines of biblical Trinitarianism, we can best describe his thought as a variant of semi-Arianism. His semi-Ariansim was neither new nor strange, since it had become a widely held theological staple of many pioneer Seventh-day Adventists, including such notables as his own father and Uriah Smith.

Furthermore, he had not fully expressed his views on the human nature of Christ. While Waggoner was abundantly clear that Jesus had never committed a sinful thought or an act of sin, he somehow understood Him to be deeply identified with the sinful infection of our collective human nature.

In the immediate aftermath of the 1888 session he did begin to emerge with fuller concepts on both issues.

The Godhead

In six articles published in March and April of 1889,[4] and later reflected in Waggoner's book entitled *Christ and His Righteousness* (1890), Waggoner explicitly displayed his semi-Ariansim. He clearly stated that Christ partakes of the divine nature and was preexistent. In addition, he plainly made the point that Christ was not created as a divine being, but he did interpret the biblical phrase "only-begotten" to mean that there had been a time when the "Son was not" and then the Father brought him forth. "In arguing the perfect equality of the Father and the Son, and the fact that Christ is in very nature God, we do not design to be understood as teaching that the Father was not before the Son. . . . While both are of the same nature, the Father is first in point of time. He is also greater in that He had no beginning, while Christ's personality had a beginning."[5]

Two years later he restated the priority of the Father over the Son in the aspect of time with somewhat less force in his 1890 book, *Christ and His Righteousness*, but with essentially the same meaning. "We know that Christ 'proceeded forth and came from God' (John 8:42), but it was so far back in the ages of eternity as to be far beyond the grasp of the mind of man."[6]

While Waggoner did believe that Christ was a divine and preexistent being, he did not accept the full eternity of Christ as a divine person. The above-cited statements obviously reveal his sympathy with a species of the semi-Arian interpretation of the nature of Christ. While he would later deal with this issue only somewhat sparingly, he would make a couple statements that would bring him quite close to the essence of the Trinitarian view of the eternal deity of Christ.[7] But one searches in vain for any place in his writings where he gave any indication of moving into a full-blown Trinitarian understanding of the full and eternal coexistence of the person of Christ with the person of the Father.

Furthermore, we must point out that during these years, when the key factors of the 1888 message were being clarified, he was a semi-Arian. And finally, the evidence indicates that he never *explicitly* repudiated his semi-Arian convictions expressed so clearly in 1889.

His limited view of the eternity of the person of Christ has disturbed many. But taken in its historical context, it should not greatly trouble contemporary Trinitarian Seventh-day Adventists, including Waggoner's most devoted partisans. As already noted, Arianism and semi-Arianism had been widespread among Seventh-day Adventists during the nineteenth and early twentieth centuries, including in its ranks such figures as James White, Joseph Waggoner, and Uriah Smith (to name just three of many). E. J. Waggoner was once more, on this issue and a number of others, the "son" of the Adventist "pioneers." And it only makes sense to see that if God had used these other leading individuals (in spite of their theological viewpoints), He could also employ Ellet Waggoner.

What seems to make such an admission quite controversial is that many of Waggoner's avid twentieth- and twenty-first-century admirers have been extremely reluctant to recognize that he had any significant theological flaws. To admit such a thing, however, is nothing new or unusual. It is simply to acknowledge that we need to assess Waggoner very carefully. We should not swallow everything that he taught as inerrant truth simply because Ellen White gave him unparalleled affirmation and support. Even Waggoner's strongest supporters have admitted this point when it comes to any number of his later views. Therefore, even though Ellen White's endorsement for both Waggoner and A. T. Jones was unequaled in comparison to any other persons whom she gave support to in her long ministry, it does not spare them from careful screening. God greatly blessed them, but they were still human, and to admit theological flaws is only to acknowledge to being mortal and subject to error.

Also we must remind ourselves that Ellen White had been quite explicit, even in one of her strongest statements of affirmation, that Waggoner and Jones were not infallible. Referring directly to them, she asked the pointed rhetorical question: "Do I place them as infallible? Do I say that they will not make a statement or have an idea that cannot be questioned or that cannot be error? Do I say so? No, I do not say any such thing. Nor do I say that of any man in the world. But I do say God has sent light, and do be careful how you treat it."[8] Even at Minneapolis she had declared that "some interpretations of Scripture given by Dr. Waggoner I do not regard as correct."[9] Ellen White never demanded inerrant, infallible doctrinal clarity before a person could be affirmed as used of God.

While we today are fully justified to look upon Waggoner's somewhat restricted view of the person of Christ with considerable theological reserve, it should not take away from the fact that God worked through him and that He also uses many of us despite our theological defects. Furthermore, we must affirm that while Waggoner did not at this time, or ever afterward, step into the light of full biblical Trinitarianism, he did come up to the very borders of it with his strong emphasis that the Father and the Son share the same substance of the divine nature. He definitely made a positive, though not a definitive, contribution to further clarification of the full and eternal deity of Christ. And for this, all Trinitarian Seventh-day Adventists should be grateful.

Instead of concentrating on some unreal demand that Waggoner be absolutely inerrant on all points, it is best to close out this assessment of his views on the Godhead with the informed observations of Jerry Moon: "Waggoner was not yet fully Trinitarian, but he saw clearly that a more exalted conception of Christ's work of redemption demanded a higher view of His being as deity." Then Moon cites the judicious words of Waggoner: "The fact that Christ is a part of the Godhead, possessing all the attributes of Divinity, being the equal of the Father in all respects, as Creator and Lawgiver, is the only force there is in the atonement. . . . Christ died 'that he might bring us to God' (1 Peter 3:18); but if He lacked one iota of being equal to God, He could not bring us to Him."[10] We do owe solemn debts to Waggoner for the progress that he had made on this subject. But he still had some distance to go before we could justly call him fully Trinitarian.

The Humanity of Christ

As to the humanity of Christ, Waggoner also came out early in 1889 with a significantly more explicit view on the sinfulness of Christ's humanity during the Incarnation. In a series of *Signs* articles that began in January,[11] he interpreted Romans 8:3 as teaching that Christ was not just accounted a sinner, but that He actually took upon Himself sinful nature. In a specific reference to the expression "likeness of sinful flesh," he said that "it must have been sinful man that He was made like, for it is only sin that causes death." Sin, however, was not just laid on Him, but "the flesh which He assumed had all the weaknesses and sinful tendencies to which fallen human nature is subject."[12] *Most certainly Waggoner had shed any ambiguities of the pre-1888 era as he now boldly said that Christ bore not only "weaknesses" but also "sinful tendencies."*

He went on to further elaborate the "sinful tendencies" concept by saying that though Christ was "sinless" and "counted as a sinner," He "actually" took "upon Himself sinful nature." Then he underscored the previous points by arguing that while children are not born condemned by the law, "they are born with sinful tendencies, owing to the sins of their ancestors. And when Christ came into the world, He came subject to all the conditions to which other children are subject."[13] *In 1890 he repeated virtually the same position in Christ and His Righteousness.*[14] Thus the clear stand he took in 1889 he once more confirmed in 1890.

As interesting and controversial as his position is, Waggoner was not through with his exposition. He would proceed to draw some most curious theological conclusions. In the same *Signs* article of January 21, 1889, he readily acknowledged that some would challenge him that there is a real danger in bringing the humanity of Christ to the very same level as all other sinful human beings. But such a reaction did not daunt him, as he then gave the astounding response that since "'God was in Christ,' . . . he could not sin. His humanity only veiled his divine nature, which was more than able to successfully resist the sinful passions of the flesh. There was in his whole life a struggle. The flesh, moved upon by the enemy of all unrighteousness, would tend to sin, yet His divine nature never for a moment harbored an evil desire, nor did His divine power for a moment waver."[15] While Waggoner has Christ and the sinner virtually sharing the same level of depraved sinful nature, the actual functioning of His divine nature during the Incarnation made it so that Christ "could not sin."

Almost immediately Waggoner anticipated the objection that "some will say, 'I don't see any comfort in this for me; it wasn't possible that the Son of God should sin, but I haven't any such power.'" Waggoner came back with a ready reply.

He began by citing Ephesians 3:14-19 and suggesting that any advantage that Christ possessed was to the believer's advantage since trusting humans can benefit from having Him abide in them: "Who could ask for more? Christ, in whom dwelleth all the fullness of the Godhead bodily, may dwell in our hearts, so that we may be filled with all the fullness of God." Thus sinful humans should not be discouraged, since through faith in the indwelling Christ they may conquer all their temptations: "All the power which Christ had dwelling in Him by nature, we may have dwelling in us by grace, for He freely bestows it upon us."[16]

His teaching is unique. While the issue of Christ not being able to sin because of His inherent deity will not receive much further development, the fact that he speaks of the indwelling Christ in believers, giving them the same victory over sin, is one of the factors that will receive increasing accent for the rest of his ministry. It was a most critical and important theme for Waggoner, as it not only provides a key to understanding his perfectionistic[17] optimism, but also gives a possible clue to his later aberrant tendencies. Waggoner's highly subjective emphasis on the indwelling Christ cries out for careful tracing over the balance of his career.[18]

A few more comments on Waggoner's position that Christ in His humanity took "tendencies to sin" are in order. We could immediately enter in a discussion of the hotly contested debate over the sinful human nature of Christ. But that is the subject for another book.

Two things, however, we must preliminarily point out: (1) Ellen White never employed the expression "sinful tendencies" to describe the human nature of Christ and His struggles with temptation; (2) the issue of the humanity of Christ never gets mentioned as being among the controverted issues contested by either side in the Minneapolis debates, before, during, or afterward. We will further explore this issue both in the present chapter and in chapter 13, when we more specifically address what the "Minneapolis message" was.

SIN AND THE ATONEMENT

Sin

We encounter no appreciable development in Waggoner's understanding of sin during this period, except his clear teaching that both sinners and their Savior were born with "sinful tendencies." While it is quite obvious that all the children of Adam did inherit such "sinful tendencies" and that this is an important component in any fully fledged understanding of sin, it is dubious to apply such an understanding to Christ. Could our Savior really be infected with "sinful tendencies" and still be our effectual advocate before the Father?

Furthermore, we need to emphasize that Waggoner's central concept of sin had to do with the guilt engendered by the rejection of God's offer of salvation. Here was a highly perceptive principle that all Bible-believing Christians can heartily approve of.

Whether or not Waggoner was superficial in his view of sin can be debated. But what is beyond dispute is that the sinner could never initiate a saving relationship with God. The initiative was solely God's. Sinners were so steeped in sin that they could not approach Him or produce real righteousness through their sin-infected human resources. They were born sinful and were already steeped in sin. Such sinfulness included sinful attitudes, tendencies, and actual acts. The only way out of this sinful condition was through the grace of God. Thus Waggoner, during this period, still saw the Decalogue very much as an instrument of the conviction of sin and that such conviction would lead the sinner to Christ.

Atonement

Now with reference to the issue of the significance of Christ's death as a means of atonement, we also fail to find any appreciable development. We will need to examine the issue in the future, as there will begin to unfold, especially in 1893, interesting concepts that will very much lean to a more subjective view of the atonement, in contrast to the penal/substitution/satisfaction ideas that had been in place in his thought through the early 1890s.

JUSTIFICATION AND SANCTIFICATION BY FAITH

As evidenced by the extensive space devoted to the issues in chapter 3,[19] Waggoner's theology of salvation clearly has two key concepts. As pointed out earlier, what often makes him hard to grasp is the way that he used the language of justification (imputation or being accounted as righteous) to effectively encompass a lot of what we normally ascribe to the work of sanctification (impartation, or to actually be made righteous in character). And thus it is often tough to tease out Waggoner's meaning when he employs the traditional terms to explain the biblical dynamics of salvation.

But if we are to clearly grasp his understanding of justification, it involves more than forgiveness and a new legal standing. It also includes the new birth and a whole new attitude to God's express commands.

As George Knight has succinctly put it, in Waggoner's thought "being accounted righteous (being justified) and having one's nature changed happen simultaneously." Knight then elaborates the point: "Being accounted righteous . . . is not a legal fiction. . . . Other writers, in talking of that beginning [of the Christian experience], verbally differentiate between the two aspects of the simultaneous experience by labeling them justification and new birth."[20] Such a characterization of Waggoner's views on justification essentially applies to his 1888-1892 understanding of justification as well as to his pre-1888 teachings.

As in the previous era, so in the 1888-1892 period, it seems that for Waggoner the refutation of the "legal fiction" idea rests on the fact that the true believer receives a "*disposition*" to do right and it is mainly what he meant when he suggested that justification "makes the believer righteous."

Another way that Waggoner sought to explain the "disposition" of the justified believer to do God's will is that there will always be plenty of room for growth from "faith to faith." In other words, the Lord will be empowering new growth and making up for the inevitable slips and slides that any new and growing Christian experiences.[21] Thus while Waggoner seemed to hopelessly conflate justifying and sanctifying grace, he was mainly seeking to qualify the faith that saves as a genuinely transforming exercise of trust in God.

Waggoner gave a rather succinct summary of the overall scope of justifying grace in the following statement: "The first of the blessings of the gospel is the forgiveness of sin. . . . The next is the writing of the law in the hearts of the people. Then comes the final blotting out of sins. . . . And then comes the close of probation, and the eternal inheritance, when 'they shall teach no more every man his neighbor, and every man his brother, saying, Know the Lord. . . .' Jer. 31: 34."[22]

Thus the genuinely justifying faith of a true believer receives forgiveness from the sins of the past, the placing of the law of God in the heart, and the final blotting out of sins in the pre-Advent investigative judgment (the Adventist version of "once saved, always saved"). Finally comes glorification, when we the faithful will forever have the law sealed sinlessly in our hearts and can at last truly say that we are sinless.

On the issue of the final blotting out of sins at the close of the pre-Advent judgment and the close of probation, we have suggested that Waggoner held to a strongly sinless perfection understanding of the sealed saints at this time. And on the question of what it means to live without a Mediator or Intercessor during this time before the second coming of Christ, he clearly suggested that the reason they will live without a Mediator is that they will be sinless. But that does not mean that they are without a "Saviour every moment."[23]

The strong impression we receive from Waggoner is that Jesus will be a Savior not in the sense of making up for any lingering "unavoidable deficiencies," but in the sense that He saves the sealed saints from death and from giving in to the terrible temptations that they will experience during the intense eschatological finale. This definitely supports (and is most likely the historical source for) the final generation vindication scheme of many of Waggoner's contemporary admirers. Thus he did fill out the concept of what it means to experience final justification and the most serious manifestation of sinless perfection victory imaginable. While now more explicit, such concepts seemed implicit in his pre-1888 views on the final justification and perfection of the sealed saints.

Thus there is, on balance, no really significantly new directions in his understanding and presentations on justification by faith. Once more, we will carefully monitor this development, as some important interpreters feel that around 1893 Waggoner took the subjective aspects of what he called "justification" too far.

Furthermore, what we have said about justifying grace is also basically true of his developing understanding of sanctifying grace. We continue to find in his writings the strong, optimistic teaching that transforming grace can accomplish great things in the life of the believer—all to the glory of God.

UNIVERSAL LEGAL JUSTIFICATION

As promised in chapter 3, we will review any developments on this issue for the balance of Waggoner's career in Adventism. Yet in this era, immediately following the 1888 General Conference session, we find no real appreciable development of his concepts. But we will dedicate a few paragraphs to review the issue and further prepare the way for changes that will come after 1892.

Many of Waggoner's twentieth- and twenty-first-century admirers claim to have detected a concept in Waggoner's teaching on justification that they have labeled "universal legal justification." By this they mean that not only has God offered justification by faith to the whole human race, but that in some sense the whole human race is truly, and legally, saved from the guilt of sin. Now if they are here simply referring to the issue of what most Arminian Christians (those who believe in graced free will—that is, that God's grace, freely bestowed on all, enables them to make a decision to respond to God's offer of salvation with either a yea or a nay response) have called prevenient grace and its blessing of probationary time (in other words, in the light of the promise of the atoning death of Christ, sinful humans are not immediately destroyed by God's just justice), then we are all in agreement. In other words, the mercy of God provides a temporary shield against the execution of His justice and grants sinners time to consider the benefits of God's great atoning work that has made full provision for salvation from the guilt of sin. Waggoner himself made this point quite clear:

"If it had not been that Christ was given for man's redemption, death would have ended all for Adam, and for the human race. But the promise of a Redeemer carried with it another probation, and so the execution of the sentence was suspended until it should be seen what use men would make of that probation. God has appointed a day in which He will judge the world . . . and until that time the sentence will be held in abeyance. . . . But those who reject the Son shall not see life, but the wrath of God will abide on them."[24] All Arminian, or freewill, Christians are clear on this. But things get a bit more complicated when one claims that God has actually justified the whole human race, not just provided them with probationary time.

What we have suggested in chapter 3 is that Waggoner saw no real evidence that God actually, legally declares all human beings justified for Christ's sake. And his writings suggest that this is true for him during not only the pre-1888 era but also the years 1888-1892. Yet a few more comments are in order to help clarify this issue.

Those who advocate this reading of both Waggoner and Ellen G. White place a lot of emphasis upon Paul's representative man concepts expressed in Romans 5: in Adam, all are declared sinful. And the reason is that all are actually sinful in nature and action. But this is reversed in Christ, and much more so, as grace is much greater than sin. Thus this interpretation claims that just as all are legally in sin and are lost in Adam, so all are legally justified in Christ, even without any exercise of faith in God's offer of salvation. The key verses are Romans 5:16-19: "For the judgment was by one to condemnation, but the free gift is of many offences unto justification. For if by one man's offence death reigned by one; much more they which receive abundance of grace and of the gift of righteousness shall reign in life by one, Jesus Christ. Therefore as by the offence of one judgment came upon all men to condemnation; even so by the righteousness of one the free gift came upon all men unto justification of life. For as by one man's disobedience many were made sinners, so by the obedience of one shall many be made righteous."

We need not go into a detailed interpretation of these verses to make the point. But the key question is this: when Paul says that "the free gift is of many offences unto justification" (verse 16) and "by the righteousness of one the free gift came upon all men unto justification of life" (verse 18), does this mean that all humans are actually justified and legally declared to be saved? Or does it just indicate that God has now offered full provision for salvation to all but that it will not be legally effective to save from the guilt of sin until there is some sort of genuine faith response or embrace of God's offer of justification by faith in the merits of Christ's atoning work?

Now, I do believe that the latter is the preferred interpretative option in the context of Paul's wider discussion of justification by faith, not only in Romans, but in his whole body of teachings contained in all of his epistles. The context of Romans 5 itself is justification by faith (verse 1—"therefore being justified by faith"), and the very next chapter speaks of the appropriate response of faith—being baptized as a sign of our faith acceptance of Christ's justifying merits. But let's lay aside those considerations for the moment.

The key question is this: Do these verses really teach that all humanity is legally justified and saved, or are the verses speaking to the profound provisions that have been made in or by Christ for the salvation of all, but that the "all" will only ultimately include those who have responded by faith and embraced God's offer of justification by faith?

Now, let's assume for the moment that the first interpretation is true: that justification has, in some sense, come legally upon the whole human race, beyond the blessings of being granted probationary time (a blessing that all Arminians agree is true). Can this actually be upheld? Here an illustration from social life will prove helpful.

All of us have had the experience of being showered with gifts (especially at Christmas and birthdays) that have been given by well-meaning but misguided friends and loved ones. Normally we accept these gifts without telling our loving donors how we really feel. It is not being deceptive—it is just being diplomatic. So while we really do have the gift "upon" us, or in our proverbial laps, we really have not embraced the gift. And often what we do is quietly give the gift away to some other person at some special occasion and hope the original giver never learns what we have done. So yes, we have the well-meant gift in our very possession, but in actual fact we have no real heart embrace of the gift, even though we usually appreciate the spirit in which the favor was bestowed.

So the question is this: Does God actually, legally bestow justification on all? Does He actually place it, as it were, in our laps? For Waggoner, it appears that during the years from before 1888 and up through 1892, the answer was no! Certainly legal justification is on offer, but unless there is a real heart embrace of the offer by genuine, living faith, we in essence spurn it. And all that has been said in chapter 3, for the pre-1888 thought of Waggoner applies to this era from 1888 to 1892.

And thus it probably comes down to a certain level of semantics. Even if one accepts the metaphor that the gift has actually been placed in your mailbox or hands (or lap), this still does not imply an embrace of the gift. And once more, here is the key issue, even for the universal legal justification interpreters of Waggoner: even if it is effectively stuck in your lap, your hands, your whatever, it is not savingly effectual unless there is the subsequent experience of what they call "experiential justification," or a real heart embrace of the universally bestowed gift of legal justification. And this is the reason that I have earlier suggested that this whole discussion has become a needless "strife about words." And what is so ironic about the whole issue is that this is one of the key issues that Waggoner emphasized about the true Bible teaching on the covenants: if there is no true heart embrace of God's free, saving grace, it will do absolutely no good.

At this stage of Waggoner's expression in his writings (up to 1892), I have simply not been able to find any evidence that he claimed that God actually places the gift of legal justification in our laps and that we are legally justified whether we want to be or not. But all of this will have some significant shift after 1892. During these subsequent years there will develop an expanding body of evidence that he did believe that God actually does place the gift in our laps or hands. Thus we encourage the reader to ponder carefully developments of this issue as we trace them in chapter 11. Yet even there Waggoner will continue to make it very clear that a true experience of legal justification is always granted only upon the condition of an embracing, heart reception of justification by faith in the merits of Christ's atoning work.

THE COVENANTS

It is hard to detect any appreciable shifts in Waggoner's doctrine of the covenants. About the only real one was that during this period Ellen White gave explicit support for the major outlines of Waggoner's position, particularly at the 1889/1990 ministerial institute in Battle Creek (review the developments in chapter 7). Thus, with the exception of some issues related to making oaths or promises to God, the major outlines of Waggoner's covenant theology were fully in place and strongly endorsed by Ellen White during this period.

One issue, however, that we need to follow with some care is the aspect of the new covenant that features the law being written on the heart of the forgiven believer. Because of Waggoner's growing emphasis on the literal indwelling of Christ in the heart via the work of the Holy Spirit, we need to examine the issue very carefully. This is particularly relevant since he will portray the indwelling of the divine Christ as producing a perfect righteousness in humans that will be reckoned as theirs. We will need to assess this development with some care, especially what he has to say after 1892.

WHAT WAS THE "MINNEAPOLIS MESSAGE"?

Now that we have covered the developments in Waggoner's basic understanding of the key salvation-related issues during this period, we need to wrestle with the question of what the "Minneapolis message" was (and was not). We have broached this subject earlier, but we now must directly come to grips with it in at least a preliminary way.

But before we introduce some of the more controversial claims as to the major components of the message of Minneapolis and its controverted aftermath, we should identify the components that all interpreters should give hearty assent to. And thus we must return to Ellen White's wonderful endorsement that we considered briefly at the end of chapter 6 (and subsequently published in *Testimonies to Ministers*, pp. 91-93).[25]

In her rather comprehensive and positive endorsement, she lays out the following prominent points. In fact, it reads like a résumé of the theological emphases of "team Minnieapolis" that we have been reviewing in previous chapters. Here they are as Ellen White distilled them: (1) The need to uplift Christ as Savior (not just lawgiver); (2) a strong focus on justification by faith in Jesus; (3) the intimate connection between the righteousness of Christ and obedience to God's commandments; (4) the need for Adventists to focus on Jesus; (5) that Christ's righteousness has an intimate relationship to the third angel's message of Revelation 14:9-12; (6) that Jesus has special "covenant blessings" for His children; (7) that Seventh-day Adventists had been emphasizing the law but neglecting Jesus and the importance of faith in His sacrifice; and (8) that God had raised up Jones and Waggoner to redirect the gaze of Adventists to Jesus and to faith in His sacrifice and merits.

Furthermore, she made another closely related, positive assessment of the message of Minneapolis nearly five months later in letter 86 (September 25, 1895), written to her son Edson White. In an unmistakable reference to the "words spoken by the messengers of God" (including E. J. Waggoner) since the Minneapolis meeting "at the campmeetings and ministerial institutes," Ellen White specifically spoke about "the light that has been shining upon justification by faith and the imputed righteousness of Christ. Those who receive and act on the light given, will, in their teachings, give evidence that the message of Christ crucified, a risen Saviour ascended into the heavens to be our advocate, is the wisdom and power of God in the conversion of souls, bringing them back to their loyalty to Christ. These are our themes: Christ crucified for our sins, Christ risen from the dead, Christ our intercessor before God; and closely connected with these is the office work of the Holy Spirit, the representative of Christ, sent forth with divine power and gifts for men."[26]

One cannot imagine a more hopeful list of subjects to charm the minds and hearts of God's people. Please note the emphasis on the atoning work of Christ, both on the cross and in the heavenly sanctuary, and the fact that "justification by faith and the imputed righteousness of Christ" are the leading points of this wonderful Christ-centered emphasis. It is a powerful confirmation of the main outlines of the ministry and message of E. J. Waggoner and those associated with him in the post-Minneapolis revival.

In addition, Ellen White was enthusiastic that the concept of justification by faith had been presented in a way that blended both law and gospel without compromising their essential and distinctive roles. She encapsulated the apex of this emphasis in her statement that the message "presented justification through faith in the Surety; it invited the people to receive the righteousness of Christ, which is made manifest in obedience to all the commandments of God." And how did one do it? By beholding the person of Christ! "Many had lost sight of Jesus. They needed to have their eyes directed to His divine person, His merits, and His changeless love for the human family."[27]

To put it as simply as possible, these are the themes that form the positive heart, or core, of the "message of Minneapolis." And if anyone is to further elaborate and interpret them, then Ellen White's meaning, in the broader context of her expositions (confirmed by Scripture, rightly interpreted), should have the final word in determining what were the central burdens of the "message of Minneapolis."

WHAT IS THE CONTROVERSY ALL ABOUT?

So now the reader might justifiably enquire, "What is it that seems to be at the heart of the lingering controversies over the meaning of the Minneapolis message?" The answer swirls around the question of what Ellen White meant when she said that the reception of "the righteousness of Christ" will be "made manifest in obedience to all the commandments of God."[28]

The attempt to provide a credible response has produced two distinct schools of interpretation. The first is what we could call the "perfectionistic"[29] approach and the second is the "effective forensic justification" view of interpretation.[30] Both schools of thought in the subsequent history of the debate have sought support from Ellen White's understanding of the proper relationship between justification and sanctification. We need to spell out this issue in further detail if we are to grasp appropriately the respective positions of the two schools of thought.

THE "PERFECTIONISTIC SCHOOL"

First of all, the "perfectionistic school" has sought to invoke various aspects of Waggoner's and Jones's subsequent developments as the key components of the message. Such interpreters claim that the later emphases are an essential and integral part of what Ellen White endorsed as the "Minneapolis message." The later developments include the following themes: (1) An emphasis on some species of "perfection" that sounds very much like sinless perfection at the close of probation and during the time of trouble. Its advocates undergird the perfection orientation with (2) a strong stress on the "post-Fall" view of the humanity of Christ, (3) a literal writing of the law on the hearts of new covenant believers, and (4) the need for a "final generation" of remnant saints to fully vindicate God against the charges of the devil that obedience to the law of God is impossible. Then (5) all of these aspects come together in the teaching that the vindication of God will take place in the closing up of the Most Holy Place ministrations of Christ in heaven just before the close of probation. And the final result of this ministry will be (6) the perfecting work of the latter-rain power of the Holy Spirit. After the mighty latter-rain power does its work, the "final generation" of sealed and perfected saints will demonstrate perfect obedience to God's law during the great time of trouble that will transpire between the close of probation and the second coming of Christ.

THE EFFECTIVE FORENSIC JUSTIFICATION SCHOOL

By contrast, the "effective forensic justification school" of interpretation has wanted to focus on justification by faith. But at the same time they have gone to some pains to emphasize that the faith that justifies is also a faith that works. Yet the results of such a working faith still always need the forensic merits of the constantly interceding Christ, who continues to make up for the "unavoidable deficiencies" of all true believers, no matter how far they have traveled on the road to perfection this side of glorification. The adherents of this position therefore do not deny the inevitable fruit that arises from the experience of sanctifying grace. They are "pre-Fall" in their views on the humanity of Christ. Furthermore, they deny that there is any such thing as unqualified sinless perfection in this mortal life and that God does not need a final generation to vindicate Himself. In addition, they readily admit that God will not save the rebellious, presumptuous sinner who cries "grace, grace" while indulging in known sin. Such attitudes evidence a lack of the genuine experience of both justification and sanctification.

A PRELIMINARY ASSESSMENT OF BOTH SCHOOLS

Now, when it comes to the position of the sinless perfection school of interpretation, one can certainly go to the teachings of Jones and

E. J. WAGGONER'S WORLD

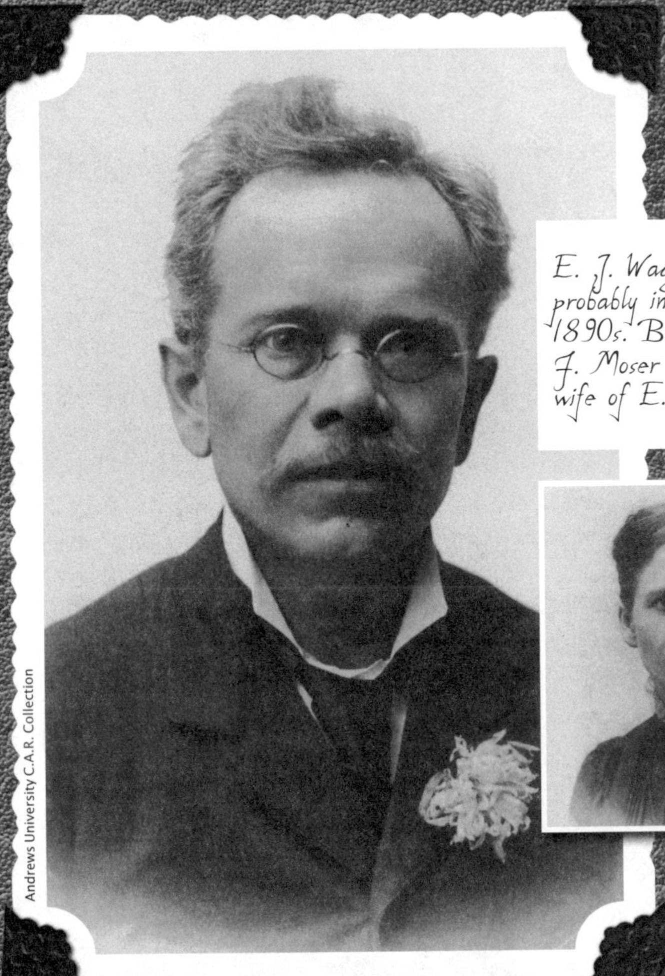

Andrews University C.A.R. Collection

E. J. Waggoner, probably in the early 1890s. Below: Jessie F. Moser Waggoner, wife of E. J. Waggoner.

Andrews University C.A.R. Collection

EGW Estate Collection

J. H. Waggoner, E. J. Waggoner's father.

The old Waggoner family home in Burlington, Michigan, originally built by Joseph and Mary(etta) Waggoner, was the childhood home of E. J. Waggoner.

W. C. White and E. J. Waggoner were friends at Battle Creek College.

The Waggoner family traveled by train from Oakland, California, to Battle Creek, Michigan, to attend a major ministerial institute (October 1890) and the General Conference session (March 1891). Pictured are E. J. Waggoner (second from left), Mrs. E. J. (Jessie) Waggoner (front right), and daughters Pearl and Bessie (front center) (c. 1889-1890). Others in photo include Elder and Mrs. J. N. Loughborough, Daniel Scoules, Elder Morrison, Maria Loughborough, and C. P. Kellogg.

EGW Estate Collection

Left: E. J. Waggoner. School days at Battle Creek College (c. 1875).
Middle: E. J. Waggoner, soon after graduation from medical school (c. 1878).
Right: E. J. Waggoner (taken from a group photo, location unknown).

Staff of the International Tract Society (ITS), predecessor of Stanborough Press, Ltd. (c. 1900). The group poses in front of the ITS offices. Front row, left to right: Mr. Pickwick, Miss Nellie Marsh, W. T. Bartlett (assistant editor and later chief editor), and Miss Wright (17-year-old sister of Dr. Gertrude Brown of Crieff). Middle row: Miss Hetty Hurd (who would later marry S. N. Haskell), W. W. Prescott, E. J. Waggoner, D. A. Robinson, Mr. Mason, and Alta Waggoner Armstrong (E. J.'s youngest sister and wife of Harry Armstrong). Back row: Mr. Ritchie (in charge of the Book and Bible House), Walter Armstrong, Mr. Bacon, W. A. Spicer (later to be General Conference president), Mr. Howarth, Harry Armstrong, and Edith Adams. This is one of only two pictures known that record the likeness of Edith Adams, and the only known photo in which E. J. Waggoner and Edith, who would become his second wife, appear together.

Ellet J. Waggoner (from ITS group photo, above).

A photo of E. J. Waggoner (center) and others in London around the turn of the century.

Review and Herald Collection

Image from Mark Peters family heirlooms

Above: The Waggoner family coat of arms (notice the spelling, "Wagner"). Left: E. J. and Jessie Waggoner, Oakland, California (c. 1883-1885).

EGW Estate Collection

A family portrait of the E. J. Waggoner family, probably taken during the mid-1890s in London. Left to right: Bessie Waggoner, E. J. Waggoner, Jessie Moser Waggoner, and Pearl Waggoner.

Jonathan Whidden

The Charles W. Lindsay farmhouse, with its original staircase, has been completely restored. It's located near the village of Burt, New York. The basic layout of the house is the same as it was in the years that Waggoner began visiting the Lindsay family.

Phillip Whidden

The Waggoners lived in three different residences during their years in London (from 1892 to 1903). This home, located at 53 Mercers Road, Islington, north London, was the last one they lived in, moving in most likely around 1897.

A conference held in Bath, England, during the summer of 1898. E. J. Waggoner is fourth from the right. The elderly man to his right (with the white beard) is J. N. Loughborough. W. W. Prescott stands to Loughborough's right.

LLU Archives and Special Collections

An elderly E. J. Waggoner and his collie dog, Bruce (c. 1915 or 1916).

E. J. Waggoner in his home study at Battle Creek.

Waggoner, in his later years, working in the medical laboratory at the Battle Creek Sanitarium (taken sometime between 1910 and his death in 1916).

Waggoner and find themes that tend in the sinless perfection direction before 1888 and that become quite definite after Minneapolis and 1888. But once more, the key question that confronts all interpreters is this: What did Ellen White understand the message of Minneapolis to be?

And here is the heart of the issue that faces any interpreter of the disputed issues swirling around the fabled 1888 General Conference session and its challenging aftermath: Whom do you trust to define these things—Ellen White and her expositions of the issues of salvation, the nature of Christ, etc.; or Jones and Waggoner and their teachings?

While such pressing issues do deserve forthright and balanced treatment, it would be, at this juncture, premature to enter into a definitive discussion of the evolution of Waggoner's larger body of theological teaching. We will return to these questions in the final chapter of this biography. In it we will seek to assess further developments in Waggoner's thought. But why this delay?

The reason is simply this: what is still to unfold in the years from late 1892 to 1916 will decisively impact how anyone can best answer the question of what *were* and *were not* the truly essential theological contents of the message of Minneapolis and 1888. We must examine the developments after 1892 before we can properly assess the overall trajectory of Waggoner's theology and legacy. And it is only when we have the full trajectory in view that we can accurately answer the question of what the Minneapolis message definitively was and was not.

WHAT WAS THE MAJOR DEVELOPMENT OF 1888-1892?

As we have already noted earlier in this chapter, most of the really positive theological developments in Waggoner's theological thought were already in place by Minneapolis, the year 1888, and the three and a half years following that momentous event. The period saw some wonderful breakthroughs in the Christ-centered presentations of the righteousness of Christ and related subjects. The clarifications on the law in Galatians and the covenants were especially gratifying. Both Jones and Waggoner had important opportunities to present their much-needed messages, and continued to receive amazingly consistent support from Ellen White, despite their failures in judgment, both practical and theological. We have seen the major outlines of the positive developments.

But there were also some serious warning signs that were lurking on a progressively hazy horizon.

Undoubtedly the most significant and portentous theological trend of the early post-Minneapolis period (1888 to mid-1892) was Waggoner's early 1889 emphasis on the indwelling Christ. When he concluded that Christ could not sin because of His inherent deity, his concept would unfold in some problematic, even troubling, directions. As noted earlier, when he sought to meet the objection that this would give Christ an unfair advantage, he concluded that Christ's advantage could be the believer's also: "All the power which Christ had dwelling in Him by nature, we may have dwelling in us by grace, for He freely bestows it upon us."[31]

In the light of the above-mentioned concept, the working theological thesis for the rest of this biography is that it would become the source for almost all of the errant theological and practical paths that Waggoner would tread for the balance of his life. His concept of the overliteralized indwelling of Christ, through the work the Holy Spirit, would become the matrix for his pantheistic-oriented blurring of the distinctions between the realms of the natural and the supernatural, his more extreme perfection emphases, his doctrine of "spiritual affinities," his flawed views on faith healing,[32] and his radical individualism when it came to his ideas on church organization. His hypersubjective emphasis would almost totally eclipse any objective points of reference in his doctrine of salvation and growing subjectivism in personal and practical matters of healing, church organization, and personal ethics. Once a person is convinced that they are the effective, literal repository of the presence of God, then it is hard to listen to any other authority except the voice of the divine that they think speaks or acts from within their soul temple.

While Waggoner would still have many special highs and important further accomplishments, his unbalanced theology had begun its insidious work by the time he departed for Britain and Europe in May of 1892. Thus it is to the decisive British years of the life and ministry of E. J. Waggoner that we now turn our attention in section 3 of this biography.

---

[1] Seventh-day Adventists often employ the expression "present truth" to refer to the church's distinctive teachings. Other words that they use almost interchangeably are the "pillars," the "landmarks," the "three angels' messages," or just simply "the truth." These

include the premillennial, literal, visible, and universal Second Coming; the ten-commandment law of God; the seventh-day Sabbath; the sanctuary doctrine with its pre-Advent investigative judgment; the unconscious state of the dead; annihilationism (hell totally destroys the wicked); the millennium; spiritual gifts, especially that of prophecy; and wholistic health reform.

[2] For these insights regarding what was "Adventist" and what was "Christian" in Seventh-day Adventism, I am indebted to George Knight, *A Search for Identity* (Hagerstown, Md.: Review and Herald Pub. Assn., 2000), p. 10.

[3] The loud cry is an expression commonly invoked by Seventh-day Adventists to describe the role of the aroused remnant church to proclaim effectively the last message of mercy and warning to the world. It will be the immediate effect of the latter-rain empowerment of the Holy Spirit. This final religious movement will polarize the whole world into two irrevocable groups—those who will have the seal of God and those who will receive the mark of the beast mentioned in Revelation 13 and 14.

[4] "The Divinity of Christ," *Signs of the Times*, Mar. 25, Apr. 1, 8, 15, 22, and May 6, 1889. The same series appeared in the Australian *Bible Echo and Signs of the Times*, Sept. 1, 16; Oct. 1, 15; and Nov. 1, 1889.

[5] *Signs of the Times*, Apr. 8, 1889.

[6] E. J. Waggoner, *Christ and His Righteousness* (Oakland, Calif.: Pacific Press Pub. Co., 1890), p. 9; compare pp. 19 and 22.

[7] We will deal with them in chapter 11 when we examine and analyze the theological developments of the 1892 to 1903 era.

[8] Ellen G. White manuscript 56, 1890, "Remarks at the Bible School," Feb. 7, 1890, in *The Ellen G. White 1888 Materials*, vol. 2, p. 566.

[9] Ellen G. White manuscript 15, November of 1888, in *The Ellen G. White 1888 Materials*, vol. 1, p. 164.

[10] In Woodrow W. Whidden , Jerry Moon, and John Reeve, *The Trinity* (Hagerstown, Md.: Review and Herald Pub. Assn., 2002), p. 195.

[11] "God Manifest in the Flesh," *Signs of the Times*, Jan. 21, 1889, pp. 38, 39.

[12] *Ibid.*

[13] *Ibid.*

[14] Waggoner, *Christ and His Righteousness*, pp. 24-31.

[15] "God Manifest in the Flesh," *Signs of the Times*, Jan. 21, 1889, p. 39. The book *Christ and His Righteousness*, just as it did with Waggoner's semi-Arianism, repeats essentially the same thought that because divine power dwelled in Christ, He could resist the inherent weaknesses of the flesh (pp. 28-30).

[16] "God Manifest in the Flesh," *Signs of the Times*, Jan. 21, 1889, p. 39.

[17] We do not employ the expression "perfectionistic" here in any negative sense. Rather we use it descriptively, not pejoratively, to refer to any theological emphasis that accentuates transforming or sanctifying grace in the experience of salvation. The pejorative is "perfectionism," employed in this biography to desribe any doctrine of transforming grace that speaks of believers coming to the place in which they cannot sin (Waggoner taught that Christ "could not sin"), or that they have received a sinless nature before glorification. Sinless character is the vision of Ellen White, but not sinless nature before glorification.

[18] Eric C. Webster offers the following, intriguing critique of Waggoner's "post-Fall" teaching on the humanity of Christ: "In his unfolding Christology and soteriology during the 1890s, Waggoner began to lay greater and greater stress on the internal and immanent Christ within the heart of the believer. . . . The existential Christ is the one who lives in the believer's heart and takes over the actual obedience. It is the faith of Christ operative in the believer that produces the law-abiding life. In this view we submit that the human

Christ who lived in Palestine and the actual nature of His humanity is not an essential element. . . . Did [Waggoner] not lose the uniqueness of the historical Jesus as he insisted on the divine Christ merging so closely with all men . . .? It appears probable that . . . Christ had become a universal principle for Waggoner rather than a historical person" (*Crosscurrents in Adventist Christology*, pp. 242, 243). Then Webster delivers his most challenging conclusion: "Waggoner's soteriology was, therefore, not really based on the concept that what Jesus Christ did in His humanity on earth man can do today by following His example and relying upon the power of God as Christ did. Rather than this 'example theology' Waggoner taught the power of the internal and existential Christ within the heart. We repeat that this concept makes the debate on the actuality or the degree of the 'sinful nature' of Christ irrelevant, at least to some extent" (*ibid.*, p. 243).

[19] In fact, the author suggests a careful rereading of the treatment of justification and sanctification by faith in chapter 3 before tackling this segment of chapter 8.

[20] G. Knight, *A User-friendly Guide*, p. 97.

[21] E. J. Waggoner, "'From Faith to Faith.' Romans 1:17," *Signs of the Times*, Apr. 1, 1889.

[22] E. J. Waggoner, "Letter to the Hebrews. Chapter 8:8-13," *Signs of the Times*, Jan. 13, 1890.

[23] E. J. Waggoner, "Bible Study: Letter to the Romans—No. 16," *General Conference Bulletin*, Mar. 25, 1891, p. 242.

[24] "The Penalty of the Law," *Signs of the Times*, Aug. 4, 1890.

[25] She wrote this important statement as letter 57, May 1, 1895, from Hobart, Tasmania, to O. A. Olsen, the president of the General Conference. It is most readily accessible in *The Ellen G. White 1888 Materials*, vol. 3, pp. 1322-1343. The key part excerpted in *Testimonies to Ministers*, pp. 91-93, appears on pp. 1336ff.

[26] The cited portion of letter 86 (Sept. 25, 1895) appears in *The Ellen G. White 1888 Materials*, vol. 4, pp. 1455, 1456.

[27] White, *Testimonies to Ministers,* p. 92.

[28] *Ibid.*, p. 92.

[29] Once again we must emphasize that we use the word "perfectionistic" not negatively, but descriptively. But if perfection is subsequently invoked in the sense of any species of teaching that involves the core of a "perfectionism," they we will be employed negatively.

[30] The word "forensic" essentially means legal standing, and "effective" indicates that such an experience of new legal standing in Christ "effectively" changes the attitudes, dispositions, and character of the true believer (working in unison with a genuine experience of sanctification). Hans K. LaRondelle has given the best statement of the concepts inherent in the "effective forensic justification" view in his perceptive chapter entitled "The Seventh-day Adventist View of the Relationship of Justification—Sanctification—the Final Judgment," published in the book *Lutherans and Adventists in Conversation: Reports and Papers Presented 1994-1998* (Silver Spring, Md.: General Conference of Seventh-day Adventists and Geneva, Switzerland: Lutheran World Federation, 2000). This relatively unknown and little-circulated report of the bilateral dialogues that took place between the Lutherans and Seventh-day Adventists is available upon request from the General Conference Office of Public Affairs and Religious Liberty. LaRondelle's essay should be more widely circulated in Seventh-day Adventist popular and professional periodicals.

[31] E. J. Waggoner, *Christ and His Righteousness*, p. 30, and "God Manifest in the Flesh," *Signs of the Times*, Jan. 21, 1889.

[32] While these troubling views have been hard to substantiate from the writings of Waggoner during the 1888-1892 period, we do have credible evidence that they were there. O. A. Olsen, in a letter to Ellen White written on March 10, 1892, complains that

A. T. Jones, E. J. Waggoner, and W. W. Prescott had used "extreme expressions" and had taken "extreme positions . . . which have not strengthened the good work that they were trying to do. . . . The positions that have been taken on healing, and some other matters, have brought about . . . quite a strained condition of things" (cited by P. Penno, *Calvary at Sinai*, p. 195). George Knight provides further documentation for the faith healing fanaticism of Jones, Waggoner, and Prescott: "[John Harvey] Kellogg felt particularly incensed at their declarations of unconditionally accomplished healing based totally on the faith of the sick individual, irrespective of God's will or remaining symptoms of disease" (*From 1888 to Apostasy*, p. 49). We will see this troubling trend on healing begin to emerge more strongly as the 1890s progress.

CHAPTER IX

THE YEARS OF EXPANDING HORIZONS AND UNSETTLING DIRECTIONS

INTRODUCTION

SIX WEEKS BEFORE Ellet Waggoner and family were to leave for their work in Britain and the European continent, Ellet had written a rather newsy but reflective personal letter to his old friend and colleague, Adventist educator Sydney Brownsberger. As he mused over his American years of service and looked forward to his new assignment as editor of the British *Present Truth*, Waggoner offered a sage observation on the phenomenon and meaning of change.

After he noted that California had been his home for many years, he then suggested that "in this work it is not a good thing for a man to be too long in one place. Our life consists in motion." Yes, for the E. J. Waggoner family the keynote had been and would continue to be "in motion." Perhaps a little too much so!

While Ellet had surmised that the workload would be lighter in his approaching London assignment, his seemingly genetic endowment with a puritan work ethic and multiple talents would not tolerate an easy schedule. In the years ahead he would continue with the grueling editorial deadlines; incessant writing; pastoral/evangelistic involvements in London and all around southern and central England; numerous trips to the European continent for institutes, camp meetings, and personal travel; four trips back to the United States for General Conference sessions; teaching in the newly founded Bible college at Duncombe Hall; and an increasing role in the developments of the organized church in Britain. And stuck between the cracks of this full and hectic schedule were the demands placed on him as a husband and father.

One of the greatest challenges in writing this biography has been the frustrating dearth of basic biographical sources (letters, diaries, and so forth).[1] This factor, combined with Waggoner's almost endemic reticence to talk much about his personal concerns, has left many a gap in the story of his life. While we know the basic outlines of his comings and goings during the British years, the details are often tantalizingly scanty. Thankfully, however, we still have the reminiscences of his adoring daughter Pearl. These recollections, which we have liberally drawn on in earlier chapters, still provide the best glimpses into Waggoner's personal life during the British years.

What follows in this chapter will basically split into two major divisions: (1) Waggoner the personal man and (2) Waggoner the public man. But before we turn to these considerations, we need to catch up with the Waggoner family as transatlantic travelers and new residents in London.

THE ARRIVAL IN BRITAIN

The transatlantic passage on board the liner *Teutonic* was apparently uneventful. After a week of travel the ship docked in the English port of Liverpool on May 18, 1892.[2] The Waggoner family, including Ellet's sister Alta (who made the trip with them), then proceeded to north London, where they settled into temporary quarters.[3]

According to the news notes in the *Present Truth*, the staff of the International Tract Society located at 451 North Holloway Road in the Islington section of north London had long anticipated their arrival: "It is almost a year since we were encouraged to hope that the Doctor would come to this field, and we are sure our friends in this country will rejoice that he has decided to do so."[4]

The "friends in this country" only numbered in the low hundreds, and the International Tract Society offices and publishing facilities were the only Adventist institutions to speak of during this relatively early period of British Seventh-day Adventist history. Thus the arrival of one of Adventism's most celebrated writers, teachers, and revivalists was truly a big deal for the fledgling British and European Seventh-day Adventist program.

But it would be a couple more months before Ellet would begin his editorial/writing, pastoral, and evangelistic tasks in England. After getting the family settled into their lodgings in north London, he, along with O. A. Olsen, departed for an extensive tour of Scandinavia and Western Europe, with stops in Norway, Sweden, Denmark, and Switzerland.[5] Not until July 17 would he return to London and begin producing a steady stream of editorials, articles, stories for children, and news notes in the *Present Truth*.[6]

While his labors at the editorial offices of the Tract Society would be his primary assignment, Waggoner would also be occupied with numerous other responsibilities. But before we review the work of Waggoner, the public person, we will seek to provide a composite sketch of Waggoner, the private and domestic individual.

THE PRIVATE, FAMILY MAN

One of Pearl's most vivid memories (among many) from this period related to an incident involving her and her father on their way to a prayer meeting one evening. While she was merrily skipping along she "inadvertently came down hard on his toes," and her misstep elicited a sudden burst of "impatient expressions" from her father. While she was nursing her resentful feelings for "some minutes," her father suddenly belted out an apology. Though he blamed the pain on his corns, he readily confessed that he had no excuse for such a hasty and impassioned reaction since the whole thing had been caused by an innocent misstep. Pearl recalled that prayer meeting as one of the most memorable of her life, offering her retrospective commentary that "he lived his religion. It was only in *physical* stature that he could be called a small man."[7]

While known mainly for his writing and speaking talents, Waggoner also possessed a fine singing voice that he could utilize in either the tenor or soprano range. During the years in Britain he often led the singing in worship assemblies or lent his versatile vocal cords to a quartet that frequently performed at numerous denominational gatherings. The quartet normally consisted of Waggoner, J. S. Washburn, E. E. Harris, and William Meredith (of Wales).

But Ellet was not only a producer of music—he was also a consumer. In a letter to his sister Ruby Canright he tells how the family attended a performance of Handel's most renowned oratorio, *The Messiah*, at the large Crystal Palace in London. The generosity of his American colleague in England, J. S. Washburn, and Washburn's brother back in Boston had made the opportunity possible. Every three years the Handel Society of London would sponsor a three-day Handel Festival, and the Boston brother had sent money to Washburn strictly dedicated to purchasing tickets for the Handel Society performances. The Washburns, who were working on the south coast of England, offered tickets to the Waggoners in exchange for lodging.

Since the tickets were not for reserved seats, the entire party left early so that they could secure a good location in the vast palace. They arrived late in the morning for a 2:00 p.m. matinee performance and were thus able to secure well-positioned seats. But that meant a wait of almost three hours. Wisely they had thought to bring their lunch along and had an enjoyable, picnic-style repast. The concert did begin on time, but lasted for four hours, including a 40-minute intermission.

The length of the performance, however, was a matter of utter indifference to the enraptured Ellet. The performance of the 4,000-member chorus and the 500-strong orchestra simply overwhelmed him. "When the vast chorus sang, it was just as though there was only one grand voice. I never heard such perfect singing in my life, and I don't suppose that better singing has ever been heard in this world since the angels sang in Bethlehem." It was certainly one of the artistic and aesthetic highlights of his life.

The musical event had its downside, however. When they returned to north London later that evening, Jesse was promptly operated on for the removal of a worrying cyst on her leg that had been slowly developing for a number of years. She survived the operation quite well, but her recovery was slow, forcing her to keep the leg propped up most of the time.[8]

Pearl's favorite experience, however, with her father's musical abilities and interests involved music at home. What she remembered and loved most were the "old hymns he used to sing to me as a very small child while rocking me at night." They included "In the Cross of Christ I Glory," "O Could I Speak the Matchless Worth," and "I Sing the Mighty Power of God." But singing was not the only family comfort and entertainment that Papa Ellet provided.

"Another thing I always enjoyed and appreciated was his frequent reading aloud to all of us" from various books, "old or new." The fare consisted of bedtime readings not just from Hans Christian Andersen's fairy tales,[9] but more memorable and substantive works, such as Wylie's *History of Protestantism* and D'Aubigne's *History of the Reformation*. She recalled these ponderous-appearing volumes as "enormous" and with "no pictures." Pearl, duly impressed with the scholarly imprint of her father's mind, recalled that by the time she was 11 she "would hurry back from school to read 'D'Aubigne'" and other "big volumes on Africa—with Stanley and Livingstone." They were among her favorite discoveries "in our big library."

But the singing and children's stories and the heavy tomes of history were not the only delights that graced the Waggoner household. Ellet also took time to play parlor games with the girls and their friends.

He especially enjoyed bringing home "some new kind of interesting quiz game." The parents often joined the children and visitors to the family circle in "testing knowledge" with these innovative parlor pastimes.

The family also indulged in some less-cerebral pursuits, much to the "shocked" dismay of "one of our good but staid English sisters when she dropped in one evening and found the 'minister' down on the floor playing tiddledywinks with his children!" The delighted Pearl remembered the incident with "amusement."

Another constant feature of the Waggoner household was the practice of generous hospitality. In fact, she characterized both her parents to be the bearers of the "soul of hospitality," "whether we were living in thirteen rooms or three." And this aspect of their family was constantly on offer to "visitors from the continent, or any missionaries passing through London to or from Africa, India or other places"—all "were welcomed at our house." And such generosity definitely implicated the girls who "more than once gave up" their room and slept on upturned tables, in a padded bathtub, on the floor, or even going "several blocks to friends who preferred us to strangers unknown."

Such hospitality, especially to missionaries in transit, made a lasting impression on Pearl, who later, along with her husband, spent most of their career in overseas mission service. This aspect of her parents' social life was one of the most positive contributions that they would bequeath to their impressionable daughter.[10]

But Ellet was not just a host to travelers. In addition to his wide-ranging teaching and revival itineraries in both Europe and North America, he did some jaunts of his own, seemingly just for the joy of the adventure.

While one could wish for more details, it is clear that he, along with his old friend A. T. Jones, traveled together to Southern Europe and Turkey during the summer of 1895.

The trip had its origins in the administrative maneuvers of the General Conference president, O. A. Olsen. In an attempt to relieve the ongoing tensions between Uriah Smith and the team of W. W. Prescott and A. T. Jones, Olsen felt that they all should get some international exposure as a part of what George Knight has characterized as "experience-enlarging field education."

Smith departed first in 1894, soon followed by Prescott and Jones in 1895. Prescott headed for Australia in the first leg of an around-the-world tour. Jones left the States on May 8, 1895, and would be gone for 10 months (returning March 8, 1896), touring 16 nations in Europe and the Near East.[11]

How those 10 months of touring meshed with E. J. Waggoner's travels is not entirely clear. For Jones's part, it was a never-to-be-forgotten trip. He had at least one other traveling partner besides Waggoner, and that was H. P. Holser, president of the Adventist organizational structure in central Europe.

Exactly how much time Waggoner spent with Jones and Holser is also not clear, though it is evident that they did tour Turkey together. But it was not one of the more propitious moments to be wandering about Turkey.

The previous months had witnessed one of the infamous Turkish massacres of the Armenian minority ethnic group. The first nation to embrace Christianity as a national group, the Armenians have a history of persecution eerily similar to that of the Jews. In Waggoner's time they were the late-nineteenth- and early-twentieth-century version of the present-day Kurdish minority in Turkey, Iran, and Iraq—persecuted by all and loved by no one. But such jittery, intimidating circumstances were not about to thwart the travel plans of Jones, Holser, and Waggoner.

They did get arrested on suspicion that they were Armenian partisans. In fact, the Armenian Christians that they met said it was not even "'safe to go out of the house,' let alone 'to be found out walking upon the hills.'" But somehow they managed to gain their freedom and continued to wander at will over significant stretches of Turkey. According to Holser, "Brother Jones seems to be in his element," once more the intrepid frontier soldier—only now doing his thing in the Near East rather than in the Pacific Northwest.[12]

While we can only wish for more reports from the pen of E. J. Waggoner regarding his adventures, he alluded a few times to his travels with Jones and Holser. In the pages of the *Present Truth* a year and three months later Waggoner reported the following:

"In September last [1895], just after the last outbreak [of the Turkish persecutions of the Armenians], the writer witnessed a baptismal scene at Constantinople. It was at a time when the Turkish soldiers were patrolling the streets night and day; one could not turn a corner without seeing a squad of them. In the open day, without asking permission of anybody, a company of Christians went through the streets to the sea, to witness the immersion of some believers."[13]

Furthermore, Waggoner did reveal, in a speech at the 1899 General Conference session in South Lancaster, Massachusetts, that he had visited Smyrna (present-day Izmir, Turkey, on the eastern coast of the Aegean Sea). It must have been a reference to his 1895 tour with Jones and Holser.[14]

Why Waggoner did not share more of his odyssey is not clear, but his family was certainly aware of the dangers involved. Pearl's report, decades later, does contain hints of his family's anxiety. The "trip through Turkey in company with A. T. Jones" and, especially their safe return, was a cause of rejoicing for "all."[15]

But not all things on the domestic front during the British years involved family pleasure and high adventure in the Near East. In addition to Jessie's cyst surgery in the summer of 1894,[16] Ellet also suffered a number of bouts with various physical maladies. He reported a fainting spell on the wedding day of his sister Alta and periodic attacks of rheumatism. But the most serious was a scary replay of the "brain fever"[17] episode that had overtaken him in Oakland a decade earlier.

Once again overwork must have triggered the dreaded "fever." Pearl recalled that even when he was away on business he "would keep in touch with the office and send in his editorials." In a classic understatement, she added that he "was a hard worker." But the "hard worker" descriptor she immediately followed with the caveat—"except for a few weeks when critically ill in hospital with brain fever."[18]

The summer of 1894 witnessed Alta's marriage to an Englishman by the name of Harry Armstrong, who hailed from Lincolnshire.[19] Her choice pleased Ellet. "Alta could [not] have done any better if she had waited a long time yet. Harry is younger than she is, but that is a very common thing in this country." While being thankful for Harry as a brother-in-law, Ellet also confided to his sister Ruby, in a moment of folksy, philosophical reflection, his opinion of the positive effects of marriage for Alta. "I am sure that it will be a good thing for her, for she was getting into set ways that people are apt to get into who stay unmarried too long."

Soon after the wedding at a nearby Anglican church,[20] the newlyweds moved in with Ellet, Jesse, and the girls. The honeymooners occupied the downstairs apartment while Ellet and family lived upstairs, an arrangement most likely entered into to mitigate the exorbitant cost of living in Islington, north London.[21]

Another interesting aspect of the home life of the Waggoner family concerned their efforts in personal evangelism. The Wright family and their four daughters lived across from them during their early years in Islington. The two families developed a strong neighborly bond, which eventuated in a lengthy period of personal Bible studies. It led to the baptism of all four girls—the first converts the Waggoners gained in England.[22] But Ellet and his family also complemented personal youth evangelism with ministry to the down-and-outers of English society.

Pearl related how the family sought to help out a pitiable little person by the name of "Sister McConnell." The woman had been a "notorious drunkard." The family faithfully brought her to church, and Jessie and Bessie would painstakingly record notes on the sermon for her since she not only was afflicted with alcoholism, but was also cursed with a hearing loss. Such a method of personal outreach involved a lot of patient struggle. But their faithful, painstaking efforts received their reward as the woman overcame alcohol and became a faithful church member.[23]

While the efforts for Sister McConnell mainly devolved on Jessie and Bessie, Ellet also had his own brush with the prevalent social debauchery of the times. In a *Present Truth* article he reported confronting "a little lad, with [a] pinched face and poorly clad" coming out of a "public house" [a pub, or bar] in London carrying "rum 'for his mother' in a teacup. Within a yard [of the public house] he drank some, and in another twenty yards, tasted again, and gave a little girl some." When the little waif shared it with the little girl, all of Ellet's fatherly, teetotal temperance[24] instincts must have welled up in a sense of moral outrage. He reports how he proceeded to prevent the two children "from having" another "taste."

Waggoner concluded his report with a note of sarcastic commentary to the effect that "no doubt the mother would have thanked him, not perhaps for preventing young children from drinking raw spirits, but for safeguarding her rum."[25] Sometimes Waggoner just could not hold back his sense of righteous indignation at the injustice of the various ills that so grated upon his sensitive social consciousness.

Perhaps we can appropriately sum up Ellet Waggoner as the personal and domestic man through a report of what must have been one of his highest days in youth evangelism—the baptism of his beloved Pearl on a New Year's Eve Friday night (1897). While Bessie had been baptized sometime during the winter of 1893/1894, the memory of Pearl's later baptism became particularly vivid through recollections shared with her some decades later by a chance meeting with a person who had witnessed the event. What stood out in the memory of the onlooker was the sight of the diminutive Pearl standing in the pool with her father, her head just barely visible above the waters of the baptistry.

One of the final news notes shared by Ellet in his July 1894 letter to his sister Ruby was that he had received an "invitation to return to America" to "teach the Bible in the college" (obviously Battle Creek). The opportunity most certainly tempted Waggoner, but he turned it down. "We did not want to go, not now, at least, and it did not seem right that we should, the work here [being] in a most interesting state. . . . I am sure that this is the place for us to stay."[26]

And most certainly the work did present some great challenges and inviting opportunities for not only the personal evangelism they were already deeply involved with, but also a wider public stage in both Britain and the European continent.

WAGGONER THE PUBLIC MAN

During the British years Waggoner made five major contributions to the denomination. They included (1) his work as a pastor, public evangelist, and teacher; (2) his opposition to Sunday laws; (3) his contributions as scholar and writer, (4) his service as a delegate to the General Conference sessions; and (5) his problematic involvements in the development of church organization in Britain during the early years of the twentieth century. We will review these interesting aspects in the above order. The balance of the present chapter will examine the first three major contributions. The following chapter will deal with the last two.

PASTOR, PUBLIC EVANGELIST, AND TEACHER

Quite soon after his arrival in London to begin his editorial duties at the British *Present Truth*, Waggoner took on the pastoral responsibilities of the Adventist congregation in north London. It mainly served the spiritual needs of the employees of the International Tract Society and printing press.

The church had been meeting in a nearby second-story hall with the wonderfully tongue-twisting epithet, the Athenaueum. But in September of 1893 the church moved from the Athenaueum to Duncombe Hall.[27] The Duncombe Hall location was just a few short blocks east of the Tract Society and editorial offices.[28] The incurably workaholic Waggoner just could not resist taking on multiple responsibilities. It appears that for most of the 11 years that he served in north London, he shepherded this congregation.[29]

Of course, the major reason that the denomination had invited Waggoner to England was to edit the *Present Truth*. As previously mentioned, the journal went to press only twice monthly when he first arrived. But not surprisingly, that would soon change under the ambitious leadership of its new editor. By June of 1893 it announced that it would become a weekly.

This undoubtedly resulted not only from the fact that Waggoner felt the need to be more extensive and intensive in the spread of Adventist beliefs, but it also provided a more regular publication for the many Adventist colporteurs (called "Present Truth agents") to sell copies to their regular customers. Employment was very hard to come by for many of the new Adventist converts in England, and colporteuring not only spread Adventism but provided a regular income for the hardworking personal evangelists.

But the economic needs of the dedicated colporteurs were not the only consideration. It was also nearly impossible to mail out copies of *Present Truth*. The British postal system simply did not feature the liberal policies of the American bulk-mail privileges granted to almost all periodicals. Therefore it was virtually a distribution necessity to utilize the services of salespeople to spread the Adventist message in Britain.[30] In effect, postal costs, the economic needs of new Adventist converts, and the evangelistic challenges of the emerging Adventist mission in Britain all dovetailed together to produce an ever-increasing number of distributed copies of *Present Truth*. But pure numbers distributed and economic necessity were not the ultimate goals of the ministry.

It was in this context that Waggoner reported to Ellen White how the periodical "agents" would seek to gather interested readers into little companies throughout Greater London. "They get the people interested in the paper, which they deliver each week, and then as they begin to ask questions, they follow up the interest with Bible readings. In some cases the Bible worker will invite them to her room for meeting, until it outgrows that place. We have now four such meetings held in different parts of London, besides our original meeting" (obviously referring to the church at Duncombe Hall).[31]

But Waggoner did not leave public evangelism just to the *Present Truth* agents and his normal church services at the Athenaueum and Duncombe Hall. He also soon began to engage in more direct public evangelistic efforts of his own. The final two weeks of December 1892 witnessed a series of public Bible studies given by Waggoner in north London (most likely at the Athenaueum). And this pattern of public appearances by the editor of *Present Truth*, though not unusually striking in sheer numbers, would prove to be a notable feature of his public evangelistic appearances in Britain for the next decade.

Such appointments did not normally include lengthy public meetings, but featured travel to various sites for brief series that lasted anywhere from 10 days to two weeks. The main strategy seemed to be to announce the intensive meetings in the pages of *Present Truth* and by the normal means of local promotions (handbills, posters, newspaper notices, etc.) in an attempt to make contact with interested readers. Afterward area church members would follow up with those who had responded to the sessions.

Such meetings occurred sporadically. The known ones were Birmingham (no date); Bath (July and August of 1898); Ashton Gate Park, Bristol (summer of 1899);[32] a meeting "on the Kentish coast" (no date given); a major London session held with W. W. Prescott;[33] and a "big meeting at Portsmouth." The latter was one of the major campaigns of the 1890s. It required attaining lodging for the staff, as the tents served only for the "meetings, dining and books [sales]."[34]

But most likely the major portion of Waggoner's travels for public appearances involved the numerous camp meetings and Bible institutes that he attended during his decade-plus European sojourn. Typical of such occasions, which had begun in the summer of 1891 (before his permanent arrival in 1892), were Bible institutes in Frederikshavn, Denmark, during the summers of 1894 and 1897. The latter was a large school that lasted most of the summer and included denominational employees from all parts of Scandinavia. Apparently the family accompanied Ellet to Denmark as Pearl fondly recalled the place for its wonderful seaside beauty and a memorable baptism.

On the way back to London the family stopped for a two-week visit at the newly acquired "royal property" in Skodsborg, Denmark. The legendary site would be the location for the famous Skodsborg Sanitarium that was to become the heart of the Adventist institutional program in Denmark until the early years of the 1990s. Denmark would also be the scene of some return engagements for the teaching skills of E. J. Waggoner, even after his permanent return to America and formal separation from church employment.

Other Bible institutes and camp meeting sites were in Norway, Sweden, Germany, Switzerland, and France. Recalling his meetings in the French-speaking Cantons of Switzerland and those in France during 1894/1895, Waggoner shared with Ellen White the blessings he had gained in picking up a fluency with French (he had already mastered Danish and German).

But the main thing that he was learning was that in teaching one cannot merely spoon-feed students by the pure lecture method. Thus he more and more felt the need to lead his institute students directly into the actual reading of the Bible for themselves: "The last two institutes that I have held . . . I have tried to teach them how to study the Bible for themselves, rather than to try to bring out any special things from the Bible. . . . We have taken some one book and gone through it. I have not told them anything, nor made any statements whatever, but have simply asked questions, and have required them to answer, from the Bible."

Waggoner was convinced that the results of such a Socratic style of pedagogy more than vindicated his method of getting students "directly into the Bible." He concluded that "truth has come out clearly as we have studied" and it had the wonderful effect of leading them to "learn for themselves."[35] It is undoubtedly one of the reasons for Ellen White's continued positive comments on Waggoner's work until at least 1900.[36]

Pearl was probably correct in her assessment of her father's abilities: "Though my father was an interesting speaker, his great fort[e], and perhaps his greatest success, was in his plain teaching, and verse drills—emphasizing the exact wording of the Scriptures, and as far as possible letting them speak for themselves."[37] Though we will later record some downsides to his interpretive principles, it was certainly true that his forte was his "plain teaching," whether in the Bible institutes on two continents, the college classroom, or in the local Sabbath school.

Waggoner's final major teaching contribution during this period was his involvement with Homer Salisbury in the founding of the Bible college at Duncombe Hall in January of 1902. The school initially went under the title Duncombe Hall Missionary College (later renamed Duncombe Hall Training College). It was the effectual beginning of what has evolved into Newbold College, the major institution of higher learning of the Seventh-day Adventist Trans-European Division.[38]

The space accommodations at Duncombe Hall were quite limited, with one large room being quartered off into four teaching venues, except for the "Bible and 'assembly' hour," which dominated the front from side to side. Quite naturally Waggoner's main teaching responsibilities concentrated on biblical studies.

But his well-honed Socratic, class-centered teaching method did have its rather peculiar challenges. Pearl described one particular student who was "inclined to be rather argumentative." He was always interrupting the class by saying, "But just supposing . . . ," to which her father would answer back, "But we are not supposing; the Bible definitely states 'thus and so.'"[39]

Next to the legacy of his Christ-centered presentations in connection with Minneapolis and his published works that still circulate, most likely the Bible teaching work of E. J. Waggoner was his most significant legacy to the development of the Seventh-day Adventist Church. It was especially the case of his desire not only to make the Bible the formal authority in all theological and doctrinal enquiry, but simply to let the pure, living Word of God speak with direct power to the students that came under his pedagogical sway.[40]

But, sadly, Waggoner's interpretations of the Bible were not always consistent with what the text truly intended to communicate. He had a certain wooden literalism that seemed to affect negatively his attempts to allow the Scriptures to speak directly to the student. It would begin to become sadly apparent in his sincere but misguided mode of opposition to the Sunday laws in London and Europe.

WAGGONER AND THE EUROPEAN SUNDAY LAW CRISES

During the mid-1890s there appeared to be a particular push on the part of the European labor movement to implement what were known as Factory Acts, not only in England (especially in London), but also in Switzerland and Norway. One of the main intentions of the Factory Acts was to protect women and children from Sunday labor.

The mania for enforcement in London began to emerge in late 1894 and early 1895. Initially the International Tract Society press operations in north London escaped the stiff enforcement of such laws and had continued to employ a number of women and young persons on a weekly schedule from Sunday through Friday.

But the lax enforcement of the Factory Act would end with a vengeance during the 1894/1895 period as the local authorities demanded that the management of the Tract Society stop the women and youth from working on Sundays.

The response of E. J. Waggoner echoed what he and A. T. Jones had earlier advocated back in the States. Instead of urging Sabbathkeeping

Adventists to refrain from confrontation through a compliant work stoppage, they felt that because of the inherently religious nature of the laws, active, nondemanding defiance was the only appropriate path to take. Waggoner, along with Jones, felt that to obey such laws was just as much a transgression of the fourth commandment as it would be to actually work on the Sabbath. Carefully follow Waggoner's rationale:

"For several weeks [the Factory Act] was complied with. . . . The women were told not to come to work on Sundays. But the inconsistency of such a course in those who are teaching the third angel's message became more and more apparent, until finally, after careful deliberation, it was decided that no difference could be made between Sunday and the other working days of the week."[41] And what was the "inconsistency of such a course" for Sabbath keepers?

Waggoner reasoned that the very obedience to a Sunday law, by refraining from work after having kept the Sabbath, is "to a degree, also [to] pay homage to the institution which has been established in opposition to the Sabbath."[42]

He further sharpened his rationale in a "resolution" submitted to the governmental authorities:

"By this commandment [the fourth of the Ten Commandments] we are strictly forbidden to labor on the seventh day of the week. Not only so, but we are forbidden to recognize any other day having a religious significance, as a day of rest; for if any other such day be to any degree recognized as a rest day, the distinction between it and the true Sabbath is to that degree broken down, and therefore the Sabbath is not kept holy or separate from other days.

"The keeping of Sunday is therefore a direct violation of the fourth commandment, the day itself being a rival of the Sabbath of the Lord, brought into the church when the pagan element gained control of it in the third and fourth centuries. We cannot therefore, without disloyalty to God, recognize Sunday in any way whatever as different from the other laboring days of the week, nor as having whatever in common with the Sabbath of the Lord."[43]

Though Waggoner's position was one of active defiance, he felt strongly that such disobedience to the laws should be in a spirit somewhat similar to the nonviolent civil disobedience advocated by Martin Luther

King, Jr., the renowned leader of the American civil rights movement during the mid-twentieth century. Thus to disobey was to simply be willing to bear the unjust penalties required of those breaking such laws. One should not demand any civil rights to the free exercise of religion. The managers of the press were to state forthrightly that to disobey Sunday laws was simply a matter of obedience to the law of God versus the laws of humanity. Repeatedly Waggoner made this point.[44]

During the same general period that the authorities enforced such regulations in London, similar campaigns went on in Basel, Switzerland, and Christiana, Norway. While it is not totally clear, the correspondence between Waggoner and the respective Adventist administrators in both of the other countries (Castberg in Norway and H. P. Holser in Switzerland) seemed to indicate that Waggoner's concept of civil disobedience to Sunday laws, based on the idea that to obey a Sunday law was tantamount to transgression of the fourth commandment, had influenced the other two leaders.[45]

The practical response to the enforcement of the European Factory Acts was that Waggoner and his associates simply refused to pay the fines levied against them for employing the women and young people in their presses. And the practical effect was that the authorities stripped the offices and the press areas of their furniture and equipment to satisfy the fines. Despite that, Waggoner repeatedly said that it never prevented them from publishing their regular press runs of the *Present Truth* and that business would "go on as usual, and with increased vigor and volume."[46]

From Waggoner's perspective, the amount of the fines and the inconveniences (the authorities even pulled up the carpets) was worth the loss: "As a direct result, more people in the United Kingdom have learned of the truth in the past year than in all the previous years that work has been carried on."[47]

The intrepid editor would go on to elaborate the advantages gained through all of the material losses and stresses:

"We could not, if the whole General Conference had spent a day in planning, have devised means by which a thousand pounds could have done so much for the work. Every paper of any importance in London has a notice of the case. Even the [London] *Times* had it. Some papers had an editorial notice as well. Of course they did not see what is in it, but in every case it is very clearly put that we rest on the Sabbath and work on Sunday, and that our work is to show people from the Bible that Saturday is the Sabbath instead of Sunday. It is also made clear that we are Christians and not Jews."

The situation did not in the least bit discourage Waggoner. In fact, he seemed to be on one of the great "highs" of his life: "I am of the best of courage. The Lord is very good, and I feel happy to be permitted to live and work at this time. I pray and trust that the Lord will guide in everything, and that infinite wisdom, not ours, may be manifested."[48]

While undoubtedly the Lord overruled in the circumstances, the whole strategy did not meet with the approval of Ellen G. White. If the logic of Waggoner's interpretation of the fourth commandment seems a bit strained to the reader, it most certainly was to Ellen White.

In an interview in Australia, on November 20, 1895, Waggoner's longtime friend and supporter could not have been more direct in her disagreements with his type of opposition strategy to the London and European Sunday laws. She plainly said that the deliberate flaunting of Sunday laws through direct, defiant disobedience was wrong.

"Refraining from work on Sunday is not receiving the mark of the beast. . . . In places where the opposition is so strong as to arouse persecution, if work is done on Sunday, let our brethren make that day an occasion to do genuine missionary work."

Now, while the original counsel had special reference to Adventist activities among African-Americans in the Deep South of the United States, the very same principle also applied to "foreign fields." In fact, the above quoted counsel from Ellen White came in direct answer to the following "*Question*: Should the same principles govern our work and our attitude toward the Sunday question in foreign fields where the prejudices of the people are so strong?" And her answer was unequivocal: "Yes; just the same."[49]

Sadly, what we have in the case of E. J. Waggoner and his opposition to Sunday laws were some of the early manifestations of a slow but steady slide into a subtle sort of extremism that would eventually take him completely out of church employment. Such well-meant and sincere misapplication and misinterpretation of the Scripture will also become more and more evident in his developing views on justification, sanctification, and church organization.

His ever-so-subtle slide into error would be on full display in his appearances at the General Conference sessions from the years 1897 to 1903 and the controversies surrounding denominational organization in Great Britain during the same period. But before we turn our attention to Waggoner's participation in these four General Conference sessions, we should briefly consider his scholarly pursuits and key book publications during the British years.

THE SCHOLAR AND BOOK WRITER

While Waggoner produced numerous books and booklets during his career,[50] most of them were edited collections of specific series of articles that he had previously published in various Adventist periodicals.

Two of his most important and enduring contributions were *The Everlasting Covenant* (1900) and *The Glad Tidings* (1900). As with his other books and booklets, both did have a lengthy history of development in his periodical articles. But his final work on the covenants had been consciously percolating in his mind as a specific book project from the early British years in the 1890s.

Another interesting aspect of Waggoner's scholarly work involved the fact that for the better part of four years he was the beneficiary of having W. W. Prescott as his next-door neighbor and coworker. The 1897 General Conference session had asked Prescott to head up the church structure in Britain.[51] It was a bit of a surprising move in Prescott's life, but he did embrace the project with some zeal. One of the things, however, that he especially enjoyed during his British years was haunting the many used bookshops in London. One can imagine him sharing many prize discoveries and purchases with his scholarly neighbor.

Many deep discussions must have taken place between these two bright minds and intense students of the Bible. As they had been theological allies, along with A. T. Jones, since the early aftermath of Minneapolis and 1888, it is not surprising that we observe numerous convergences in their theology. But clearly their neighborly and evangelistic collaboration during the years from 1897 to 1901 further solidified their areas of agreement.[52]

The alliance between Waggoner and Prescott would last until the church reorganization crisis following the 1903 General Conference session. While Prescott would veer away from their more individualistic and congregational views on church order, Waggoner and Jones would persist to the end, and eventually sided with Kellogg and his forces. Although Waggoner, Jones, and Prescott appeared to gain some support for their views on church organization during the 1897, 1899, and 1901 General Conferences sessions, they would ultimately be defeated at the 1903 Oakland session. By 1903 Prescott had parted company with them.

During the Kellogg crisis after 1903 Prescott finally turned away from teachings that were essentially a perilous pathway to "Christian anarchy,"[53] a development inherent in the radical individualism, congregationalism, and pantheistic tendencies of Jones and Waggoner.

Sadly, both Jones and Waggoner would go on to ally themselves with Kellogg instead of their old friend, W. W. Prescott. The major venues reflecting those developments were the last four General Conference sessions of Waggoner's Seventh-day Adventist denominational experience.

SUMMARY

Truly the early British years were a time of expanding horizons in the domestic and public life of Waggoner and his talented, deeply dedicated family. In many ways he was an exemplary father and man of the house. He continued to unfold as a faithful pastor, dedicated editor, productive writer, and innovative evangelist. The continued swelling of the distribution numbers for the *Present Truth* and its use as an effective means to make friends for the Adventist message were most gratifying. His work as an institute and college Bible teacher was innovative and effective. Such factors made his expanding service in Great Britain and continental Europe bright with positive accomplishment and even greater possibilities. But there also lurked the seeds of unsettling theological directions.

The gathering clouds on the horizon, especially as they began to outwardly reveal themselves in his Sunday law opposition, would filter over into other areas of his life and thought. They would become especially evident in his work as a leader of the church in both North America and Britain during the latter years of the nineteenth and the earliest years of the twentieth century. To these telling but troubling and unsettling directions we now turn our attention.

[1] Two possible reasons for this lack of biographic materials were: (1) the inexplicable loss of trunks and boxes of books containing keepsakes that the family had left in London during the return to the States in 1903; and (2) the destruction of Pearl Waggoner Howard's heirlooms in a barn fire in Tennessee where she and her husband had left many of their family relics for storage during their years of mission service. In a letter to L. E. Froom she lamented the barn fire and would have most likely shared many items of biographical interest with him. She willingly cooperated with Froom and A. V. Olson in their search for biographical information related to her notable father (see Pearl Waggoner Howard to L. E. Froom, Oct. 30, 1956, Froom PC 48: archives of the General Conference of Seventh-day Adventists, Silver Spring, Md.).

[2] *Present Truth*, May 19, 1892.

[3] The exact number of different Waggoner residences is not known. But it appears that aside from this early temporary residence, they had at least three others: (1) 33 Parolles Road, Highgate Hill, London North (E. J. Waggoner to Ruby Waggoner Canright, July 13, 1894); (2) 53 Mercers Road, Islington, London North. Waggoner also mentions that they lived in (3) the "Mission House," with "sixteen in the family. This is pleasant, but it throws a great burden on my wife" (E. J. Waggoner to E. G. White, Dec. 31, 1895). It is not clear as to what the "Mission House" was and where it was located. When they made the move from Highgate Hill or the "Mission House" to 53 Mercers Road is not known. By the time of the 1900 census they were at 53 Mercers Road, Islington, north London.

[4] *Present Truth*, Apr. 21, 1892, cited in C. Wahlen, "Selected Aspects," p. 112.

[5] "General Conference Proceedings, Twenty-fourth Meeting," *General Conference Bulletin*, Mar. 26, 1891.

[6] *Present Truth*, July 28, 1892.

[7] Pearl Waggoner Howard to L. E. Froom, Oct. 30, 1956.

[8] E. J. Waggoner to Ruby Canright, July 13, 1894.

[9] She confessed to liking Hans Christian Andersen, but offered that she and Bessie "abhorred fairy tales." The Waggoner household seemed to have a predilection for the more serious type of tomes.

[10] *Ibid.* All of the preceding litany of domestic memories appeared either in her letter to Froom or in her "Biographical Sketch."

[11] G. Knight, *From 1888 to Apostasy*, pp. 160-162.

[12] *Ibid.*, p. 161. Jones had become a Seventh-day Adventist while serving in the Army in the Pacific Northwest.

[13] "The Turkish-Armenian Question," *Present Truth*, Dec. 17, 1896.

[14] *General Conference Bulletin*, Feb. 23, 1899, p. 58.

[15] Pearl Waggoner Howard, "Biographical Sketch."

[16] E. J. Waggoner to Ellen White, July 13, 1894, cited in P. Penno, *Calvary at Sinai*, p. 207.

[17] We remind the reader that "brain fever" was most likely the nineteenth-century version of encephalitis or spinal meningitis.

[18] Pearl Waggoner Howard, "Biographical Sketch." The timing of Waggoner's bout with "brain fever" is not evident from Pearl's report of the episode, except that it took place during the British years.

[19] Alta's marriage to Harry Armstrong was a union destined to include extensive pastoral/evangelistic service during the coming years. The Armstrongs served in north Britain, Wales, and India. Following the untimely death of her husband, Alta returned to the United States, where she lived out her final years, mainly in southern California (Alta Waggoner Armstrong obituary, *Review and Herald*, Mar. 31, 1949).

[20] During the Victorian era British law required weddings to be conducted in an Anglican church.

[21] E. J. Waggoner to Ruby Canright, July 13, 1894 (archival source of the letter is unknown; it is most likely located at a White Estate Research Center). Greater London is still no bargain place to stay, and Islington is still pricey, even by current London standards. The asking price for the Waggoner's last Islington residence at 53 Mercers Road, though modest in every appearance, would be far beyond the reach of the average middle-class resident of the early twenty-first century.

[22] Pearl Waggoner Howard, "Biographical Sketch." One of the girls, Gertie Wright, went on to a career as a medical doctor in Edinburgh.

[23] Pearl Waggoner Howard to L. E. Froom, Nov. 7, 1961 (letter located in Pearl Howard Waggoner File, Document File 236b, Ellen G. White Estate, Silver Spring, Md.).

[24] "Teetotal" temperance is an old term to describe total abstinence from any form of alcoholic beverages, not just moderate consumption that avoids drunkenness.

[25] E. J. Waggoner, "What of the Night," *Present Truth*, Oct. 5, 1899.

[26] E. J. Waggoner to Ruby Canright, July 13, 1894.

[27] *Present Truth*, Sept. 7, 1893.

[28] With the very able assistance of British Adventist church historian Brian Phillips (president of the Welsh Mission in 2005), the author was able to locate the original site of Duncombe Hall. A Catholic technical college now occupies it. The school staff was very kind and helpful to us, but it was next to impossible to determine if the site still retained any original structures from the days when it was Duncombe Hall. In the first two years of the twentieth century it would be the site for the beginnings of the Bible school that was the forerunner of present-day Newbold College. Phillips and I were also successful in locating the 53 Mercers Road residence of the Waggoner family, though we were not able to gain entrance to the house. On a return visit a few days after initially locating the house, I did meet the elderly couple who presently live there. As they had just returned from their summer "holiday," they were in no mood to entertain total strangers for a look-see into the parlor—even after we explained the historic significance of their residence for British Adventist history. We might have been more successful if we would have introduced ourselves as having just landed in London on a visit from Mars!

[29] Pearl claimed that he "was pastor always of the north London church at Duncombe Hall" (Pearl Waggoner Howard to L. E. Froom, Nov. 18, 1960).

[30] Report given by D. A. Robinson at the 1895 Battle Creek General Conference Session regarding the high postal costs for newspapers that necessitated the use of colporteurs (*General Conference Bulletin*, Feb. 9, 1895, p. 93).

[31] E. J. Waggoner to Ellen G. White, Dec. 31, 1895 (archival location not noted, but most likely the White Estate or the General Conference archives).

[32] Notices given in *Present Truth*, July 21 and Aug. 18, 1898, and Aug. 10, 1899.

[33] The London meeting was W. W. Prescott's first public evangelistic series in Britain after his arrival to "superintend" the work in Great Britain. The results "yielded a few young women converts" (G. Valentine, *The Shaping of Adventism*, p. 104).

[34] Pearl Waggoner Howard, "Biographical Sketch."

[35] E. J. Waggoner to Ellen G. White, Dec. 31, 1895.

[36] Ellen G. White letter 77, Aug. 26, 1898, to "Brother and Sister Waggoner," and letter 28, Feb. 17, 1900, to "Brother and Sister Prescott" (see Ellen G. White, *Manuscript Releases*, vol. 14, pp. 158-167, and vol. 17, pp. 216-220).

[37] Pearl Waggoner Howard to L. E. Froom, Oct. 30, 1956 (PC 48: archives of the General Conference of Seventh-day Adventists).

[38] For background on Newbold College, see "Newbold College," *Seventh-day Adventist Encyclopedia*, vol. 11, pp. 176, 177.

[39] Pearl Waggoner Howard to L. E. Froom, Oct. 30, 1956 (PC 48: General Conference

of Seventh-day Adventist archives).

[40] In fact, the Bible and its educative power was the theme of the last General Conference lecture that Waggoner would ever make. "Study of Education" was the lecture title of a discourse presented on April 7 at the Oakland General Conference session of 1903 (*General Conference Bulletin*, Apr. 11, 1903, pp. 175, 176; Apr. 13, 1903, pp. 189-192; Apr. 14, 1903, pp. 198, 199).

[41] E. J. Waggoner, "The Publishing House in London and the Sunday Law," *Review and Herald*, Dec. 3, 1895.

[42] E. J. Waggoner, "The Sunday Laws in London," *Present Truth*, Feb. 21, 1895.

[43] E. J. Waggoner, "Statement and Appeal," *Present Truth*, Feb. 28, 1895.

[44] A good example of his rationale appears in his letter to Ellen G. White from London, Apr. 12, 1895.

[45] E. J. Waggoner, from London, to "Brother Castberg" in Christiana, Norway, Apr. 10, 1895.

[46] E. J. Waggoner, in *Present Truth*, Dec. 5, 1895.

[47] E. J. Waggoner, "The Publishing House in London and the Sunday Law," *Review and Herald*, Dec. 3, 1895.

[48] E. J. Waggoner, quoted by D. A. Robinson in the article "Persecution in Great Britain," *Review and Herald*, Mar. 5, 1895.

[49] Ellen G. White manuscript 22a, 1895 (produced from an interview with Ellen White in Australia, Nov. 20, 1895), published in *The Southern Work* (Washington, D.C.: Review and Herald, 1966 [reprint]), pp. 69, 70.

[50] See appendix A for a bibliography of all of Waggoner's book and booklet publications.

[51] Appropriately enough, E. J. Waggoner was the person who made the motion at the 1897 General Conference session that Prescott be sent to Great Britain.

[52] Valentine, *The Shaping of Adventism*, pp. 104-106.

[53] The expression "Christian anarchy" is George Knight's. See *From 1888 to Apostasy*, pp. 178ff.

CHAPTER X

WAGGONER THE CHURCHMAN: THE PERNICIOUS PATH TO SEPARATION

INTRODUCTION

THE MOVE TO EUROPE created a significant break in Waggoner's involvement with the ongoing General Conference sessions. After 1889 the sessions convened every other year. Thus the 1891 assembly was the last that Ellet would attend for six years. But then he would attend each biennial meeting from 1897 through 1903.[1]

They must have been exciting trips for the overseas missionary. Being able to see old friends, coworkers, and family members (especially in the greater Battle Creek area and at the Lindsay farm in western New York) made them all much-anticipated gatherings.

But for the focused Waggoner such journeys were mainly about the business of preaching, teaching, committee work, and weighing in with his ideas on church order. The popular, somewhat romantic vision of Waggoner's public persona paints him up as the great prophetic voice of righteousness by faith. And this version of the Waggoner legend does have much truth to it. But Waggoner was also an individual who had always taken a keen interest in his church, its local concerns, its missionary outreach, health ministries, and publishing houses, and the administrative affairs of the General Conference. His and his father's work had focused mainly on building up the denominational network of institutions for the more effective advancement of the gospel and its final proclamation via the mission of the three angels of Revelation 14.

A subtle shift, however, had been occurring since the early 1890s as

Waggoner began to develop a concept of ecclesiology that would tend to be less embracing of the corporate forms of the church (especially its organizational structures and institutions). The reasons for the growing shift away from the visible and organized body to a much more individualistic understanding of the church are not entirely clear. But two factors merit consideration.

One could be that he had just grown weary and somewhat disenchanted with the structures of a church whose leaders had brought upon him so much grief and opposition. Even though he and Jones had received unprecedented access to its key venues of influence, the sensitive Waggoner had paid a pretty steep price in terms of the amount of criticism, questioning, and serious disagreement that many of his most prized theological positions had encountered.

The second possible factor would be that his theology was developing in such a way that it would naturally tend to the internal, the subjective, and the highly spontaneous expectations of the ideally Spirit-led and filled individual life. These evolving, mystical aspects of Waggoner's theology were markedly open to the internal dynamics of what he considered the increasingly victorious believer.

There certainly appears to be some validity to both suggestions. But before we seek to come to terms with the theological rationale that undergirded Waggoner's personal spirituality and his ecclesiology, we need to take a good look at how he actually functioned in the councils of the church, both in the United States and in Britain during this period. We begin our survey of his leadership in the church with a review and an analysis of his involvement with its General Conference sessions.

THE GENERAL CONFERENCE SESSIONS OF 1897, 1899, 1901, AND 1903

The 1897 College View, Nebraska, Session

The thirty-second General Conference session convened at College View, in suburban Lincoln, Nebraska, on the campus of Union College. Waggoner was present for the opening session and was seated as a delegate from England.[2]

The key feature of his public participation in this conference was that he was the main speaker for the daily Bible study hour. His 18 studies on the New Testament book of Hebrews would be the last major series that he would ever present at a General Conference session. While he would make Bible study presentations, preach, and give special talks at the three subsequent biennial sessions, he would never again be the chief presenter. His talks on the book of Hebrews were fairly standard fare, featuring the usual Waggoner emphases on Christ and personal salvation. But they did contain a strong element of panentheism.

While the session appointed him a member of the "Committee on Plans and Resolutions," he was not noticeably active in the floor discussions, very much in contrast to the later 1899 and 1903 sessions, when he would make numerous speeches.

In addition to the series on Hebrews, it was reported that he did present one Sabbath sermon on March 6. It stressed the theme of the vindication of God by His last-day saints. While it is true that Waggoner never used such terminology as "final generation vindication" or "last generation theology" (common since the days of M. L. Andreasen),[3] his concepts were essentially the same as Andreasen's. Waggoner's March 6 sermon was very forthright that "God has left the vindication of His character to His children. He has, as it were, risked His character with men." And how can this be? The balance of his sermon expounds his, by now, well-honed theme of the Christ who dwells in His believers, and it is the indwelling Christ who, through His followers, vindicates the Father's character.[4]

About the only other items of note were the report that *Present Truth* now had an annual circulation of 13,000 and that W. W. Prescott had been asked to go to Britain to superintend the challenging field. We have already, in the previous chapter, explored some of the effects of this action of the 1897 General Conference session and how it literally put W. W. Prescott right next door to Waggoner in north London.

The 1899 South Lancaster, Massachusetts Session

The thirty-third General Conference session convened at South Lancaster, Massachusetts, on Wednesday, February 15, 1899. Waggoner attended as a delegate at large.[5] Interestingly enough, he did not serve on any session committees. But his presence would make itself strongly felt both through his public talks and his speeches made from the floor.

His official public appearances consisted of three solo presentations (lectures, or Bible studies), one devotional, and one very telling and interesting dual presentation made with W. W. Prescott.

Once more, the overriding themes of Waggoner's talks reflected the major concepts that he had been writing about for most of the previous decade. His Bible study, entitled "Spirit of Prophecy," continued to feature his version of the vindication of God by the last-day saints through the power of the indwelling Son of God.[6] The speeches he made from the floor were, for the most part, variations of the theme of the indwelling Christ via the dynamic work of the Holy Spirit. Only now he strongly emphasized that the translation faith of the last-day saints would overcome all illness and death.[7] In subsequent speeches from the floor he continued to emphasize the need for believers to allow God to live in them in such a way that the indwelling presence will powerfully resist any advance of disease. In fact, he called the whole process "justification by faith."[8]

But the most controversial themes were yet to come. In his third solo lecture or study, entitled "The Water of Life," we have some of the clearest evidence of a developing tendency to strongly blur the realms of the natural and the supernatural. Eventually others would label it pantheism. We will review these developments in more depth in the next chapter. But suffice it to say, at this juncture, that at the very least Waggoner was skirting close to panentheism. Yet the theme that was to set the stage most prominently for the major impending conflicts in Britain and the 1903 General Conference session at Oakland stemmed from his emphasis on the almost literal indwelling of Christ and how this affected his understanding of church organization.[9]

In the dual presentation given by Waggoner and Prescott, they made it extremely clear that Christ was "the only head" of "each member" of the church. Thus "each member [is] perfect in Him, and independent of every other member." Aside from the independent headship of Christ in each person there was simply "no other proper organization." And Waggoner reinforced the concept through a strong emphasis on the Holy Spirit's dwelling in each person. Such Spirit-filled persons were truly individual "temple[s] of the Holy Ghost."[10] Quite apparently the two next-door neighbors from London had done their homework together during the previous two years and had polished their common theological views to the point that they could make a forceful team presentation.

Thus the stage was clearly set for the looming struggles about church organization. The controversy would unfold both in England and in North America. The latter burgeoned into the titanic struggles that would emerge from the fabled 1901 General Conference session at Battle Creek. Its controverted aftermath starkly manifested itself at the deeply conflicted 1903 session and the later Kellogg schism directly resulting from the actions taken during the 1903 Oakland session. And the panentheism and marked subjectivism of Waggoner would seemingly draw him inexorably into the clutches of Kellogg and propel him away from the church that he had served devotedly for two and a half decades.

In the light of these conceptual developments, one has to grant some credibility to Gilbert Valentine's interpretation of Ellen White's interest in having the Waggoners spend some time in Australia in 1899. He has suggested that Ellen White sensed "that Waggoner might be running into difficulty" and that his decision not to go to Australia indicated a developing pattern of disregard for her guidance. "He declined, preferring to think that England needed him more. That decision, in hindsight, may have set a pattern of resistance to Mrs. White's counsels."[11] While the Ellen White letters to Waggoner during this time give no explicit support to Valentine's thesis, the outcome tragically fits his more sinister interpretation of Waggoner's decision not to visit Australia.

The 1901 Battle Creek Session

Next to the fabled 1888 session at Minneapolis, this was the most important General Conference gathering in Adventist history. Under the strong influence of administrative pressures that had been building for some years, as well as the powerful support of Ellen White, who had just recently returned from Australia, the sessions would set the church onto a clear path to structural reorganization. It would also lead to the election of A. G. Daniells as the new president of the General Conference.

A gifted and adept leader who had been closely associated with Ellen and W. C. White in Australia, he was undoubtedly the man for the times. Following his election, he promptly and effectively proceeded to give strong leadership in (1) implementing the new restructuring policies and

(2) squarely and forcefully meeting the Kellogg crisis ominously looming on the Adventist horizon.

Interestingly enough, Waggoner, Prescott, Jones, Kellogg, and their sympathizers made no strong protests against the 1901 organizational reforms. Most likely they felt that with the diffusion of greater decision-making latitude to the newly conceived union conferences and the longstanding local conferences, the church was headed in their direction.

At this session Waggoner and Prescott represented the British church as delegates.[12] Once more, while his public presentations were relatively few in number, they revealed his unfolding theology.

Waggoner commenced his public presentations with a Bible study on April 3,[13] followed by a sermon on April 6. Waggoner laced his first sermon of the 1901 session with his usual themes of the indwelling "Spirit of God." But the emphasis now had almost a robotic aspect to it: the presence of God was so overpowering that "as God thinks, the body will move."[14] Then he reinforced his version of the powerfully controlling effects of the Spirit of God with a subsequent Bible study on 1 John 1, given on April 11. Once more he invoked his most often cited proof-text reference, Galatians 2:20 ("Christ liveth in me"). Promptly and predictably he followed up with the claim that when "we receive the life into us, and let that life live in its own way," spiritual victory was sure.

What proved interesting was that Waggoner felt the need to confront directly the suspicion that what he was teaching was pantheism. But pantheism or not, he proceeded to suggest that the indwelling power of God can keep the believer from disease.[15]

While he reportedly preached in the college chapel on Sabbath, April 13 (on the "power of Christ's life, by which the Christian lives and overcomes"),[16] his final major sermon occurred on April 16 at 7:00 p.m. The discourse, based on Hebrews 10:4-10, was a fitting finale to the major emphases that he had been steadily unfolding during the session. Only now he approached his "victory through the indwelling power of God" theme via the subject of the sinful human nature of Christ. And quite predictably, he capped off his exposition with a powerful emphasis on the final vindication of God by His last-day people, punctuated with the terse line—"sinless lives in sinful flesh."[17]

While Waggoner's presentations might have impressed a number of the delegates,[18] he did not sway Ellen White. "During the General Conference of 1901 the Lord warned me against sentiments that were then held by Brethren Prescott and Waggoner. . . . These sentiments . . . have been as leaven put into meal. Many minds have received them. The ideas of some regarding a great experience . . . supposed to be sanctification have been the alpha of a train of deception. . . . Because of some overdrawn expressions frequently used by Brother E. J. Waggoner . . ., I was led to speak words intended to counteract their influence. If ever there was a time when our brethren should blend in unity it is now."[19]

But Waggoner's "overdrawn expressions" regarding "sanctification" did not reveal the full depths of even more disturbing ideas developing in his mind in 1901. At least one other thought would soon bear tragic consequences.

Definitely referring to ideas that Waggoner wanted to share with her during the 1901 General Conference session, Ellen White later reported that he was "enthused with what" he "supposed to be precious spiritual light." She did not leave it to anyone's imagination what his "supposed light" might have been: "Dr. Waggoner was then departing from the faith in the doctrine he held regarding spiritual affinities."[20] Quite obviously, if the recollections of Ellen White were correct, disaster lurked ahead for the ministry and family of Ellet Waggoner. But these destructive thoughts were not to bear public fruit until four years later.

During the historic 1901 session Waggoner made two other less-theological presentations. The first was a report on "The Work in England," in which he revealed that the annual circulation of the *Present Truth* had swollen to 17,500 and that the Adventist constituency in Britain had risen to 892 believers. His speech must have made a strong impression on the interested delegates and visitors. Following his report those who surged forward to greet him spontaneously gave him more than $100 for the church program in England.[21] The other presentation was a personal testimony given during the closing service praising God for the gift of unity in Christ. Furthermore, Ellet blessed this moving time of buoyant testimony with his musical gifts as he sang "On the Cross."

Aside from the sermons, Bible studies, testimonies, and the special music, only one other notable action of the conference involved

Waggoner—it elected him as one of the 25 members of the newly expanded General Conference Committee.[22]

Finally, in marked contrast to the 1899 session, Waggoner gave only a couple low-key speeches during the floor discussions. All of that would change as he, the incumbent member of the General Conference Committee, would come to his final General Conference session at Oakland in 1903.

The 1903 Oakland Session

The thirty-fifth session began on March 27, 1903.[23] Waggoner was present as a delegate from the British Union Conference and was appointed to serve on the Committee on Plans and Constitution and the Committee on Education.[24] The most fateful appointment was the first one.

While Waggoner made three formal public presentations during the session, his most memorable contributions occurred during the debates in the public working sessions. But before we get to the controversial and decisive public debates, we need to review briefly his three scheduled talks.

The first was a sermon entitled "The Gospel of the Kingdom," delivered on March 30, 1903. Undoubtedly many of the locals who had known him from his Oakland years (1883-1892) were present. It must have felt like old-timers' day for the Oakland Adventist community, who had not seen their former pastor in more than a decade. The key thought of his sermon was that the gospel is proclaimed through Christ being manifest in the lives and ministry of each individual believer. He succinctly summed up the idea with the epigrammatic phrase—"the truth as it is in Jesus, in ourselves."[25] Waggoner had condensed years of subjective exposition into this terse but revealing phraseology.

On April 5 he delivered a report entitled "Great Britain" to the delegates. It would be the last one that he would ever make on the progress of the church in the British Isles. British Adventism had made some notable progress in the previous decade. The weekly circulation of *Present Truth* had grown from 1,500 in 1892 to 20,000 in 1902. Even though a number of discouraging circumstances hampered the growth of Seventh-day Adventism in Britain, these figures did evidence some slow yet gratifying forward motion.[26] The labors of the British years had not been in vain for the hardworking editor and evangelist.

His final formal public lecture was entitled "Study of Education," and he presented it to the conference on April 7, 1903. As previously noted, it would be the last public discourse (be it Bible study, sermon, or thematic lecture) he would ever make to a General Conference session. This study on education was remarkably unremarkable. But the rest of Ellet's public contributions were much more dramatic. And these compelling speeches just seemed to flow spontaneously from the depths of his inmost convictions and into the testy and trying debates over the proposed new constitution of the General Conference.

The two years following the storied 1901 reorganization session at Battle Creek had seen a number of controversial developments. We need not let all of the fascinating details detain us. Yet it is important, for the purposes of the E. J. Waggoner story, that we do highlight and elaborate on two of the key controverted questions:

1. Should the church be headed up by a president, or should it be run by the General Conference Committee under the leadership of a less-empowered "chair"? A. G. Daniells had felt that the whole situation needed clarification, as he had discovered that many legal documents that he had to sign called for the signature of a genuine chief executive—most readily understood under the title of president. Thus Daniells once again began to have himself referred to as president. The practice did not sit well with the A. T. Jones and Kellogg forces.

2. Furthermore, there was the whole question as to who would own church properties, especially the relatively vast holdings of the Medical and Benevolent Association—the wing of the church that had been under the leadership and effective control of Dr. John Harvey Kellogg.

Thus, when the Plans and Constitution Committee presented its majority report with its constitutional recommendations that made provision for the church to hold title to all properties, the controversial fat had been definitely flung into the fire of sizzling debate. The ensuing contentions precipitated one of the most memorable moments in General Conference history. The majority report recommendations appeared to the Waggoner, Jones, and Kellogg forces to be a retreat from the principles of the 1901 reorganization actions and their wider dissemination of decision-making responsibilities. And not surprisingly, after the reading of the report on denominational ownership of institutions, Kellogg and Waggoner responded in a strongly negative way.

Kellogg was incensed, and Waggoner was moved to wax theological/philosophical. Once more, on the floor of the session, he outlined his idealistic laundry list of subjective ideas that envisioned individual persons, not hierarchical structures of authority and ownership, as the best embodiment of the essence of the church. For Waggoner, the main thing was the individual who is indwelt by Christ—the Lord of the church who unerringly guides and directs such persons as to their individual duties and relationships.[27] The collective results were to be left to the somewhat mysterious providences of God.

One of the most dramatic moments of the conference, however, arrived when E. J. Waggoner, Dr. David Paulson, and Percy T. Magan presented a "Report of the Minority of the Committee on Plans and Constitution." It proclaimed that the majority recommendation (with its call for denominational ownership of institutions, especially the medical ones) was contrary to the "principles" promulgated at the 1897 and 1901 General Conferences sessions. Their minority report conclusion was simply that "we cannot possibly subscribe to it."[28]

Waggoner and his cohorts then moved that their report be accepted. The delegates rejected their motion.[29] But the opposition to the new constitution had generated at least one significant amendment: that the new constitution recommended by the majority report had to be approved by 75 percent of the delegates.[30]

Following the vote on the minority report, Waggoner arose and proceeded to make a lengthy floor speech, in a last-ditch effort to win at least the needed minority of delegates over to his highly subjective version of church order. Because of the required 75 percent majority, he sensed that the "minority" opposition could defeat the new constitution.

His floor speech was an unvarnished appeal for a highly congregationalist view of church order. Waggoner ominously warned that the direction that the majority of the body was moving toward involved a "fixed creed constitution." With his typical controlled passion, he pleaded that to do away with such creedal "constitutions" was not a move toward disorganization. To the contrary, to embrace his vision for the church would allow the collective whole of the individual believers to be open to the grand ideal that the body of Christ would act "just as the Spirit of God shall move."[31] These final words had succinctly encapsulated the core of the Waggoner, Jones, and Magan vision of church order.

Waggoner's speech almost carried the day as it sparked an extended debate on the motion to accept the entire majority report on the constitution. The intense discussion featured numerous speeches by Magan, Jones, and their supporters, and notable replies by A. G. Daniells, G. I. Butler, and J. N. Loughborough (to name the most prominent) in support of the new constitution.

Finally, the vote on the majority report recommendations occurred on April 9. One of the most decisive moments in the life of E. J. Waggoner and the history of the Seventh-day Adventist Church had arrived. Because of the 75 percent stipulation, the vote turned out to be a classic cliffhanger victory for the majority forces led by Daniells and a telling reversal for the position of Waggoner, Jones, Magan, and Kellogg. Not only had the delegates rejected the minority report, but the majority report had passed 85 to 20.[32] The raw numbers, taken in their sheer weight, represented not just a defeat for Waggoner, but a resounding disavowal of his views on church order.

While the Oakland General Conference session would soon end, the struggle over church order was not over—neither in North America nor in Great Britain. In principle, Daniells and his allies had won. But the war had not ended. The mopping-up operations conducted by the Daniells forces in North America would take another four years, not being effectively wrapped up until 1907. But the situation in Great Britain would be decided in just a few weeks, following Waggoner's return to England from his 1903 General Conference session sojourn in North America.

THE ADVENTIST "BATTLE OF BRITAIN" FOR CHURCH ORDER

Brief Background on British Adventism and Organization

While Adventist progress in Britain had been slowly moving forward since 1879, only minimal formal organization existed before 1902. The exceptions were the editorial and publishing enterprises of the

International Tract Society and the British Conference in north London. The British Conference existed mainly, however, in the persons of such able leaders as W. W. Prescott and O. A. Olsen, both of whom had given de facto organizational direction to the evangelistic outreach of the young, slowly developing church.[33] This form of informal organization, however, would begin to change during the first three years of the new century. An August 1902 conference at Leeds formed the British Union and the North and South England conferences. The move toward formal church structures occurred under the strong leadership of the new General Conference president, A. G. Daniells.[34] O. A. Olsen was named the first president.[35]

But the formation of the British Union and its two constituent conferences (and three associated Missions—Irish, Scottish, and Welsh) had largely proved to be only the barest "shell" of an organization. The reason for this state of affairs was that Daniells had not been able to institute an effective constitution for these newly formed structures. The de facto disorganization situation largely resulted from the stiff opposition of Waggoner and his allies.

Yet one of the interesting ironies of this whole story was that at Leeds in 1902, Waggoner had been appointed vice-president of the British Union[36] and elected the first president of the newly formed South England Conference. Furthermore, the person chosen as the secretary/treasurer of the South England Conference was his "assistant editor" at the *Present Truth* and the woman who would become his second wife, Miss Edith Adams. We will return to the Edith Adams facet of this story in chapter 12.

The Swansea Conference

The really decisive battle for effectual church organization, however, would not take place until the fateful 1903 Swansea conference on the south coast of Wales. It was the first annual joint meeting of the British Union Conference and the South England Conference. The joint sessions lasted from May 29 to June 7, 1903.[37] The staff of the Welsh Mission was also invited to participate. The session would prove to be the decisive Adventist "battle of Britain" and the struggle "for organisation."[38] It was here that Waggoner would make his last formal stand against what he saw as "fixed creed constitutions." But we need to back up and get some further background.

What follows I have largely drawn from the memoirs of one of British Adventism's most respected early-twentieth-century ministers and able administrators—the Welshman William H. Meredith. At the time that the organization crisis began to come to a head during the last years of the nineteenth and the early years of the twentieth century, Meredith was a relatively young minister. Despite his age, though, he had already risen to membership in the important councils of British Adventism.

Sadly, it became the lot of Meredith to become an unwilling expert in dealing with prominent Adventist defectors. During this early period of his ministry he was associated with both E. J. Waggoner and Albion F. Ballenger. Meredith would find himself inexorably and intimately drawn into the initial stages of their separation from the Seventh-day Adventist Church during the latter years of their British ministry.

Meredith's first workers' meeting was at Duncombe Hall in 1896. His early interactions with Waggoner had left the young Welsh minister with a highly favorable impression of him. But this period of almost unquestioning respect for the talented editor and teacher would only last until a troubling workers' meeting held at "Redhill" during February of 1900. Present at this meeting were Waggoner, Meredith, and a number of other prominent church employees, including W. W. Prescott, J. N. Loughborough (a venerable pioneer of both American and British Adventism), E. E. Andross, H. E. Armstrong (brother-in-law of Waggoner), H. Champness, and J. S. Washburn.

The meeting had been progressing for four days, with Prescott and Waggoner serving as the main speakers. But each day the "situation grew more tense" as J. N. Loughborough began to express his disagreements with Prescott and Waggoner over "slitting remarks" regarding the authority of Ellen White. The clashes were especially tense between Waggoner and Loughborough, with Waggoner being described as quite "aggressive and dogmatic." In marked contrast, Loughborough exhibited meekness, yet it was meekness tempered with a demeanor that was "very decisive and sure" in his responses to Waggoner.

The whole situation deeply disturbed Meredith. He confessed that though he had been "bound to" Waggoner's "mind," he was drawn to the "spirit" of Loughborough. The confrontation between Waggoner and Loughborough was so intense in Meredith's mind that he confessed that he nearly lost his grip on matters, even life itself. It was only through a remarkable experience of providentially opening his Bible to Colossians 1:13 that he felt himself "delivered . . . from the power of darkness, and . . . translated . . . into the kingdom of His dear Son."

Quite obviously the central issue dealt with the authenticity and authority of Ellen White's prophetic messages. Meredith had little doubt in his mind that Waggoner and at least one other individual were raising "subtle opposition to the Testimonies."[39] But the deeply disturbing and depressing experience was only the first act in an unfolding spiritual trauma.

While deeply shaken in the face of Waggoner's perceived opposition to Ellen White, he could not totally lose his deep respect for someone who had added so much through his teaching, writings, and faithful editorial work. Meredith still regarded him as "a giant among men, though small of stature." The young minister had placed Waggoner on a high pedestal. But his confidence was in for a further blow.

The second act came at a workers' meeting sometime in the spring or summer of 1902, just before the historic Leeds conference.[40] When a particularly perplexing question began to plague the mind of Meredith, he had somewhat instinctively sought counsel from Waggoner. To his utter dismay, when he "laid the question before him," Meredith "was taken back by his abrupt way in replying. I was made to feel very small, and yet no attempt was made to solve the problem. I left the brother [Waggoner] feeling as if I had received a stunning blow; I was shaken, shocked, and very troubled. The man I had thought could make no mistake had failed me badly." The only solace that the chagrined Meredith could draw from his experience was the lesson that "it helped me not to put my trust in men, and led me to rely more upon God for help."[41]

The Dynamics of the Swansea Conference

But it was the events and actions of the third act of the protracted drama that would prove decisive. It played out at the previously mentioned Swansea conference of 1903. Under the leadership of O. A. Olsen and G. A. Irwin, both former General Conference presidents, the time had arrived to settle on a constitution for the newly founded union and local conferences. In the wake of the inability of Daniells to institute a guiding constitution for each of the new administrative units in 1902, Olsen and

Irwin must have sensed that the time had come to meet the situation head-on. Undoubtedly they perceived that in the aftermath of the Oakland General Conference session of 1903, with its defeat of Waggoner and his allies, the opportunity demanded that they strike for a more constitutionally based church order in Britain.

Waggoner, however, was not about to give in easily. He stoutly opposed the "idea of putting down rules to govern the conferences, and for some days took at least one meeting each morning to teach that when the Spirit of God ruled there was no need for rules to govern churches, missions, or conferences. Every day he read the scriptures purporting to uphold his view, and there was a real division in the conference so that it became painful to attend the meetings when the subject" was up for discussion.[42]

The stressful debates had dragged on for the better part of seven days when Olsen and Irwin finally put their leadership foot down and "said the matter must be settled that day by vote of the conference." Waggoner "was doing all he knew not to have a vote taken." When the morning session ended, it was announced that a vote would occur at 2:30 in the afternoon following the lunch break. Once more the sensitive Meredith found himself thrown into agony over the stressful dilemma of church order and Waggoner's persistent opposition to it.

But as the delegates made their way out of the morning session for the noon break, Meredith caught Waggoner and drew him aside for a heart-to-heart discussion of the older man's ideas of "the Spirit leading and ruling." After gaining Waggoner's attention, he led him away to a nearby park where they took a seat on a convenient bench. It was then that Meredith promptly proceeded to launch a most incisive challenge. It was as if years of pent-up reflection released themselves in a spontaneous reaction to Waggoner's ecclesiastical subjectivism. The Meredith challenge to Waggoner's ideas was quite direct.

"I want you to settle this matter for me. . . . You have been teaching all this week about the place of the work of the Holy Spirit, and I accept the texts you quoted and read to us; I have no doubt as to their force. But these other men, while accepting the scripture, make clear that a form of rules, a constitution, is necessary because we are many members not all having the same office and sometimes liable to be led by another spirit, or not always controlled by the Holy Spirit. I now ask you to put your theory into practice. Tell me how your theory would work with a dozen men, not all seeing eye to eye, not all agreeing on certain matters. I can see how the plan of these other men can work, for they have rules that govern or control, but I am still at a loss to see how your theory would work under certain conditions. How can I know what to do this afternoon when the vote is taken?"

Waggoner's reply was simply that "those men don't know anything." The discussion continued until the meeting time. Meredith was in a deep dilemma, filled with such "love for this man and that which I felt I could not understand." What finally seemed to settle in on him was that Waggoner "could not, or did not try to, give an example of the working of his theory; he only made me feel more and more unsettled." Then the young minister really put it to the senior editor and mentor: "I want to be led by the Spirit; you say you are led by the Spirit; how is it you can't help me to understand?"[43]

The struggle was seemingly unremitting in Meredith's mind. He was so frustrated and torn by the ordeal that he even finally decided not to attend the scheduled 2:30 meeting and its crucial vote. After having walked about in "real misery" for quite some time, he decided that he would go on to the next scheduled meeting at 4:00 p.m., at which Dr. David Paulson[44] would give a talk on a health topic that vitally interested Meredith.

But when he returned to the meeting hall he discovered that the discussion on church order was still in full swing—"the matter had not been settled." It was then that he decided that he needed to accept the responsibility of personally discerning the leading of the Spirit in the important matter. The ensuing discussion made it clear that the spirit of the opposition was one of strange domination and harshness. It stood out in stark contrast to the patient, steady, and reasoned leadership emanating from Olsen and Irwin—"fathers indeed" who sought "to lead and guide, but never drove."

The outcome was that once again Waggoner and his subjectivist principles went down to defeat by a "good majority." But Meredith's dismay with Waggoner would further intensify.

A little while after the decisive vote, he found Waggoner sitting in another room calmly writing. When Meredith questioned Waggoner as to whether he was aware of what had just taken place in the meeting hall, it became apparent that the man had simply boycotted the meeting and had done so in a spirit of dismissive disdain.

His whole attitude utterly astonished Meredith, who felt duly provoked to offer a final, indignant challenge to Waggoner: "My brother, if I had been speaking as you have been speaking every day this week, I feel I should have been there to record my vote, if I had died in doing so. I then said, 'Goodbye, brother.' "[45]

Waggoner and the Outcome of the Swansea Conference

The ultimate outcome of the Swansea Conference was that it was Waggoner who would soon bid goodbye to Britain. Knight suggests that the more immediate reason for Waggoner's late 1903 permanent departure from Britain was because " 'the brethren . . . could no longer sanction' his 'teaching that was tearing down all order and organization.' [From Waggoner's perspective,] he believed that the denomination was well on its way to papalism."[46]

While we cannot conclusively demonstrate Knight's contention, it was most likely the back-to-back defeats at the 1903 General Conference session and the subsequent Swansea British conference that caused Waggoner seriously to begin to contemplate a return to the States. By this time a teaching position at the newly founded Emmanuel Missionary College in Berrien Springs, Michigan, had already been in the works, being negotiated by W. W. Prescott, Ellen White, and the administrators in Battle Creek and Berrien Springs. The British years were regrettably coming to an end with a dismissive sigh of disdainful resignation.

The Sun Sets on the European Horizon

If we take the testimonies of both Ellen G. White and W. H. Meredith seriously, it is apparent that Waggoner was in not just an ecclesiastical free fall but also a troubling spiritual, theological, and moral descent. The actions described by Meredith were strangely contrary to the nurturing patterns and sensitivity that had made Waggoner such a winsome man at the hearth and a Christian gentleman in the public councils of the church. The analysis of Ellen White was, at bare minimum, alarming and shocking. Most certainly the time of "troubling directions" was inexorably enveloping the confused, troubled, and defeated proclaimer of the "glad tidings." Such theological seeds would soon germinate in Ellet Waggoner's life to produce a crop of withered fruit.

The Final Months in England

Without doubt the previously mentioned defeats at both the March/April Oakland General Conference session and the later May/June Swansea conference in Wales during the first six months of 1903 led Waggoner to seek permanent return to the States. Ellen White felt a growing sense of apprehension that things were degenerating in the life and thought of her old friend and protégé. She was already aware of his fanciful views on sanctification, faith healing, and church organization as well as his pantheistic tendencies. But she was also aware that the tentacles of such views, tinged with spiritualistic "theories," had begun to envelope him in the form of his ideas on "spiritual affinities" and the disastrous directions that such spiritual sentimentalism were leading to.[47]

But she would continue to labor for his restoration just as she had for his father's family life and ministry at important junctures of the latter's career. Thus she would ultimately throw her support behind the plan to bring Waggoner and his family back from Europe to labor at the newly developing school in Berrien Springs, Michigan.

Beginning in the summer and running on until the end of 1902, a series of lengthy and complex letter exchanges took place between key officers of the General Conference and the leadership of the board and administration at Emmanuel Missionary College regarding a proposal to bring Waggoner there to teach Bible.

The idea seems to have originated with A. G. Daniells, who had taken a vital interest in the new college.[48] He felt that it was crucially important to have a strong Bible teacher in a school that its leaders were deliberately developing as a model of what a real Bible school should look like. Magan and Sutherland, along with W. W. Prescott, were supportive of the plan.

The issue, however, became greatly complicated when Waggoner shared his ideas on training the faculty and expressed his wish to control the curriculum. Regrettably, he stated it all in a rather hastily drawn-up letter. Waggoner was probably sincere when he later said that his letter was only a preliminary sketch and that he was not at all intending to demand control of either the faculty or the curriculum.

But when others brought the hastily composed letter to the attention of Magan and Sutherland, it did not come across well. The whole tenor of the letter appeared to these fervent young reformers (and their board) as a rejection of their efforts and as a demand for full control. The board, much to Prescott's dismay, rejected the idea. Prescott was so upset about the board's response that he even threatened to resign as its chair. But in spite of Prescott's protests, by the last days of 1902 the damage had been done and the issue seemed to be dead in the murky waters of unintended misunderstanding.[49]

It thus appeared that circumstances would keep the Waggoner family in Britain for a few more years. But sometime between mid-1902 and the late summer of 1903. Waggoner's own convictions about his vocational directions would clearly shift.

Probably the best documentary evidence for his change of heart regarding the possibility of teaching in North America appears in a letter to A. G. Daniells and W. W. Prescott in September of 1904.[50] The letter clearly stated that by August of 1902 he was already contemplating a career shift and that the events of the first half of 1903 had reinforced his sense that such a change was the way to go.

Feeling overwhelmed with his heavy and varied duties in Britain and reeling from the sting of the Oakland and Swansea defeats, Waggoner began to give serious consideration to a return to medical studies and practice. In fact, he reminded A. G. Daniells that in 1902 he had already "talked freely with him about my settled purpose to renew my long-broken-off medical studies in order that I might be more efficient in my work of teaching."

He claimed that it was not just some whim that he had cooked up—if he were to do otherwise he would "be crippled" in his "work" if he did "not go on in the line of light that the Lord had opened up to me."[51] Already he had investigated the possibility of retooling in London for a renewed career in the practice of medicine, but the high cost of living (including the commuting expenses to and from downtown London) made that alternative seem prohibitive.[52]

But he also expressed to Daniells and Prescott a clear sense of rejection that had complicated his circumstances in Britain: "Do you wonder, then, that when, without having changed in any particular, either in my views or my plans, I found myself regarded as at least quite at variance with the body, if not almost an apostate. I was sorely perplexed."[53]

While we can only speculate why he chose to accept a teaching position, it seems most likely that he concluded that it would provide the best avenue of return to North America. After such a stint, he then would move on to Battle Creek, where he could then get back up to professional competency as a physician. Additionally, he felt that Battle Creek would provide the best educational and employment possibilities for his two late adolescent daughters.[54]

Thus when he sensed that the time had come for a more permanent change, he must have simply sent communications that he and his family were ready for something different and let it be known that he would work with the leadership of Magan and Sutherland and their board. Furthermore, it could well be that the deciding factor for Magan and Sutherland to receive Waggoner into their faculty was the counsels and appeals of Ellen White. For her this also represented a change of heart.

W. C. White had kept his mother informed regarding the failed negotiations of the last seven-plus months of 1902. She was also initially quite negative about the possibility of Waggoner coming to teach at Berrien Springs. His unfortunate and misunderstood letter had also struck her as arrogant and demanding. In fact, she had communicated her reaction to both Waggoner and Prescott in unmistakably clear terms.[55]

But during the late summer of 1903 she must have sensed that something of a more decided and direct nature needed to be done for Waggoner. And it was then that she began to make appeals to Magan and Sutherland at Emmanuel Missionary College to give him another chance. "I have had much confidence in Brother Waggoner, but I know that just now he is in special danger. He is in danger, as many others are, of accepting incorrect views of God, as set forth in the new book 'Living Temple.'"[56]

She refused to let the issue just play itself out without a strong redemptive effort. In her typically "err on the side of mercy" way, she directly appealed to Magan and Sutherland to "take him into the school at Berrien Springs. My counsel regarding his work is that you help him to place his feet on solid ground, even the Rock of Ages." Then she followed up her appeal by expressing her hopeful and optimistic belief "that he will recover his former clearness and power."[57]

Her optimistic and redemptive counsel apparently turned the tide of opposition during the late summer months of 1903 and paved the way for the Waggoner family to head back to North America.

By late September they were packing, securing reservations for the return passage, and saying their goodbyes to a host of associates and friends in England. Waggoner's British and European ministry was ending, but there were also fresh venues of recovery and redemption beckoning from the Midwest of the United States.

PERSPECTIVE AT A KEY TURNING POINT

For E. J. Waggoner these were the most critically decisive months for the latter years of his life and ministry. Few persons in Adventist ministry had accomplished as much and been granted as great a sphere of influence as this talented man. And few had also benefited as much from the persistent and prodigiously redemptive efforts of Ellen G. White. Waggoner stood at a significant juncture in his life and ministry. A career launched by an inspiring vision of the cross of Christ now hung in the balance as he faced the dilemmas that would present themselves at this key crossroad. Which way would he turn?

---

[1] It has been suggested that he attended the 1895 General Conference session, but we have no known evidence from Waggoner and no mention of him appears in the General Conference Bulletin. In the light of his active participation during previous sessions and his presence as a delegate at the subsequent sessions (from 1897 to 1903), the complete lack of reference to him in the 1895 Bulletin argues strongly that he was simply not there.

[2] *General Conference Bulletin*, Feb. 12, 1897, p. 16.

[3] M. L. Andreasen was the leading Adventist theological teacher and writer of the 1930s and 1940s. The only biography of Andreasen is Virginia Steinweg, *Without Fear or Favor: The Life of M. L. Andreasen* (Washington, D.C.: Review and Herald Pub. Assn., 1979). Andreasen would later become a major participant in the controversies that have swirled around the publication of the book *Seventh-day Adventists Answer Questions on Doctrine* in 1957. Andreasen's theology strongly focused on the "final atonement" that would feature the final vindication of God's requirement of perfect obedience against the charges of the devil that obedience to the law of God by sin-affected humans is impossible. Roy Adams has given the best analysis of Andreasen's theology in *The Sanctuary Doctrine: Three Approaches in the Seventh-day Adventist Church* (Berrien Springs, Mich.: Andrews University Press, 1981). Additionally, George Knight has further illuminated his

ideas in the "Historical and Theological Introduction to the Annotated Edition," *Seventh-day Adventists Answer Questions on Doctrine: Annotated Edition* (Berrien Springs, Mich.: Andrews University Press, 2003), pp. xiii-xxxvi. Numerous other twentieth- and twenty-first-century Seventh-day Adventist teachers and writers (the most notable being Herbert Douglass, Robert Wieland, Dennis Priebe, and, more recently, Larry Kirkpatrick) have strongly advocated the issue. It seems that the father of this theology was none other than E. J. Waggoner. We will give this issue more detailed attention in chapter 11.

[4] *General Conference Bulletin*, First Quarter, 1897, pp. 54ff.

[5] *General Conference Bulletin*, Feb. 16, 1899, p. 5.

[6] *General Conference Bulletin,* Feb. 17, 1899, pp. 13, 14.

[7] *General Conference Bulletin*, Feb. 22, 1899, p. 53.

[8] *General Conference Bulletin,* Feb. 23, 1899, p. 58.

[9] For a helpful overview of the late-nineteenth- and early-twentieth-century debates about the reorganization of church structures, see Richard W. Schwarz, *Light Bearers to the Remnant* (Mountain View, Calif.: Pacific Press Pub. Assn., 1979), pp. 271-298. For more specific treatments of the struggles involving Waggoner, Jones, and Prescott from 1897 onward, see George R. Knight, *From 1888 to Apostasy,* pp. 171-193, and *Organizing to Beat the Devil: The Development of Adventist Church Structure* (Hagerstown, Md.: Review and Herald Pub. Assn., 2001), pp. 86-131.

[10] *General Conference Bulletin,* Feb. 26, 1899, pp. 85-88.

[11] G. Valentine, *The Shaping of Adventism,* p. 106.

[12] *General Conference Bulletin,* Apr. 3, 1901, p. 18.

[13] *General Conference Bulletin,* Apr. 5, 1901, p. 78.

[14] *General Conference Bulletin*, Apr. 9, 1901, p. 148.

[15] *General Conference Bulletin,* Apr. 14, 1901, p. 220.

[16] *General Conference Bulletin,* Apr. 15, 1901, p. 225.

[17] *General Conference Bulletin,* Apr. 22, 1901, pp. 406, 407.

[18] In those days the stenographic records of public presentations often recorded spontaneous expressions of approval from the audience.

[19] Ellen G. White letter 269, 1903, from Elmshaven, California, to A. G. Daniells, Dec. 14, 1903.

[20] Ellen White letter 224, 1908, to W. W. Prescott, written at Sanitarium, California, June 24, 1908. The sobering letter apparently never went to W. W. Prescott (a handwritten note across the top of the transcribed copy says "not sent"). But the letter is authentic, and Ellen White did sign it. The communication is quite straightforward: she said to Prescott that during the time he was connected with E. J. Waggoner he was in "peril." One even gets the impression that Prescott had developed an enthusiasm for "spiritual affinities," though she never made this explicit. She said that both Prescott and Waggoner "were desirous of presenting" to her (at the 1901 General Conference session) what she felt were "dangerous, misleading fables, and that I must have no conversation with you regarding these ideas that were filling your minds." It is then, in the very next paragraph, that she gave the stunning revelation that the ideas they were excited about were similar in nature to the fanaticism that she had to face in the immediate aftermath of the second great disappointment in 1844. Next she delivered the shocking line that in 1901 "Dr. Waggoner was then departing from the faith in the doctrine he held regarding spiritual affinities." How widely Waggoner (and possibly Prescott) spread these views on "spiritual affinities" during the 1901 session is not known. The published records of the 1901 session reveal nothing about "spiritual affinities" in any of his public presentations. The "spiritual affinities" idea suggested that a person could have a special relationship with another person who was not their spouse here on earth, and then be married to that individual in heaven.

For further insights from Ellen White, see *Testimonies for the Church* (Mountain View, Calif.: Pacific Press Pub. Assn., 1948), vol. 8, pp. 291-296. The final two chapters of this biography will provide more analysis of the "spiritual affinities" theme.

[21] *General Conference Bulletin,* Apr. 21, 1901, pp. 364ff.

[22] *General Conference Bulletin,* Apr. 22, 1901, p. 377. Aside from this election, we have no record that he served on any regular working committee of the session.

[23] *General Conference Bulletin,* Mar. 31, 1903, p. 17.

[24] *General Conference Bulletin,* Apr. 1, 1903, p. 37.

[25] *General Conference Bulletin,* Apr. 3, 1903, pp. 68-72.

[26] *General Conference Bulletin,* Apr. 9, 1903, pp. 137ff.

[27] *General Conference Bulletin,* Apr. 7, 1903, pp. 99, 100.

[28] *General Conference Bulletin,* Apr. 10, 1903, pp. 146-149.

[29] *Ibid.*, p. 147. The *General Conference Bulletin* does not record the margin of defeat, and this has led to some historical confusion.

[30] George Knight has footnoted a key letter from Daniells to George A. Irwin on Oct. 5, 1904, that made reference to the voted amendment requiring a 75 percent majority for passage (*Organizing to Beat the Devil*, p. 116). The 1903 *General Conference Bulletin* reports of the debate do not mention the amendment.

[31] *General Conference Bulletin,* Apr. 10, 1903, p. 148.

[32] *General Conference Bulletin,* Apr. 11, 1903, p. 173. Thus the new constitution carried by only a small percentage of the delegates. According to the recollection letters of S. P. S Edwards, the margin of victory was even slimmer. Edwards had taught at Battle Creek College and Emmanuel Missionary College. During the mid-1950s Emmanuel Missionary College church historian E. K. Vande Vere sent a number of enquiries to Edwards. He collected Edwards' replies and entitled them "Letters of Dr. S.P.S. Edwards Relating to Denominational History" (located at the Center for Adventist Research, James White Library, Andrews University). Drawing on the eyewitness accounts of an Elder Wight, Edwards shared the following regarding the 1903 Oakland General Conference session: "There were Kellogg and Jones and many others [who] did not like this plan [the proposed new constitution]. They felt that it was concentrating too much power at the head. They favored a central advisory head with no executive power, the president merely a presiding officer . . . The big question was control. When we reached Oakland, there were Kellogg and Jones with a group of some 40 followers, well organized to revise the constitution adopted at Battle Creek in 1901 so as to change the organization in line with what I have before stated. There was a lot of campaigning all through the conference, and not until the last day of the conference did the matter come to a vote and the sentiment was so divided that on the standing vote it was a tie and Elder Daniells as presiding officer cast the deciding vote against the change" (p. 12). Since no other documentary evidence has surfaced to confirm Edwards' (and Wight's) account of events, the published vote figures given in *General Conference Bulletin* are the preferred version of the margin of victory.

[33] The *General Conference Bulletin,* Third Quarter, 1897, p. 109, lists, under the heading of "Great Britain," W. W. Prescott as director and Edith Adams as secretary and treasurer, with an advisory committee of W. W. Prescott, J. S. Washburn, Isaac Bell, E. Piednue, and W. A. Spicer. Waggoner was listed among the ministers, and Edith Adams was the Sabbath School Association secretary and treasurer.

The *General Conference Bulletin,* First Quarter, 1899, p. 15, lists under the heading of "British" and the subheading "Conference," W. W. Prescott as president and Edith E. Adams as secretary and treasurer. The executive committee roster and the list of ministers both included the name of E. J. Waggoner.

The *General Conference Bulletin,* Second Quarter, 1900, p. 130, lists, under the heading of "British," and the subheading "Conference," W. W. Prescott as president and Mary Jacques as secretary and treasurer and also secretary of the Sabbath School Association. Edith Adams had been relieved of her offices, though she would be elected secretary/treasurer of the newly formed South England Conference in 1902. Waggoner was not a member of the executive committee but was listed as a minister.

[34] What follows I have largely drawn from a manuscript copy given me by Brian P. Phillips, the president of the Welsh Mission of Seventh-day Adventists. Edited by Phillips, this manuscript is entitled "'Pages From a Minister's Diary,' by William Henry Meredith, President, 1926-32, British Union Conference." Archival copies are available at the Center for Adventist Research, James White Library, Andrews University. It provides one of the few available, intimate glimpses into Waggoner's interactions with and relationships to other church employees and the (dis)organized church in Britain during his last years in England.

Other sources for this brief history of the formation of the British Union and its local conferences and missions are (1) the article "Great Britain and Northern Ireland," especially the subsection entitled "British Union Conference," in *Seventh-day Adventist Encyclopedia*, vol. 10, p. 625. Further helpful information and interesting photos were gleaned from (2) an article entitled "South England Conference" in the "Special Historical Number" of *The Missionary Worker* (organ of the British Union Conference of Seventh-day Adventists), July 15, 1924 (original archival copy located at Ellen G. White Research Center, Newbold College Library, Binfield, Bracknell, Berkshire, United Kingdom), pp. 7ff. and (3) a "Centennial Historical Special" of the *Messenger* (official organ of the British Union Conference), published in 1974 by the Stanborough Press, Ltd., Alma Park, Grantham, Lincolnshire, for the British Union Conference, Stanborough Park, Watford, Hertfordshire (a personal copy is in the possession of the author, with other original archival copies located at Ellen G. White Research Center, Newbold College library, Binfield, Bracknell, Berkshire, United Kingdom). Only the Meredith diary will be footnoted.

[35] Calvin W. Edwards and Gary Land, *Seeker After Light* (Berrien Springs, Mich.: Andrews University Press, 2000), p. 72.

[36] *Ibid.*

[37] *Ibid.*, p. 73. Meredith suggested, but not explicitly, that the meetings took place at "Easter time" ("Minister's Diary," p. 34).

[38] "Minister's Diary," p. 34.

[39] *Ibid.*, pp. 25, 26.

[40] *Ibid.*, p. 31.

[41] *Ibid.*, p. 31.

[42] *Ibid.*, pp. 31, 32.

[43] *Ibid.*, p. 32.

[44] *Ibid.*, p. 34.

[45] *Ibid.*, p. 33.

[46] In Knight, *From 1888 to Apostasy*, p. 180.

[47] See especially Ellen G. White letter 230, Oct. 2, 1903.

[48] Paul Penno, Jr., has presented convincing documentation (especially Daniells' letter to E. J. Waggoner, Jan. 6, 1903, written from Graysville, Tennessee) that the General Conference president was not only enthusiastically interested in bringing Waggoner to EMC in 1902, but that he had even grander ideas in mind. When it became apparent to Daniells that the plans for Berrien Springs were not going to work, he conceived of an alternative one. It envisioned that young people preparing for mission service would be sent to England to study under Waggoner at the newly forming mission training school in

north London for their final two or three years. But this plan never materialized (taken from a private manuscript that Penno shared with the author entitled "Waggoner's Final Years," p. 6).

[49] The best overall discussion of the 1902 efforts to bring Waggoner to Berrien Springs is Gilbert Valentine's newly revised biography of Prescott entitled *W. W. Prescott: Forgotten Giant of Adventism's Second Generation,* pp. 158-162. The following letters provide the key primary sources for the story of the botched negotiations of 1902: A. G. Daniells (from London) to A. T. Jones, May 15, 1902; A. G. Daniells (from London) to Brethren Prescott and Sutherland, May 15, 1902; A. G. Daniells (from London) to W. C. White, May 15, 1902; W. C. White (from Sanitarium, Napa County, California, to A. G. Daniells, May 30, 1902; E. J. Waggoner (from London) to A. G. Daniells, June 1, 1902; P. T. Magan (from Berrien Springs, Michigan) to A. G. Daniells, June 23, 1902; E. A. Sutherland (from Berrien Springs, Michigan) to A. G. Daniells, June 24, 1902; W. C. White (from Sanitarium, Napa County, California) to A. G. Daniells, July 3, 1902; W.W. Prescott (from Battle Creek, Michigan) to A. G. Daniells, July 3, 1902; W. W. Prescott (from Battle Creek) to E. J. Waggoner, July 3, 1902; W. W. Prescott (from Battle Creek) to P. T. Magan, July 3, 1902; A. G. Daniells (from Battle Creek) to W. C. White, Aug. 22, 1902; E. J. Waggoner (from London) to A. G. Daniells, Dec. 24, 1902 (all located in the presidential files, General Conference archives, Silver Spring, Md.).

[50] Letter from E. J. Waggoner (at Battle Creek) to "Brethren Daniells and Prescott," Sept. 5, 1904 (Center for Adventist Research, James White Library, Andrews University).

[51] A sense of direct revelation from God would also manifest itself in the story of his growing "affinity" with Edith Adams. More on this issue when we take up his divorce from Jessie and his marriage with Edith in chapter 12.

[52] E. J. Waggoner (from Battle Creek) to "Brethren Daniells and Prescott," Sept. 5, 1904.

[53] *Ibid.*

[54] *Ibid.*

[55] Ellen G. White letter 101, June 30, 1902 (from "Elmshaven," Sanitarium, California), to E. J. Waggoner; Ellen G. White letter 102, June 30, 1902 (from "Elmshaven," Sanitarium, California), to W. W. Prescott.

[56] Ellen G. White letter 214, Oct. 9, 1903 (from "Elmshaven," Sanitarium, California), to "Brethren Magan and Sutherland." (Ellen G. White Estate Research Center).

[57] *Ibid.*

CHAPTER XI

THE THEOLOGICAL DIVIDE CLARIFIES

INTRODUCTION

THE PERIOD FROM 1892 TO 1903 was the most decisive of Waggoner's career. The previous two periods saw the most positive developments, but now they would be overshadowed by troubling theological directions that have forever complicated and even compromised Waggoner's legacy as a theologian and revival figure in Seventh-day Adventist history. Even his most ardent admirers and defenders have acknowledged a number of them, especially his growing tendency to blur the realms of the natural and the supernatural.

In this crucial chapter we will trace the same basic themes that we looked at in the previous two chapters dealing with theological developments (chapters 3 and 8) and will examine how they continued to unfold. While we have already anticipated some of them in the two narrative chapters of this section (chapters 9 and 10), the present chapter will review and augment those themes.

We urge the reader to follow the various developments closely. The issues can be quite challenging, but the attentive reader will certainly profit from the effort. Even if some feel led to disagree with the interpretations given here, the exercise should prove stimulating, because we are here dealing with some highly controversial but crucially fundamental issues. If we can get a handle on the key concepts involved, we can make significant progress toward separating the wheat from the chaff in a lot of the debates that have swirled around Seventh-day Adventist theological developments since the passing of E. J. Waggoner. With these thoughts in mind, we now turn to the definitive, clarifying theological "divides" in the life and thought of E. J. Waggoner during the British years.

THE GODHEAD AND THE NATURE OF CHRIST

Trinitarian Thought

As previously noted, by 1892 Waggoner's views on the Trinity and the full deity of Christ were quite well formed. He had come to the very borders of a Trinitarian understanding of the person of Christ. But in 1893 he would seem even closer to a Trinitarian position, as evident in his reflections on the parallels between the unity exemplified by the Father and the Son and that possible between believers.

"The union of the Father and the Son is union of Spirit. We cannot comprehend this union, but we may know that it is not a forced union, but that it results from their very nature. They have one life. Their thoughts and purposes are the same, not because they come together and compare notes and agree to be alike, but because one life is in them both . . . The life of the Father and the Son in each member of the church will produce the most perfect union in the whole body."[1]

The most intriguing comment, however, that Waggoner made during the 1892 to 1903 era was his declaration that Christ "did not first become a mediator at the fall of man, but was such from eternity."[2] The statement seems to come not only to the borders of a Trinitarian concept of the deity of Christ, but could possibly indicate that he had crossed the frontier from the land of semi-Arianism. Yet such an assessment might be a bit too optimistic: it could still be that the eternity of Christ as mediator was bound up with the eternity of the Father's nature within which He was allegedly enfolded before He was "begotten" as a separate and identifiable personal, divine being. Most certainly the eternal nature of the Father possessed the all-knowing and loving heart of an advocate for those whom He knew would reject His love, and the alleged emergence of the Son from the Father would also feature this same advocating and mediating love.

Intriguing and insightful as these statements are relative to both the eternal mediatorship of Christ and His profound union with the Father, Waggoner still seems to lean toward a position that is an interesting variation of the semi-Arian view. It was a position, clearly articulated in early1889 and reinforced in 1890, that he simply never repudiated. Once more, in all fairness to Waggoner, we need to repeat that even though he made many wonderful statements that spoke of the full equality of the Father and the Son, he never clearly and explicitly taught that they were eternally coexistent, divine persons.

It could well be that while he sensed the vital importance of the full equality of the shared natures of both the Father and the Son (for a clear understanding of the meaning of Christ as atoning sacrifice and mediator), Waggoner never seemed to fully appreciate the importance of the doctrine of the Trinity for its emphasis on the coeternity of the three persons of the Godhead. If they were not coeternal in time, then there would have been a time that the Father would not have been in a fully interdependent, mutually submissive, self-sacrificing, yet creative and redemptive outflowing relationship of eternal social love. The issue is absolutely critical to the meaning of divine love and its power to make atonement and effectively communicate redemption to the sinful human race.[3] And this assessment could also be true of the Holy Spirit.

The Person of the Holy Spirit

Thus far in the chapters devoted to theological developments, we have given no direct attention to Waggoner's view of the Holy Spirit. But the issues that would soon surface in relationship to developments in Waggoner's atonement theology make a brief discussion of the Holy Spirit in Waggoner's thought seem more relevant. What follows is Eric C. Webster's stimulating summary of Waggoner's thought on the Holy Spirit.

When we contemplate Waggoner's theology, we do not find "a clear and forthright doctrine of the Holy Spirit. At least the personality and deity of the Holy Spirit as a part of the Godhead is not emphasized. The prevailing attitude toward the Holy Spirit in Adventist circles at the time of Waggoner's work was anti-Trinitarian, accepting the Holy Spirit as a divine influence from God. . . . In the light of the above it is not surprising that Waggoner was influenced by his contemporaries in regard to the doctrine of the Holy Spirit. In his developing Christology, Waggoner gave greater emphasis to the abiding presence of Christ in the heart and could it be that without a clear teaching on the Deity or personality of the Holy Spirit, Christ took over the work of the Holy Spirit in Waggoner's thinking? In time this led to a lessening of the emphasis on the historical work of Christ in His earthly life and death. The historical Christ was almost lost in the form of the existential Christ, who usurped the work and role of the Holy Spirit in the heart."[4]

Perhaps Webster is right regarding Waggoner's doctrine of the Holy Spirit, though it is hard to be dogmatic. But in the light of the highly subjective developments in Waggoner's atonement convictions and the great emphasis on the immanent Christ, his suggestion that "without a clear teaching on the Deity or personality of the Holy Spirit, Christ took over the work of the Holy Spirit" is a most tempting thesis. But in the final analysis, the lack of clear evidence for the full deity and personhood of the Spirit fits in well with the rest of Waggoner's semi-Arian views and his wariness in fully embracing Trinitarian categories of theology.

One of the last statements that Waggoner would ever make on the subject of the Trinity clearly evidenced that he did not appreciate the biblical, historical, and theological significance of the issues swirling around this very foundational subject. He reflects a type of sincere but misplaced biblicism that held the following assumptions: if (1) Scripture does not explicitly use a theological term and (2) it has had a background of controversy stemming from the deep mystery of the subject, then such a subject is not worthy of serious consideration by Bible-believing Christians.[5]

Such a stance by Waggoner was one of the saddest manifestations of the heritage he received from his Adventist version of American Restorationism.[6] In actual fact, the doctrine of the Trinity is quite biblical and contains absolutely essential truth if we are to grasp fully the depths of the doctrines of the atonement and the gospel of Christ. But let us look at how Waggoner dealt with the subject.

In a published response to a question sent to the *Present Truth*, "Do you believe in the Trinity?" Waggoner offered the following reply: "If I knew what you meant by the term, I might tell you; but from the days of Athanasius[7] until now all discussion about the Trinity has been an attempt to define the indefinable and the incomprehensible. Thousands have been put to death for not professing belief in a formula which even its professors could not comprehend, nor state in terms that anybody else could comprehend. The Scriptures reveal 'One God and Father of all,' our Lord Jesus Christ, who is the brightness of the Father's glory, and 'the eternal

Spirit' through whom Christ offered Himself and was raised from the dead; but we do not profess any knowledge of them beyond what the Scriptures give us. In teaching and preaching the gospel we always confine ourselves strictly to Scripture terms and language; those who manufacture terms must be looked to for definitions of them. It is best not to presume to define what the Bible has not defined, nor to attempt to explain infinity."[8]

Quite apparently, Waggoner just never really devoted any sustained attention to the study of the issue. Furthermore, it seems that he gave scant attention to Ellen White's growing body of pro-Trinitarian testimony.[9] When it came to the doctrine of the Trinity, he came close to full truth, but still remained a son of the semi-Arian Seventh-day Adventist pioneers. Thankfully, Ellen White, with the strong help of such individuals as W. W. Prescott, was able to break out of this rationalistic, anti-historical Restorationism and step into the full light of a truly biblical doctrine of the Trinity.[10]

The Humanity of Christ

On the humanity of Christ, Waggoner's position was fully clarified during the 1888 to 1892 era. Although he would comment on the subject numerous times, his essentially "post-Fall" Christology remained unchanged during the British years. Yet one interesting development (coming in December of 1900) evidenced that he had been wrestling with an important implication of his position that Christ was born with sinful propensities or tendencies to sin and yet was sinless in thought and behavior.

While Waggoner believed that if Christ's humanity "was not like ours it would involve the idea of the immaculate conception," he would then proceed to take the position that "it was Christ's miraculous birth[11] which neutralized the evil tendencies of His evil ancestry."[12] Webster has raised some interesting questions regarding this somewhat surprising development in Waggoner's long-held position that Christ had taken sinful flesh, which included evil tendencies. "One does wonder whether it is possible to hold together a Christ with sinful flesh possessing evil tendencies from an evil ancestry, and at the same time, a spotless Christ as a result of a 'miraculous birth'? When Waggoner goes on to state that godly parents could also, through the power of the Holy Spirit, give birth to a similar child, one wonders if the unique distinction between the birth of Christ and all other children is not destroyed."[13]

Possibly we could state Waggoner's conundrum this way: How can you censure those who hold the "immaculate conception" doctrine, when you have come up with a doctrine that could be justifiably called the "immaculate reception" of a "miraculous birth"? Not surprisingly, a number of Waggoner's twentieth- and twenty-first-century admirers have taken essentially the same "miraculous birth" route in attempting to explain how Christ could be born sinful but be the only human baby ever born who did not commit acts of sin.

But "miraculous birth" perplexities aside, we need to make one last point regarding Waggoner's doctrine of the humanity of Christ: the overall effect of his teachings on the humanity of Christ was to highlight the role of Christ as a sympathetic example who can aid the subjective victory of the true believer over temptation. It is just one more doctrinal component that had, for Waggoner, a primarily subjective, sanctifying role to play in his salvation theology.

Furthermore, his post-Fall concept of the humanity of Christ has always been understood as intimately tied in with a vision of some total victory over sin. This version of sanctification experience teaches that there will emerge a final generation of perfect believers who vindicate God's claim that obedience to the holy law of God is possible for fallen but graced sinners. As in so many other areas, so it was in his Christology that the implications overwhelmingly point to the subjective work of God in the soul of the struggling believer, not to the issues of imputation and objective legal standing before God. While we must never see the issues of the subjective and the objective as opposed to one another, it is also absolutely necessary that they not swallow up one with the other. And for Waggoner, there seemed to be a real danger that the subjective and relational would swallow up the objective and the imputational.

THE COVENANTS

Although Waggoner would publish his summary opus on the covenants in 1900 (*The Everlasting Covenant*), it added nothing substantively original to his covenant theology. His concept of the subject had reached its full maturity by the end of 1890.

Yet one feature that would somewhat supplement his covenant theology emerged in 1894: "When do we need consolation? When we flee for refuge to Christ as priest in the holy places. Within the veil He ministers as high priest; and it is the oath of God that gives us courage to believe that His priesthood will save us. Then our consolation comes from Christ's priesthood, and so from the oath which made Him priest. Therefore the oath of God to Abraham was identical with the oath that made Christ high priest."[14] Here, for the first time, Waggoner connected his views on the covenants with Christ's priestly ministry in the heavenly sanctuary.

Paul Penno, Jr., has succinctly summed up the significance of this development: "All the blessings and fulfillment of the new covenant were ministered by Christ, the high priest from the heavenly sanctuary" and thus all the blessings "of Christ's sacrifice upon the cross were ministered from the sanctuary."[15] This final, helpful insight will later take on added significance when Waggoner will make some strange turns in his understanding of the ministry of Christ in the heavenly sanctuary during the setting of the final, most holy place, phase of His high priestly intercessions. We will carefully need to weigh it as we ponder (in chapter 13) the significance of his last written document left on his desk just prior to his untimely death. But as far as the positive developments of his covenant theology, the major outlines were fully in place by 1894.

Without a doubt Waggoner's views on the covenants were a positive advance in Seventh-day Adventist theology. This has been especially true of his emphases that the eternal covenant of grace transcends all dispensations and that the experience of this covenant is a matter of a deep, heartfelt embrace of the grace of God. Here is the true core, or essence, of the subjective truths involved in any genuine Christian experience of the gospel of free grace.

But we must also mention that Waggoner has bequeathed to subsequent generations a certain accent on this truth that has been a channel for subjective, perfectionistic emphases that can lead to imbalance and even fanaticism. While the real truth of the eternal covenant is that God is both the one who forgives sins and who writes His law on the hearts of true believers, Waggoner's slant on the latter concept has been more especially open to some vexing extremism.

While abuse never cancels legitimate use, there has surfaced the not-so-subtle suggestion that the writing of the law of God on the heart involves a sinless sort of perfection emphasis. Now once more, here is an issue in which the "the track of truth lies close beside the track of error."[16] Most certainly there is a legitimate doctrine of sanctification that leads to a genuine understanding of the true biblical doctrine of Christian perfection. But does this include some sort of a subjective purging away of sin that will bring a type of perfection that has no more need for Christ to be making up for the unavoidable deficiencies of true believers (before the experience of glorification)? Waggoner strongly suggested that there was.

He left the distinct impression that through the indwelling Christ (via the ministry of the Holy Spirit), the believer could have the law of God so embossed on the heart that there would be no more sin. And such an emphasis has produced a lot of needless division in the church. Such division and brushes with extremism seem to find their key sources in Waggoner's views on sin and atonement.

SIN AND THE ATONEMENT

Sin

Waggoner's understanding of sin would remain essentially the same as it had been during the previous eras. He regarded it as a condition of profound derangement that afflicted every person ever born into the world with selfish and depraved propensities to do the wrong thing. Waggoner defined sin as the acts of disobedience to the law of God manifested when the unbelieving, distrusting sinner encountered temptations. While the law had plenty of power to expose sin and define righteousness, it could neither deliver from the pull of the sinful propensities nor beget any truly perfect obedience. Such perfect obedience could arise only out of a relationship of faith in Christ and out of the fruit of His marvelous forgiveness and transforming power. Thus the sinner needed not only forgiveness of sins to deliver from the guilt of sin, but also gospel grace to rescue from the power of sin.

Thus to sum up, sin includes a profound warping of human nature that lead to acts of sin.

But during this period Waggoner would add a new wrinkle (in

December of 1894) regarding the sinful "flesh": the "flesh" of sinful human nature will never be changed until glorification (though character can be perfected).[17] But the fleshly propensities of sin and the guilt of sin could be overcome through the atoning work of Christ and the power of God's grace flowing from the life and death of Christ, the atonement maker.

The Atonement

During the years leading up to 1888 and the four years following, Waggoner had clearly taught the essential outlines of the penalty, substitutionary, satisfaction model of the atonement. But in 1892 this would all change. Sometime before 1891 Waggoner had adapted the theory of Brooke Foss Westcott (1825-1901)[18] that the blood is life and that Christ died in order to be able to communicate His life to sinful human beings. By October of 1892 Waggoner "repeated Westcott's theory that the blood means the life of Christ rather than the forfeited life—violent death—of Christ."[19] This very subtle teaching would lead Waggoner away from the more objective models of the atonement into the subtleties of a more subjective and "mystical" understanding of the death of Christ.[20] The word "mystical" here refers to some spiritual substance that is infused into the soul, as opposed to a change in attitude brought about by a profound sense of new legal, motivational, and family relationships established by the work of Christ for the soul.

On September 21, 1893, Waggoner began to lay out his new insights into the redemptive significance of the death of Christ. And they would cause him to abandon totally the idea that Christ's death was needed to bear the just penalty of sin as the sinner's substitute in order to satisfy the just demands of God's justice. In other words, the just penalty for sin is eternal death, and Christ bore this penalty as the substitute for the sin of the whole human race in order to meet the legal demands of God's nature of justice (what the Bible refers to as His just "wrath," or revulsion, against sin).

In order for the reader to get the full flavor of this strategic theological development in Waggoner's thought, we will extensively cite his 1893 article "Why Did Christ Die?"[21]

"'But,' someone will say, 'You have made the reconciliation all on the part of man; I have always been taught that the death of Christ reconciled God to man; that Christ died to satisfy God's justice, and to appease Him.' Well, we have left the matter of reconciliation just where the Scriptures have put it: and while they have much to say about the necessity for man to be reconciled to God, they never once hint of such a thing as the necessity for God to be reconciled to man. To intimate the necessity for such a thing is to bring a grave charge against the character of God. This idea has come into the Christian church from the Papacy, which in turn brought it from Paganism, in which the only idea of God was of a being whose wrath must be appeased by a sacrifice. . . .

"Consider further what reconciliation means. It means a change on the part of the one reconciled. If one has enmity in his heart toward another, a radical change must take place in him before he is reconciled. This is the case with man. 'If any man be in Christ he is a new creature; old things are passed away; behold, all things are become new. And all things are of God, who hath reconciled us to Himself by Jesus Christ.' 2 Cor. 5:17, 18. But to speak of the necessity for God to be reconciled to man is not only to say that He cherished enmity in His heart, but to say that God was partially in the wrong, and that a change had to take place in Him as well as in man. If it were not in the innocence of ignorance that men talked about God's having been reconciled to man, it would be blasphemy. This is one of the 'great things and blasphemies' that the Papacy has spoken against God. Let us not echo it."

Clearly Waggoner was denying a whole galaxy of related ideas inherent in penalty/substitution/satisfaction models or theories. But he was not through with his extensive attack on this venerable Christian explanation of the death of Christ:

"Sometimes this idea of propitiating the wrath of God has taken an easier form—that is, easier for the worshipers. Instead of sacrificing themselves, they have sacrificed others. Human sacrifices have always been to a greater or less extent connected with heathenism. Men shudder as they read of the human sacrifices offered by the ancient inhabitants of Mexico and Peru, and by the Druids: but professed [not real] Christianity has its awful list. Even so-called Christian England has made hundreds of burnt offerings of men, for the purpose of turning away the wrath of God from the country. Wherever there is religious persecution to any degree, it springs from the mistaken idea that God demands a victim. This is shown by the words of Christ to His disciples: 'The time cometh, that whosoever killeth you will think that he doeth God service.'" John 16:2. All such worship has been devil worship, and not worship of the true God.

"Just here somebody has remembered that it is said in Hebrews 9:22, 'Without shedding of blood is no remission'; and this makes him think that after all God did demand a sacrifice before He would pardon man. It is very difficult for the mind to rid itself of the idea received as a legacy from paganism, through the Papacy, that God was so angry at man for having sinned, that He could not be mollified without seeing blood flow; but that it made no difference to Him whose blood it was, if only somebody was killed: and that since Christ's life was worth more than the lives of all men, He accepted Him as a substitute for them. This is almost a brutal way of stating the case, but it is the only way that the case can be truly presented. The heathen conception of God is a brutal one, as dishonouring to God as it is discouraging to man; and this heathen idea has been allowed to color too many texts of Scripture. It is sad to think how greatly men who really loved the Lord have given occasion to His enemies to blaspheme."[22]

Clearly Waggoner here presented an unabashed caricature of the penalty/substitution/satisfaction theories or models of the atonement. The truthfulness of his position on the atonement, however, is not the issue we are concerned about at the moment. But what is truly relevant is to see just how this "mystical" teaching of the meaning of the death of Christ worked and how it might have influenced his understanding of justification and sanctification. Waggoner was quite forthcoming with his explanations:

"But how is it that the shedding of blood, even the blood of Christ, can take away sins? Simply because the blood is the life." After citing Leviticus 17:11 ("For the life of the flesh is in the blood"), Waggoner proceeded to say that "we know it means that no sins can be taken away except by the life of Christ. In Him is no sin; therefore when He imparts His life to a soul, that soul is at once cleansed from sin. . . .

"God gave Himself, and you will see that a sacrifice was not demanded to satisfy God's outraged feelings, but that, on the contrary, God's inexpressible love led Him to sacrifice Himself, in order to break down man's enmity, and reconcile us to Himself.

"'But why could He not give us His life without dying?' That is to say, Why could He not give us His life, and still not give it? We needed life, and Christ alone had life to give; but the giving of life is dying. His death reconciles us to God, provided we make it our own by faith. We are reconciled to God by the death of Christ, because in dying He gave up His life, and He gave it to us.[23] Being made partakers of the life of God, through faith in Christ's death, we are at peace with Him, because one life is in us both. Then we are 'saved by His life.' Christ died, but He still lives, and his life in us keeps us united to God. The imparting of His life to us frees us from sin and the continuing of it in us keeps us from sin."[24]

Quite obviously Waggoner had abandoned the closely connected concepts of imputation and punishment, which so clearly point to the satisfaction of the penalty demanded by the just wrath of God. McMahon was quite correct that such views inevitably tend to a downgrading of the historic death of Christ. This downgrading of objective categories then gets supplemented by the confounding of the actual history of Calvary with "the cross of suffering and self-denial that the believer bears as he follows Jesus."[25]

In a subsequent piece (February 1894) Waggoner would lay it out very clearly: "The failure with many people is that they make a distinction between the cross of Christ and their own crosses."[26] In other words, the saving efficacy of the cross of Christ had to do with the experience of the cross within the heart and mind of the believer. Waggoner made the subjective implications very clear:

"Christ is the present Saviour of all men . . . The knowledge that the cross is set up in every heart, that He is crucified for us, makes a delight of the crosses which come to us, all the burdens to be borne, all the habits to be given up which are as taking our life, because they are our life. The knowledge that now Christ is crucified for us, that now are we crucified with Him, not in fancy, but in fact, makes the presence of the cross a joy to us, for there we find Christ, and are brought into fellowship with His death, and live with Him. Being reconciled by His blood, we know we shall be saved by His life. To take up the cross is to take Him. To deny self is to own Him. To crucify self indeed is to take His life."[27]

Now, we could certainly say much more on the issue of the atonement. But what Waggoner in essence has done is to combine elements of Westcott's "mystical" view of the meaning of the sacrificial blood (as actually, mystically imparting new life to the sinner) with the elements of Abelard's moral influence model that taught that the only reason Christ had to die was to change the mind of the convicted sinner that God really does love us and is not just bent on getting His just vengeance. The death of Christ then seeks to change the attitudes of the sinner so that they can be mystically imbued with and transformed by the life of Christ offered through His death and shed blood.

And what is the central point? When we clearly grasp these highly subjective teachings on Christ's atoning death, we come to see that the ever-flowing blood of Christ, through the heart and mind of the individual believer, purges away sin (and its ill effects). In other words, the mystical presence of the death-imparted blood (life) of Christ removes all sin (the guilt and the power of it) from the believer. And when we combine this idea with Waggoner's continuing emphasis on the concept that it is through the indwelling Christ that the divine power of Christ gets mediated, it forms a powerful axis through which all temptation to sin is overcome. Thus Waggoner's theology was on a remarkably subjective track. And the thought of divine power personally dwelling in every believer can very much open the way for all sorts of subjective mischief.

And finally, it comes as no surprise that Waggoner would throughout the balance of his career manifest a growing emphasis on the need for believers to be "made righteous" by the indwelling Christ. The net effect of this whole procession of ideas was the teaching that God can declare believers to be righteous because they have been effectively made just and right with God through the subjective, mystically cleansing presence of Christ and His lifegiving blood.

It is therefore appropriate that we must soon turn our attention to Waggoner's highly subjective views of justification and sanctification. But before we do that, we need to clarify one other element that needs clarification during this period. And that involves the nature and influence of his developing pantheistic tendencies and how they affected (or infected) not only his views on the atonement but also his increasingly subjective views of justification and sanctification.

WAS WAGGONER A PANTHEIST?

When any researcher begins the attempt to sort out Waggoner's doctrine of God, it does not take long to realize that he or she has entered one of the most elusive and tangled thickets of his multifaceted teachings. What then are the factors that can be readily affirmed and what are those that we should treat with some reserve? Was Waggoner a pantheist, or was he not?[28]

It is abundantly evident that Waggoner was, after 1893, moving "toward a more pronounced blurring of grace and nature."[29] Webster has convincingly traced the basic outlines of this development through the balance of Waggoner's career.[30] Yet Waggoner persistently denied that any of his "blurring" tendencies were pantheistic.[31] And he was, technically speaking, correct in his firm denials that he was a classic pantheist. Kellogg would manifest the same defensive posture when charged with pantheism. Before we proceed any further, it will prove helpful to define "pantheism," and its closely related philosophical worldview, "panentheism."

Pantheism "embraces a variety of different views bound together by a common belief that God and all that exists are identical" and that God is thus "the full totality of all existent things."[32] In some limited differentiation from pantheism, panentheism "denotes the belief that the reality of the world and the whole created order does not exhaust the reality of God. . . . Yet it also holds in common with pantheism that God's presence and active agency permeates the world, actively sustaining it in every part. It expresses the *omnipresence* of God as immanent in the world. Panentheism is still more sharply to be distinguished from *deism*, which tends to exaggerate a one-sided emphasis on divine *transcendence* in such a way as to make God remote from the world and from daily life. Panentheism stresses first and foremost divine *immanence*, but without excluding divine transcendence."[33]

In the light of these helpful definitions and the somewhat precise differentiations offered, it is easier to grasp Waggoner's teaching. Thus it is not surprising that he ostensibly developed his position in opposition to what he perceived to be an understanding of the person of God that was essentially deistic. In other words, God made the worlds, but then simply walked off and left them to operate under their own inherent powers and the autonomous laws of nature. He considered such a concept to be a theistic version of paganism. What he claimed to be seeking to convey was that God's power and life-imparting, personal influence pervaded all of nature as He manifested Himself in His various roles as a creative, sustaining, and redeeming presence.

Furthermore, God (the Creator) was not to be directly identified with nature (what He had created). The latter position he correctly identified as pure pantheism. To teach that God and nature are one and the same leads to idolatry in the sense that creation, understood as god, is then worshipped. He was clearly not guilty of the classic or cruder doctrine of pantheism.[34]

If Waggoner was not a full-blown, classic *pantheist*, then the fairest way to categorize his thought is with the terminology and thought forms of *panentheism*. Ellen White gave a pretty good clue. She did clearly warn Waggoner about entertaining "pantheistic" sentiments. But was she describing classic pantheism, or was it a variety of teaching that only tended in a pantheistic direction? What follows is her most informative statement on the substance of Waggoner's teachings on the immanence of God and one that clearly points to Waggoner's *panentheism* (though she did not use the term itself):

"Had God desired to be represented as dwelling personally in the things of nature—in the flower, the tree, the spear of grass—would not Christ have spoken of this to His disciples? To take the works of God, and represent them to be God, is a fearful misrepresentation. . . . The theory that He is an essence, pervading everything, is one of Satan's most subtle devices."[35] Quite obviously, the key to understanding Waggoner's position was the idea that God was "dwelling personally in the things of nature" and that God is "an essence, pervading everything." Ellen White called the concept "one of Satan's most subtle devices." Is there clear evidence that her observations were justified and that Waggoner's teachings were of the *panentheistic* genre of thought?

After considerable reflection on the allegations of pantheism, Paul Penno, Jr., has provided a helpful summary of Waggoner's doctrine of God during the last years of his public ministry. After quoting Ellen White's previously cited warning to Waggoner, Penno makes the following points:

"Indeed, Waggoner had been incorporating detectable panentheism into his writings. . . . In *The Everlasting Covenant* he wrote: 'Nothing is done merely to represent something else. . . . So in the Lord's Supper we partake of the body of Christ, and not of a mere representation of His body. . . . It is utterly useless to spend time arguing . . . that the priest has not the power to change the bread into the body of Christ; for the Scripture tells us that it is that already' (E. J. Waggoner, *The Everlasting Covenant* [London: International Tract Society, Ltd., 1900], pp. 254, 255)." After the citation from *The Everlasting Covenant*, Penno continues his commentary on this somewhat elusive issue:

"Waggoner was not a pantheist. Pantheism believed God had no personality. Rather God was everything and everything was God. Waggoner was a panentheist. Ellen White said this theory reduced God to an 'essence.' Waggoner believed everything was in God. God was immanently present in all things and yet He was transcendent. This would tend to incorporate Satan and evil into God. Hence Ellen White labeled it spiritualism."[36]

Penno's interpretation does seem to do the most justice to the documentary evidence from both the writings of Waggoner and Ellen White. Very clearly Waggoner did present abundant evidence for his panentheistic views, especially from 1897 onward. What follows will be a summary overview of his unfolding accentuation of the immanence of God as it emerges in his panentheistic expressions.

After some initial intimations during 1894 and 1895,[37] he would break forth at the General Conference session of 1897 with an undeniable emphasis on the idea that God personally pervaded all nature.

In his fourth lecture at the 1897 General Conference session he claimed that "God's power is in everything" and that the gospel is evident in the natural world.[38] Then during his sixth lecture he once more spoke of God's power in humanity, even that Christ was in fallen human beings: "He [fallen man] is brought face to face with the power of God in him, keeping him alive. It is Christ in fallen man, it is Christ in cursed man, it is Christ with the curse on him, it is Christ crucified."[39] But the concept of "power" was then evolving into the "divinity of God": "We see the power and the divinity of God in the trees and grass, and in everything that God has made, and see it clearly, too."[40]

By his seventh lecture, however, what had been subtly evolving finally got quite explicit. Speaking of God's life in the grass, he asked: "But what was that power?—God's own life, His own personal presence there, doing in the grass just what He designed for the grass; it was God that was working in it, both to will and to do of His own good pleasure."[41] The concept of God's "personal presence" Waggoner reaffirmed in his eighth lecture: "The Lord Jesus is in everything that He has made. He upholds all things, because He is in them. He is cohesion even to inanimate nature. It is the personal, powerful presence of God that keeps the mountains together, and the stones from crumbling to pieces; because God is there with His personal power."[42] And such cohesion in inanimate nature identified Christ with light: humans should "simply drink in the light, and that is the life of Christ."[43]

But the whole tendency to blur the natural with the all-pervading supernatural became extremely explicit when he claimed that God and Christ are manifest as a force in all nature: "God Himself is personally present in all His works. He Himself is the energy that is manifest in all creation. God Himself is force, the force that is manifest in all matter."[44]

What proves interesting is the way that Waggoner proceeded quite logically to integrate his panentheistic tendencies with his already clearly manifest, highly subjective and passive views on sanctification: "And how will many do right? By the obedience of One. Well, then, if I am made righteous by His obedience, if I do right by His obedience, where does He obey? In me. What am I doing? Letting Him, submitting to the righteousness of God."[45]

And the ties between his extremely subjective, passive, and mystical views of sanctification were explicitly related to his ideas that Christ is a force that pervades the whole of the natural world: "There is work enough for us, then, to hold still, and let the Lord fill us with His Spirit, and work us. That does not mean laziness; it is passive activity, if you please; it means being just as active as the Lord Himself was; because Christ Himself living in us will be just the same as He was when He was here on the earth.

"Then God will live in us, and will choose for us just the same as in the tree. We do not know anything, but He will think for us."[46] Most certainly McMahon is correct to conclude that here "pantheism, quietism, and perfectionism were all blended."[47] Furthermore, it should come as no great surprise that Waggoner would integrate this galaxy of passive, mystical panentheistic sentiments with his views on the vindication of God. During a sermon on March 6 he laid it out in clear language:

"If anything less than the fullness of God be in us, we cannot witness for Him. God's faithful witnesses, seen in the starry heavens, bear continual testimony to His glory; but they speak no word. So with us. The strongest witness we can bear to the character of God is a life that is consistent with that character. . . . And this life can only be lived through the power of the Spirit of Christ dwelling in us. . . .

"The power of God in us seeks for utterance and expression. It has been too long repressed. The Lord still waits for us. He does not become impatient with us; and bears with us because He has His character at stake. The only way in which He can demonstrate the perfection of His character, and take away His reproach, is in perfecting a people to His praise. He is able to accomplish this in us. Shall we let God have a chance? Shall we let the people know that God is with us, that they may see Him and know Him."[48] Most clearly, in 1897 his mystical views on the atonement, his subjective views on justification, and his panentheistic impulses were all meshing together into a potent mix of quietism and perfectionism. Waggoner was not a man to leave matters hanging about at loose ends—he clearly had the power of a highly integrative thinker.

During the 1899 General Conference session at South Lancaster he would continue the unfolding of his panentheistic sentiments. In his presentations the most evident, even startling, manifestations had to do with the implications of divine immanence for healthful living. In fact, he plainly claimed that if Christ dwells in our sinful flesh in the same manner that He did in His own sinful flesh in Palestine, the life of Christ in us would be lived just as sinlessly and free from disease as He was during the incarnation: "Just as you cannot conceive of Jesus' losing a day's work from sickness, so it ought to be conceivable of Seventh-day Adventists' losing a day's work from sickness. . . . Then if the life of Jesus is manifest in our mortal flesh, we shall be in this world the same as He was."[49] Waggoner was so deeply convicted of the truthfulness of his position that he confessed that in recent months the Lord had taught him "how to live forever" and that he even announced that he expected "to live forever."[50]And Waggoner was not just suggesting eternal life by faith to be granted at the Second Coming, but was clearly claiming that he truly possessed it now, through the indwelling presence of Christ.

Another revealing concept was his teaching that the life of Christ is literally in the food we eat.[51] And then he went on to claim that when Christ spoke of the bread of the Lord's Supper, "This is my body," it was literally true. In a recorded exchange with a person in the audience, Waggoner made his views quite explicit:

"A voice: Is the life of God in the bread?

"E. J. Waggoner: Yes.

"A voice: What is the difference, then, between this and the position taken by the priest?

"E. J. Waggoner: They are diametrically opposite. Christ said, when He took the break, and broke it, 'This is my body'; but the priest says, 'I will take this bread, and make it the body.' The priest denies the truth of God. The Lord's Supper is simply the model meal. . . ."

In the very next paragraph of the published report of this exchange, Waggoner then clears up all ambiguity: "Christ took the piece of bread and said, 'This is my body.' Whoever really recognizes Christ in the bread ought to cut off everything from his table that which is not purely of Christ, and that does not have the pure life of Christ in it." Two paragraphs later he reinforces the matter. When the grain is made into bread the "life is in it still. We do not see the life, but it is there, and it is the life of God. It is His body, and we take His body and get life. . . . If you see in it His body, then in every meal to which we sit down, we see the body of Christ."[52]

Waggoner's view of the Lord's Supper and the eating of bread was not just a passing fad. Later he would repeat the same literalistic and panentheistic views in *The Everlasting Covenant.* He would once more state that the Papacy's claim to turn the bread into the body of Christ was erroneous, as the bread was already the body of Christ.[53]

But it was not just bread that Waggoner referred to in order to express his highly literalistic and mystically driven panentheism. He also invoked the water and the light that we use every day for seeing, drinking, and washing: "We have a drink of water here—living water. Where does it come from? The throne of God, where Jesus Christ, the Lamb slain, is. It flows from His heart. It is the blood of Christ, which cleanses from all sin. The blood of Christ is a real thing.

"That water which flows from the throne of God is His life; and His life is the light. 'If we walk in the light, as he is in the light, we have fellowship one with another; and the blood of the [Son of God] cleanseth us from all sin.' Is that a real thing? Or is it only a figurative expression—a mere form of words? Can we actually bathe in the blood of Christ, and live by it? Yes; for what is the blood? It is the life. The life is in the blood. By whatever means Christ conveys the life to us, that is the blood, the life. . . . Water is life, and it has life-giving powers."[54]

But Waggoner was applying these matters not just to the Lord's Supper or to one's personal devotional time. He also claimed that such views had even transformed his normal drinking and bathing habits into deeply spiritual experiences: "O, I delight in drinking water, as I never have before; I delight in bathing. . . . A man may get righteousness in bathing, when he knows where the water comes from, and recognizes the source. . . . Just bathe in the word. That is not figurative, that is not sentimental; God wants His people to live now as seeing the Invisible, so that they will walk in the sight of the river of God, and drink from the throne of God, and all they do will be eating and drinking in His presence. . . .

"Let us drink in the water every day. Then we are living in the presence of God."[55]

What is stunning, yet fascinating, is that no one present seemed troubled by all of such outrageous panentheistic literalism. But thankfully one significant manifestation of concern did emerge—and that came from Ellen White in faraway Australia, who wrote a letter of warning to the delegates regarding subtle doctrines about God and nature.[56]

The 1901 General Conference session in Battle Creek was the next major public venue at which Waggoner continued to unfold his panentheism. As a speaker during it he reiterated his conviction that Christ's life is immanent throughout the creation, including the air, food, water, and the light.[57] Once again he denied that he was a pantheist. But that belied his profoundly pervasive panentheism. One more venue from the late years of the 1890s and the early years of the 1900s would give clear witness to these concepts. And this was the publication of *The Glad Tidings.* The bulk of the chapters had appeared earlier as a series of articles in the *Signs of the Times* from November 24, 1898, to May 17, 1899. And this well-known publication also reflected the other panentheistic currents in his thought from these years. What follows is a sampling of these sentiments:[58]

To believe "on His name [Christ] means simply to believe that He dwells personally in every man—in all flesh. We do not make it so by believing it; it is so, whether we believe it or not; we simply accept the fact, which all nature reveals to us."[59] "On the cross Christ bore the crown of thorns. Therefore, all the curse, every trace of it, is borne by Christ—by Christ crucified. Wherever, therefore, we see any curse, . . . whether we see it or not, there is the cross of Christ."[60]

Clearly, all of these panentheistic expressions in Waggoner's unfolding theology from the mid-1890s onward were the ultimate, stark manifestations of his unrelenting exposition of the immanent Christ. Therefore, a key question presents itself for further reflection: Were these panentheistic tendencies the natural outgrowth of the larger outlines of his subjective emphases, including his views on effective justification through the immanent, indwelling Christ? Or were they less sinister, being merely a parasite not inherent in his teachings on righteousness by faith?[61]

It seems quite apparent that the panentheistic attributes represent a logical outgrowth within the context of his long-developing, strongly subjective teachings on personal salvation. If one is going to feature a strong doctrine of an immanent Christ who literally inhabits the souls of those He is seeking to "make righteous," pantheistic tendencies are a natural, though not necessarily inevitable, temptation.

Now, as to whether Waggoner was his own source for the evident pantheistic flavored views or whether Kellogg or something else deeply influenced him, we will probably never know for sure.[62] But the tendencies were abundantly apparent and readily resonant with the rest of his highly subjective emphases undergirded by his vision of the immanent Christ dwelling in the believer.

The final issue raised by Waggoner's panentheism is whether it was a factor contributing to the "spiritualistic" fantasies that led him into "a heavenly 'free-loveism.'"[63] Paul Penno, Jr., has suggested a profound linkage (might we say "affinity"?) between his panentheism and the immorality that Ellen White warned him about.[64] Penno might be right, but we will tackle the question of the moral implications of Waggoner's immanent views of God in the final two chapters that more directly deal with

Waggoner's doctrine of "spiritual affinities" (the obvious pretext for his "free-lovism").

Now with Waggoner's views on the atonement and panentheism in place, we are much better prepared to review and assess his unfolding views on justification and sanctification by faith.

JUSTIFICATION AND SANCTIFICATION BY FAITH

The reader will recall that in chapter 3 we presented an extended discussion of Waggoner's views on justification. While much debate has raged on the exact nature of his views, especially his often-repeated claim that justification "makes" sinners "righteous," we concluded that he did have the essential core of the doctrine of justification by faith alone in the imputed merits of Christ.

In the light of his pre-1888 understanding of the penalty/substitution/satisfaction models or theories of the atonement, it seems clear that Waggoner used concepts that presented justification as declaring, reckoning, or accounting a person as just because of the legal substitution of the perfect life and atoning merits of Christ's death. Such merits were then put in place of the sinner's failures and justly deserved death. In other words, Christ vicariously substituted His righteousness in place of the sinner's failures, and the result is that the penitent believer can be reckoned or declared forgiven and just for Christ's sake.

Yet as Waggoner's thought unfolded during the years 1892 and 1893 he made a noticeable shift to the concept that being "made righteous" involved more than the inevitable *fruit* of the genuine *root* of a "faith that works." But before we directly address the heart of Waggoner's fully developed thinking on subjective justification, we need to give one last review of the developments in Waggoner's thought regarding the issue of universal legal justification.

UNIVERSAL LEGAL JUSTIFICATION

According to the advocates of this theme, Waggoner set forth the strongest evidence for this teaching during the middle and latter parts of the 1890s. Once more we need to review briefly the issue. The claim for Waggoner is that he taught that the entire human race has been universally, legally justified by Christ through the "provisions" of the atonement.

Thus while all are justified and such justification has some sort of saving efficacy, it will not become finally effectual unless individual believers embrace their status of legal justification through what proponents call experiential justification by faith.

As was pointed out in chapters 3 and 8, it is not at all clear how universal legal justification justifies the believer beyond providing the temporary and needed shelter of probationary time so that the legally justified can become experientially justified. We have suggested that all who believe in some sort of graced free will[65] (broadly identified as Arminianism) fully agree with the idea that the atoning work of Christ does grant all humanity a time of probation. But beyond this we have little evidence that Waggoner intended to teach that all have received any additional benefits that precede the essential experience of a heart embrace of justifying grace through faith.

Thus whatever benefits humanity gained through this legal or forensic justification were not conclusively and finally effective without experiential justification.

Therefore little or no difference exists between such an alleged sequence and the basic Arminian/Wesleyan teaching on free grace. And for this reason we have characterized the whole debate as a classic "strife about words" that reveals no truly substantive disagreement. So what were the developments during this period?

The leading advocates of universal justification claim that the following published statements present the strongest evidence for their interpretation of Waggoner. After presenting each, we will offer some assessments and then explore other interesting developments related to such a concept in Waggoner's thought.

The first statement (in October 1894) involves an exposition of Romans 5:15-18. The reader will recall that theologians have considered this biblical passage as the prime canonical basis for universal legal justification. And we do find some semblance of evidence in Waggoner's exposition that did amount to some such an interpretation of Romans 5: "There is no exception here. As the condemnation came upon all, so the *justification comes upon all.* Christ has tasted death for every man. He has given Himself for all. Nay, he has given Himself *to every man.* The free gift has *come upon all.*"

On the face of it, the case seems quite convincing. Especially the expressions "justification comes upon all" and "to every man" seem to point to something that is universally placed in the hands or laps of "all." But that is not the full story. More is yet to come.

While the "gift of righteousness and life in Christ has come *to every man on earth,*" it is also true that "there is not the slightest reason why every man that has ever lived should not be saved unto eternal life, except that they would not have it." Thus salvation "unto eternal life" is conditional upon believers actually having it. So there is an essential, saving condition that must be experienced if the alleged universal, legal bestowment is to prove effective for the receipt of "eternal life."

Thus far, the universal justification interpreters are consistent, recognizing that whatever God gives or offers is ultimately effectual only if the believer claims it by faith. But Waggoner is not through with his exposition of the conditional qualification of salvation to "eternal life." He promptly goes on to say that "so many *spurn the gift offered so freely*" and that "the free gift comes upon all, but all will not accept it, and therefore all are not made righteous by it."[66]

The reader should carefully note the expressions "spurn the gift offered so freely." The "to every man" and the coming "upon all" means to receive an "offer" that can be "spurned." This definitely qualifies the seemingly unconditional force of the words that appeared to suggest the "free gift" has been placed "upon all" or given "to every man." A significant difference exists between an "offer" that can be "spurned" and something that is actually and legally bestowed into the hands or laps (as it were) of "every man" on earth. Thus the case is not nearly as self-evident as the universal legal interpreters of Waggoner and Romans 5 claim it to be.

Once more, in November of 1895, Waggoner writes in a manner quite similar to the just-cited article of 1894: "Jesus is the light of the world; so He is the true light, 'which lighteth every man that cometh into the world.' Or, as some render it, In coming into the world, He lights every man. The point is that all do have the light. . . . That life-giving light has shone upon all, and is still shining." And once more he cites the key Romans passage: " 'By the righteousness of One the free gift came upon all men unto justification of life.' Rom. 5:18. God's love embraces all the world, and every man in it. To all He has given 'His unspeakable gift.'

What a sad awakening it will be at last when men realize what was within their grasp, and what they let go."[67]

While his 1895 exposition has a bit more force to it in support of the argument of Waggoner's admirers, it is also not compelling. It is one thing to have light shining upon someone and sense that God's love is embracing all the world, but quite another to be actually justified. Furthermore, the expression "what was within their grasp" does not necessarily mean to actually have something for sure—it can also mean to be in a position to actually be able to receive what the light has illuminated. In other words, the tragedy is that what was in the clear realm of possibility was "let go." To reject light is to "let go" the offer of a lifetime. Thus it seems more natural to see Paul's "justification of life" to be the offer of salvation that has been spotlighted as something that is "within the grasp" of the truly responsive believer, but is also an opportunity that one can "let go" of or neglect.

In October of 1898 Waggoner again cited the verse from Romans: "The free gift comes upon all men unto justification of life, but many reject the gift. It is evident, then, that God cannot be charged with unrighteousness. If men will not take what he freely gives, He is clear . . . and the fact that many utterly refuse His loving mercy, does not in the least diminish it."[68] Again we can easily understand the "free gift" as coming upon all men in the sense that an offer is being made, not that something is actually, legally bestowed. And thus human beings can reject or refuse the offer of "justification of life." This is simply the more natural and normal way to interpret Waggoner's language.

Again, let's assume, for the sake of further illustration, the interpretation that the universal legal justification advocates place on Waggoner's expositions. Even if there is some sort of new legal standing, beyond the temporary forgiveness that allows for probationary time, the actual placing of a gift in someone's hands is no guarantee that the person will appreciate or genuinely receive it. In chapter 8 we gave the illustration of the way that many people receive well-meant, but not really needed or appreciated, gifts.

But do we find any further evidence for the concept? And the answer is that, in fact, there is some rather convincing evidence for universal legal justification. But it seems to show up in some interesting yet disconcerting settings. Consider the following.

At the 1897 General Conference session, Waggoner presented a series on the New Testament book of Hebrews. The following concepts are quite revealing: "The Word is nigh thee, even in thy mouth and in thy heart—in thy flesh; confess this fact, and 'thou shalt be saved.' This teaches the presence of Christ in every soul, waiting for recognition, in order that he may save.

"'Then you would make no difference between a sinner and a Christian?' Oh, yes, indeed; all the difference in the world, or, rather, all the difference between the world and heaven. Christ has come in the flesh—that is, in all mankind, for man is flesh (Gen. 7:3)—but while he dwells in the sinner without recognition, and is held down in unrighteousness (Rom. 1:15), in the Christian He dwells "*by faith*." Eph. 3:19."[69] Clearly he teaches the "presence of Christ in every soul," not just standing by offering, but actually in the soul. But this concept would become even more explicit as the years after 1897 unfolded.

In Waggoner's series on Galatians (eventually released as *The Glad Tidings*) that he published in both North America and England in the latter part of the 1890s, we find the following (January 1899): "The difference, then, between the sinner and the Christian is this: that, whereas Christ is crucified and risen in every man, in the sinner He is there unrecognized and ignored, while in the Christian He dwells there by faith.

"Christ is crucified in the sinner, for wherever there is sin and the curse, there is Christ bearing it. . . . Faith in the eternal power and divinity of God, that are seen in all the things He has made,[70] will enable anyone to grasp this mystery."[71] In a subsequent article (March 1899) in the same series, Waggoner elaborates the issue of who are among God's children:

"What a blessed thing it is that God counts even the ungodly, those who are in the bondage of sin, as His children! Wandering, prodigal sons, but still children. God has made all men 'accepted in the Beloved.' This probationary life is given us for the purpose of giving us a chance to acknowledge Him as Father, and to become sons indeed."[72]

In these three statements we encounter unmistakable evidence that Waggoner definitely taught that Christ was "crucified and risen in every man" and that He is "bearing" their "sin" and that even the "ungodly" are counted as "His children" and are "accepted in the Beloved." This is far beyond an "offer" to them or the possibility of "spurning." And while it is not the same status as those who "acknowledge Him as Father, and . . . become sons indeed," they are still "His children" and are "accepted in the Beloved" (justified). So the question then arises: Why the change in Waggoner's thought?

The answer is actually quite simple. As was demonstrated in the previous section of this chapter, beginning in 1894 and then flooding forth like a tidal rush of muddy water from 1897 and onward, Waggoner clearly evidenced pantheistic tendencies. In this seemingly vibrant worldview the "eternal power and divinity of God" are "seen in all the things He has made." Such a worldview, however, contained subtle theological darkness that would ultimately lead Waggoner into the sloughs of deadly deception.

But with reference to our present issue, the rationale is quite simple: if the "eternal power and divinity of God" are "in all the things He has made," then it is one easy, logical step to conclude that He dwells in the "ungodly" and thus view them as "accepted in the Beloved."

Is there a doctrine of universal legal justification for the ungodly? Yes, there clearly is, and it appears to be the offspring of the pagan philosophy of pantheism. Thus it is quite clear that these darkening currents of pantheistic-related ideas were clouding and confusing the clarity of Waggoner's views on salvation by faith.

What then are we to make of this teaching? While we could possibly interpret the prepantheistic Waggoner as teaching universal legal justification, the evidence is not compelling that he actually did. Furthermore, we need to reiterate that the alleged doctrine can be largely classified as a "strife about words." But aside from its clear emergence in the setting of Waggoner's later pantheisitic distortions, the doctrine has one other interesting downside. Here is the problem as I see it.

The interpreters of Waggoner who have touted this doctrine as somehow the most wonderful discovery in the history of the doctrine of salvation by faith have unwittingly employed his allegedly glorious discovery to legitimate Waggoner's numerous other theological directions. In other words, he has come up with this great discovery, and the net effect is to lead many to fail to realize the terrible directions that Waggoner's overall theology was moving toward after 1889 and especially after 1893. I know that this is not what is intended, but it is the unwitting net effect.

So what is the sum of the matter? It is simply a doctrine that we can do without. The positive thrust regarding the granting of temporary forgiveness, in the interest of making room for a time of probation (in which sin-confused sinners can weigh their options in view of the fact of God's gracious calling and convicting initiatives), has already been laid out by the vast majority of Arminian Christians, including John Wesley and the pre-1888 Ellen G. White. And while Waggoner did make some truly significant contributions to theological clarity, they all were essentially in place by 1888, not afterward. In fact, what comes later (especially after 1892) is, on balance, a body of theology that descends into theological confusion and error in just about every major issue he sought to highlight. And the alleged universal legal justification clearly emerges only when enveloped in the mists of panentheism.

With this issue in perspective, it is now appropriate that we turn our attention to Waggoner's truly definitive doctrine of justification by faith that seemed to develop so naturally out of his views on the atonement and his increasingly panentheistic worldview.

JUSTIFICATION GOES SUBJECTIVE

During the years 1892 and 1893 Waggoner seemed to have evolved to an understanding of justification in which the faith that works subjectively produces a righteousness that makes the believer actually and inherently just. Thus the just demands of God's righteousness are met through the victorious, obedient lives of the faithful believers. And Waggoner placed the whole process in the context of an increasing accent on the work of the indwelling Christ.

When he put his emerging "mystical" views of the atonement into the context of the subjective theme of the internal and immanent Christ who abides in the heart of any repentant soul, the stage was set for a full-blown doctrine of "effective justification." Furthermore, this version of "effective justification" greatly reflects the position of the Roman Catholic Council of Trent and the subjective justification views of the post-Reformation Lutheran scholar Andreas Osiander.[73] While the views expressed in these similar sixteenth-century teachings took some subtly different routes, they both essentially ended up at the same place: the subjectively accomplished, or infused righteousness of Christ effectively makes the believer righteous so that the believer is justified by the fruits of a transforming, internal work of grace. To put it simply, the *fruit* of sanctification forms the *root* basis for God's act of justification, not vice versa.

While Waggoner's thought during the 1892-1916 period did have some seeming glimmers of forensic imputation from time to time, we can best understand such expressions as the results of the work of the immanent, indwelling Christ via the ministration of His shed blood. This mystical communication of blood effectively absorbs the guilt of sin and delivers believers from the power of sinful impulses. As a result the working of the immanent, internally dwelling Christ declares the believer just and righteous for His sake.

We take this position because it best reflects the weight of evidence in Waggoner's unfolding theology (especially after 1893). Furthermore, two other factors augment the above interpretive position: (1) we find in his writings of this period few, if any, unequivocally clear statements of objective, forensic justification by faith alone in the legally reckoned righteousness of Christ (mediated from the heavenly sanctuary). But not only do we have a lack of clear positive teaching, there are also (2) numerous statements in his published writings that directly and pointedly deny that Christ accounts or reckons sinners to be righteous in any objective, legal sense.

When any interested reader moves methodically through the writings of Waggoner during the 1892-1903 period, he or she is struck with the predominance of this sort of subjective, mystically communicated righteousness. We find page after page of this type of emphasis. If the writer started listing representative samples from each year, it would fill many pages. The concept simply saturates Waggoner's thought.

INTERPRETIVE PRINCIPLES

Furthermore, Waggoner undergirded the whole set of mystical concepts by a definite approach to the interpretation of certain key passages from the New Testament. Thus, before we present some representative examples of Waggoner's views on justification during this period, it will prove helpful to lay out how his key scriptural evidence and his hermeneutics (principles of interpretation) produced his highly subjective teaching on the indwelling, justifying presence of the redeeming Christ.

When one reviews Waggoner's scriptural support and the way he interpreted his key proof texts during this period, we encounter a few passages that he repeats so often that their use becomes quite predictable. The text he invoked most often was Galatians 2:20. Then come 2 Corinthians 5:21 and Ephesians 3:14-19 (to name the three most often cited). Let's begin with Galatians 2:20 as his key supporting text:

"I have been crucified with Christ; it is no longer I who live, but Christ lives in me; and the life which I now live in the flesh I live by faith in the Son of God, who loved me and gave Himself for me" (NKJV). Waggoner interpreted such passages quite literally. Thus he would say that Christ, through the communion of the Holy Spirit, literally "lives in me"—that is, in the hearts and minds of responsive believers. And the indwelling Christ does His work of making righteous—that is to say, He justifies through His internal accomplishments of righteousness that then get reckoned as belonging to the believers.

We find the same basic interpretive rationale applied to Ephesians 3:14-19 and 2 Corinthians 5:21: "For he hath made him to be sin for us, who knew no sin; that we might be made the righteousness of God in him" (KJV). Thus, since Christ was literally made sinful in nature (though He never sinned by thought or act), the believer is then literally made righteous in character.

ANALYSIS OF INTERPRETIVE PRINCIPLES

What should we make of this mode of interpretation? A little further reflection will reveal that what Waggoner failed to realize was a very important interpretive principle—that we must take the verbal and thematic context of these passages into account!

Milton Hook has given a helpful analysis of Ellet's approach to interpretation: "Waggoner exercised a high degree of literalism in his articles. He wrote, 'God does have a tangible structure in heaven for His occupancy. . . . The ten commandments literally form the basis, or foundation, of the throne of God.' This same literalism was carried over into expressions such as 'Christ in us.' His understanding was tantamount to a personal entrance of Christ, by the Holy Spirit, into a Christian's being, rather than the phrase 'Christ in us' signifying the motivational power of love as the fruitage of justification (Eph. 3:14-21). He did not recognize that the locution 'Christ in us' is obviously, by context, a figure of speech (Gal. 2:20; 4:19)."[74]

Not only did Waggoner fail to give proper consideration to the context of such important figures of speech, it also never seemed to enter his mind what effect it would have if one brought the same assumed literalism to bear on other, closely related expressions—such as "raised us up together, and made us sit together in the heavenly places in Christ Jesus" (Eph. 2:6, NKJV). Does anyone want to argue that true believers are literally swept away to heaven at conversion in order to be seated next to Christ as a manifestation of their intimate faith relationship to Jesus?

So here we have the literalistic interpretive keys that undergirded Waggoner's highly subjective, effective, and immanent view of the Christ who justifies. Thus he would continue his arguments with the further thought that Christ does His work by taking control of the yielded will, and with the will under His effectual control, He then proceeds with His work of sowing His obedience into the characters of the indwelt believers.

WAGGONER'S VERSION OF AUTOMATIC, ROBOTIC OBEDIENCE

But the whole concept has still another interesting wrinkle to it: Waggoner portrayed the process of subjective transformation as an automatic, virtually puppetlike or robotic accomplishment in the believer. While he did not see this transformation as instantaneous, he regarded it as progressive. As the immature believer more and more yields the will to Christ and grows in grace, the mystically present Jesus was understood to be constantly, through the life-giving power of His shed blood, absorbing the guilt of the continually advancing, spiritually growing individual.

Furthermore, the process reveals almost no hint of Christ ministering the merits of His righteousness to the account of the believers in the heavenly sanctuary as an objective advocate before the Father. Rather Waggoner conceived everything as dynamically taking place in the heart of the passively responsive and yielding believer. For Ellet, the only function of Christ's high priestly intercession was to dispatch the Holy Spirit to dwell in the believer. All the rest was accomplished in the subjective temple of the converted human soul.

THE HEALING NARRATIVES OF JESUS AND JUSTIFICATION

But Waggoner did not restrict his biblical rationale to Pauline passages. He would also supplement (in May of 1894) the "Christ in you" or "in Christ" passages with a very literalistic understanding of Jesus' physical healings, especially those accompanied by His assurance that the sins of those who had been healed were forgiven.

His favorite Gospel story was the healing of the woman with the issue of blood: "Here we have something that our mind can lay hold of, and our sense can appreciate. A real thing was done. Something real went from Jesus into the woman. It was not imagination; it was not a figure of speech." And what did Jesus communicate to the woman? It was "the righteous life of Christ." Waggoner did not just understand the story as being *illustrative* of the healing power of justification; he put it forward as an actual *portrayal* of it:

"For the words of Jesus to that poor woman show that she was healed in the same way and by the same means by which we are justified and have peace with God. He said unto her, 'Daughter, be of good comfort: thy faith hath made thee whole; go in peace.' Luke 8:48. If we should apply the word of the Apostle Paul to her particular experience, we might read, 'Therefore being made whole in body by faith, she had peace with God through our Lord Jesus Christ.'[75] Perhaps this may enable someone to grasp more fully the reality of the righteousness which comes by faith of Jesus Christ. Nothing is said about forgiveness of sins in this instance, but we may be sure from other instances that such faith as the poor woman had brought healing of soul as well as the body."

But Waggoner was not through with his exposition of justification. He became even more explicit in his views:

"Just as something real, although invisible, went from Jesus into the person of the diseased woman, making her perfectly well and strong, even so we are to know that something real comes from Christ into the person of the repentant sinner, making him whole, and free from sin. That something is nothing less than the actual life of Christ." While his position is quite clear, Waggoner still had more to say! The mystical affirmations and imputational denials became even more explicit:

"The forgiveness of sins is too often thought to be illustrated by the payment of a poor man's debt by a rich friend. If a rich man pays the debt of a poor man, then the shopkeeper credits the poor man with the sum, and the record on the books shows that the debt is canceled. Of course the poor man is benefited, but he does not actually receive anything that will keep him in the future. But it is different when God for Christ's sake forgives sin. . . .

"His life is given to be manifest in our mortal flesh. 2 Cor. 4:11. Just as the sap flows through the vine to the farthest branches, and just as the life of Christ went into the poor, diseased woman, to make her perfectly well, so the sinless, endless, inexhaustible life of Christ flows into those who have faith in Him, to cleanse them from sin, and to make them walk in newness of life."

But now comes the most stupendous denial of all: "He fulfilled the righteousness of the law. Matt. 5:17. That is the fullness, the perfection of the law, appeared in His life. And it is by this life that we are saved. *It is not that we are accounted righteous because Jesus of Nazareth was righteous eighteen hundred years ago, but because 'he ever liveth,' 'the same yesterday, and to day, and for ever,' to save, by the power of His endless life, all that come to Him.*"[76]

Thus literal physical healing actually portrays subjective spiritual healing through the effective deliverance of the sinner from the guilt and power of sin. And one can readily see how Waggoner, through his emphasis on the therapeutic stories of the Gospels, complemented and undergirded his views on justification with his mystical views of the death of Christ. Thus the shed blood contains life that can actually purge away the guilt and the power of sin.

Now, with the basic outlines of his understanding of effective justification before us, powerfully evidenced in his interpretation of the healing of the woman cursed with hemorrhaging, we are now prepared to consider a few representative examples of his interpretations of the Pauline writings in which he also prominently displayed his subjective, effective view of justification. Once more the reader needs to realize that we could cite scores of examples. We have chosen the following as the most representative.

SAMPLES OF EFFECTIVE, SUBJECTIVE INTERPRETATION

Appropriately enough, the first example came quite early (October 1892) in the British years. After citing Romans 5:1, Waggoner asked:

"What does this mean? What is it to be justified?" He then proceeded to point out that many assume that it is "a sort of halfway house to perfect favor with God" while others regard it as "a substitute for real righteousness. They think that the idea of justification by faith is that if one will only believe what the Bible says, he is to be counted as righteous when he is not. All this is a great mistake." Next he followed up with his usual definition of justification as "making just" or "to be righteous. Therefore since the just man is the one who does the law, it follows that to justify a man, that is, to make him just, is to make him a doer of the law. Being justified by faith, then, is simply being made a doer of the law by faith."

In order to leave no doubt as to his meaning, he proceeded to claim that justification "does not mean that Christ's righteousness which He did eighteen hundred years ago is laid up for the sinner, to be simply credited to his account, but it means that His present, active righteousness is given to that man." And how does the believer receive such righteousness? "Christ comes to live in that man who believes, for he dwells in the heart by faith. So the man who was a sinner is transformed into a new man, having the very righteousness of God."

In the very next paragraph he claims that "there can be no higher state than that of justification. It does everything that God can do for a man short of making him immortal, which is done only at the resurrection."

Thus in one fell swoop he argued that justification completely encompasses sanctification and perfection of character, not just the settling of legal accounts. And to make the point unmistakably clear that justification is the result of the working of the indwelling Christ, Waggoner concluded that the "one who obeys is the Lord Jesus Christ, and His obedience is done in the heart of everyone who believes. And as it is by His obedience alone that men are made doers of the law, so to Him shall be the glory forever and ever."[77]

This important article, along with the previous comments on the healing of the hemorrhaging woman, were the most comprehensive statements that Waggoner would ever offer on the subject of effective justification. But he presented the concept frequently, even sometimes apparently tinged with his almost universalistic, panentheistic view that Christ dwells in even sinners. Consider the following from February of 1898:

"To believe that He [Christ] is the Son of God means to believe that He is come in the flesh, in human flesh, in our flesh, for His name is 'God with us'; so to believe on His name means simply to believe that He dwells personally in every man—in all flesh. We do not make it so by believing it; it is so, whether we believe it or not; we simply accept the fact, which all nature reveals to us." Here he came extremely close to suggesting that Christ dwells even in unbelievers and that His indwelling will be redemptively efficacious (effective), even if unbelievers will not believe.

But he then went on to claim that the indwelling Christ is the justifier: "It follows then as a matter of course that, believing in Christ, we are justified by the faith of Christ, since we have Him personally dwelling in us, exercising His own faith. All power in heaven and earth is in His hands, and, recognizing this, we simply allow Him to exercise His own power in His own way. . . . The Gospel is no dead thing, no abstract doctrine, no 'works done in righteousness, which we did ourselves' (Titus 3:5, RV), but a personal acceptance of the personal Christ, who alone has power to work salvation. Christ as a living Savior, always and everywhere present, always active and mighty to save."[78]

Possibly the best statement that Waggoner made that appears the most to speak of an objective justification came in 1899. Yet even it was consistent with his often-repeated view that justification makes the believer righteous (and, seemingly, accomplished almost instantaneously):

"Men are saved only by the righteousness of God in Jesus Christ. It is not abstract righteousness, but the righteousness of Christ's real life 'unto all and upon all them that believe: for there is no difference' (Rom. 3:22), that saves us. The instant any man, however sinful he may be, believes on the Lord Jesus, and confesses Him, he is counted righteous. God declares him righteous, and that makes him righteous. If he should die that very hour, as was the case with the thief on the cross, he would be saved, and would appear in heaven as though he had never sinned. Thousands will appear in the kingdom of God without fault, who never in their lifetime knew all the commandments of God, nor all that is involved in the faith of Jesus. Consequently not all the righteousness of the law has been exhibited in their lives. They have unconsciously been living in violation of some precepts of the law, but from all these secret, hidden faults they have been cleansed."[79]

While these words sound highly imputational ("counted" and "declared righteous"), we must point out that the person whom "God declares . . . righteous" is someone whom His declaration "makes . . . righteous." Furthermore, such a believer has been "cleansed." The effective note stands out, even here in a statement that at first glance seems imputational.

One last exhibit (from May 1903) should suffice: "'By the obedience of one shall many be made righteous.' Rom. 5:19. Notice that it is not simply that by the obedience of One we are accounted righteous, but that it is by Christ's obedience that we are actually *made righteous*. His obedience is not a substitute for our disobedience, but it is actually our righteousness. Oneness with Christ is the Christian standard. . . . He set the example when He was on earth, and now He comes to walk over the same road in us."[80]

Clearly Waggoner conceived of justification by faith as "effectively" accomplished through the indwelling Christ. And it is Christ who transforms the character of the believer so that it is made righteous enough to be declared the means of justification via the subjectively produced righteousness of Christ. Furthermore, we find him consistently downgrading any elements of accounting or reckoning, which he caricatured as "abstract" righteousness.

While there certainly exists a false and "abstract" notion of justification by faith alone, there is also a version of it that is the real thing. Waggoner just never seemed to be able to grasp the powerful biblical notion of effective, forensic justification (received by a faith) that truly and objectively declares the believer to be just for Christ's sake, based on objective accounting of what He had accomplished historically 2,000 years ago.

SANCTIFICATION

In the light of his highly subjective teaching on justification, what then was Waggoner's understanding of sanctification? It is abundantly evident that sanctification has "effectively" been assumed under his transformative view of justification. Thus he has not just blurred the distinguishing features between justification and sanctification—he has almost totally obliterated them.

Now, could it be that Waggoner was simply trying to say that a faith that saves is a faith that works? Quite possibly the key point to be made in support of the interpretation laid out in the preceding paragraphs is that his understanding involved a powerfully subjective manifestation of the immanent Christ who effectively justifies. And it was part and parcel of Waggoner's entire theological trajectory during this decisive period.

To what end does all of this subjectivity tend? The ultimate goal seems to be the vindication of God by a final generation of saints. But before we ponder Waggoner's thinking on divine exoneration, we need to trace the unfolding of his teachings on the earthly sanctuary.

THE LITERAL OLD TESTAMENT SANCTUARY: A "WITNESS" TO "UNBELIEF"?

One other revealing manifestation of Waggoner's pervasive subjective emphases during his British years had to do with the construction of the desert tabernacle. He explicitly taught (in May 1901) that if the people of Israel had received God's ideal of Christ dwelling by faith in every person, there would have been no need for a literal, earthly sanctuary for Him to dwell in:

"Search the Scriptures through and through, and you will find that the intelligently believing Jews understood from the first that the tabernacle was only an object lesson, made necessary on account of the unbelief of the people. It was the 'tabernacle of witness,' but its witness was not that which is effectual among the nations, to bring the end. It was a witness against the Jewish people, rather than to the world, testifying to the fact that their unbelief shut God out of their hearts. Those who believe the Lord receive Him; but Israel did not believe. Yet God did not cast them off, nor become discouraged with them, but said, 'Let them make me a sanctuary; that I may dwell among them.' Ex. 25:8. They would not allow Him to dwell in their hearts by faith, so He would in a special manner manifest His presence nearby . . ."

The ultimate thrust of his argument comes four paragraphs later:

"The life of Christ is being seen as never before as the efficient power to cleanse body as well as soul, so that a sinless, healthy people—a whole people, a holy people—are being prepared as a sign to the world. Soon sin will be eradicated from the universe. That glorious end will be attained as soon as every soul on earth has made his final decision as to whether or not he will consent to be filled with the divine life."[81]

Waggoner felt so strongly about the issue that he even deemed it important to seek to communicate the concept to the "little ones" among his readership (in September 1901):

"Do you think that this was the Lord's own choice—to dwell in a tent separate from the people, though among them? No, for He tells us plainly what the house is that He has chosen: 'Know ye not that ye are the temple of God, and that the Spirit of God dwelleth in you . . . ?' Yes, we are His dwelling place, for He fills all things. How large, then, is the house of God? It is as large as the universe—a living, growing temple. . . . Thus we dwell in God, who is 'our dwelling place,' in whom 'we live, and move, and have our being,' and He dwells in us, filling us with His universal Spirit of life."[82]

Yet Waggoner's most graphic expression of his teaching against the literal tabernacle was still to come (in February of 1902): "There was and is a perception of truth that is not seen by all Christians. 'When Israel went out of Egypt, the house of Jacob from a people of strange language; Judah was his sanctuary, and Israel his dominion.' Ps. 114:1, 2. Not until they lost their faith and zeal did they have to build a house of dead material. . . . It is living temples, more than dead ones, that God's cause wants now. Who will supply them?"[83]

It is beyond the scope of this chapter to critique his interesting interpretation. But suffice it to say that what we have here is just one more example of his powerful emphasis on the indwelling Christ, the immanent one who is to be so manifested in the individual souls of the people of God that they no longer need houses of worship. In fact, even to have a literal tabernacle of "dead material" erected is a witness to the "lost" "faith and zeal" of Israel. This whole line of thought has persistently and obviously emerged in every single phase of Waggoner's biblical and theological expositions from the early 1890s and into the year 1903.

VINDICATION OF GOD BY LAST-DAY SAINTS

While this theme received little, if any, expression in the years before 1890, it would receive increasing attention as the 1890s and the early years of the twentieth century unfolded. We have already, in the previous chapter, noted some instances of Waggoner's expositions of his theme during the General Conference sessions of 1897, 1899, and 1901.[84] What follows is a review of Waggoner's advancing thought on it from 1890 onward.

He began (in August of 1890) his exposition of the theme with some quite sound, straightforward observations that clearly proclaimed that the major reason the Bible teaches that there will be a judgment according to works is that God's fairness in judging has been called into question. So very "evidently" in the "judgment God's righteousness will be made manifest" and it will "appear that he is indeed true and that everything opposed to him is a lie. Thus God will be clear when he judges" (in other words, He will be vindicated). And therefore "God condescends in all His ways to submit them to the judgment of the people, and thus He educates their sense of right and wrong," even including the "wicked," who "will thus acknowledge God's justice."[85]

Probably no Seventh-day Adventist who believes the basic outlines of Ellen White's expositions of the great controversy theme would take any issue with Waggoner's sound teaching on the reasons for a judgment. And while Waggoner would then go on in a subsequent article (in December 1893) to suggest how important the witness of the changed lives of the believers will be when displayed in the great judgment,[86] he also made some interesting statements to the effect that God does not really need any human witnesses to vindicate Himself against the charges of the devil that obedience is impossible. In later articles he made this point unmistakably clear:

"Men have nothing to do with giving Christ His kingdom. All they are called upon to do is to yield themselves to the Holy Spirit, that they may be fashioned into a fit subject for the kingdom which the Lord God will give unto them."[87] But the next two pieces of commentary are even more explicit:

"What if all the professed Christians in a province apostatized, and his work seemed to have been entirely in vain? 'Nevertheless the foundation of God standeth sure.' The truth is no more true because many men, and even great men, believe it; and it is no less true because many reject it. Jesus was just as much the Son of God when all forsook Him and fled as He was when the multitude followed Him, shouting, 'Blessed be the King that cometh in the name of the Lord.' "[88] "The gospel does not derive its character from the character of men who profess it. It comes from God. Men may live ungodly lives, but that does not disprove the Bible. On the contrary, it makes the truth the more vivid by the contrast. Men may deny the faith; they may apostatize and say that it is all a sham; but that does not shake the gospel any more than it would make the fortress of Gibraltar fall down if some of the men who are now stationed there should desert, and say that it is built on cardboard. It is solid rock, no matter what may be said of it."[89]

Now, if his statements of God's sovereign ability to vindicate Himself, without the help of either friend or foe, were quite clear, the following is even more explicit about God's sovereign, independent capacity to take care of the issues of His own vindication: "His honor is at stake. He has declared that the table shall be filled, and the inheritance fully occupied. He has pledged His very existence to that. Therefore, 'Some must enter therein.' So necessary is it, that if all the men on earth should refuse to come, God would raise the children to Abraham from the stones of the ground. Matt. 3:9."[90] So God will have witnesses; but if need be, in the face of universal apostasy and rejection, He will produce them from the very "stones."[91]

The thought expressed in the latter statement seems to bring an interesting wrinkle to the discussion. Even though Waggoner had earlier said that God does not need any witness from any person, he now says that the sovereign God will get them, even if He has to manufacture unilaterally such witnesses from the ground, the "stones" of the earth. But his strong emphasis on divine sovereignty would noticeably change as his "vindication" theology continued to unfold.

And such modifications would come at the previously mentioned Lincoln, Nebraska, General Conference session of March 6, 1897: "God has left the vindication of His character to His children. He has, as it were, risked His character with men." The sovereignty of God no longer rests on His ability to raise up "stones" as vindicating witnesses. Rather, now he views God as almost totally dependent upon human beings—"He has, as it were, risked His character with men."

But he would state the case in even more unmistakable terms in December of 1898.

Referring to the "work" of the 144,000 of Revelation 14, he made God totally hostage to their witness: "In them He sees the work that He designed to do for men, and He is willing that these shall be known everywhere as the proofs of His saving power. He is willing to be judged by these results and He puts His own seal upon them. . . . His commandments are known to them as life everlasting, and Christ dwells in them, so that they have the faith of Jesus. They are His perfect representatives."[92] But Waggoner was just warming up in these initial comments in the same number of the *Present Truth*:

"God has never left Himself without witness in what he termed the works of nature; but that witness is insufficient; man, the highest of God's creatures, must witness to Him as well as the lower things that God has made. . . . It is not merely single individuals, but a body of people 'called out'—the congregation, the church—that constitutes God's house. Before the end comes, and at the time of the coming of Christ, there *must* be a people on earth, not necessarily large in proportion to the number of inhabitants of earth, but large enough to be known in all the earth, in whom 'all the fulness of God' will be manifest even as it was in Jesus of Nazareth. God will demonstrate to the world that what He did with Jesus of Nazareth He can do with anyone who will yield to Him."

Waggoner could not leave this demonstration as a matter of some extra, bonus witness. In one of the most astonishing arguments ever entertained by his fertile mind, he would go on to claim that without the witness of the end-time followers of Jesus, not even the life of Jesus was sufficient to vindicate the justice and mercy of God! Carefully weigh the sentiments expressed in the next paragraph:

"Jesus Christ was the perfect temple of God; but if He were to be the only one in whom such fullness is revealed, then the too-common idea that Jesus was a unique specimen, not made in all things like unto His brethren, and that it is impossible for anybody else to be in all things like Him, would be warranted; and Satan would not fail to charge God with incapacity and failure, saying that He is not able to make a man born in sin, and bring him to perfection. Day after day he is making this charge through men who, either despondently or in self-justification, say that 'Christ was different from us, for He was begotten by the Holy Ghost, and being born sinless had the advantage of us.' The Lord wants all to understand that the new birth puts men in the same position that Christ occupied on this earth, and He will demonstrate this before all the world. The life of Jesus *is to be perfectly reproduced in His followers,*[93] not for a day merely, but for all time and for eternity."[94]

What is truly remarkable about his claim of God's need for an end-time group to reproduce the life of Jesus perfectly in themselves was that he would later, paradoxically, once more make it seem that everything rode on the perfect obedience of Jesus. What follows (in May 1899) is the most astounding statement that I have ever read on the issue:

"If Christ had failed or become discouraged because of the difficulties of His task, God's oath would have been broken; but if God's oath would have been broken, God's own life would have been forfeited; and since He is the Creator and upholder of all things, everything would have ceased to be. Now we can see how well tried is the foundation upon which we are asked to build. God placed Himself and the weight of the entire universe upon it, and it stood the test. Therefore, we can rest upon it in confidence. It is a precious stone to those who believe."[95]

If the faithfulness of Christ settled all questions about God and His governance of the universe (even the very existence of the universe itself was seen to be at stake), what further need would there be for any other "must" witness from His church? Here is a paradox if not even an unmistakable contradiction in the thought of Waggoner. Was God at risk? The better part of Waggoner's thought was to throw all of the weight of the risk onto the faithfulness and obedience of the person of Christ. The more questionable proposition of God staking His vindication on the performance of His church is one of the more disingenuous moments in the doctrinal history of E. J. Waggoner.

Tensions would always remain in Waggoner's mind between the concept of the sovereign God putting the exoneration of His character and the moral governance of the universe at stake through the accomplishments of His Son and that of His alleged putting His reputation on the line through the witness of His church. But it was the latter version of a human-centered, subjective, "victory over sin" vindication of God that ultimately triumphed in Waggoner's thought. Carefully ponder the later developments in his "vindication" teachings (June 1899):

"Who is to clear the Infinite One of Satan's accusations? God created the world to be inhabited with a race of beings who would reflect His image, who would be loyal to Him. He has such confidence in man, whom He has created, that He is willing to risk His character with him, and to this end He calls upon men to be His witnesses, witnesses of His loving-kindness, of His great mercy, of His willingness and power to forgive sin—witnesses who will tell the truth, the whole truth, and nothing but the truth."[96]

In May of 1901 Waggoner unequivocally laid out the "must" vindication of God through the "mortal flesh" of His professed people:

"Before this corruptible body is made incorruptible, and the natural, sinful body is exchanged for the spiritual, sinless body, God will demonstrate what He can do in spite of corruption and mortality. He has condemned sin in the flesh, showing that even in sinful flesh He can live a sinless life. His perfect life will be manifested in mortal flesh, so that all will see it. . . . *This wonder must be worked out in sinful man, not simply in the person of Jesus Christ, but in Jesus Christ reproduced and multiplied in the thousands of His followers.*"[97]

While the paradoxical thought of Waggoner seemed to finally land on the side of a mandatory demonstration of the vindicating, faithful obedience given through the last-day people of God, he did lay out (in April 1901) a more positive, practical, and down-to-earth possibility for the witness of God's professed people:

"But before probation ends, there will be a people so complete in Him that in spite of their sinful flesh, they will live sinless lives. They will live sinless lives in mortal flesh, because He who has demonstrated that he has power over all flesh lives in them—lives a sinless life in sinful flesh, and a healthful life in mortal flesh, and that will be a testimony that can not be gainsaid—a witness than which no greater can be given. Then the end will come. This will be the kingdom of God manifested to all nations for a witness to God's power. 'The kingdom of God is within you.'"[98]

In these last two statements a number of themes present themselves for a succinct summary.

First of all, the positive motif that God wants to use the end-time witness of His sanctified servants as a practical missionary witness to a doomed and hopeless world is most laudable. One could only wish that Waggoner would have stuck to this sort of motivation for living "sinless" lives in "sinful flesh." To claim that such victorious living was a "must" demonstration to get God off the hook of Satan's claim that obedience is impossible, however, places a horrible burden on God's struggling people.

But we need to consider still another matter rising from Waggoner's constantly repeated theme of redemptive subjectivity: "They will live sinless lives in mortal flesh, because He who has demonstrated that He has power over all flesh lives in them" and such living of "sinless lives in mortal flesh" will be a "witness to God's power. 'The kingdom of God is within you.'"

While such a vindication thesis has many positive aspects, the real point was that it provided Waggoner one more additional occasion to promote and elaborate the great overriding theme of his concept of salvation, especially during this last phase of his public ministry in the Seventh-day Adventist Church. And what was that theme? It was that Christ literally dwells in His followers—the immanent Christ is the very embodiment (in redeemed sinful flesh) of "the kingdom of God within you." The subjective aspects of the presence of the immanent Christ once more revealed themselves as the all-consuming feature of his salvation theology. But the ultimate manifestation of subjectivity was yet to emerge fully. And that was Waggoner's contorted theological and philosophical dance across the slippery rocks of pantheistic tendencies![99]

SUMMARY

While numerous interesting developments appeared in Waggoner's theology during his British/European years, the two that were the most decisive were his expositions on the atonement and justification by faith. The two developing themes were intimately interrelated to each other. While Waggoner had always had a preoccupation with the issues of obedience and the inner workings of the Holy Spirit, by 1894 something had really changed. During the period 1891-1894 there emerged an emphatic embrace of the "mystical atonement" views inspired by his reading of Brooke Foss Westcott. And it was this "mystical" embrace that proved decisive in leading him to espouse effective justification through the forgiving, cleansing, healing work of the immanent, indwelling Christ.

The result was a clear rejection of any objective categories of the doctrine of the atonement (such as the penal/substitution/satisfaction models or theories). The most obvious outgrowth was a more "mystical" understanding and teaching about justification. His embrace of the idea of the "mystically" communicated Christ who dwells quite literally in the soul reflects a highly literalistic method of interpreting the Bible. Both the key passages of Paul that speak of the "In Christ" (or Christ "in me") theme and the healing narratives of Jesus Waggoner interpreted as indicating that Christ is really in the soul and that Christ's healing was not just an *illustration* of justification, but seemed actually to *portray* a literal cleansing of the soul from both the guilt and the power of sin. Thus he almost completely identified the dynamics of justification with what Protestant Christians have traditionally called the experience of sanctification. In fact, sanctification by grace effectively absorbs justification by faith, for all practical purposes extinguishing any distinction between them.

The rest of the themes dealt with in this chapter either played the role of a supporting cast or background chorus, or they were the logical creations of his effective, subjective justification views and the concept of the immanent Christ. But whether in the role of supporting cast or logical outgrowth, each of the concepts in this complex network of ideas enhanced the central subjective and effective components of Waggoner's theology.

Thus the humanity of Christ, the new covenant idea of writing the law on the heart, the final "must" demonstration of perfect obedience by God's end-time saints (the 144,000 of Revelation 14), the downplaying of the importance of the Old Testament literal sanctuary in favor of the indwelling of Christ in the temple of the soul of every true Israelite, and the ongoing blurring of the spheres of grace and nature through the invocation of panentheistic terminology—all of them focus on the same key development(s).

The entire issue of salvation has become an almost totally subjective accomplishment in the soul of the believer who is in-dwelt by the immanent, healing, transforming Christ. While there may be a few other complementary themes,[100] the developments traced in this chapter provide the core ideas that drove Waggoner's theology and ethics.

As we now move to the narrative of the final years of Waggoner's life and ministry (1903-1916), we will see how all of this played out in not only his theology but also his ethics—his personal life. It seems abundantly evident that his immanent views of the indwelling Christ, fueled with his panentheistic philosophy, did play a vital role in the development of his spiritualistic doctrine of "spiritual affinities" and their "free-love" tendencies. But the key question is this:

Did Waggoner's developing doctrines of the "mystical" model or theory of the atonement and its accompanying views of the immanent, indwelling Christ lead to his panentheistic views? We will not, at this juncture, venture an answer. It seems best to save those considerations until after we have more clearly grasped the developments of his final years. And it is those absorbing events that will next occupy our attention.

---

[1] *Present Truth*, Apr. 20, 1893.

[2] *The Glad Tidings* (Oakland, Calif.: Pacific Press Pub. Assn., 1900), p. 141.

[3] For a fuller reflection on these important issues, see W. W. Whidden, J. Moon, and J. Reeve, *The Trinity,* especially pp. 239-271.

[4] E. C. Webster, *Crosscurrents in Adventist Christology*, pp. 239, 240, footnote 248.

[5] If we take this same principle to its logical conclusion, we must exclude all discussion of the "millennium" since that word does not appear in Scripture and the subject has always been vexed with controversy. But most certainly the book of Revelation discusses the concept of a 1,000-year period. So, by parity of reason, while Scripture does not contain the word "Trinity," the concepts that make up the substance of the doctrine are clearly in there. Waggoner was simply engaging in a disingenuous quibble about words.

[6] For some background on the North American religious movement called Restorationism, see chapter 4, endnote 18.

[7] Athanasius was one of the leading figures in the church of the fourth century A. D. who doggedly supported the position that Christ possessed the same substantial deity as that possessed by God the Father. In fact, his defense of this position was so well known and important to Trinitarian developments that someone coined the phrase "Athanasius against the world."

[8] *Present Truth*, July 30, 1903.

[9] This is really quite surprising in the light of W. W. Prescott's presence, right next door to Waggoner in London, from 1897 until 1901. Prescott, during his lengthy stay in Australia (in the mid-1890s) had been instrumental in helping Ellen White and her staff to clarify the full and coeternal personhood of the Father with the Son. See G. Valentine, *W. W. Prescott: Forgotten Giant of Adventism's Second Generation*, pp. 119-122. If Waggoner and Prescott ever discussed the subject of the Trinity, we have no evidence that Prescott had any influence on Waggoner's thought on the subject.

[10] For a well-researched and clearly stated narration of Ellen White's pilgrimage on the issue of the Godhead, see Jerry Moon's excellent, informative chapters in Whidden, Moon, and Reeve, *The Trinity*, pp. 190-231.

[11] We find some tantalizing similarities between Waggoner's "miraculous birth" concept "which neutralized the evil tendencies of His evil ancestry" and the thought of early-nineteenth century British Adventist leader Edward Irving. Writing to a "Mr. McDonald," Irving says regarding "the human nature of our blessed Redeemer": "The human nature of our Lord was of the virgin's substance, perfectly and completely sanctified in the genera-

tion of it by the work of the Holy Ghost, and underwent no process or progress of purification." He then proceeded to deny that this was "a physical work, changing the natural substance of His humanity, whereas it is the whole truth to believe that it was a divine indwelling of Godhead power, and not a physical change in the created thing, in the creature part" (Margaret Oliphant, *The Life of Edward Irving: Minister of the National Scotch Church* [London: Hurst and Blackett, 1862], pp. 123, 124). One wonders if Waggoner had been reading Irving. There will be some further evidence of his dependence on the thought of Irving when we deal with Waggoner's concept of the reason for an end-time vindication of God. I am indebted to my doctoral student, Ricardo Gonzalez, for these statements from Edward Irving.

[12] Webster, pp. 200, 201. The Waggoner reference for this interesting, even paradoxical concept was "The Miraculous Birth," *Present Truth*, Dec. 20, 1900.

[13] Webster, p. 201, footnote 144.

[14] "Studies in Romans. The Surety of the Promise," *Present Truth*, Oct. 4, 1894.

[15] P. Penno, *Calvary at Sinai*, p. 210.

[16] Ellen G. White, *Selected Messages* (Washington, D. C.: Review and Herald Pub. Assn., 1958), book 1, p. 202.

[17] Waggoner articulated an interesting dualism between "flesh" and "Spirit." In the "flesh" humans are sinful, but in the "Spirit" they are sinless: "The Spirit never yields to the flesh, and the flesh never gets converted. The flesh will be of the nature of sin until our bodies are changed at the coming of the Lord. The Spirit strives with the sinful man, but he yields to the flesh, and so is the servant of sin. Such a man is not led by the Spirit, although the Spirit has by no means forsaken him. The flesh is just the same in a converted man that it is in a sinner, but the difference is that now it has no power, since the man yields to the Spirit, which controls the flesh. Although the man's flesh is precisely the same that it was before he was converted, he is said to be not 'in the flesh,' but 'in the Spirit,' since he through the Spirit mortifies the deeds of the body." ("Studies in Romans. Sons of God. Rom. 8:9-17," *Present Truth*, Dec. 6, 1894.

[18] Westcott, a well-known English New Testament scholar at Cambridge University, was later elected the Anglican bishop of Durham. He is most well known for his work, along with F.J.A. Hort, on the text of the New Testament, and the history of New Testament studies refers to them as "Westcott and Hort" (*The New Testament in the Original Greek* [Cambridge: Macmillan and Co., 1881]).Westcott is also highly regarded for his often-cited commentary on the book of Hebrews (*The Epistle to the Hebrews* [Grand Rapids: W. B. Eerdmans and Co., 1892, 1952]). For a helpful biographic sketch, see the article "Westcott, Brooke Foss (1825-1901)," in Walter E. Elwell, ed., *Evangelical Dictionary of Theology*, 2nd ed. (Grand Rapids: Baker Academic, 2001), p. 1270.

[19] D. P. McMahon, *The Myth and the Man*, pp. 133, 134. Cf. E. J. Waggoner, "Saved by His Life," *Present Truth*, Oct. 6, 1892.

[20] For a helpful summary analysis and critique of the mystical theory or model of the atonement, see appendix C for the observations and insights of systematic theologian L. Berkhof. In fact, a thoughtful review of them will be beneficial before reading Waggoner's observations in the succeeding paragraphs of this section of the present chapter.

[21] "Why Did Christ Die?" *Present Truth*, Sept. 21, 1893.

[22] *Ibid.*

[23] It was about as close as Waggoner would come to giving any credence to the alleged doctrine of "universal legal justification" that many of his most ardent twentieth- and twenty-first-century admirers have credited to him. But it is interesting that Waggoner did not call this giving of "His life . . . to us" justification and is explicit that His death will not prove redemptively effectual unless we "make it our own by faith." Once more, this giving

of His life seemed to be the Waggoner version of "prevenient grace" offered to all sinful human beings. But its eternal, saving efficacy is totally dependent on a faith response from the convicted sinner.

[24] *Ibid.*

[25] McMahon, p. 138.

[26] "The Cross and Crosses," *Present Truth*, Feb. 22, 1894.

[27] *Ibid.*

[28] For an interesting and enlightening portrayal of the somewhat parallel pantheistic developments in the thought of Dr. John H. Kellogg, see Jerry Moon's very helpful chapter 14, "Ellen White's Role in the Trinity Debate," in *The Trinity* (pp. 204-220, with special reference to pp. 212-218). The thoughts of Waggoner and Kellogg are very similar.

[29] E. L. Webster, p. 207.

[30] *Ibid.*, pp. 210-216.

[31] He issued such denials in various published writings and his presentations at the General Conference sessions from 1897 to 1901. Cf. E. J. Waggoner, "The Everlasting Gospel: God's Saving Power in the Things That Are Made," *Present Truth*, June 30, 1898; "Sight for the Blind. John 9:1-17," *Present Truth*, Aug. 9, 1900; "The Law of Life. The Second Commandment," *Present Truth*, Mar. 28, 1901; "Bible Study," *General Conference Quarterly Bulletin*, Apr. 14, 1901, pp. 220-224; "Present Truth," *The Medical Missionary*, 12, no. 11 September 1903.

[32] Anthony C. Thiselton, "Pantheism," *A Concise Encyclopedia of the Philosophy of Religion* (Grand Rapids: Baker Academic, 2002), p. 222.

[33] Thiselton, "Panentheism," *A Concise Encyclopedia of the Philosophy of Religion,* p. 221.

[34] "Breathing in the Gospel," *Signs of the Times*, Oct. 10, 1895; "Studies in Romans. God's Revelation to Man. Rom. I. 21-25," *Present Truth*, July 12, 1894; "'Brain-Power' of Plants," *Present Truth*, Sept. 6, 1894; "The Everlasting Gospel: God's Saving Power in the Things That Are Made," *Present Truth*, June 30, 1898; "The Gospel of Isaiah. Strength for the Helpless. Isa. 40:25-31," *Present Truth*, Sept. 28, 1899; "The Law of Life. The Second Commandment," *Present Truth*, Mar. 28, 1901; "Why Does Sap Ascend?" *Present Truth*, June 20, 1901.

[35] Ellen G. White letter 230, Oct. 2, 1903, to E. G. Waggoner, quoted in E. G. White, "The Danger of False Views About God," *Manuscript Releases* (Silver Spring, Md.: Ellen G. White Estate, 1993), vol. 21, p. 172.

[36] P. Penno, Jr., "Waggoner's Final Years."

[37] One of the best examples is the following: "The man of faith is able to see God in all things; for God is in all things, and faith does not teach men fables, but simply enables them to see and know the truth" ("Seeing the Life," *Present Truth*, Jan. 24, 1895). Such an expression would evolve into the following: "'God is in heaven,' but He is also on the earth; for He fills all things. He is a person indeed, but not confined to one certain place. His personality is everywhere" ("The Editor's Private Corner. The Spirit That Witnesses," *Present Truth*, Feb. 6, 1902).

[38] "Studies in the Book of Hebrews-No. 4," *General Conference Bulletin* , Feb. 15, 1897, p. 46.

[39] "Studies in the Book of Hebrews—No. 6," *General Conference Bulletin,* Feb. 18, 1897, p. 71

[40] *Ibid.*

[41] "Studies in the Book of Hebrews—No. 7, *General Conference Bulletin,* Feb. 19, 1897, p. 87.

[42] "Studies in the Book of Hebrews—No. 8," *General Conference Bulletin,* Feb. 22, 1897, p. 102.

[43] "Studies in the Book of Hebrews—No. 9," *General Conference Bulletin,* Feb. 25, 1897, p. 159.

[44] "Studies in Hebrews—No. 18," *General Conference Bulletin,* First Quarter, 1897, p. 13. The context clearly shows that Jesus Christ is the wisdom and power of God, who also pervades all nature. Thus Jesus is a force that also fills all sinners and nature.

[45] "Studies in the Book of Hebrews," *General Conference Bulletin,* Feb. 25, 1897, p. 156.

[46] *Ibid.*, pp. 157-159.

[47] McMahon, p. 158.

[48] "Witnesses for God," *General Conference Bulletin,* First Quarter, 1897, pp. 55-57.

[49] *General Conference Bulletin,* Feb. 22, 1899, p. 53.

[50] *Ibid.*

[51] *General Conference Bulletin* , Feb. 23, 1899, p. 58.

[52] *Ibid.*

[53] E. J. Waggoner, *The Everlasting Covenant*, pp. 254-256.

[54] "The Water of Life," *General Conference Bulletin,* Feb. 24, 1899, pp. 79, 80.

[55] *Ibid.*

[56] "The True Relationship of God and Nature," *General Conference Bulletin,* Mar. 6, 1899, pp. 157-160.

[57] "Bible Study," *General Conference Bulletin,* Apr. 14, 1901, pp. 220-224; and "Sermon," *General Conference Bulletin,* Apr. 9, 1901, p. 148.

[58] An edited version of this book appeared in 1972 from Pacific Press (edited by Robert Wieland). Wieland, well aware of the pantheistic sentiments in the book, simply edited out many of Waggoner's most "blatant pantheistic sentiments." But in his foreword to the book he never bothered to inform his readers that he had done so. The reason for this is that Wieland felt that Waggoner's pantheistic sentiments were only mildly "parasitic" in relationship to his central message of Christ and His righteousness. We will deal more on this later in the section dealing with Waggoner's panentheism.

[59] Waggoner, *The Glad Tidings,* pp. 80, 81.

[60] *Ibid.* p. 85.

[61] The metaphor of a somewhat benign "parasitism" comes from Robert J. Wieland, employed to try to protect the alleged orthodoxy of Waggoner's salvation views. In other words, Wieland has argued that Waggoner's pantheistic tendencies were an essentially harmless irrelevancy to Waggoner's already developed views on Christ as our righteousness (see Webster, p. 235, for documentation of Wieland's benign parasite defense of Waggoner's salvation teachings).

[62] For a sampling of the debate over the source(s) of Waggoner pantheistic ideas, see Webster, pp. 210, 211, footnote 181.

[63] Paul Penno, Jr., "Waggoner's Final Years."

[64] *Ibid.*: "Evidently Waggoner was using panentheisitic beliefs to fantasize a heavenly 'free-loveism.'"

[65] "Graced free will" is the idea that all humans, because of the infection of sin, do not naturally possess freewill. But the goodness of God's grace awakens the sin-deadened sinner to the realities of new life and Christ, and this is what frees the will to the possibility of being able to choose the life that God offers in Christ.

[66] "Studies in Romans. The Free Gift. Rom. 5:12-19," *The Present Truth*, Oct. 18, 1894. The same article was republished under the very same title in *Signs of the Times*, Mar. 12, 1896. (Italics supplied.)

[67] "The Word of Life and Light," *Present Truth*, Nov. 21, 1895.

[68] "'His Mercy Endureth For Ever,'" *Present Truth*, Oct. 20, 1898.

[69] "Lessons From the Book of Hebrews. The True Confession of Faith," *Present Truth*,

Nov. 25, 1897.

[70] Compare this with the following: "The fact that a man lives and has breath . . . is proof of the presence of God in his flesh" ("Studies in the Gospel of John. Words of Comfort. John 14:1-14," *Present Truth*, Apr. 13, 1899).

[71] "Studies in Galatians. The Ever-Present Cross. Gal. 2:17-21; 3:1," *Signs of the Times*, Jan. 18, 1899.

[72] "Studies in Galatians. The Adoption of Sons. Gal. 4:1-7," *Signs of the Times*, Mar. 8, 1899.

[73] For helpful explanations of the Roman Catholic Council of Trent, the sixteenth-century Protestant Reformers, and the thought of Andreas Osiander, see Alister E. McGrath, "The Doctrine of Justification by Faith," *Reformation Thought: An Introduction,* 3rd ed. (Oxford, Eng.: Blackwell Publishers, 1999), pp. 101-131, and Justo L. Gonzalez, *A History of Christian Thought: From the Protestant Reformation to the Twentieth Century,* rev. ed. (Nashville: Abingdon Press, 1975), Vol. III, pp. 114-118, 150, 151, 155, 275.

[74] Milton R. Hook, "The Message of E. J. Waggoner," Arthur L. Ferch, ed., *Towards Righteousness by Faith: 1888 in Retrospect* (Warburton, Australia: Signs Pub. Co., 1989), p. 39.

[75] Waggoner's interpretive paraphrase of Romans 5:1.

[76] "A Lesson From Real Life," *Present Truth*, May 31, 1894. (Italics supplied.)

[77] "Being Justified," *Present Truth*, Oct. 20, 1892.

[78] "The Epistle to the Galatians. 'Justified by the Faith of Christ,'" *Present Truth*, Feb. 10, 1898.

[79] "The Gospel of Isaiah. Deliverance of God's People. Isa. 25:1-9," *Present Truth*, Apr. 13, 1899.

[80] "The Editor's Private Corner. 'As He walked,'" *Present Truth*, May 7, 1903.

[81] "Jesus Our High Priest in Heaven. Heb. 9:11-14, 24-25," *Present Truth*, May 23, 1901.

[82] "For Little Ones. A Living Temple," *Present Truth*, Sept. 12, 1901.

[83] "The Most Beautiful Sanctuary," *Present Truth*, Feb. 27, 1902.

[84] What follows is a brief review of the General Conference session presentations (1897, 1899, and 1901) on this theme given in the previous chapter:

The March 6, 1897, talk at Lincoln went like this: "God has left the vindication of his character to His children. He has, as it were, risked His character with men." The balance of his presentation featured his well-honed theme of the Christ who dwells in believers and that it was the indwelling Christ, working through His followers, who would vindicate the Father God's character (*General Conference Bulletin,* First Quarter, 1897, p. 54).

Waggoner repeated the same basic idea at the 1899 General Conference session in South Lancaster. His presentation entitled "Spirit of Prophecy" followed the rationale of his 1897 emphasis on the vindication of God being effected by the last-day saints through the indwelling Christ via the dynamic activity of the Holy Spirit (*General Conference Bulletin,* Feb. 16, 1899, pp. 13, 14).

At the famed 1901 Battle Creek session Waggoner based his final sermon (on April 16) on Hebrews 10:4-10. In his fitting finale for his major emphases on the "power of Christ's life, by which the Christian lives and overcomes" through "the indwelling power of God," he further elaborated the concept through the theme of the sinful human nature of Christ. Then, almost on automatic cue, he climaxed his exposition with a strong emphasis on the final exoneration of God by His last-day people. His key, terse punch line was "sinless living in sinful flesh" (*General Conference Bulletin,* Apr. 22, 1901, pp. 406, 407).

[85] "Romans 3:9-12. (Concluded)," *Signs of the Times*, Aug. 25, 1890. A similar line of thought came nine years later: "In order that rebellion shall be put down forever, never

more to have any possibility of arising, every creature in the universe must see and acknowledge the righteousness of God. . . . The great Judgment is not for the purpose of enabling God to judge of the character of men, but to cause men to see the true character of God. . . . The time will come when every secret thing will be brought to light. Then all will see that God has always been true and just. Every knee will bow, and every tongue will confess" ("The Gospel of Isaiah. The Great Case at Law," *Present Truth*, Jan. 5, 1898).

[86] "Witnesses for God," *Present Truth*, Dec. 14, 1893.

[87] "The Authority of Christ," *Present Truth*, Apr. 12, 1894.

[88] "The Gospel Does Not Depend Upon Man," *Present Truth*, May 10, 1894.

[89] "Not of Man," *Present Truth*, June 7, 1894.

[90] *Present Truth*, Aug. 30, 1894.

[91] He would repeat the same point some three years later: "So absolutely necessary is it that some must enter into the rest that God has prepared, and which can be entered into only by faith, that even if every man should be false and faithless, God would still remain true to his promise (Rom. 3:3, 4), for He could take some of the ground and raise up children to Abraham. Matt. 3:9" ("Lessons From the Book of Hebrews. The Rest That Remains," *Present Truth*, Nov. 11, 1897).

[92] "Notes on the International Sunday School Lessons. The Captivity of Judah. Jeremiah 52:1-11," *Present Truth*, Dec. 8, 1898.

[93] Most of the twentieth- and twenty-first-century advocates of Waggoner's end-time vindication theology have employed this phraseology. Documentary evidence to the contrary is welcomed, but it does appear that Waggoner is the exclusive source of this theology. This writer knows of no other writer who was a precursor of this type of final generation vindication thought in nineteenth- or twentieth-century Seventh-day Adventism.

[94] "The Sanctuary of God," *Present Truth*, Dec. 8, 1898. (Italics supplied.) Edward Irving expressed a somewhat similar type of thought: "I believe that in the minds of many the edge of this mighty trial is taken off by a certain vague apprehension that He was helped to bear it by the new power which He had received from heaven; but this is a notion against which we protest, as totally unsupported by Scripture, and defeating one chief end of His coming in the flesh, which was to conquer every form of wickedness and trial that could come against Him from the cradle to the grave, and to set us an example that we might follow His steps. If His humanity bore not His human encounter, but needed the aid of His superior faculties, then how serveth it as an encouragement or an example to us who are mere men, and have no such divinity to bear us up? His humanity sustained Him against all earthly encounters; and whatever His divinity served Him, it served not to lighten the load which lay heavy upon His shoulders" (Gavin Carlyle, *The Collected Writings of Edward Irving* (London: Alexander Strahan and Co., 1864), vol. 2, p. 220. Again, could it be that Waggoner was reading Irving? We will probably never be able to answer this question, as his library has completely vanished.

[95] "The Gospel of Isaiah. The Sure Foundation. Isa. 28:14-18," *Present Truth*, May 11, 1899. A somewhat similar line of thought appears in Ellen G. White's reflections on the great test brought by Satan to Christ in Gethsemane: "Everything was at stake with him [Satan]. If he failed here, his hope of mastery was lost; the kingdoms of the world would finally become Christ's; he himself would be overthrown and cast out. But if Christ could be overcome, the earth would become Satan's kingdom, and the human race would be forever in his power. With the issues of the conflict before Him [Christ], Christ's soul was filled with dread of separation from God" (Ellen G. White, *The Desire of Ages* [Mountain View, Calif.: Pacific Press Pub. Assn., 1898], p. 687). The following passage also refers to the terrible struggle of Christ in Gethsemane: "The awful moment had arrived which was to decide the destiny of the world. The heavenly hosts waited the issue with intense inter-

est. The fate of humanity trembled in the balance" (Ellen G. White, *The Spirit of Prophecy* [Battle Creek, Mich.: Steam Press of the Seventh-day Adventist Publishing Association, 1878], vol. 3, p. 99). And finally: "For a period of time Christ was on probation. He took humanity on Himself, to stand the test and trial which the first Adam failed to endure. Had He failed in His test and trial, He would have been disobedient to the voice of God, and the world would have been lost" (*Signs of the Times*, May 10, 1899, cited in *The Seventh-day Adventist Bible Commentary* [Washington, D.C.: Review and Herald Pub. Assn., 1956, 1980], vol. 5, pp. 1082, 1083). Ellen G. White seemed a bit less apocalyptic than Waggoner. For him, the cosmic universe could have imploded as a result of Christ's possible failure. But Ellen White saw it as causing just the loss of sinful humanity.

[96] "God's Witnesses," *Present Truth*, June 1, 1899.

[97] *Present Truth*, May 9, 1901. (Italics supplied.) A similar expression would appear about six weeks later: "Now, however, are we sons; and God will demonstrate His mercy and His power, and vindicate His righteousness before all the universe, by demonstrating that He can work that which is good and well pleasing in His sight in a corruptible body as well as in an incorruptible one" ("The Editor's Private Corner. The New Birth—A Spiritual Man," *Present Truth*, June 20, 1901).

[98] "Sermon," *General Conference Bulletin*, First Quarter, Apr. 9, 1901, p. 147.

[99] Webster, p. 207.

[100] More particularly, Waggoner's ideas that the indwelling Holy Spirit can directly guide each person in all matters. But we will consider more about this intriguing manifestation of subjective impulses in the final section's two chapters.

SECTION FOUR:
The Years of Decline

CHAPTER XII

THE FINAL YEARS: 1903-1916

INTRODUCTION

THE NEWLY ESTABLISHED Emmanuel Missionary College, in October of 1903, felt more like a strictly run Adventist boarding academy than a newly developing model Bible college. The buildings were not all that adequate, and the newly arrived Waggoner family bore the brunt of the obvious limitations. Their first accommodations consisted of unfinished dormitory rooms, with the girls housed in a room on the floor above Ellet and Jessie, and the student dining room occupying the floor below. It is not hard to imagine that the conditions were a bit crowded and that noise drifted up from the student diners below. But the dorm rooms must have seemed like a penthouse compared to what became their more permanent quarters. The latter soon acquired the unflattering nickname of the "holey" quarters.

The title had little or nothing to do with the newly ensconced family's growth in grace. It rather reflected the fact that the house was simply filled with holes! And the only thing that possibly contributed to the "holiness" of the Waggoner family was the patience they must have developed while enduring the cold blasting through the cracks in the walls, doors, and windows. Pearl vividly recalled snow blowing through the frigid fissures and that the family had to pack all of the doors with shirts to insulate against the cold winds and snow filtering through with bone-chilling effect.[1]

The family's return to the states had occurred during the lovely, crisp days of autumn with its stunning fall colors that make this time of year, in both the Northeastern states and southwest Michigan, among the most enjoyable of the four seasons. But the striking palette of fall colors soon gave way to the barren limbs of the now-denuded maples and oaks and the graying skies of early winter. The brutal Michigan winter had begun to descend. And in many ways the passing of the season was a doleful harbinger of the approaching "winter of discontent" for the Waggoner family and a deep-freeze effect that would effectively end Ellet's public ministry as a Seventh-day Adventist minister. It was a truly sad, even chilling ill-wind that would soon engulf the newly returned missionaries.

The previous decade and a half had witnessed an amazing rise to prominence and usefulness on two continents. But now the troubling indications of change pointed in a direction that would be anything but rewarding and positive for the domestic tranquillity and public effectiveness of Ellet J. Waggoner.

But first we need to catch up with the Waggoner family in their travels from Great Britain and the events of their few months in Berrien Springs—especially their life outside of the "holey" quarters.

THE TRIP FROM GREAT BRITAIN TO BERRIEN SPRINGS

While the British years ended on somewhat of a down note for the public ministry of Ellet Waggoner (especially his ignominious defeat at the Swansea conference and the growing disenchantment with him by a number of the leaders in Britain), the boat trip back to the States was even worse. The passage across the northern Atlantic was undoubtedly the worst of Waggoner's numerous transatlantic crossings. The family departed England in late September of 1903, and the steamship voyage must have taken seven days or less.[2]

But the crossing was unceasingly stormy. Pearl reported that the family occupied two cabins, with Jessie and the girls housed in one and Ellet in another across the hall. The girls included both Bessie and Pearl, along with cousin Irma Waggoner, who had come to Britain with her uncle in the early spring of 1903. The family became extremely ill, especially the girls. Undoubtedly they suffered from seasickness as a result of the persistently stormy conditions on the high seas. Pearl claimed that she was under the weather during the entire passage. Jessie and Ellet must have spent considerable time caring for their little clutch of retching young women. The seasickness was bad, but the incessant confinement must have also been a most gloomy and wearing ordeal.

Thankfully, the seemingly unrelieved misery of the sea passage ended with their arrival in the States (most likely the port of New York City). The sight of New York City must have greatly lifted the spirits of the family, and one can readily imagine them gladly fleeing the claustrophobic cabins of the ship. They then boarded the spacious cars of a passenger train bound for western upstate New York. Most certainly the bracing effects of the breathtaking beauty and the fresh, crisp atmosphere of both the fall-festooned villages and the numerous vistas of the lakes, hills, and valleys of rural New York State buoyed the spirits of the weary passengers as the train made its way to Niagara County.

In a relatively few hours the weary days of the storm-cursed Atlantic passage were a distant memory as the family reveled in a sunny interlude at the friendly confines of the Lindsay farm in Burt, New Fane Township, New York. As mentioned previously, the Lindsay family and its commodious farmhouse had provided the venue for many happy layovers for Ellet and his well-traveled family.[3] While Ellet had undoubtedly seen the Lindsay family on a number of occasions during his trips to the General Conference sessions from 1897 to 1903, it had been more than 11 years since the ever-hospitable Lindsays had spent any time with Jessie and the girls. These enjoyable days must have passed relatively quickly, and then it was back to the train and on to Berrien Springs and the challenges of the 1903/1904 school year on the campus of Emmanuel Missionary College.

THE 1903/1904 SCHOOL YEAR AT EMC

The family arrived in Berrien Springs on October 20, 1903, to an Irish welcome from the cheerful and upbeat Percy T. Magan, cofounder of the newly minted college. While Magan and E. A. Sutherland had expressed serious reservations about having Waggoner come to teach, Magan had apparently all but forgotten it. While he and Sutherland would soon leave Berrien Springs for Madison, Tennessee, and new educational reform adventures in the American South, the balance of the school year at EMC seemed to unfold in a manner profitable for all.[4] While the previously mentioned living circumstances left much to be desired, both Ellet and the family enjoyed the challenges of the school year. Pearl took organ lessons, in addition to working in the printing department of the college during the afternoons, and Bessie took courses in physiology.

One of the more interesting facets of life on campus involved the stringent rules governing their personal life. Such regulations were not only strict for the students, but also impinged on the goings and comings of the faculty, staff, and their families. Pearl recalled that the college required written requests for any trip off campus, even for shopping trips to secure such menial items and services as shoelaces and haircuts. Yet the restrictions did not appear to dampen their spirits. Pearl's report of the overall circumstances of the school year was, on balance, upbeat. We find no indication of tension between Ellet and the faculty and the students. The stay in Berrien Springs, however, would be relatively brief.

Why the family remained only until the end of the school year in the late spring of 1904 is not readily apparent. But soon all headed to Battle Creek. Pearl and Bessie departed first, followed a few weeks later by Ellet and Jessie. It was during the late spring or early summer of 1904 that the family finally reunited in a house of their own in Battle Creek. And it was in the new home at Battle Creek that, during the next 18 months, the family would come to a sad breakup and Ellet would separate from denominational employment.

THE EARLY BATTLE CREEK YEARS: 1904-1906

The move to Battle Creek had been contrary to the counsels of Ellen White.[5] She had strongly suggested that if Waggoner did not continue teaching at EMC, he should go into evangelism. During this period she urged that the church needed to reach the masses of the burgeoning cities of North America.

But it was not just evangelism that concerned her about the service placement of Ellet Waggoner. She also worried about the influence of Dr. John Harvey Kellogg on the increasingly fragile Waggoner. Not only did Kellogg's pantheistic tendencies disturb her, but also his ill-advised plans for the medical program—not only in Battle Creek but for the entire denomination.

By mid-1904 the defeats that Kellogg, Waggoner, and their allies had experienced at the earlier 1903 Oakland General Conference session had spurred the stubborn Kellogg into a more combative mode. His longtime relationship with Ellen White rapidly deteriorated. She was deeply concerned about the spiritual and theological state of both Kellogg and Waggoner. But Waggoner also seemed to manifest little if any inclination to pay much attention to her counsels. Other voices seemed to have his attention, ones that he found to be either more authoritative or more appealing. During the ensuing 18 months any positive influences from Ellen White would seem to come to naught in the life and work of E. J. Waggoner. While the employment record is not entirely clear, it does seem that Kellogg hired Waggoner, either in the Sanitarium or possibly teaching (and studying) at Kellogg's American Medical Missionary College.[6]

Yet the most conspicuous issue was not where or for whom he worked. Rather it involved the tangled and controversial circumstances of Ellet and Jessie's marriage and their tragic divorce in late 1905 or early 1906. And not only would this divorce conclusively end the marriage—it would also effectively provide the circumstances that would forever terminate Ellet's formal Adventist ministerial connections. It is to this sad, even scandalous, episode that we must now turn our reluctant attention.

Divorce

During a brief visit to Pearl in Hinsdale, Illinois, sometime in the early spring of 1905, Jessie shared the "flooring announcement" that "she was going to start proceedings." Pearl added that there was "no real reason at all, except the planned marriage to E. S.[7] 'Nothing' could stop it."[8] Quite obviously it came as a complete shock to the daughter. Pearl was quite right that Jessie's intentions seemed unstoppable. She formally filed the application for divorce on September 11, 1905, in Calhoun County, Michigan.

The subsequent three-and-one-half month proceedings were relatively devoid of any public acrimony. The main reason for the apparent lack of rancor was that Ellet did not legally contest the divorce. In fact, it seems that he even went into somewhat of a retreat mode during much of the period, spending considerable time at the Lindsay farm in New York.[9] The proceedings finalized on December 31, 1905.[10]

Though Ellet had not legally contested the actual divorce proceedings and they were not contentious, the aftermath of the legal decree was anything but passive and uncontested. When the official grounds for the divorce were published as part of the legally required public record, there ensued one of the most sensational public "scandal(s) Adventists had had."[11] The official papers listed the "alleged cause for divorce" as "adultery." But before we go into those unseemly and notorious aftershocks, we should give some attention to the background of the wrenching breakup itself.

Possible Contributing Causes of the Divorce: Overwork, Long Separations, and Poverty

From time to time in the preceding chapters we have commented on the heavy work (including prodigious multitasking) and travel schedules of both Ellet and Jessie. Certainly Jessie had a great capacity for work herself, but we can only describe Ellet's appetite for it as Olympian! Especially since the early days in Oakland (beginning in 1883), he variously wrote, edited, pastored, sold denominational books door to door, taught Bible classes at Healdsburg College, and engaged in extensive itineraries up and down the Pacific coast, in which he attended camp meetings, ministerial gatherings, and other church-related assemblies. After 1885, however, the pace would quicken, as he not only played an active part in local and regional church affairs but also became deeply involved in the annual and then biennial General Conference sessions and the increasingly important and prominent national religious liberty projects. His heavy work schedules allowed him few breaks.

His travels especially increased after the fabled 1888 General Conference session. During many stretches he would not see his family for numerous months on end (including the terrible times of the virtual back-to-back losses of his father and infant son just before the Johnstown flood disaster). Those lonely travels involved mainly intense speaking schedules, all in addition to maintaining much of his editorial responsibilities at the *Signs of the Times* as well as other editorial labors at Pacific Press.

While he anticipated that he would have some letup in his demanding work schedules when he transferred to England and Europe, we have little evidence that he ever subsequently spent any consistently significant time with his wife and family in intentional vacations and days of rest. We have noted the interaction he had with his daughters in parlor games, reading, and singing. But there are few, if any, reports of Jessie and Ellet spending personal time together.

Furthermore, in a highly complimentary letter written by J. S. Washburn to Ellen White in 1899 (sent in response to her proposal that the Waggoners spend some time working in Australia), Washburn referred to Waggoner's heavy work burdens.

In addition to the heavy workload, he also mentioned that the self-sacrificing Waggoner had received little royalty for his numerous book publications. This lack, coupled with his selfless generosity and the family's almost constant hospitable tendencies, all added up to what Washburn characterized as a "constant necessity of" economic "pinching."[12]

Furthermore, not only did they endure poverty, but the hospitable spirit of the Waggoner family seemed to give them little time simply to be together as husband and wife. Somebody always seemed to be visiting, or they had some couple living with them (recall that Alta stayed with them for many years, even after her marriage to Harry Armstrong in England). While Jessie did travel with Ellet in both the United States and Europe from time to time, it seems they were so busy with their public presentations (he to ministerial and camp meeting audiences and she to Sabbath school workshops) that they really took little or no time just to nurture their own marital relationship.

In addition to the work and hosting and entertainment challenges, they occasionally struggled with illness (both in the 1880s and 1890s), much of which seemed a result of their unremitting work schedules, further compounded by the almost-incessant multitasking. When we put all of this together, it should not surprise anyone that marital stresses and cracks would develop. While we will note other contributing factors, the simple dearth of quality time together as a loving and nurturing couple seemed to be the most obvious source of the tensions that would ultimately cost them their marriage and significantly contribute to the premature end of Ellet's denominational career.

The Mary(etta) and Joseph Waggoner Infidelities

While every researcher needs to move with the utmost care in seeking to assess parental impact on the lives of children and lineal descendants, the respective affairs of Ellet's parents could not have been a positive influence. This was especially true of the notorious affair during the mid-1880s in Oakland that tarnished the ministerial reputation and domestic stability of Ellet's father, Joseph Waggoner.

While we have gone into Mary(etta)'s adulteries and narcissistic episodes in more detail, we have up to this point sought to be more circumspect regarding the infidelities of Joseph Waggoner during the 1880s. The reason for this is that his father's troubles seemed, at the time, to play only a limited role in the immediate life and ministry of Ellet Waggoner. But in the light of subsequent developments in the son's faltering domestic circumstances, the father's episode suggests some further elaboration and analysis.

The reader will recall that the Joseph Waggoner affair transpired during the early public career of Ellet Waggoner in Oakland and featured a protracted romantic involvement with a local Adventist woman by the name of Chittenden. Ellen White's correspondence with Joseph Waggoner, Mrs. Chittenden, and leading church administrators, agonizing over how to relate to the delicate situation, reveal his unwise involvement in some detail.[13]

We have no interest in going into any of the salacious aspects, but only pause to address the issue for two key reasons: to assess (1) the impact of the incident on the marital life and the subsequent divorce of Ellet, and (2) the persistently redemptive efforts that Ellen White exercised in behalf of both the father and Ellet.[14]

Furthermore, Joseph Waggoner's protracted (it had gone on for "several years")[15] and notorious "spell" (his infidelity had become "a by-word" in Oakland)[16] is also relevant in order to identify the way that Joseph responded and related to the persistent rebukes, pleas, and threats of Ellen White as she sought to pull him out of the clutches of his "affinity"[17] with Mrs. Chittenden. The redemptive efforts of Ellen White for both him and his paramour were unrelentingly persistent.

While Joseph Waggoner did eventually depart from the West Coast (and the attractions of Mrs. Chittenden) and finally ended up doing productive work in Europe, his "dallying" neglect of and slow response to the stern counsels of Ellen White left an indelible stain on his legacy. But even worse, his example eerily replayed itself in the life of his son Ellet in later years.

Yet there was one major difference: Ellet did not eventually pull himself out of the clutches of the one with whom he developed a "spiritual affinity." One of the fascinating details of Ellen White's counsel to Joseph Waggoner was her use of the word "affinity" to describe his illicit affair. In the light of Ellet Waggoner's later advocacy of the adulterous teachings called "spiritual affinities," Ellen White's use of the word "affinity," in the setting of the father's adultery, seemed almost uncannily to anticipate similar episodes in the later experience of his son.

Once more we need to repeat a note of interpretive caution. It is very hard to assess role-modeling influences on subsequent developments in the lives of lineal descendants. But the infidelities of Joseph Waggoner and his foot-dragging response to Ellen White's appeals to break off his protracted friendship with Mrs. Chittenden were quite possibly not lost on Ellet. At bare minimum, it was definitely an episode that any adult son should have been spared. It was most certainly not a helpful precedent when things began to go sour in Ellet's relationship with Jessie. The old adage seems, in this case, to be sadly true—that acorns do not seem to fall very far from the limbs of their parental oaks.

Were the tragic affairs of his parents decisive in Ellet's subsequent affair? Probably not. But the similarities are sobering and most certainly contributed nothing positive to the domestic destiny of Joseph Waggoner's son and his family.

But what then are we to make of the charges of adultery directed at both Ellet and Jessie?

Ellet and His Association With Edith Adams

While both Ellet and his daughter Pearl persistently denied the charges of adultery (more on this later), testimony from two important witnesses indicates that such denials were not valid. The allegations center around his relationship with the woman who would eventually become his second wife, Edith Eliza Adams. But first we need to get some background on the woman who would become Waggoner's second wife.

Our knowledge of the early life and work of Edith Eliza Adams is a bit sketchy. We know that she was born to John and Mary Adams in London, England, on March 20, 1869, and that she was survived at the time of her death by an unnamed brother and sister back in England.[18] Joining the Adventist Church as a young adult, she subsequently found employment at the International Tract Society in north London. The available records do not make it clear as to the type of work she did. But since she was elected as the secretary/treasurer of numerous institutional entities of the fledgling church organization in Britain, it suggests that her duties at the Tract Society headquarters in London were most likely clerical and financial. Records indicate that she received some sort of financial remittances during the years 1892 until December of 1899 from the International Tract Society in London.[19]

As already noted, she received appointment to a number of fairly high profile offices in the fledgling church organization in Great Britain.[20] She was both the secretary and treasurer of the Great Britain Seventh-day Adventist Church and secretary and treasurer of the Sabbath School Association of the British Conference in 1897.[21] Furthermore, denominational sources also list her as secretary and treasurer of the British Conference in 1899.[22] She was not, however, listed as holding either of the previous positions in the *General Conference Bulletin* of 1900;[23] yet she was subsequently elected the first secretary/treasurer of the newly formed South England Conference in 1902, at the same Leeds conference that chose E. J. Waggoner as president. It is thus evident that we are not dealing with a person who was some unknown minor figure in late-nineteenth-century British Seventh-day Adventism.

But, ultimately and fatefully, it must have been sometime in the later 1890s (at least by 1898 or 1899) that she began working more directly with Ellet as his literary assistant or unofficial "assistant editor."[24] According to the best records available, however, the masthead of the British *Present Truth* never listed her as an "assistant editor."

There exist only two known photographs of her from sometime between the late 1890s up to early 1906. The first is a group shot of the "staff of the International Tract Society" that included both Edith and Ellet (though not seated together—see photo pages after page 208). The approximate date of this photo is "about 1900."[25] In this photo both she and Ellet are well-dressed and composed. To say the least, Edith gave every indication of culture and attractiveness.

The only other known photographic record of her appeared with the sensational front-page headlines and gossipy news story of Ellet and Jessie's divorce in an "Extra Edition" of the Chicago *Evening American* of

January 8, 1906. The photo also suggests a self-composed and pleasant-looking woman.[26]

The record is fairly clear that sometime between 1902 and 1904 Edith migrated to the United States and secured a job at the Battle Creek Sanitarium. J. S. Washburn claimed that Ellet arranged for her transfer to Battle Creek sometime before the Waggoners' return to the States, while Pearl alleged that she came to Battle Creek after the Waggoners' arrival back in the country.[27]

But by the time the family settled in Battle Creek in 1904 it appears that Edith was already there and employed by the Sanitarium (probably as a medical librarian).[28] It is in this setting of the years 1904 and 1905 that the divorce unfolded. But was there credible testimony to sustain the allegations of "adultery"? Ellen White and J. S. Washburn were convinced that the relationship was adulterous and have left their unmistakably clear testimonies on the documentary record.

Until 1901 Ellen White's recorded testimonies had been quite positive in her assessments of Waggoner and his work.[29] After the 1901 General Conference session in Battle Creek, however, she became quite apprehensive of his "views." She plainly warned him about his pantheistic tendencies, calling them "fanciful views of God" similar to a "misrepresentation of God" that she had had to oppose at the "beginning" of her work.[30]

On October 2, 1903, she not so subtly suggested that such "fanciful views" would result not only in "apostasy [and] spiritualism," but also in scandalous "free-loveism."[31] Three days later, she minced no words in directly confronting Waggoner's subtle, but adulterous philosophy: "[Satan] hopes to lead you into the maze of spiritualism. He hopes to wean your affections from your wife, and to fix them upon another woman."[32] These initial warning shots were but the opening round in what would develop into a withering volley of fire in the later paragraphs of the same frank and revealing letter. Such troubling observations, coming from E. J. Waggoner's longtime supporter and family friend, merit a rather extensive citation:

"The enemy of souls has gained much when he can lead the imagination of one of Jehovah's chosen watchmen to dwell upon the possibilities of association, in the world to come, with some woman whom he loves, and of there raising up a family. We need no such pleasing pictures. All such views originate in the mind of the tempter."[33]

"Stop, for Christ's sake, stop right where you are. You are on forbidden ground. Repent, I entreat of you, and be converted."[34]

"To married men I am instructed to say, It is to your wives, the mothers of your children, that your respect and affections are due. Your attentions are to be given to them, and your thoughts are to dwell upon plans for their happiness."[35]

Then followed one of Ellen White's most direct and unmistakable admonitions. The aroused and concerned prophet pulled no punches when she addressed the adulterous tendencies of the relationship between Ellet and Edith:

"My brother Ellet, remember that the woman who receives the least manifestation of affection from a man who is the husband of another woman shows herself to be in need of repentance and conversion. And the man who allows his wife to occupy the second place in his affections is dishonoring himself and his God. This thing is one of the signs of the last days. But surely you do not desire to fulfill this sign. This is the part that the wicked are to act. Christ will take charge of the affections of those who love and honor God, causing them to center upon proper objects.

"My brother, your wife has her faults, but so have you. She is your wife still. She is the mother of your children, and you are to respect, cherish, and love her. Guard yourself carefully, that impurity may not abide in mind or heart."[36] Then two pages later, the address once more became quite direct in identifying adultery:

"Brother Waggoner, your case was presented to me some time ago, but I have delayed writing, thinking that I might see you and talk with you. You are being imprisoned with a dangerous sentimentalism, and this has nearly spoiled you and the one also who has permitted you to make her your favorite. You need not ask God to bless you in pursuing this course. In this matter your mind has been worked by the enemy, who stands ready to control those who give place to spiritualistic affection.

"You have a wife, and you are bound to her by the law of God."[37] And finally she reiterated the "spiritualistic" nature of his subtle sentimentalism: "You have been imbibing spiritualistic ideas."[38]

Her comments, so plain that they need little or no commentary, were later supplemented in 1908 when she reiterated the concept that Waggoner's ideas were "similar in character to those we had met and rebuked in several places where we met fanatical movements after the passing of time in 1844." Then she bluntly stated that "Dr. Waggoner was . . . [in 1901] departing from the faith in the doctrine he held regarding spiritual affinities."[39]

Once more, we must keep in mind that along with the unmistakably stern warnings of 1901 and 1903, Ellen White still continued to work for Waggoner's recovery. But she was not the only concerned figure who labored with Ellet. We now turn to the recollections of his longtime colleague and friend J. S. Washburn.

J. S. Washburn: The Firsthand Report of a Concerned Witness

The reader will recall the earlier pleasant associations of the Waggoner and Washburn families as they attended the performance of Handel's *Messiah* in the mid-1890s at the Glass Palace in London. The Washburns had arrived in England a year before the Waggoners. Thus by 1899 there had been at least seven years of ministerial and social interaction between the two men and their families. Furthermore, what lends added credibility to the following recollections is how positive Washburn's assessments of Ellet had been as late as May 29, 1899. His upbeat and complimentary attitude included a clear affirmation of both Waggoner's teachings and the overall tone of his work. So it comes as somewhat of a shock to ponder the following recollections regarding events that apparently began to unfold by late 1899 and would eventually culminate in the 1905 divorce.

Washburn was widely respected and probably the most effective Seventh-day Adventist public evangelist in Britain from 1891 until his return to the States in early 1902. While he could get a bit overwrought on such issues as the controversial debate over the meaning of the "daily" of Daniel 8, he was a firm believer in the prophetic authority of Ellen G. White and gave evidence of honesty. What follows we have taken from an interview with Robert Wieland in 1950 and a letter written by Washburn to his old colleague, G. B. Starr, on January 1, 1942. The similarities of Washburn's observations to the insights of Ellen White are quite striking. As we did with Ellen White's letters to Waggoner, we here cite extensively from Washburn's recollections.

He claimed that Jessie did not "always treat" Ellet "sympathetically" and that both "feared" that the other "loved someone else." Washburn also recalled a conversation with Jessie in which she said that she "knew what it was to love and have no love returned." We find further confirmation of Jessie's feelings of rejection in the claim that Ellet had said "that his wife had no more attraction for him than a stick."[40] In an even later recollection Washburn once again repeated Waggoner's alleged testimony of rejection of Jessie's efforts to save the marriage: "He said she was trying to win him to her, but she was only a stone to him."

As painful and dysfunctional as these initial reports were, worst was yet to come: "He [Ellet] told me of their terrible quarrels. How both of them had threatened to commit suicide."

Such utter desperation is nothing short of heartrending. Here were two highly talented and deeply dedicated persons who had obviously known love, but who now felt so trapped by the prospect of both lost and frustrated love that they saw no way out except one of the most unthinkable of possible alternatives. They both undoubtedly felt driven to imagine that none of the other alternatives appeared viable. Jessie seemingly contemplated nothing but a dark future with or without her husband, and Ellet could only sense that his loss of passion for Jessie could not portend anything but bad alternatives. Clearly Washburn's sympathies sided with Jessie. His final report of her feelings in the matter was that "Sister Waggoner was very forgiving and charitable."[41]

Washburn's description is clearly that of a seriously dysfunctional relationship. As for the reasons the marriage had come to such grief, Washburn would lay most of the blame on what appears to be Waggoner's solution to the terrible dilemma of his loss of affection for Jessie and a developing "affinity" for a woman that he had to know was not easy to justify.

Most certainly, in his better, biblically based ethical moments, he had to admit that his illegitimate "affinity" would not pass the test of the holy law of God. But it seems that Waggoner was beginning to run short of such moments. And it is thus that we must now turn our attention to Washburn's shocking report of Waggoner's rather far-fetched self-understanding—his claim to have special God-revealed views on "spiritual affinities."

What follows is the most detailed report of Waggoner's philosophical and theological views on marriage during this period. He undergirded them by a clearly articulated rationale for what would become the ultimate "solution" to his lost-love, new-love dilemma. And while he would come to the conclusion that his rationale would finally enable him to be with his new love here on earth, it would prove to be a "solution" that would cost him dearly.

According to Washburn, Waggoner "believed that he was led by the Spirit. He would say unusual, strange things, and I would ask him how he knew those things, things not in the Bible, and he would say God made it plain to me or 'God told me.'"

Regarding himself as one privileged with direct revelations from God, Waggoner then proceeded to outline his views on "spiritual affinities": "He said that nearly all marriages were mistakes, [that they were] only human marriages. But somewhere in the world God had made a certain woman for every man and a certain man for every woman. If they were led by the Spirit they would find the right one. But if they had been mistaken in the choice for a companion, if they were led by the Spirit they would first see that they were mated wrong. And that God had revealed to him that the woman he had married was not his true wife. So it would be sin, adultery for him to live with Jessie Moser as his wife. . . . She was not his God-given companion."

At this point Washburn interjected a report on Waggoner's views that in a man-woman relationship, the "male was active, the female wholly passive. A woman who was not passive in the hands of her husband was not the true God-ordained wife."[42] Washburn later elaborated on the concept in his interview with Wieland: "E. J. Waggoner knew the Lord was with him. 'The Lord spoke to me.' Had spiritual impressions. Then [he] began to study sex under his microscope (was an M.D.). Sex in plants. Would show J. S. Washburn pictures of microorganisms united together under microscope."[43] Next Washburn returned to his recital of Waggoner's more "focused" and extensive views on the dynamics of "spiritual affinities."

"Then he proceeded to say that if a man lived still closer to the Lord he would not only reveal to a couple that they were wrongly mated [,] but the Lord would reveal the right divinely appointed one. People who were near to God would stumble along doing the best they could with the wrong mate. But those who drew nearer to God would find out the fact they had the wrong mate [written in the margin of the letter appears the following parenthetical caveat: "So the nearer you lived to God, the more apt you would be to have your wife and find the true mate"]. Those who drew still nearer to God would find the right one." And now the experience of "special revelation" seemed to reach its logical destination:

"He [Waggoner] said he had visions of eternity and he was not alone, Edith Adams was his God-formed, God-intended eternal companion. I said, 'Brother Waggoner, God says, "Love your wife"; how can you love another woman?' He said if God commands [him] to love another woman he [Waggoner] must obey. [Out in the side margin, written perpendicular to the main text of the letter, was the following note: "I asked if a man could be married twice or three times in God's plan. He said no, only one marriage was right"]."[44]

So here we have the troubling, even deeply disturbing reports of Ellen White and J. S. Washburn. While it seems almost impossible to believe that Waggoner could have fallen so far from obedience to the clearest statements of Jesus in the Sermon on the Mount and the seventh and tenth commandments, the reports of Washburn and White are strikingly similar when it comes to the gist of the insights and counsels they both shared: Waggoner was caught up in an adulterous relationship!

Furthermore, the fact that both White and Washburn had been Ellet's longtime friends and colleagues and had been highly supportive of his ministry attest to the integrity of their reports. Additionally, it was only around 1901 that both of them became extremely apprehensive about Waggoner's relationship with Edith. Neither testimony comes from some longtime enemy who had some mean-spirited ax to grind. They were not cranks intent on ruining the reputation of an innocent man, but well-meaning friends and admirers who had sought to reclaim one that they had cared for and supported!

One other factor that attests to their credibility is the complementary revelations of the young Welsh minister W. H. Meredith, that we have already surveyed in chapter 10. While Meredith, during the time he was involved with Waggoner, gave no hints that he was aware of any infidelities, he did describe a man who was going through a period of strange, unprecedented behavior and attitudes that seemed markedly out of character. As noted earlier, the verbal portrait that Meredith painted was of a man who was in not just an ecclesiastical but also a spiritual free fall during this very same period of the developing infatuation with Edith. Quite clearly something was seriously wrong with Waggoner, and a likely explanation could well be a deeply divided set of spiritual and domestic conundrums.

When we collate all of the evidence, the resulting conclusion is quite disconcerting but sadly credible. All of these three witnesses were either longtime friends, supporters, and colleagues or, like Meredith, had simply commenced their relationship with a sense of deep respect and admiration. And when all three rather abruptly changed their attitudes at approximately the same time, we have to take their collective witness very seriously.[45]

Furthermore, it is not a terribly great stretch to see how Waggoner's views could be a rather shocking but quite logical extension of his already-developed concept that each person should be literally indwelt and directly controlled by the Holy Spirit. Waggoner's subjective emphasis had already taken him into errant views on healing and the gift of prophecy, and unbalanced positions on sanctification and church organization (every member should be under the direct guidance of the Holy Spirit and thus there should be no church constitution and organizations to control the free, Spirit-led individual believer). Such "mystical" views of the literally indwelling Christ, mediated through the Holy Spirit, had already troubled the history of Seventh-day Adventists and had led to the most bizarre practices and claims to justify the grossest acts of sexual immorality.

Ellen White had been quite explicit when she warned Waggoner that his ideas were already tending in the same direction as those early post-Millerite fanatics and their attempts to prove that they could live without sin. When they gathered in groups in which all were completely naked to demonstrate that they could not sin, it should come as no shock that sexual immorality did happen. Then it was that they took the next logical step: if they could not sin, then it must be that what they were doing was not a sin.[46] And the same sinister, deceptive, highly subjective, effectively antibiblical rationale had apparently, in principle, taken control of the mind and affections of E. J. Waggoner. The almost inexorable result was that he could claim that since he was literally indwelt and directly guided by the Holy Spirit, he could then proceed to claim a species of special revelation to justify his own adulterous affections for Edith Adams and declare the whole thing to be a justifiable "special affinity" not only for time but for all eternity.

Thus it was not surprising that he could, with the most facile pen, tell the world that he had not engaged in any adulterous attitudes and behavior with Edith Adams. The public proclamation of his innocence took the form of a published defense in the Battle Creek newspapers following the official notice of the finalized divorce decree and the previously mentioned scandalous newspaper reports. Both the Battle Creek *Morning Enquirer* and the Battle Creek *Daily Journal* of January 15, 1906, published identical texts of Waggoner's pained and defensive response to the charges of adultery. The piece that appeared in the *Morning Enquirer* carried the title "A Worthy Statement by E. J. Waggoner," with the subtitle "Showing That Innocent Parties Have Been Seriously Misrepresented: The Story—The Outgrowth of Recent Publications About a Divorce."

Probably Waggoner did have some justification for his claim that he and Edith had been victimized by a broken promise, and he was thus very careful to make the point that it was his understanding that there would be no legal contest of the divorce from his side if the formal grounds were "incompatibility" rather than adultery.

But he claimed great shock and dismay when the published legal reports of the decree listed "adultery" as the grounds. He then went to some length to demonstrate that it was his understanding with Jessie and her friend "Eddie" that they had both assured him that adultery would not be the grounds claimed.

Now, as to why the "adultery" charge was inserted into the divorce papers, we will probably never know. Waggoner chose to believe it was some sort of ploy by Jessie's attorney for reasons know only to him.[47]

Waggoner, however, not only sought to demonstrate de facto betrayal through either broken promises or legal mismanagement, but also directly proclaimed his and Edith's innocence in the face of the now widely published allegations of adultery. "For the benefit of my friends . . . and in the interest of simple justice, that the name of an innocent woman may be cleared of the cloud thrown upon it, I wish to make the following brief statement."

After clearly affirming his understanding that there would be no charges of adultery entered into the divorce proceedings, he proceeded to declare that "on this assurance, and from the consciousness of my innocence, not supposing it possible that anybody could ever think of making the charge of adultery, I made no defense."

But he did not consider one claim of innocence sufficient. Thus once more, in his "Worthy Statement," he declared: "Regarding the charge mentioned in the paper, I will say that I stated definitely to the lawyer that no matter what circumstances might come out, I positively knew that there had been no adultery."

If the insights of Ellen White (shared more than two years before) and the firsthand reports of J. S. Washburn's conversations with both Ellet and Jessie have any semblance of validity, Waggoner's "Worthy Statement" was, at bare minimum, disingenuous.

Furthermore, we find the frame of mind exhibited by Waggoner (and possibly his alleged advisors) further in evidence when he then proceeded to marry Edith in April of 1907. Pearl claimed that her father married the woman on the advice of some of the church elders and friends. As their rationale they claimed that since Edith's name had been so besmirched, it was therefore his duty to marry her. But that was at best curious and implausible reasoning.[48]

Whether Ellet was the source of Pearl's explanation we cannot know for sure, but his and Edith's subsequent marriage could only add more fuel to the already-overheated fire of the adultery allegations. At bare minimum the marriage gave the appearance of evil, and the suggestion that there had been no adulterous "affinities" had to ignore some pretty compelling testimony from some highly credible witnesses. In the light of common sense and Ellet's persistent claims of innocence, it would have been best for him and Edith simply to have parted company—in a manner that both Ellen White and J. S. Washburn had so forcefully (and wisely) suggested years before the whole tragic divorce had become a reality.

The above background raises the question of how best to relate to the persistent claims of Pearl and her husband, Ellis, that Jessie had largely caused the divorce. While we must grant all due respect to the highly loyal Pearl and her unflagging support for her father's claims, the most informed response to such claims is that we must gently and reluctantly call them into question in the light of the strong testimony of both Ellen G. White and J. H. Washburn. But what were Jessie's contributions to the sad breakup?

The Jessie Waggoner and Eddie Spicer Affair

When Ellen White had offered the observation to Ellet Waggoner that "your wife has her faults," she once more proved to be an uncanny analyst of their disintegrating marriage. While Ellet had manifested inexcusably bad judgment in his relationship with Edith, Jessie had displayed it on any number of counts in her involvement with her young male friend Eddie Spicer.

Most of what we know about the relationship between Eddie Spicer and Jessie comes from Pearl's recollections.[49] But we also have confirmation of his role contained in the published newspaper defense given by Ellet Waggoner in which he explicitly mentioned Eddie as being with Jessie in Illinois when the divorce was finalized and the fact that the younger man seemed to have played a rather significant advisory role in her divorce strategies. But who was Eddie Spicer?

According to Pearl he was a teenager (about 17 years old) who had been a member of either Jessie's Sabbath school or Sunday school groups in London. He was also an employee of the International Tract Society. To what extent they were involved with each other before the departure to the States is not clear. But it must have already taken on some proportions of an emotional involvement, as he was on the same ship with the Waggoner family coming to America.

He then proceeded to Battle Creek, where he, as did Edith, found employment at the Sanitarium. If Pearl's shock at her mother's announced intention to seek a divorce was genuine (and it appears to have been such), Jessie must have kept the illicit side of the relationship with Eddie well concealed from the girls. His being on the same ship must have seemed to Pearl to be just one more effort on the part of her parents to help a needy young person have a chance at a better lot in life.

But by the early spring of 1905 Jessie must have already concluded that any possible weaning of Ellet's affections away from Edith was hopeless. And it seems that Eddie had, at least by this time, become a most willing partner in encouraging her feelings for him and suggesting that the time had come to end the marriage with Ellet. By now Eddie could not have been more than 20 years of age. Not only was the relationship morally compromising, but Jessie's desperation must have also led her to abandon any sense of practical judgment by entering into a serious relationship that featured such a marked disparity in age.[50]

In fact, Pearl explained her mother's poor practical and moral judgments as a symptom of mental disturbance.[51] She thus laid the cause of Jessie's uncharacteristic and irresponsible behavior on her illness and Eddie's willingness to manipulate the allegedly ailing and vulnerable Jessie.

Mental disturbance or not, the unsurprising outcome was that Jessie was sent through what she later described as her Gethsemane.[52] While the divorce did legally free up Jessie to marry Eddie, her hopes would soon be dashed. After she spent some time with him in both Kankakee, Illinois, and Toledo, Ohio, he ended the relationship. It left her completely embarrassed and scorned by yet a second man who found the affections of another woman more enticing. While Jessie would recover from her love losses, she would never remarry.

Review of the Divorce

Most certainly both Ellet and Jessie had brought much of their marital tragedy down on their own heads. At bare minimum Ellet was just as much at fault for the divorce as she was. Yet blame is not really the business of this biography.

The key cautionary burdens of this sad domestic and spiritual tragedy have more to do with how the whole thing could have been prevented. Certainly the previously mentioned factors of workaholism and its persistent neglect of the nourishing factors that must be invested in any viable marriage had a large role in the breakup of the marriage. Ellet and Jessie failed to heed the profound insights of Jesus that it is just as much a sin to nurture thoughts of illicit desire as it is to engage in the actual fulfillment of them. And we must not forget the less-than-stellar role-modeling of Ellet's parents.

But the most controversial factor involved Ellet Waggoner's theological trajectory. Can we justifiably claim that his unfolding theology during the 1890s and the first five years of the twentieth century played a significant part in his subsequent "fall"? We will save a fuller assessment of the theological aspect for our next, and concluding, chapter.

THE LATER BATTLE CREEK YEARS: 1906 TO 1916

Loss of Credentials and Church Membership

Sadly, we know more about the details of the divorce of E. J. Waggoner than we do about his work during the final decade of his life. Sometime during the years of 1904 and 1905 he lost both his formal ministerial standing and his membership in the Seventh-day Adventist Church. Unfortunately we simply have no known records as to when the events took place nor as to exactly what the reasons were for either of the disciplinary actions.[53]

Pearl claimed that he was dropped "from organized work—because of notoriety, etc., but *not* because of any change in his teachings or in his love of the truth, and his adherence to it."[54] But during the years 1904 and 1905 he did write and publish articles on a regular basis for the Kellogg periodical *Medical Missionary*.[55] When the divorce was finalized, it is not clear what sort of employment he had. But apparently it was not very steady.

On a lighter note, one notable family event took place in Battle Creek in March 1906—the marriage of Pearl's sister, Bessie, to Henry Harrower. Pearl recalled the ceremony as a "beautiful" home wedding held on the premises of a family friend who was a physician. It must have been a time of somewhat mixed emotions for Ellet and Jessie, though Pearl does not mention if either of them attended.

Aside from the sketchy information of Ellet's work and the pleasant notation on the wedding of Bessie, the year 1906 apparently passed quite uneventfully. But the pace of things would gather speed in 1907.

Marriage to Edith Adams and Two Years in Europe: 1907-1909

Ellet's marriage to Edith took place in April of 1907.[56] Following it they spent a few weeks at the Lindsay farm in western New York. And it was during this time that final arrangements took place for the newly married couple to leave for Denmark. Apparently the work had only been recently contracted. Pearl suggested that he was "expected to teach English to university students—private lessons."[57] She then went on to cite a letter received from her father from the farm in New York in which he said that their departure for Denmark had developed "rather sudden[ly]," even though the negotiations had been going on for some months.

He expressed his regrets at not being able to return to Michigan to bid farewell to his aging mother before sailing, and since they were "short of money," the visit "would be too short anyway."[58] All of this hinted at some difficult financial circumstances. Most likely Ellet later regretted his penny-pinching decision not to make a quick trip back to Michigan to spend some time with his aging mother before departing for Denmark. His mother would pass away during his last European sojourn.[59]

Ellet and Edith left the Lindsay farm on April 30 in order to board the ship for passage to Denmark on May 2, 1907. What exactly he did beyond teaching English in Denmark for the next two years remains largely unknown. The newlyweds did visit Skodsborg often. Apparently the ties that had developed during the earlier European years offered some good social outlets, if not some teaching employment, at Skodsborg. Beyond the above-mentioned items, the two years in Europe remain largely unsketched.

The Last Years in Battle Creek: 1909-1916

While exact dates of the return from Europe to Battle Creek are also unknown, it is clear that by April 14, 1909, Ellet and Edith were back in Battle Creek. The following notice appeared in a Battle Creek newspaper on that date with the headline "Will Resume Practice—Dr. E. J. Waggoner, who has been doing missionary work for a number of years in Europe for the Seventh-day Adventists, has returned from Denmark, and is now at the Sanitarium. He will attend classes of the American Medical Missionary College this year, and review his studies with a view of resuming practice again."

Whether Ellet actually did enter medicine again is not at all evident in any subsequent records. It does appear that he did work for the Sanitarium in various capacities—doing laboratory tests, engaging in some chaplaincy ministry, and so forth. Pearl put it this way: "He accepted a position at Sanitarium—in laboratory mostly" and until 1916 continued this work at Battle Creek Sanitarium. Taught as chaplain, and in Sabbath school, etc."[60]

They were the among the most tranquil years of a life that had been lived at a hectic pace. With the departure from Berrien Springs in the spring of 1904 and the events surrounding the divorce from Jessie, the truly historically significant public ministry of Ellet Joseph Waggoner was over. It is a sad thought that the once-mighty messenger of Christ and His righteousness had now found himself relegated mostly to "laboratory" work.

Surely he must have accomplished much good in such more technical work and in his institutional ministry as chaplain and Sabbath school teacher. But it is hard to believe that it was the destiny the Lord had in mind for the last public years of professional service in the life and ministry of Ellet Waggoner!

The Time of Departure Cometh With an "Awful Shock"

The life of Ellet Joseph Waggoner had a number of cruel twists. He had endured bitter opposition from leading church administrators when he was at the apex of his influence and had suffered the wrenching back-to-back losses of his father in faraway Europe and his infant son during a lengthy itinerary to the East Coast in the spring of 1889. But such cruel twists were also the occasional lot of his loyal and adoring daughter Pearl. While the shock of her mother's declaration of intention to divorce her father was wrenching, what was about to unfold was to prove even more cruel for a new bride.[61]

During the spring of 1916 Pearl had just about completed the school year at Washington Missionary College in Takoma Park, Maryland. She and her fiancé, Ellis Howard, had just accepted an appointment to do overseas mission service near Lake Titicaca, Peru. They looked forward to serving at a mission station founded by one of the most legendary couples in the history of Seventh-day Adventist overseas missions—the indomitable Fernando and Ana Stahl.

The deeply dedicated young couple was married at 2:00 p.m. on Wednesday, May 24, in Takoma Park—just two days after the school year ended. That evening following the wedding they left for what they intended to be a combination honeymoon and farewell tour to visit their friends and family before departing for their initial term of overseas service.

For anyone who has ever taken such a trip, it is a heady, exciting time—filled with numerous and mixed emotions. Especially in those days, people exchanged goodbyes with the sobering knowledge that it could be as much as seven to 10 years before overseas mission appointees might see their loved ones again. In more recent times furloughs have evolved into annual leaves, and all sorts of communication media assist families and friends to stay well connected. But furloughs in the early twentieth century were relatively few and far between. Quite understandably, such farewell visits have traditionally been extremely poignant. And Pearl and Ellis's initial farewell tour was no exception.

Their journey would include stops in Hinsdale, Illinois, and Nashville and Graysville, Tennessee, but the first stop was to be at Battle Creek, where the mission-bound honeymooners were scheduled to spend a week with Ellet, Edith, and the numerous Waggoner kin and friends in south-central Michigan.

Pearl and Ellis arrived without incident on Thursday evening, May 25, to an "overjoyed" reception from the ever-composed but affectionate father. He was glad to meet his new son-in-law for the first time and was deeply gratified that his daughter had proved faithful to her childhood dream of overseas mission service. Pearl would later relate that mission service "was in his own heart too and he wished us all Godspeed."

But some apprehension soon tinged the happy reunion as during the next few days Pearl and Ellis noted some quick "spasms of pain" crossing her father's "face while his hand went to his heart." Even though the pain "was over in a moment," the always-attentive Pearl insistently urged "a thorough examination." The ever-calm, somewhat-diffident father responded with the news that he had "already had" an examination "and the doctors could find nothing wrong," suggesting that it "might be a touch of neuritis or something."

With the children put somewhat at ease by Ellet's assurances, the weekend unfolded in a most pleasant manner. On Sunday afternoon Ellet took Pearl and Ellis on a tour of his prized strawberry bed. Earlier in the day he had confided to Ellis that he was beginning to contemplate retirement and was giving serious consideration to moving about 20 or so miles to the west in the vicinity of Kalamazoo, where the soil was alleged to be very rich and conducive to outstanding gardens. For the relaxed Ellet, the sunset years of life seemed to beckon him to horticultural pursuits. On that afternoon he seemed "hale and hearty as ever."

But that evening another of the tragic twists that had earlier in life overtaken Ellet, the sometime-grieving young son and father, would now swoop down on Ellet, the aging father. But such dark shadows were now also about to envelop his beloved daughter caught up in her lifelong dream of mission service. As Pearl would later put it, "the shock was awful—such a sudden one, when before midnight he was gone."

Soon after retiring that Sunday evening, May 28, 1916, Ellet let out a groan that immediately alarmed Edith. She quickly checked him over and immediately called for Pearl and Ellis. But Ellet's groan was the result of a severe heart attack. In a moment the life of 61 years was over.

Three days later, on May 31, his funeral service took place at the Battle Creek Tabernacle. Appropriately enough, his old "blood brother in the blood of the everlasting covenant," A. T. Jones, was able to travel to Battle Creek and preach the funeral homily. Jones rose to the occasion and was in fine rhetorical form as he celebrated the life and character of his colleague, a true comrade in arms with whose name he will be forever indelibly associated in the annals of Seventh-day Adventist history as "Jones and Waggoner" of "Christ our righteousness" fame.

"Only those who knew Dr. Waggoner intimately were prepared to properly estimate his real worth," Jones declared. "He was so unassuming, so gentle as not to attract attention to himself. His knowledge of the Scriptures was broad and profound, and he carefully put all that knowledge to practical use in his own life. As a preacher and expositor of the Bible he was excelled by very few. As a comrade and a brother he was most obliging and kindly—this I personally know from the relationship of a friend and brother of thirty-two years. Never a word of criticism or unkindness concerning others escaped his lips or were permitted to dwell in his heart."[62]

So it was that in the wake of a heartfelt eulogy from his well-known covenant brother, E. J. Waggoner was laid to rest in the old Burlington cemetery just a few hundred yards to the west of the little Michigan town that had been his childhood home. His earthly sojourn had come to an end—the time of departure had arrived suddenly and quite unexpectedly.

His untimely death leaves one with many moving yet conflicting thoughts as Waggoner's spiritual and theological heirs ponder the legacy of this herald of the "glad tidings" of "Christ and His righteousness." E. J. Waggoner has not always been an easy person either to trace or fully to comprehend. But in the flow of Seventh-day Adventist history we simply cannot ignore his somewhat-elusive life and challenging thought. It commands attention and calls for the most careful assessments. And it is to this legacy that we now turn our attention in the final chapter of his life and theological pilgrimage.

---

[1] The revelations about the "holey" quarters, travels from Britain, and the arrival in Berrien Springs in the fall of 1903 appear in a letter by Pearl Waggoner Howard to L. E. Froom, dated October 15, 1961, and located in the Pearl Waggoner Howard File, Document File 236b, Ellen G. White Estate. The materials contained in this file can be reported on only in general terms, and are not to be extensively quoted, as per agreement by the White Estate with the donors of such letters. I have tried to abide by the spirit of this agreement and the White Estate's attempts to honor their agreements with the donor family. As this chapter unfolds, it will become readily apparent as to why we must handle such sensitive letters with discretion.

[2] The exact dates and ports of the family's departure and arrival and the steamship line taken are unknown. Mark Peters, the enthusiastic Waggoner family researcher (and lineal descendant of E. J. Waggoner), has been unable to locate the exact travel circumstances. While a wealth of this sort of information is available on the Internet, extensive searches have so far proved futile.

[3] Pearl Waggoner Howard to L. E. Froom, Document File 236b, Oct. 15, 1961.

[4] *Ibid.* Pearl claims that it was during this school year that Magan and Sutherland left for Madison. P. T. Magan would go on to legendary fame in the development of the new College of Medical Evangelists, the present-day Loma Linda University in southern California. He was certainly one of the most colorful characters in the history of twentieth-century Adventism. For more on Magan, see Merlin Neff, *Invincible Irishman: A Biography of Percy T. Magan* (Mountain View, Calif.: Pacific Press Pub. Assn., 1964).

[5] For this claim the author is dependent on L. E. Froom, *Movement of Destiny,* p. 530, and A. L. White. For a similar account of Ellen White's counsel to Waggoner during this time of transition from Britain back to the States, see A. V. Olson, *Through Crisis to Victory 1888-1901* (later republished as *Thirteen Crisis Years*), pp. 312-316, especially p. 315. Arthur L. White, then secretary of the Ellen G. White Estate, prepared the brief review of the later histories of Jones and Waggoner published in Olson as "Appendix B."

[6] Kellogg operated the American Medical Missionary College in both Chicago and Battle Creek from the years 1895 to 1910. See "American Medical Missionary College," *Seventh-day Adventist Encyclopedia,* vol. 10, p. 63.

[7] "E. S." is a reference to Eddie Spicer, Jessie's young male friend, with whom we will

shortly become more familiar as we explore his and Jessie's contributions to the pending divorce.

[8] Pearl Waggoner Howard, "Biographical Sketch and Background," Document File 236, E. G. White Research Center, Andrews University, Berrien Springs, Michigan.

[9] Pearl Waggoner Howard to L. E. Froom, Document File 236b, Oct. 15, 1961.

[10] The formal divorce document is available from the Library of Michigan, Microfilm F565, Summary of Returns Relative to Divorce [in Michigan], Bay 1905 to Wayne 1906, Calhoun County, from the Circuit Court, Record Number: 179. The author is once again indebted to lay Adventist family historian, Jean Davis of Battle Creek, Michigan, for locating the official court documents.

[11] These are the words of J. S. Washburn, a colleague of Waggoner's for most of the British years. They appear on page 9 of the report on an interview with J. S. Washburn conducted by R. J. Wieland at Hagerstown, Maryland, on June 4, 1950. The report is on record in Document File 242, at the Center for Adventist Research, James White Library, Andrews University. The contents of this interview will also shed some further light on the reasons for the divorce.

[12] J. S. Washburn to Ellen G. White, May 29, 1899, located in the incoming letter files of the Ellen G. White Estate, Center for Adventist Research, James White Library, Andrews University.

[13] The most informative background on this affair comes from the following Ellen White correspondence: letter 74, 1886, written January 25, 1886, to "Sister Chittenden" from Basle, Switzerland; letter 73, 1886, written January 16, 1886, to "Brother (G. I.) Butler" from Basle, Switzerland; letter 76, 1886, written sometime in April of 1886 to "My Brethren [Joseph] Waggoner, Loughborough, A. T. Jones, and E. J. Waggoner" (place of origin not listed); letter 51, 1886, written September 6, 1886, to "Brother Butler" from Basle, Switzerland; Letter 116, 1886, a fragment written around December 1886, probably to Elder Butler.

[14] George Knight has done a nice job in telling the story of how Ellen White worked so persistently, firmly, and mercifully to pull her old comrade in arms, Joseph Waggoner, out of the fires of his affair. Through her influence Joseph did finally leave Oakland sometime in 1886 and by June of 1887 he was preaching with Ellen White in Norway. The last two years of his career he spent heading up the editorial program at the Adventist publishing house in Basle, Switzerland. See George R. Knight, *Walking With Ellen White* (Hagerstown, Md.: Review and Herald Pub. Assn., 1999), pp. 48-51.

[15] Joseph Waggoner had been pastorally involved with Mrs. Chittenden and her husband from at least as early as November of 1878 (letters dated November 19 and December 2, 1878, written to W. C. White from Oakland, California, and located in Document File 236a, Ellen G. White Estate files, Center for Adventist Research, Andrews University).

[16] The quoted words in this sentence come from Ellen White letter 74, 1886, written January 25, 1886, to Mrs. Chittenden from Basle, Switzerland. My use of the expression "notorious" and Ellen White's word "byword" are clarified by the following Ellen White caveat: in a context of ironic jest, the question is asked: "Where is Brother Waggoner?" The commonplace answer given: "I do not know unless visiting Sister Chittenden." The whole affair had come to the attention of church leadership when Joseph Waggoner's estranged wife, Mary(etta) Hall Waggoner, had discovered letters that he had written to Mrs. Chittenden. Mary(etta) had threatened church leaders that she would turn the letters over to the leadership of a Protestant denomination well known for its attacks on Seventh-day Adventists if the denomination did not take some action. Apparently she did not make good her threat. This sad set of circumstances was just one of a number of embarrassing

and discouraging affairs involving prominent Seventh-day Adventist ministers during the period. Such scandals were just one of numerous heavy burdens that fell on the beleaguered administrative head of the embattled General Conference president G. I Butler (see Bert Haloviak's unpublished manuscript "From Righteousness to Holy Flesh: Judgment at Minneapolis," chap. 4, pp. 17ff.).

[17] Ellen White uses the intriguing phrase "his affinity" to refer to Joseph Waggoner's persistent "preferences for Mrs. Chittenden's society, and his intimacy with her," an "intimacy" that Ellen White pointedly said "was sinful as in the light of the word of God" (quoted from letter 51, 1886, written September 6, 1886, to "Brother Butler" from Basle, Switzerland). Ellen White employs the term a number of times in her unpublished letters and manuscripts and always uses it to refer to some sort of illicit intimacy.

[18] The basic biographical facts are drawn from her obituary, "Mrs. Ellet J. Wagner [*sic*]," published in the Battle Creek *Enquirer and News,* Wednesday, June 12, 1945 (p. 2, col. 3).

[19] The "Ledgers/Journals of the International Tract Society" have been preserved in the Heritage Room of the Newbold College Library. These records cover the years from 1892 to 1901. Edith received financial compensation on the following dates: August 31, 1892; from January to November of 1893; in January, September, October, November, and December of 1895; from January to December in the successive years of 1896, 1897, 1898, and 1899. Her records appear on pages 271, 270, 284, 307, 371. E. J. Waggoner received compensation recorded from July 31, 1892, to May of 1896, and his records appear on pages 170 and pages 211 to 214. Why and how they were subsequently compensated after these dates is unknown.

[20] While Edith Adams did work for the International Tract Society, the minutes of the annual meetings of the International Tract Society that were held once a year from September 1894 to August 1904 never mention her in any manner. Copies of the minutes are in the personal files of the author and were reproduced by David Marshall from the originals, in the possession of the Stanborough Press, Ltd, Alma Park, Grantham, Lincolnshire, NG31 9SL, England.

[21] *General Conference Bulletin,* Third Quarter, 1897, p. 109.

[22] *General Conference Bulletin,* First Quarter, 1899, p. 15.

[23] The *General Conference Bulletin,* Second Quarter, 1900, p. 130, lists under the heading "British" and the subheading "Conference," W. W. Prescott as president, and Mary Jacques as secretary and treasurer, and also secretary of the Sabbath School Association. But those who have worked for the church know that such records are not always reliable or kept up to date.

[24] Quite possibly, her new duties at the editorial offices of the British *Present Truth* precluded Edith from bearing the work of her two previous offices.

[25] The group photo appeared in a "Centennial Historical Special" of the *Messenger* (official journal of the British Union Conference, Stanborough Park, Watford, Hertfordshire, England) that was effectively a historical review of British Seventh-day Adventism entitled *A Century of Adventism in the British Isles: A Brief History of the British Union Conference of Seventh-day Adventists* (Grantham, Eng.: Stanborough Press, Ltd., 1974).

[26] Edith did project an attractive appearance, especially when compared to the unflattering portrait of Jessie that appeared just below Edith's dominant photo on the same front page. The alleged photograph of Ellet just below Edith's is not at all a convincing likeness of him. The likeness of Jessie is somewhat convincing, but I know of no photos of her from the years 1905 and 1906.

[27] Washburn's claim that Waggoner "had sent Edith Adams out some time before" his own return to the States appears in the Robert Wieland interview with J. S. Washburn (p. 9), and Pearl's claim that Edith came to the States after the Waggoner family had

returned is alleged in her letter to L. E. Froom, September 20, 1961, in Document File 236b.

[28] The obituary in the Battle Creek *Enquirer and News* said that she had served for 40 years as a medical librarian. The figure seems to be in approximate concert with her arrival sometime during the years 1904 or 1905. The highly sensational account in the Chicago *Evening American* claimed that she served as a nurse at the sanitarium and then became an "editor of the Review and Herald." We have no evidence to support such a claim, and the article makes a number of other outlandish allegations.

[29] Letter 77, 1898; letter 28, 1900; and manuscript 81a, 1901, Center for Adventist Research, Ellen G. White letter files, James White Library, Andrews University.

[30] Letter 230, 1903, in Ellen G. White, *Manuscript Releases,* vol. 21, pp. 171-173.

[31] *Ibid.*

[32] Letter 231, 1903, in Ellen G. White, *Testimonies on Sexual Behavior, Adultery, and Divorce* (Silver Spring, Md.: Ellen G. White Estate, 1989), p. 200.

[33] *Ibid.*

[34] *Ibid.*

[35] *Ibid.*

[36] *Ibid.*, pp. 200, 201.

[37] *Ibid.*, p. 201.

[38] *Ibid.*, p. 202.

[39] Letter 224, 1908, in Ellen G. White, *Manuscript Releases,* vol. 10, p. 358.

[40] Robert J. Wieland interview with J. S. Washburn, pp. 7-9.

[41] J. S. Washburn to G. B. Starr, Jan. 1, 1942.

[42] *Ibid.*

[43] Robert Wieland interview with J. S. Washburn, p. 8.

[44] J. H. Washburn to G. B. Starr, Jan. 1, 1942. The document contains other even more bizarre incidents regarding Waggoner's ill treatment of J. S. Washburn and the attempts by Waggoner to induce Washburn into an "affinity" experience of his own. But we will spare the reader these further revelations, as the reports already related clearly make the point of Washburn that Waggoner was, by at least 1901, deeply alienated from Jessie and heavily involved with Edith, and that Ellet sought to justify the affair by claims to special revelations from God that Jessie was not his right wife and Edith was his true "affinity."

[45] Former General Conference president G. A. Irwin shared similar reports of Waggoner's attitudes and behavior to those of Meredith. Irwin, who along with O. A. Olsen had presided at the Swansea conference in the late spring of 1903, sent the following observations regarding Waggoner to the General Conference president A. G. Daniells. Written from Friedensau, Magdeburg, Germany, on July 19, 1903, Irwin writes in reference to the recent "victory" gained for church "organization" at Swansea and a notable subsequent development: "We have learned recently, that Brother Waggoner has resigned, and is going back to the States, and this will leave all the brethren, save Brother Champness, in harmony on these points in that field, and *it is my opinion that unless he gets a new conversion, and that soon, he will not remain with the denomination very long*" (letter located in the General Conference archives, A. G. Daniells File 4, 1903; italics supplied).

[46] Ellen White related the following insights into the immoral tendencies of the "spiritualist" Millerites in the aftermath of the 1844 disappointment: "T. was exerting his influence to discourage and close up my way by spreading lying reports concerning me. H., who had been made so happy as he received my testimony, fell under the influence of T., and as his mind turned, he became unsettled, then unstable. It was evident that he was rejecting the counsel of God against himself. He seemed unhappy, and finally went into the spiritual view of the second advent, and received the grossest errors, neglected his family,

took a spiritual wife, and his lawful wife died of a broken heart" (Ellen G. White, *Spiritual Gifts* [Battle Creek, Mich.: James White, 1860]), p. 68. A. L. White gave a brief background review that further elaborated the scandalous nature of the "spiritual" explanation of the Second Coming: "On this trip [to Topsham, Maine, in early 1845] Ellen was again confronted with fanaticism, the result of the teaching of the spiritualizers, who claimed that as they were sanctified, they might have a spiritual wife (Document File 733). They averred that if they loved one another as Christians, they were perfectly safe. Some took the matter a step further and taught that since they were perfectly sanctified, they could do whatever they wanted to without sinning. A few attended meetings in the nude, and a few exchanged wives. They thought it right to show their love for one another and that what they did was perfectly innocent" (*Ellen G. White: The Early Years,* p. 82). For a convenient overview of the larger outlines of the distorted views and activities of the sinlessly perfect fanatics, see George Knight, *Millennial Fever* (Boise, Idaho: Pacific Press Pub. Assn., 1993), pp. 245ff. and pp. 295ff.

[47] In communicating with Jessie and Eddie, he sought to absolve them of the blame: "I am compelled to believe that your lawyer made the charge up to suit himself" ("Waggoner's Statement: Adventist Elder Issues a Statement in Defense of Himself and Miss Adams in the Recent Divorce Case," Battle Creek *Daily Journal,* Jan. 15, 1906).

[48] Pearl Waggoner Howard to L. E. Froom, Document File 236b, Sept. 20, 1961.

[49] I have based my brief account of Jessie and Eddie's ill-conceived relationship on material from Pearl Waggoner Howard's "Biographical Sketch and Background," her letter to L. E. Froom of October 15, 1961, and a personal note to Froom on October 6, 1961, that took the form of a postscript to a letter of September 20, 1961. All of these letters and notes are located in Document File 236b.

[50] Jessie was born June 8, 1860, and thus would have been 45 at the time she initiated the divorce—at least a 25-year age differential with Eddie.

[51] Pearl's husband, Ellis Howard, later described Jessie's condition as a "time of physical weakness." His statement comes from a defense of both E. J. Waggoner and A. T. Jones, and those pages of his document in the possession of the author are only a portion of a longer, seemingly untitled piece. It most likely originated in the files of the White Estate or the Heritage Room of the Dell Webb Library of Loma Linda University.

[52] This expression, used to describe the sad experience of divorce from Ellet and rejection by Eddie, appears in Jessie's correspondence when she was filing for increased sustentation support from the General Conference of Seventh-day Adventists (Mrs. J. F. Moser to Brother [H. H.] Cobban, Oct. 21, 1924, located in the sustentation files of the General Conference of Seventh-day Adventists).

[53] Paul Penno, Jr., claims that Waggoner discontinued denominational employment in 1904 and was dropped from church membership in 1905. But he offers no documentation. Most likely he is dependent on Pearl's letter to L. E. Froom written November 18, 1960, for the approximate times Waggoner ceased denominational employment. In the letter to Froom she says: "Though later in 1904 or early 1905 he was not actively engaged in denominational work as such" (located in PC 48 at General Conference archives). It seems that when he moved to Battle Creek from Berrien Springs he began working for Kellogg in some capacity.

[54] Pearl Waggoner Howard, "Biographical Sketch and Background."

[55] See *Medical Missionary, Seventh-day Adventist Encyclopedia,* vol. 11, p. 48.

[56] Pearl never gave any details about the marriage ceremony of Ellet and Edith, such as the exact date, the place, or the circumstances. Adventist family historian Jean Davis of Battle Creek has not located any legal documents on the marriage from Calhoun County Michigan.

[57] Pearl Waggoner Howard, "Biographical Sketch and Background."

[58] *Ibid.*

[59] Mary(etta) (or Mariette) Waggoner died February 8, 1908, in Burlington, Michigan, as a result of physical complications from a broken hip sustained in a fall (obituary of "Mariette Waggoner, widow of the late Elder J. H. Waggoner, aged 84 years, 1 month, and 28 days," *Review and Herald,* Mar. 5, 1908).

[60] Pearl Waggoner Howard, "Biographical Sketch and Background."

[61] I have based the narrative of the next few paragraphs largely on the letters of Pearl Waggner Howard to L. E. Froom, Oct. 30, 1956; Nov. 18, 1960; Nov. 7, 1961; and Dec. 1, 1961.

[62] "Funeral Service," *The Gathering Call* 4, no. 5 (November 1916): 5.

CHAPTER XIII

WAGGONER'S THEOLOGICAL LEGACY: AN ASSESSMENT

INTRODUCTION

OUR FINAL CHAPTER will serve three key purposes. First, we will review theological developments during Waggoner's final years (1903-1916). The best way to do this is to begin with the claims that he made in the last piece of writing that he left on his desk at the time of his death.

The second purpose of this chapter is to assess the overall legacy that Waggoner has bequeathed to Seventh-day Adventist history and theology.

And finally, the third purpose will be an effort to define what *is* and *is not* the "1888 message of Minneapolis."

While the story of his life has proved to be quite interesting in its own right, the real significance of Waggoner ultimately involves his biblical expositions and the theological themes contained in them. The latter teachings all centered in the person of Christ and His life, death, and heavenly intercession. Yet Waggoner's main preoccupation was always with how Jesus has communicated His saving merits to lost sinners.

As we have previously noted, Waggoner was certainly concerned about matters of ethics, church life, and ministry. But his all-consuming core passion arose from his abiding interest in the doctrines of Christ and His righteousness. And it dominated him from the time of his "vision" of the crucified Savior in 1882 until the last "confession of faith" left on his desk at the time of his death. What should we make of his body of teaching?

THE "CONFESSION OF FAITH" OF DR. E. J. WAGGONER

The first issue that we need to address was whether this document actually came from the hand and mind of Waggoner. Apparently it resulted as a response to some communications sent to him by his old colleague M. C. Wilcox. Internal evidence abundantly indicates that it did come from the pen of Waggoner. Breathing his "spirit" of calm, straightforward reply to an old friend, it is not confrontational and reveals no anger or animosity (in his own words, Waggoner was never a "belligerent"). Rather, it is just what it calls itself: a "confession of faith" given by someone settled in his convictions. It does not reveal a "frustrated, perplexed, [and] confused" man.[1] Though he was suffering chronic heart problems, we have no evidence that his physical health contributed to any doctrinal aberrancy evident in the last document. Furthermore, all the leading Waggoner scholars have agreed that it is genuinely his.

Now having made the point of its authenticity, the really relevant question is: Did the views expressed by Waggoner in his "confession" represent his settled convictions that had been in place by 1891 or as late as 1894?

To answer our question, we need to get a little more of the context of the "confession of faith." M. C. Wilcox had stayed in touch with his old colleague during the intervening years since Waggoner's departure from formal ministry in the Seventh-day Adventist Church. Wilcox had, along with others, held out the hope that Waggoner could return to the ranks of the full-time Adventist ministry. In the light of such wishes on the part of his friends, it appears that Waggoner had felt that the time had come to clear the air about his true convictions. And one can be quite sure that Wilcox would be deeply disappointed in his fervent desire for a restored Waggoner. Not only was he to be grieved by Waggoner's sudden death, but he also must have been deeply saddened when finally granted access to the contents of Ellet's last "confession of faith." Surely, neither eventuality was what Wilcox had hoped for.

As noted above, Waggoner was polite yet firm in expressing his convictions. The "confession" was essentially his formal but gracious declaration that a return to the ranks was out of the question. And when one gets into the body of the confession, it becomes quite apparent why that was the case: Waggoner simply no longer held to the traditional outlines of the sanctuary doctrine, its pre-Advent investigative judgment, and the legitimacy of the 2300-day prophecy with its fulfillment date of 1844. And furthermore, it is this revelation that has created some difference of opinion regarding *when* his loss of conviction regarding this unique Adventist doctrine came about.

But before we deal with the question of *when* Waggoner lost his belief in the major outlines of the traditional sanctuary doctrine, we need to let him share his own telling testimony about the reasons behind it.

After a somewhat extended review of his "mystical" ideas of the atoning death of Christ and that sin is an "entity" more akin to a viral disease of the soul than a commodity that can be transferred from a sinner to the holy places in the heavens, he then proceeded to narrate the loss of his traditional Adventist convictions on the sanctuary.

"Twenty-five years ago,[2] these truths [about Christ as the mediator who works in each individual soul], coupled with the self-evident truth that sin is not an entity but a condition that can exist only in a person, made it clear to me that it is impossible that there could be any such thing as the transferring of sins to the sanctuary in heaven, thus defiling that place; and that there could, consequently, be no such thing, either in 1844 A. D. or at any other time, as the 'cleansing of the heavenly sanctuary.'

"'Then what took place in 1844?'

"That question puzzled me for many years; for I had been so thoroughly indoctrinated with the idea of a 2300-year period ending in 1844, that it never occurred to me to doubt it. Indeed, I never did doubt it for a moment; but one day the light dawned upon me, and I saw that that period had no foundation whatever, and then of course I simply dropped it."[3] And not only did he abandon the teaching of the "cleansing of the heavenly sanctuary"—he also rejected the application of the year-day principle to the 2300 days of Daniel 8:14, suggesting that they were not days at all, but "the evening and morning sacrifices."[4]

Thus he clearly states that by 1891 he had abandoned his once dearly held convictions about the essential outlines of the doctrine. Now, what makes this claim controversial is that certain leading Waggoner defenders have argued that his loss of conviction resulted from his "embittered, defeated and confused" state of mind at this time and "that he overstated his case." They have based their interpretation on the following points.

The argument is essentially threefold: (1) "on the grounds of silence"—between 1891 and 1902 "there is not a line in Waggoner's writings . . . to indicate that he had abandoned the sanctuary teaching"; (2) on the grounds "of Ellen White's endorsement of his message between 1891 and 1896"; and finally (3) on the grounds that "Waggoner did teach the distinctive Adventist sanctuary doctrine during the period from 1891 to 1902," as witnessed by at least two or three articles, especially one in *Present Truth*, May 23, 1901.[5]

What should we make of these arguments that we must discount Waggoner's claim to have lost faith in the Adventist sanctuary doctrine by 1891 or simply not accept it at face value?

The first alleged ground simply proves nothing. Waggoner himself clearly said in his "confession of faith" that when he came to the conclusion that the doctrine was indefensible in his mind, he "simply dropped it."[6] It proves not that he was dishonest but only that he chose to hold his peace. Thus it is one thing to drop a subject quietly and quite another to fight polemical battles over the issue. Later on in his confession he frankly elaborated what he meant when he said that he "dropped it" as he sought to explain to Wilcox how his 1916 convictions would make it impossible for him to return to Adventist ministry formally. Waggoner stated that he "was never a belligerent, and as I always held, and do still, what I deemed to be the really essential truths of the message, I contented myself with teaching them, and holding my peace concerning things that I knew were not biblical. . . . I have always believed that the best way to uproot error is to sow very thickly the seeds of truth. For that reason I have never undertaken, and never shall undertake, any propaganda against the denomination. This letter is only a private expression of my views on one line, and I have no intention whatever of making it public."[7]

The above is pure vintage Waggoner. He was sensible enough just to "drop" the issue and go on proclaiming what he felt was the true doctrine of the sanctuary and the atoning work of Christ. His lack of mention of the topic, instead of being an argument from silence, is exactly the way Waggoner would have had it—don't do direct battle with error, just try to choke it out with what he deemed to be the "seeds" of truth.

The second ground offered for not fully accepting Waggoner's confession and the timing (1891) of his loss of faith in the Adventist sanctuary teaching rests on the assumption that Ellen White would endorse only someone doctrinally infallible on all points. But we have no good evidence that God granted her a form of prophetic "omniscience" regarding all of Waggoner's questionable teachings. She was simply unaware of his "dropped" convictions on this matter. Later on in this chapter we will deal with the claim that her endorsement of Waggoner assumed that he was totally "orthodox" on all major points of Christian and Adventist doctrines.

The basic thrust of Ellen White's support for Waggoner was that he certainly had powerful truth urgently needed by the people of God. He was, however, not doctrinally infallible. God has always used men and women (Adventist and non-Adventist Christians) who have done a great work, in spite of their doctrinal and moral failings. And Waggoner was no exception to this pattern, one reflective of how God has always elected to work with specially chosen human vessels.

The third ground for rejection is probably the most amazing one. First of all, it is significant that Waggoner's key defenders can point only to four articles dealing with the issue during the period 1891-1902. So few articles in a journal edited and published for the purposes of presenting Seventh-day Adventism's "present truth" teachings! And furthermore, only four articles during an 11-year span on the foundational truth of all "present truth" teachings is simply the more intriguing, even arresting argument from silence that Waggoner had indeed truly "dropped" the issue.

But furthermore, when one really takes an in-depth look at each of these articles, especially the one cited by Wieland ("Jesus Our High Priest in Heaven. Heb. 9:11-14, 24-25," *Present Truth*, May 23, 1901), the "silence" grows even more telling. We will briefly take a look at each article offered in support of the claim that Waggoner continued to believe in the traditional sanctuary doctrine.

But before we take a look at the post-1888 articles, we need to point out that up to at least 1888 Waggoner had been very much in agreement with Adventist sanctuary teaching.[8] But that would diminish during the 1890s.

The first significant article would come in September of 1893. And truly Waggoner did explicitly speak about "the great work of cleansing the true sanctuary, into which have been brought the sins of the people" and that it is here that the "final disposition of their sins" "will be made."[9] So we have good evidence that until at least 1893 he still expressed the core of the doctrine.

The next article appeared in June of 1896. It is not a full-blown exposition of the sanctuary doctrine, but simply a statement that heaven keeps a record of the deeds, words, and thoughts of every human being.[10] But we must point out that Waggoner never denied that a record of every person's deeds exists in heaven. So while he does affirm a part of the sanctuary doctrine, it does not prove that he had kept the other key components of the traditional Adventist perspective. What Waggoner taught was that those records do not need to be wiped out in heaven—they need to be wiped out only in the individual soul. So in essence his 1896 article proves nothing as to whether he still held to the major outlines of the sanctuary doctrine. Additionally, Waggoner clearly taught a judgment according to works (so that God could demonstrate the wisdom and fairness of the disposition of each case). But what he came to deny was that such a judgment cleansed anything in heaven and that it was pre-Advent. Thus we now consider the final two articles.

The third article, specifically cited by Wieland, is probably the most important one during the period following 1891. But it is also anything but a ringing endorsement of the Adventist sanctuary doctrine! It is one of the great examples in Adventist doctrinal history of what we can justifiably term "damnation by faint praise."

The first thing that we must note about the article is that it was a "commentary" on the then current Sabbath school lessons dealing with the subject of the sanctuary. It was not a subject that Waggoner picked, but one that he was called upon to elaborate for the benefit of the readers of *Present Truth*. And what proves interesting was how Waggoner treated the issue.

Essentially what he did was simply to acknowledge the Adventist sanctuary doctrine in passing, and then promptly proceed to present his own views on the sanctuary issue from his "mystical" atonement perspective. And once again, he took the opportunity to downgrade the importance of the literal Israelite sanctuaries and make just about the whole issue turn on his view that the real sanctuary is the individual human soul that is mystically indwelt and healed (cleansed) by the presence of the Mediator. Please note the way he short-shrifts the traditional doctrine by faint but passing praise:

"The eighth chapter of Daniel contains the record of a vision of events reaching to the end of time. After telling about the great apostasy, the prophet says [he then quotes Daniel 8:13, 14]."

Then came the truly telling commentary: "We have not time nor space to enter into details, but it must suffice to say that a comparison of Dan. 9:24-26 with Ezra 7. shows that the days mentioned in prophecy began [in] 457 B.C. and so reach to A.D. 1844. That is the latest date referred to in any prophecy of Scripture, so that all attempts to find a Scripture basis for fixing time for the coming of the Lord are merely speculation and fancy." So far, so good. But then came the key "drop" point in his exposition:

"But some will ask, What connection has 1844 with the cleansing of the sanctuary? Since all things are cleansed only by the blood of Christ, and that blood is no more efficient at one time than another, how can it be said that at a certain time the sanctuary shall be cleansed? Has not the blood of Christ continually been cleansing the living sanctuary, the church?" And there you have the key, fundamental point of Waggoner's reinterpretation of the traditional sanctuary teaching.

The issue has not to do, in the final analysis, with cleansing heavenly things, but rather with subjectively, mystically purifying the "church" on earth. And the very next paragraph speaks of the "cleansing" of the "church as a whole" through "the presence of the life of the Lord, showing Christ manifest in the flesh."

So what of 1844 and the cleansing of the sanctuary spoken of in connection with this important date, on which Adventists held that the pre-Advent investigative judgment began, which would lead to the cleansing of the heavenly sanctuary? Waggoner has a ready answer, but it is one that almost completely ignores the original intent of the standard, Ellen White-confirmed, interpretation:

"Now it is a fact that since the middle of the last century new light has shone forth, and the truth of the commandments of God and the faith of Jesus is revealed as never before, and the loud cry of the message, 'Behold your God!' is being proclaimed. The life of Christ is being seen as never before as the efficient power to cleanse body as well as soul, so that a sinless, healthy people—a whole people, a holy people—are being prepared as a sign to the world. Soon sin will be eradicated from the universe. That glorious end will be attained as soon as every soul on earth has made his final decision as to whether or not he will consent to be filled with the divine life."

In the very next paragraph Waggoner continued on to make it extremely plain that the "cleansing" referred to in Daniel 8:14 is exclusively "one with the work of preparing a people free from all defilement. . . . Christ is not a ritualist; He is not, like a Roman Catholic priest . . . with His back toward them, doing something in which they have no part, and of which they have no understanding; but all He does for the people He does in them."

What we have here is an almost total subjective, effective version of justification via the mystical cleansing of the blood of Christ! We find no objective reference to any real cleansing going on in heaven. In fact, Waggoner pejoratively labels any heavenly cleansing as being more akin to papal ritualism than to the true gospel of subjective cleansing.

In 1902 we have the final article of the period that dealt with "the blotting out of sin." And the message is pretty much a replay of the just-reviewed 1901 article. Using numerous metaphors that refer to the blotting out of sins, Waggoner wrote about the "slate," the "ledger," the "account," the "wiping out of the record," the "tearing of a leaf out of a book," "the burning of the book containing the record," and the "blotting out the account of it" (all seeming to affirm an objective, written account of the sins of the people). With these multiple metaphors in place, he then promptly and effectively proceeded to negate any significance they might have with reference to any literal heavenly purging of the accounts:

"We need to be on our guard against the idea that the blotting out of sin is merely as the passing of a sponge over a slate, or an entry in a ledger, to balance the account. *This is not the blotting out of sin.* An ignorant man who saw a thermometer for the first time thought to lessen the heat by breaking it. But how much effect did this have upon the weather? Just as much as the wiping out of the record of his sin has upon the sinner. The tearing of a leaf out of a book, or even the burning of the book containing the record, does not blot out the sin. The sin is not blotted out by blotting out the account of it, any more than throwing my Bible into the fire abolishes the Word of God."

Could words be plainer? In effect, his allusions to records in heaven are merely a pretext to get to the real location and business of cleansing.

But it ultimately has nothing to do with any heavenly cleansing in the Most Holy Place during the pre-Advent investigative judgment!

Waggoner then proceeded to make the point explicit as to where the real cleansing is taking place. And yes, it should come as no surprise to us—only in the subjective confines of the individual soul.

"The blotting out of sin is the erasing of it from the nature, the being of man. The blood of Jesus Christ cleanses from all sin. Our bodies are but the channel, the border, the sand upon the shore, of the river of life. Impressions have been made upon us by sin. At the seashore, when you see a smooth piece of sand, your first impulse is to make some mark on it, to write some characters upon it. Then the sea comes up, and each wave that passes over it helps to obliterate the impression until it is entirely blotted out. Even so the stream of life from the throne of God will wash away and blot out the impressions of sin upon us.

"The erasing of sin is the blotting of it from our natures, so that we shall know it no more. 'The worshipers once purged'—actually purged by the blood of Christ—have 'no more conscience of sin,' because the way of sin is gone from them. Their iniquity may be sought for, but it will not be found. It is forever gone from them—it is foreign to their new natures, and even though they may be able to recall the fact that they have committed certain sins, they have forgotten the sin itself—they do not think of doing it any more. This is the work of Christ in the true sanctuary, which the Lord pitched, and not man—the sanctuary not made with hands, but brought into existence by the thought of God."[11]

In actual effect, Waggoner has totally placed the cleansing of the sanctuary as exclusively transpiring in the individual soul, the "sanctuary" "brought into existence by the thought of God." Now, even if Waggoner does mention real records of sin in heaven, it is not any point of ultimate significance. Why? While he did admit that heaven might contain records, they really have no more to do with the cleansing of the soul from the disease of sin than do the medical records of a hospital actually healing any patient in the hospital.[12]

For all practical and theological purposes, what we have in these final two articles of 1901 and 1902 was an almost total replay, in principle, if not in a nearly exact verbal form, of Waggoner's understanding of justification that we outlined in chapter 11. Please recall that there we reviewed his telling and significant salvational developments from 1892 to 1903. And what we have in Waggoner's last "confession of faith" is a condensed replay of his salvation scenario as it unfolded during those very years. And when we couple this fact with his confession that he had "dropped" his views on the sanctuary doctrine, the whole thing makes perfect theological sense and is basically true to the chronological timing of his movement away from the central pillar of "present truth" Seventh-day Adventism.

Was Waggoner's last statement of faith true to his real convictions that began in 1891? The answer has to be a firm, though slightly qualified, yes! Yes, it could well be that it was not until 1893 or 1894 that the full contours were complete; but clearly the whole subjective move was under way by sometime between 1891 and late 1892. We can have, therefore, little doubt that his "confession of faith," on balance, truly reflected the core of his "mystically" driven, subjective version of the healing, cleansing work of the immanent Christ who indwells the responsive human soul—the real and true tabernacle, sanctuary, or temple of God!

And while the timing as Waggoner remembers it might not be totally accurate, his "confession of faith" recollections of 1916 are in the chronological time zone of significant change for his fully developed subjective gospel of cleansing. But it had little or nothing to do with any cleansing of the heavenly sanctuary.

The author is quite aware that honest and good individuals can disagree. And while Waggoner's defenders, who want to downplay the accuracy of his last 1916 recollections, do have some semblance of support for their interpretation, in the final analysis the evidence gives only that—a "semblance" of support! The actual documentary evidence from Waggoner himself, from 1892 to 1902, strongly confirms the accuracy of his last written testimony regarding the nature and timing of his effectual "dropping" of the most central components of the traditional Seventh-day Adventist sanctuary doctrine.

SUMMARY OF KEY THEOLOGICAL DEVELOPMENTS: 1903-1916

So here we have the key theological development of the years from late 1903 until 1916. And the only thing that seems to have changed was that during this final period Waggoner had finally stepped out of the shadows of silence into the full light of total personal disclosure of the telling implications that his core teaching had for his views on the Adventist sanctuary doctrine. If followed to their logical conclusion, all one has left of Christ's heavenly mediation is that He stands in the Holy of Holies to dispatch the Holy Spirit so that He (the mystically present Christ) can be subjectively communicated into the heart and mind of every responsive soul. And it is in the heart and mind that the real "cleansing" takes place, not (as he pejoratively put it) in some celestial "ritual." Is there really anything objectively that needs to transpire in heaven beyond the dispatch of the Holy Spirit? For Waggoner the answer is simple: Not one single thing!

WHAT ARE WE TO MAKE OF WAGGONER'S LEGACY?

The Larger Contours of Adventist Controversies About Salvation

As one reflects on the issue of Waggoner's convictions from the perspective of subsequent developments in twentieth-century Adventist theology, there begins to loom up a surprising parallel. When one looks at Waggoner's reinterpretation of the sanctuary doctrine, it has some interesting counterparts to a later twentieth-century attempt to reinterpret the doctrine—the teachings of Desmond Ford during the late 1970s and early 1980s!

In fact, I suggest that the entirety of the twentieth- and twenty-first-century Seventh-day Adventist debates and struggles over the doctrine of salvation (and its attendant complementing doctrines of the Trinity, the humanity of Christ, the person and the work of the Holy Spirit, the atonement, and the interpretation of the doctrines of justification, sanctification, and perfection) have essentially been reactions to Ford and Waggoner. And while the two came to widely differing conclusions (as have their partisans), the one thing that they both held in common was a rejection of the traditional Ellen White-endorsed sanctuary doctrine. In actual fact, it is ironic that Ford explicitly cited Waggoner's abandonment of the traditional sanctuary as a precedent for his own rejection of it.[13]

Furthermore, they were both initially circumspect until they fully acknowledged that rejection. But when it did come, they both made interesting attempts to reinterpret the doctrine to suit their respective teachings on justification and sanctification.

While both would abandon almost all of the traditional interpretations of Daniel 8 and 9, including the application of the year-day principle to the 2300 days, the core of their rejection was that the doctrine of the pre-Advent investigative judgment undercut genuine gospel assurance and cleansing from sin. But both would then go on to reinterpret the Adventist sanctuary doctrine as raising consciousness regarding the truths of their respective gospels of justification by faith. And here is where the contrasts came in and the parallels basically ended.

For Waggoner the gospel is that the indwelling, immanent Christ, dispatched from the heavenly sanctuary through the creative, healing work of the Holy Spirit, makes believers so perfect that they can be declared just before God (because they are truly just in character). In other words, the gospel for Waggoner essentially encompassed the work of sanctification, and sanctification effects justification.

For Desmond Ford,[14] the good news is that God justifies the believer through the imputed merits of Christ. Now, while Ford did present some solid and sensible reflections on the profoundly practical and spiritual interrelationship between justifying and transforming grace, most of his followers went on to construe his doctrine of justification as something done abstractly through faith, a faith seen as mere mental assent in accepting the forensic, accounted merits of Christ. Now, whether one accents the subjective or the more objective aspects of the experience of the gospel, fine balancing must always be played out in the delicate interrelationship between these two aspects of genuine Christian faith.

And this leads us to a careful consideration of just what is the gospel of Jesus Christ. Do we have to choose between the particular emphases of Waggoner and Ford and many of their disciples? Quite obviously we do not have to select their dropping of the traditional doctrine of the sanctuary. Seventh-day Adventist biblical and theological scholarship, since the wrenching days of the Ford crisis in the late 1970s and early 1980s, has made outstanding progress in vindicating the essential outlines of the sanctuary doctrine and its prophetic framework (as laid out in the climactic chapters of Daniel 7-12 and Revelation 12-14). Thus Seventh-day Adventists have nothing to apologize to anyone about these great doctrines; and Ford and Waggoner were simply biblically and theologically deficient in both their prophetic and theological interpretations.

But what of their respective versions of justifying and sanctifying grace? Do we really have to choose between an abstracted, scholastic faith (as mental assent, with no heart implications) version of the gospel and Waggoner's highly subjective, effective version of justification through the mystically mediated merits of Christ? I think not! Where does the truth really lie?

I suggest that the basic truth is best expressed (and experienced) by the doctrine of effective, forensic justification. It teaches that salvation becomes effective when penitent sinners unite themselves to Christ by faith and receive Him in all of His highly distinctive, but profoundly inter-related offices—as both justifying Savior and transforming (sanctifying) Lord.[15] The essence of this position is that neither the objective view of justification by faith nor the intimately related work of sanctification in the soul should be negated. True, balanced Christian experience just cannot come to be without the necessary contributions of both essential roles of the redeeming Christ. Thus salvation must include what is legally done *for* and what is effectively accomplished *in* the soul of the "true believer." And this suggestive observation leads us to a much needed evaluation of Waggoner's salvation teachings.

A Critique of Waggoner's Salvation Emphases

As we've repeatedly pointed out in the preceding chapters, Waggoner's concentration on the issue of graced obedience was quite legitimate and natural. The Seventh-day Adventist Church, which had nurtured him from his very birth, proudly called itself God's commandment-keeping remnant—those who "keep the commandments of God, and the faith of Jesus" (Rev. 14:12). And even though Waggoner would place great emphasis on the "faith of Jesus," he never was very far removed from the challenge of how the "faith of Jesus" can produce the genuine righteousness of Christian obedience.

If any one great spiritual phobia seized nineteenth-century Seventh-day Adventism, it was the specter of any teaching that would nullify the ten-commandment law of God. Thus Seventh-day Adventists have always been very careful in the way that they have sought to explain justification by faith alone, lest any presentation give off the scent of "cheap grace," the presumptuous attitude that "in grace I am now free from obedience to the law."

Thus it is not surprising that the underlying theme of graced obedience was a consistent component of Waggoner's writing and teaching. He was always keen to show that the faith that saves is a faith that works. And while his expositions on justification by faith alone would always accentuate the theme that justifying grace "makes the believer righteous," he was initially quite clear that justification also "made" the true believer "righteous" in an objective and legal sense of the word, not just in a subjective sense. Thus from 1883 until sometime around 1892 he maintained a sensible balance in his teaching on justification by faith alone. And while there were aberrant aspects of his developing theology (such as his semi-Arianism), he was "gracefully" and steadily moving in the right direction.

In the years following 1888, however, there began a subtle slide into an unhealthy subjectivism that never seemed to halt. The critical developments came in the years 1889 and 1892. But by 1893-1894 the slide was reaching precipitous levels. He would then, under the influence of his newly acquired mystical views of the atonement, set aside his previously articulated penal/substitution/satisfaction models of the atonement and continue his seductive descent into the enveloping embrace of the mystical model of the atonement and its subjective mysticism. And what would be the net effect?

His drift into mystical perspectives would eventually overwhelm just about the whole dynamic of his teaching on justification by faith alone. Such a conceptual perspective teaches that the transforming work of the immanent Christ will work directly in the soul to make the believer righteous. And furthermore, the subjective righteousness produced by the mystically indwelling Christ provides the justifying merits. Such internally bestowed merits need nothing of the work of Christ as advocate or mediator in heaven, in which He is constantly making up for the deficiencies of the true believer. And why not? Because everything is being fully accomplished in the soul of the believer.

Now, the reader might be thinking, What is so bad about all of this subjective transformation? Isn't sanctification a legitimate and actual work of God in the soul to create anew the believer's character into the likeness of Christ? And the ready response of any informed student of the Bible and Ellen G. White is a hearty "Amen." But we must never confuse the work of sanctification with that of justification. While we should never separate them, we must always carefully distinguish each!

Furthermore, it is also true that any believer who exercises genuine faith will always be the beneficiary of both blessings of grace. And while these blessings are complementary, one cannot compromise the primacy of justification in the process of conversion and regeneration. Unless the true believer can be sure that an absolutely perfect righteousness undergirds the whole process, there will be disastrous results.

This very issue that we are seeking to clarify was at the center of the controversies that the apostle Paul struggled with, especially in Romans and Galatians—justification by grace, through faith alone. But it was also the central contested point in the Protestant Reformation of the sixteenth century. Thus one of the best ways to get an explanatory handle on this matter is through a brief review of the theological situation in which the Protestant Reformers found themselves.

In their struggle with Rome the issue was not that the Papacy taught a graceless Christianity, but how its teachers understood the way in which grace justifies. What created the crisis of the Protestant Reformation was Rome's claim that grace is infused into the believer through the sacraments of the church, and this grace helped the faithful communicant to become good enough to be effectively justified. The Protestants replied with the doctrine of justification by grace through faith in Christ alone, not by any good works that any system of grace can produce in the soul.

Let's be very clear about what the Protestant Reformers meant when they articulated the doctrine of justification by grace through faith alone.

First of all, they were not saying that grace destroyed the law. They were simply declaring that the only way for a person to be truly justified was not by works of obedience to the law, but by faith in the imputed, accounted merits of Christ's righteousness mediated to the believer by Christ, the one and only high priest in heaven. Such justifying righteousness is reckoned to the believer's account. The believer then stands forgiven and accepted for Christ's sake and has a new objective, legal standing as totally sinless before God.

The Reformers felt that this was the great teaching of not only Christ and Paul but also the prophets of the Old Testament (see especially Rom. 3; 4; Gal. 2; 3). They did not deny sanctifying or transforming grace, but properly held it to be the accompaniment of receiving Christ by faith.

Furthermore, the experience of union with Christ by faith would produce the peaceable fruit of righteousness grounded in the justifying root of Christ's imputed righteousness.

Once again, we must confront the question of what is so crucial about this issue.

First of all, along with Luther, it has been the overwhelming testimony of countless believers that if justification is the result of sanctification (faith plus works, not a faith that works), how would a sensitive individual (such as Luther) ever be sure if his or her subjective obedience and good works would be sufficient to satisfy the infinite demands of divine justice?

The usual, baleful fruits of the concept of a subjectively induced justifying righteousness are twofold and closely related:

1. For those with highly sensitive consciences,[16] without the assuring knowledge of an objective righteousness that is imputed, or accounted to their records in heaven, the end result will be despair. The fruit of unrelieved despair works a strange destruction of the law: the despairing believer, without a clear grasp of imputed righteousness, simply throws in the towel and does away with the law. Soon we hear the plaintive cry—"Who is sufficient for such a righteousness? Let's give up and 'eat, drink, and be merry, for tomorrow we die.' Since we cannot perfectly obey the law, we should just give into our lusts and get as much as we can out of life before sinking into an eternity of oblivion."

2. The second terrible condition that can result is "pharisaism." The dynamics of this tragic state of mind work like this: since sinners instinctively realize that they are never in full conformity with the law of God, what one has to do is slice the law down to size and make it such that sinful humans can convince themselves that they have now met its scaled-down demands.

The pharisaic route to justification is the most subtle way of degrading the law of God. Under the guise of maintaining the law, it really compromises it. If the basketball basket were seven feet high, I could probably become a pretty good slam-dunk artist! And this is what the pharisee always does—he or she lowers the standard of the divine law in order to gain some sense of accomplishment!

In addition to lowering the bar, this method of salvation also involves the sad phenomena of "externalism." By "externalism" we mean the approach to righteousness preoccupied with meeting the mere "letter" of the law in a sterile, mechanical obedience. Not realizing the infinite nature of the righteousness of the law of Christ, we can easily convince ourselves that we have met the law's demands (moral, ceremonial, legal, or what have you). In actual fact, all that we have done is go through the motions in Christless self-deception.

What is truly ironic about either sad condition is that they seem to be just the opposite of what the average person thinks would or should happen. Since the time of Jesus and Paul, those who have proclaimed justification by grace through faith alone, not by works of the law, have consistently found themselves accused of doing away with the law (see especially Rom. 3:31). Yet it is only when believers clearly understand the biblical doctrine of justification by faith alone that they can find a sure cure for the curse of both despair and pharasaic self-righteousness.

Now, when it comes to the issue of effective, subjective generated righteousness, it does not really matter to the great adversary whether it is generated through crass pagan sacrificial offerings, Eastern Orthodox ceremonialism, legalistic Jewish conformity to the Torah, Roman Catholic merit infused through the sacred sacraments of the church, pre-1888 legalistic Adventism and its version of salvation through human-originated obedience, or the very beautiful-sounding mystical subjectivism (righteousness infused by the indwelling, allegedly immanent Christ) of the post-1888 Waggoner. It all comes down to the same deal—you are justified by a righteousness infused into or generated within the sincere but subtly deceived believer. Such concepts all have a wonderful appeal, but they are all false gospels.

And unless the Christ who works in the soul via the presence of the Holy Spirit is graciously complemented with the Christ who is the advocate with the Father in the heavenly sanctuary, the steady onslaught of despair or pharisaism cannot be too far away!

Can Sanctified, Perfected Believers Know They Are Sinless?

We need to consider one final aspect that all of these subjective models of justification fail to grasp: it seems that one of the absolutely necessary corollaries of this teaching is that the subjectively perfected believers ought to also be granted the gift of infallible insight that the indwelling Christ is effectually getting the perfection job done so that they will not be subject to a lapse into despair. But what such alleged insight usually descends to is pharisaism—that I am really good enough to be saved.

One of the lesser-known but highly instructive vignettes of the public ministry of Waggoner during the 1890s took place at the 1897 General Conference session. During a question-and-answer period a certain "Elder Lane"[17] put the following question to Waggoner: "I was asked yesterday if I thought you were teaching that although we lived very near to God, and had much of his blessing, we would ever come to understand the minds and very motives as Christ did. This was a question which resulted from the statement you made that Christ had no more than we may have. It says in regard to Him that He knew what was in man. So if we have enough faith, can we reach the same point?"

Waggoner's reply was really no answer at all. What he did was to proceed to suggest that the gifts of the Spirit should be abundantly present in the church: "the gifts of the Spirit will be in the church because every living soul will have some gift of the Spirit. The Spirit divides to every man severally as He will. Discerning of spirits is one of these."

What his reply paid no attention to is the fact that not everybody has every gift of the Spirit. Paul, in 1 Corinthians 12, makes it very plain that not everybody is privileged with a particular gift, and the gift of the "discerning of spirits" is no exception. So what about those who do not have this gift? Will they just be left to despair or pharisaism because of lack of discernment?

Totally ignoring the fact that not even one of the gifts of the Spirit is the special province of every believer, Waggoner then pushed ahead with the blithe assurance that "we do not need to explain as to the operation of the Spirit. The essential thing for us is the acceptance of the Spirit. Then whatever the Spirit is pleased to work in us, we will give God the glory. . . . There is no difference; the same things are given to us that were given to Jesus, for we are joint heirs with Him. . . . It is not depreciating Christ, but it is the Spirit endeavoring to give us a conception of the wonderful height to which God lifts man."

Quite apparently, Waggoner simply did not have a credible answer. It is little wonder then that he abruptly cut off his little response by declaring that "He [God] wants us to see and know these things."

At this juncture a serious question presents itself for our consideration: What things must the Christian know? Should even average Christians be able to reach the place where they will know that they are sinless enough in character to be declared just before the infinite demands of God's holy requirements? Such an assumption would simply go against the plainest declarations of God's Word—"If we say that we have no sin, we deceive ourselves, and the truth is not in us" (1 John 1:8).[18]

It is thus not surprising that Waggoner seemed to realize that his answer was simply going nowhere fast and he thus abruptly ended the exchange with a "let's change the issue" tactic—"Is there another question?"[19]

Most certainly not one sinful person, this side of glorification, could ever receive the conviction that they are sinless. In fact, one of the truly telling signs of a genuine conversion experience is that such a soul will feel even more sinful as he or she comes closer to Jesus. Such a response is a sure sign that the spiritual perceptions are becoming much clearer. It is not that the true believer will live a defeated Christian lifestyle, but it is just the facts of earthly spiritual life that God does not instantly perfect anybody before glorification.

Back to the Nagging Questions

Now, all of the preceding discussion leads us back to a couple nagging questions that we have been pondering for the past few chapters of our story: Can it be justly said that Waggoner's mystical, subjective views of the justifying work of the immanent Christ led him into the mazes of panentheism? And we would suggest that it most likely did.

While such theological and spiritual developments are always extremely complex, both in individual and group contexts, we do seem to find a dark thread of troubling theological and philosophical tendencies that quite naturally lead in the direction of a mystical, diffused panentheism. All the subjective elements seem to point in one direction—it is that God in you can then make you a demigod, able to define sin in such a way that it is no longer sin! And thus when anyone takes the leap out of the protective house of the biblical doctrine of justification by faith alone, before long such individuals find themselves edging toward the deadly pit of subtle, even spiritual mystical subjectivism. And very tragically, such was the trajectory of E. J. Waggoner.

There exists a terrible downward path from an unhealthy subjective emphasis, deeply colored by a false understanding of the death of Christ, that easily, even naturally, results in the panenthistic concept that whatever I think and do is God doing it in us. But is it truly God in us? Wherefore by their fruits you shall know them!

What Is Waggoner's Enduring Legacy?

Most certainly Waggoner's major legacy arises out of his teachings that sparked the revival of "Christ and His righteousness" in the late 1880s and its very positive contributions to what Ellen White called a revival that was the beginning of the "loud cry" message that God intended to be the last outreach of mercy to the world. Once more we need to review the positive contributions outlined by Ellen White in *Testimonies to Ministers* (pp. 92ff.).

The Positive Legacy

Waggoner's insights and contributions include: (1) his call to uplift Christ as Savior (not just lawgiver); (2) a strong focus on justification by faith in Jesus; (3) the intimate connection between the righteousness of Christ and obedience to God's commandments; (4) the need for Adventists to focus on Jesus; (5) that Christ's righteousness or "righteousness by faith" has an intimate relationship to the third angel's message of Revelation 14:9-12; (6) that Jesus has special covenant blessings for His children; (7) that Seventh-day Adventists had been emphasizing the law but neglecting Jesus and the importance of faith in His sacrifice; and (8) that God had raised up him and Jones to redirect the gaze of Adventists to Jesus and to faith in His sacrifice and merits.

Now, most certainly I do not know of any minister of the gospel who would forsake such a ringing testimony to the positive effects of his or her ministry. It is one of the most positive assessments that Ellen White ever gave to any minister. Yes, there was and is much to praise the Lord for in the ministry of E. J. Waggoner and A. T. Jones. And we will elaborate and highlight even more before we close.

But Waggoner's legacy also includes a heritage of perfectionistic subjectivism that has been not just mildly problematic but also highly damaging. And it is in the context of these troubling emphases that we need to sort out not only what the 1888 message of Minneapolis *is* positively, but also what it *is not*. Thus it is to this final, sobering question that we now turn our attention.

WHAT THE 1888 MESSAGE OF MINNEAPOLIS IS NOT

The Arguments From Silence

So what is the meaning of the 1888 message of Minneapolis? Especially, who has the better part of the argument or debate between the perfectionistic and the effective, forensic justification advocates? In answer to this pressing question, we offer the following.

The first key point is this: When Ellen White discussed the meaning of Minneapolis, she did not give any *explicit* support for the emphases of the "perfectionistic" school of interpretation. Now, most certainly some can bend certain of her statements in that direction. But whenever she discussed Minneapolis and its positive aspects, she never once mentioned the "post-Fall" nature of Christ, sinless perfection, and the "final generation" corporate vindication of God.

In fact, one searches the writings of Ellen White in vain to find anything like such emphases. I simply challenge the reader to do it for yourselves and see if what we have claimed here is true or not. The extensive collection of her comments, entitled *The Ellen G. White 1888 Materials,* is the most detailed compilation of her statements on the 1888 Minneapolis General Conference session meetings ever assembled by the Ellen G. White Estate. And in these voluminous documents she never said one word about the post-Fall nature of Christ. I have personally read it through numerous times and have looked in vain for such references.

Furthermore, her interpretation of the covenants never featured the sinless perfection spin when she discussed the putting of God's law "in their mind" and the writing of it on the "hearts" of the new covenant saints (Heb. 8:10). It is the specialty of the perfectionistic school of new covenant interpretation, not Ellen G. White. Any honest reader will readily recognize that she has an extremely high view of Christian perfection, but it is always tempered with warnings against the claims of those who would push final generation perfection.[20]

And finally, we find not one explicit word from her pen or the Bible that God is in desperate need of vindication in the great controversy that has been raging over the issue of whether obedience to all of His moral requirements is possible. Most certainly God is validating His divine rule through His decisions in the heavenly pre-Advent judgment. But He has no need for us to get Him off the hook of any of the charges leveled by the devil against His character. Jesus, according to Ellen White, has already taken care of that issue during His incarnate life and atoning death (on this issue, carefully and prayerfully ponder what I have called the "Most Holy Place" of the writings of Ellen White: *The Desire of Ages*, pp. 761-764).

So much for Ellen White's deafening silences on these issues. Let's now turn to some troubling trends in the thought of Jones and Waggoner (especially Waggoner) that might help us more accurately determine *what is* and *what is not* in the "1888 message of Minneapolis."

The Arguments From False Teachings

As has been mentioned in earlier chapters, most of those interested in the teachings of Jones and Waggoner agree that they had later aspects that were not sound. And for the sake of the point being made, we will lay out a few of them for the reader's consideration. We do not do so to take anything away from their already-acknowledged positive contributions. Rather we only seek to clarify what the "Minneapolis message" *is*, and *is not*.

First of all, as already pointed out, Waggoner was a semi-Arian. Now, I have gone to some lengths to locate him in his time and affirm his positive directions away from the classic Arianism of many of the Adventist pioneers. Furthermore, we have affirmed the fact that he came right up to the borders of biblical Trinitarianism, especially on the doctrine of the full deity of Christ. But the documentary evidence is very clear that in the immediate aftermath of Minneapolis he advocated semi-Arian views that clearly denied the eternal personal existence of the Son with Father.

It could be that he later tacitly repudiated such a position, but as noted in chapter 11, one searches in vain to find evidence of such a shift.

But the fact remains that in the two years immediately following the 1888 General Conference session, he was a published semi-Arian. Does this then mean that his semi-Arianism was an integral part of the 1888 message? I think the answer is quite obvious to all (unless you happen to be an anti-Trinitarian). Most obviously E. J. Waggoner is in need of authoritative "screeners" to test the validity of any claim that semi-Arianism belongs in the 1888 message.

Next, it is quite clear that E. J. Waggoner taught that Christ "could not sin" because of His inherent deity. Does anybody want to argue that this idea is part of the 1888 message? Not if you take Ellen White and the Bible seriously. Once more, one could argue that he tacitly repudiated his claim made in early 1889, but the evidence is equally obvious that in the immediate aftermath of 1888 it was still his position.

Both Jones and Waggoner advocated that it was just as bad to refrain from work on Sunday when a Sunday law was in force as it was to labor on the Sabbath. In fact, Jones argued that if someone refrained from work on Sunday in such a circumstance, that individual was receiving the mark of the beast. As we saw in our narrative of the British years, Waggoner made a big deal of having the employees at the British International Tract Society work on Sunday in direct defiance of the London Sunday law being aggressively enforced in the 1890s. Such actions went directly against the clear counsels of Ellen G. White[21] and the principles of Scripture. Is such petulant opposition to refraining from work on Sunday a part of the 1888 message?

We have clearly documented that during the course of the 1890s both Jones and Waggoner advocated highly antiorganizational ideas regarding properly constituted church order. In 1894 Ellen White explicitly stated: "Elder Waggoner has entertained ideas, and without waiting to bring his ideas before a counsel of the brethren, has agitated strange theories. He has brought before some of the people ideas in regard to organization that ought never to have had expression."[22] The two men persistently agitated such concepts for the balance of their public careers as Seventh-day Adventist ministers. Are these ideas on the doctrine of the church a part of the 1888 message?

In 1893 A. T. Jones recklessly put forth the idea that "there were no conditions" in salvation. Ellen White rebuked him and plainly told him that the Bible is replete with conditions. Is his position a part of the 1888 message, or do we need to screen it out?

What about Waggoner's later panentheistic emphases and his teaching on "spiritual affinities" (the idea that a person could have such an "affinity" with someone not their spouse in time and later be married to them in eternity)? Are these ideas such that anyone would want to include them in the 1888 message? It might be "present truth" for certain segments of nineteenth-century Mormonism, but this was and is not something that Seventh-day Adventists had or have any business embracing.

Thus it is extremely apparent that we must clearly establish the following point:

While Ellen White gave the two men unparalleled support, she did not grant them any sort of canonical authority ultimately to define anything. They were always subject to more authoritative, inspired sources. Did God use them mightily? Yes, He did! But they were individuals who needed counsel and correction, and we are not to take their word for anything without bringing them to the clear test of a "thus saith the Lord."

Furthermore, I want to reinforce the principle of "screening" them through inspired authorities, and that includes closely examining their ideas on Christ and His righteousness. Just because they taught such and such on justification, sanctification, perfection, final generation vindication, or what have you, that does not mean that they are the final word on those subjects any more than they were on their defective views of the Godhead, the impossibility of giving into temptation (even for Christ), the conditions of salvation, church organization, Sunday laws, pantheism, or "spiritual affinities."

While God mightily used the young ministers, who were two of the key players on the revival "team Minneapolis," they were not infallible. We need to heartily embrace every precious truth that God led them to give us, but we cannot emphasize enough that their teaching was a body of thought that needs careful sifting and testing. Let's seek to avoid either extreme of being overly critical or naively embracing without sanctified discrimination.

The fruits of their ministry were extremely positive and the possibilities were so great. But the errant directions were also extremely sad, and the long-term effects of these tragic misdirections have proved to be highly negative for both Jones and Waggoner personally and for the church corporately. And this sad consideration leads us to some final troubling questions.

WHO IS TO BLAME FOR THE FALL OF JONES AND WAGGONER?

Honesty compels us to recognize plenty of blame to spread all around for their failures. Most definitely those fomenting the persistent opposition in Battle Creek will face a day of sober reckoning. But we cannot finally lay the cause of Jones and Waggoner's errant directions at the door of the Battle Creek leadership or the authors of the "West Coast" conspiracy theory. The responsibility for their errant tendencies will ultimately rest on Jones and Waggoner themselves. While they were in a number of ways victimized, they were also greatly blessed with abundant support and caring guidance. And for the advantages that they squandered, they will have to give an account before God.

WHY BRING UP SUCH NEGATIVE ISSUES?

Some might raise the following issue: Why are you pointing out all of these negative issues? And the answer is simply to be able to tell the whole story, one that includes not only the triumphs but also the tribulations and the tragic failures. To do otherwise is to distort the historical record. The Bible has done this very same thing, and with brutal honesty (David, Moses, Abraham, and on and on it goes). Furthermore, while we need to take great care, the terrible truth is that doctrines usually get either vindicated or exposed by the fruit that they produce. And the lives of both Jones and Waggoner present a troubling and cautionary tale. More particularly, Ellen White was explicit in the case of Waggoner: his flawed ideas on "spiritual affinities" were the direct result of his panentheistic ideas. Yes, bad theology does produce bad ethics. This is why we should be leery, for instance, of the palpably rotten fruit of the terrible doctrine of irresistible perseverance (popularly known as "once saved, always saved"). It is truly a doctrine that has produced truckloads of presumptuous sinning.

IF THEY WERE SO FLAWED, WHY DID ELLEN WHITE SUPPORT THEM?

Some have asked: If Jones and Waggoner were so flawed, why was Ellen White so supportive of their efforts when they veered off into such troubling directions? While we have already broached this issue earlier in this chapter when we dealt with the issue of Waggoner's quiet rejection of the sanctuary doctrine in the early 1890s, it deserves a further, forthright response. I would venture the following key factors in providing the gist of a credible reply.

First of all, Ellen White was not nearly as doctrinaire as many would imagine. She certainly held strong convictions about doctrinal and ethical truth, but she never saw herself as a primary authority in such matters. While she certainly did exercise a vigorous corrective role from time to time, usually she sought to lead the church into a deeper study of the Word when doctrinal controversy loomed. And that is what she expected others to do in the case of Jones and Waggoner. In fact, the great tragedy of Minneapolis was the failure of the Battle Creek leadership to respond positively to her appeals that they give Jones and Waggoner a fair and helpful hearing.

She did not expect Butler, Smith, Morrison, and their allies just to roll over and mindlessly put their stamp of approval on every aspect of their teachings. But she did appeal for them to come close to Jones and Waggoner, embrace them as Spirit-led brothers in Christ, and receive the major positive points of their most important message.

But tragically, the otherwise-able Battle Creek leaders would not have it. They were so fixated on their own understanding of truth that they could not see the dynamic movement of the Spirit of God as He opened up broader vistas of new light that were so readily perceived by Ellen White. And thus their fierce opposition was a terrible blow to "team Minneapolis" and an insult to the person of Christ and to the Holy Spirit.

Not only did the church and its leadership need the many positive, Christ-centered themes so freshly presented by Jones and Waggoner, but the two men themselves required a number of the insights that others could have given them if the latter would have responded to the appeals of the Holy Spirit sent through Ellen White. A spirit of earnest searching for the truth, in deep mutual respect, could have avoided many errors and practical pitfalls. And according to Ellen White, such a course could have brought down the latter-rain power of the Holy Spirit.

But sadly, Christ was once more wounded in the house of His friends through the fierce opposition manifested by those that could have given great support and corrective guidance. Ellen White earnestly sought to head off all of this with repeated appeals for mutual respect and a Spirit-guided, corporate searching of the Word of God.

Once more, we must emphasize that she was normally quite reluctant to short-circuit such group efforts with authoritative, interpretive fiats. If the leading lights of Battle Creek would have obeyed Ellen White, they could have helped Jones and Waggoner (and themselves) and saved all concerned much grief down the road.

Second, Ellen White was redemptive, almost to a fault. And she did bear long with the foibles of Jones and Waggoner. When she developed alliances with persons whom she understood to be especially chosen for any particular work, she was always quite persistent in seeking to encourage and to bring correction to such Spirit-designated coworkers. A good case in point is Uriah Smith.

Having worked together with him for many decades, she deeply cared for Smith and greatly rejoiced over his many talents and dedicated service to the church in his multiple roles as writer, editor, preacher, and administrator. But his constant undermining of those involved in the revival of Minneapolis deeply troubled her. As we have seen, he was extremely stubborn in his resistance, and even after he repented of his actions he still never really embraced the truths of the message of Minneapolis. While Ellen White continued to *write* him messages of rebuke and correction, she never *wrote him off*.

In fact, it borders on the profoundly ironic that she was deeply grieved when denominational leadership replaced him as editor of the *Review and Herald* with A. T. Jones in 1897. It was not because she was upset with Jones in particular. She just felt that Smith was the best man to edit the good old *Review*, feeble and defective though he was. When the church reinstalled him in 1901, she greatly rejoiced, and this despite the fact that he was totally unrepentant about his doctrinal views on salvation, his superficial repentance for his terrible opposition to her, Jones and Waggoner, and his persistent semi-Arianism.[23] Yes, Ellen White could be quite tolerant of persons in whom she had invested great time, developmental effort, and positive backing. Just because somebody was theologically errant did not mean God could not use them. And thus it was with Jones and Waggoner.

The last factor in our vindication of Ellen White's staunch support of them is the fact that the embattled prophet was desperately looking for ready, willing, and able allies to share the proclamation of the new emphasis on Christ, His atoning work, and His justifying and transforming grace. The best and most responsive men in this time of great need and providential opportunity were Jones and Waggoner—"warts and all." And isn't this the way that God has always tended to work? Would you and I have chosen the deceiving Abraham and Jacob, the failed and disgraced Moses, the halting and grasping Balaam, the erratic, moody, and idolatrous Gideon, the immoral and suicidal Samson, the murderous and adulterous David, the whining Elijah, the theologically immature John the Baptist, and the Christ-denying Peter? They probably would not have cut it in the present-day church, but they did in Christ's!

And so it is that God has always used the best men and women who were available. And Jones and Waggoner were two such individuals, feeble and defective though they were. Their defects included not only their temperaments and practical judgment, but also significant theological errors.

But Ellen White, like the God of heaven, always saw persons for what they could become, and embraced their spirit of inspired adventure to attempt great exploits for God. When they failed, she did not give up on them easily. It meant on a practical level that she would write them strong messages of rebuke and correction. But she would always balance it with words of encouragement, affirmation, and renewal in the service of the gospel. Finally, she would leave them to their self-destructive devices only when it became utterly apparent that they would no longer receive her messages of rebuke and support. And tragically, that is what both Jones and Waggoner wound up doing.

Was it, however, Ellen White's fault that they persisted in such a course? Absolutely not! Furthermore, she made it clear that if they should be "overthrown," it was no evidence that the basic thrust of their positive message was false.[24] While they did embrace faulty views, the positive core of their message stands in its integrity, despite their later misadventures in practical and theological errors that lead to their tragic apostasies.

It is not our business to judge their souls. That we will leave to the merciful and just God. But their end was clearly not what Ellen White and the Lord intended. I must confess that in the writing of this biography I have felt moments of such intense sadness that I have been reduced to almost-unmitigated sorrow for all the losses suffered by Waggoner. But I have also been greatly inspired and encouraged by the persistently redemptive efforts of Ellen White and the wonderful way that she sought to save these men and their adversaries from themselves and the clutches of the great adversary. And it is in this spirit that I would like to bring this account to a conclusion.

A THEOLOGICAL AND INTERCESSORY FINALE

As we close the story of the life and thought of E. J. Waggoner, we should once more review the positive contributions of his ministry. Four merit final, special consideration.

We should be grateful for Waggoner's persistent but flawed attempts to draw attention to Christ and His great sacrifice. Second, his emphasis that the law is a powerful instrument of the conviction of sin was a major advance in the Adventist appreciation of the doctrine that God reaches out to all sinners. Third, his attempts to put the "faith of Jesus" at front and center of the proclamation of the great three angels' messages of Revelation 14 was wonderfully pathbreaking.

And finally, I have come to agree with Paul Penno, Jr., that Waggoner's positive teachings on the covenants were his most profound and enduring contributions to Seventh-day Adventist theology and personal Christian experience. While he would interject some panentheistic ideas into his final opus on the theme, it should not take away from his legitimate emphasis that we must have a true heart embrace of God's constant offer of salvation. All the theology, religious observances, and ethical accomplishments in the Christian life will come to naught without a deep heartfelt embrace of the person and merits of Jesus. It is for these, if for no other reasons, that we can all be grateful for the life and teachings of E. J. Waggoner.

I want to conclude this story by offering up a prayer of hope: O Lord of creation and redemption, in the spirit of redemptive mercy, so persistently manifested by Ellet's mentor, Ellen G. White, I plead Your mercies for all of us and earnestly request that we, along with E. J. Waggoner, might one day soon be able to sit down together at the feet of Jesus and talk over these precious themes with the Lord, whom Ellet J. Waggoner so earnestly sought to exalt. Maranatha!

---

[1] R. Wieland, *The 1888 Message: An Introduction*, p. 181. Most certainly Waggoner was confused from the perspective of standard Seventh-day Adventist teachings on the sanctuary and his "mystical" views of the atonement, but he was not confused as to what his true convictions were. In a remarkable manner, he was very logical in working out the implications of his thoughts so that they became consistent with his foundational principles regarding the person of Christ, the atonement, and his unbalanced views on justification by faith.

[2] That would put the events described at 1891.

[3] *The "Confession of Faith" of Dr. E. J. Waggoner* (originally published by Albion F. Ballenger, the editor of *The Gathering Call*, n.d.; Document File 236, Ellen G. White Estate, Loma Linda Branch Office, Dell Webb Library, Loma Linda University), pp. 14, 15.

[4] *Ibid.*, p. 16.

[5] Wieland, *The 1888 Message*, pp. 180, 181. Compare Wieland's position with Eric C. Webster's presentation of it in *Crosscurrents in Adventist Christology*, pp. 244, 245, footnote 257. Webster presents the gist of Wieland's argument, along with the arguments and suggestions of others who have tended to agree with Wieland. When we compare Wieland's 1980 Edition of *The 1888 Message: An Introduction* to the revised and enlarged edition of 1997, we find no apparent revisions of his positions.

[6] "*Confession of Faith*," p. 15.

[7] *Ibid.*, pp. 30, 31.

[8] E. J. Waggoner, "The Sabbath School. Acts 3; 4:1—3," *Signs of the Times*, Apr. 26, 1883; "The Commentary. Review and Temperance," *Signs of the Times*, June 15, 1888.

[9] "Looking Unto Jesus," *Present Truth*, Sept. 28, 1893.

[10] "The Judgment," *Present Truth*, June 18, 1896.

[11] "The Blotting Out of Sin," *Review and Herald*, Sept. 30, 1902. (Italics supplied.)

[12] The hospital medical records metaphor is Waggoner's.

[13] Desmond Ford, *Daniel 8:14, The Day of Atonement, and the Investigative Judgment* (Casselberry, Fla.: Euangelion Press, 1980), pp. A-1—A-6. The basic outlines of Ford's reinterpretation of the sanctuary doctrine are succinctly portrayed in the following pages of his Glacier View document entitled "Daniel 8:14, The Day of Atonement and the Investigative Judgment," pp. 646-653, 662, 667, 668, 671, 672, and the following pages in the appendexes: Appendix One, pp. A-1—A-67 and Appendix Thirty, pp. A-1—A-86. Besides Ford's published version of his Glacier View manuscript, it is also available at the General Conference archives and most Adventist university and college libraries around the world.

[14] For a further brief review of Ford's reinterpretation of the sanctuary doctrine, see

Robert W. Olson, *One Hundred and One Questions on the Sanctuary and on Ellen White* (Washington, D.C.: Ellen G. White Estate, 1981), pp. 19, 20. For some background perspective on the "Ford crisis," see *Ministry* (Special Sanctuary Issue, October 1980), pp. 4-10 (back issues of *Ministry* are available online).

[15] As noted previously, the best theological expression of this balanced teaching comes from Seventh-day Adventist theologian Hans K. LaRondelle's presentation made to the conferees of the Lutheran World Federation during the bilateral "conversations between Lutherans and Seventh-day Adventists in the years 1994-1998." LaRondelle's paper is on exhibit for the convenience of the reader in Appendix D. It is entitled "The Seventh-day Adventist View of the Relationship of Justification—Sanctification—the Final Judgment" and has been published in *Lutherans and Adventists in Conversation: Report and Papers Presented 1994—1998.*

[16] Both Luther and Ellen White are prime examples.

[17] Most likely S. H. Lane, president of the Illinois Conference.

[18] In his answer Waggoner ignores not only the Bible but the plain declarations of Ellen G. White: "There is in the religious world a theory of sanctification which is false in itself and dangerous in its influence. In many cases those who profess sanctification do not possess the genuine article. Their sanctification consists in talk and will worship. Those who are really seeking to perfect Christian character will never indulge the thought that they are sinless. Their lives may be irreproachable, they may be living representatives of the truth which they have accepted; but the more they discipline their minds to dwell upon the character of Christ, and the nearer they approach to His divine image, the more clearly will they discern its spotless perfection, and the more deeply will they feel their own defects" (*The Sanctified Life* [Washington, D.C.: Review and Herald Pub. Assn., 1937), p. 7).

[19] "Studies in the Book of Hebrews—No. 15," *General Conference Bulletin*, Mar. 5, 1897, pp. 269-275.

[20] We especially urge the reader to read carefully the amazing testimony recorded in *Selected Messages*, book 1, pp. 176ff., in which she specifically warned against any teaching that will speak of a purer, holier people coming out at the time of the end (and she gave her sobering warning in May of 1890, right at the height of the post-1888 revival of Christ our righteousness).

[21] Ellen G. White, *Last Day Events* (Nampa, Idaho: Pacific Press Pub. Assn., 1992), pp. 138, 139.

[22] Ellen G. White to A. T. Jones, Jan. 14, 1894. Cited in G. Knight, *A User-friendly Guide*, p. 75.

[23] For a succinct review of the up-and-down relationship of Ellen White and Uriah Smith, see Knight, *User-friendly Guide*, pp. 136-139.

[24] Ellen White stated: "It is quite possible that Elders Jones or Waggoner may be overthrown by the temptations of the enemy; but if they should be, this would not prove that they had had no message from God, or that the work that they had done was all a mistake" (Ellen White to Uriah Smith, Sept. 19, 1892; cited in Knight, *User-friendly Guide*, p. 141).

APPENDIX A

PUBLISHED BOOKS AND PAMPHLETS OF ELLET JOSEPH WAGGONER

Listed in Chronological Order

The Honor Due to God. Oakland, Calif.: Pacific Press Pub. Co., 1884.

A Series of Readings Covering a Portion of the Ground Embraced in the Bible Course at Healdsburg College, 1883-1884. 1st and 2nd ed. Oakland, Calif.: Pacific Press Pub. Co., [n.d.]. 2 vols.

The Gospel in the Book of Galatians: A Review. A letter to George I. Butler, dated Feb. 10, 1887. Oakland, Calif.: Pacific Press Pub. Co., 1888. Republished by the Judgment Hour Publishing Company, 309 Chevallum Road, Palmwoods, Queensland, Australia.

Fathers of the Catholic Church. Oakland, Calif.: Pacific Press Pub. Co., 1888.

Prophetic Lights: Some of the Prominent Prophecies of the Old and New Testaments, Interpreted by the Bible and History. Oakland, Calif.: Pacific Press Pub. Co., 1889.

Baptism: Its Significance. Bible Student's Library, No. 79. Oakland, Calif.: Pacific Press Pub. Co., 1890.

Christ and His Righteousness. Oakland, Calif.: Pacific Press Pub. Co., 1890. In 1972 Southern Publishing Association, Nashville, Tennessee, issued a facsimile reproduction of the original edition.

The Full Assurance of Faith. Bible Student's Library, No. 64. Oakland, Calif.: Pacific Press Pub. Co., 1890.

Living by Faith: Christian Growth. Bible Student's Library, No. 75. Oakland, Calif.: Pacific Press Pub. Co., 1890.

The Sure Foundation and the Keys of the Kingdom. Bible Student's Library, No. 63. Oakland, Calif.: Pacific Press Pub. Co., [1890?].

Bible Studies on the Book of Romans. Baker, Ore.: A. L. Hudson, [n.d.]. A facsimile reproduction from the 1891 *General Conference Bulletin.*

Sunday: The Origin of Its Observance in the Christian Church. Bible Student's Library, No. 80. Oakland, Calif.: Pacific Press Pub. Co., [1891?].

How to Get Knowledge. Apples of Gold Library, No. 4. Oakland, Calif.: Pacific Press Pub. Co., 1893.

The Rest That Remains for the People of God. Bible Student's Library, No. 101. Oakland, Calif.: Pacific Press Pub. Co., 1893.

The Power of Forgiveness. Oakland, Calif.: Pacific Press Pub. Co., 1894.

The Gospel in Creation. London: International Tract Society, 1895.

The Cross of Christ. Apples of Gold Library, No. 15. Oakland, Calif.: Pacific Press Pub. Co., 1894.

Foreknowledge and Foreordination. Apples of Gold Library, No. 41. Oakland, Calif.: Pacific Press Pub. Co., 1897.

Letter and Spirit. Apples of Gold Library, No. 37. Oakland, Calif.: Pacific Press Pub. Co., 1897.

Salvation in Jesus Christ. Apples of Gold Library, No. 64. Oakland, Calif.: Pacific Press Pub. Co., 1899.

The Everlasting Covenant. London: International Tract Society, 1900.

The Glad Tidings. London: International Tract Society, 1900. Republished by the Judgment Hour Publishing Company in unedited and unrevised form.

The Glad Tidings. Edited and revised by Robert J. Wieland. Nashville: Southern Pub. Assn., 1972.

Confession of Faith. [n.p.] [1916]. Copy located at Andrews University, Berrien Springs, Mich. James White Library, Center for Adventist Research.

Posthumous publications: reprints of series of articles from Adventist periodicals of Waggoner's day have appeared during the past few years. For a complete list of such publications, contact either Glad Tidings Publishers, 8784 Valley View Drive, Berrien Springs, Michigan 49103 or Teach Services, Brushton, New York (the Teach Services Web site is www.tsibooks.com). The reprints include his series on the books of John, Romans, Ephesians, and Isaiah.

APPENDIX B

WHAT BECAME OF JESSIE F. MOSER[1] AND EDITH ADAMS WAGGONER?

WHAT FOLLOWS ARE BRIEF SKETCHES of the lives of Jessie Moser Waggoner and Edith Adams Waggoner, following their respective marriages to E. J. Waggoner. While neither ever re-married, they lived out their later years in a relatively quiet and productive manner.

JESSIE FREMONT MOSER WAGGONER[2]
1860-1944

Following her divorce from Ellet Waggoner and her failed relationship with Eddie Spicer, Jessie resided for a number of years with her daughter Bessie and her husband in Kankakee, then Chicago and Park Ridge, Illinois. Her health had taken a turn for the worse during the period following the divorce, and her daughter and son-in-law were quite instrumental in helping her to recover.

In 1912, after Bessie and her husband returned to England, Jessie received an invitation to live in Takoma Park, Maryland. She would reside in the Greater Washington, D.C., area for six years. During this period the General Conference granted her denominational retirement support (known as "sustentation" in those years). But the amount was initially woefully inadequate (she fed herself on 10 cents a day). When Mrs. A. G. Daniells "accidentally" found out about her virtual starvation regimen, the well-connected wife of the General Conference president appealed in her behalf, and her intercessions proved effective. The church granted Jessie a "generously" increased amount.

The Washington/Takoma Park years were relatively productive. During them she wrote teachers' notes for the *Worker*, Sabbath school lessons for the children, and lessons for camp meeting children's meetings. She was also the Sabbath school superintendent of the Memorial church in Washington during most of these years (participating in numerous Sabbath school conventions) and was also the president of the Dorcas Society (the original name for the local Adventist welfare organization, now known as Community Services). But her hard work in such volunteer positions began to tell on her health.

In August of 1918 it became clear to her that she should move to southern California, where she could be near her children. It would prove to be a wise decision, as she found new life and service in sunny California, nurtured by her daughter Bessie and her husband, who had settled there upon their return from England.

When she arrived in California she weighed only 96 pounds. While her physical health did improve, her seemingly inherent workaholism once more got the best of her. She resumed work on the Sabbath school teachers' notes for the *Worker*, but such "hurry, hurry" work to keep ahead of the printer wore on her nerves to the point that she nearly had a nervous breakdown. The relapse caused her to seek relief from the strain of deadlines and allowed her "to write some things" that required no deadline, things that she "had long had on" her "mind and never could get time for." The projects included a series of senior lessons and "a lot of illustrated articles on the law of God" that she produced for non-SDA consumption in *Signs of the Times*. Along the same lines, she prepared a book on illustrations for Sabbath school teachers called "Scissors and Chalk," and another book for children called "Nuggets and Pearls for Boys and Girls." And she did all of it while engaging in "a good deal of hard work in the Glendale SDA Church Sabbath school."

Jessie herself probably rendered the best summary of her public activities in her 1924 letter to H. H. Cobban that sought to "classify" her work, which had been so different from most other women sustentation beneficiaries: she simply claimed that "I have been a Sabbath school worker and nothing else, yet it has sometimes run out in so many different directions that I did not know how to call it." On balance, she should have just left it as "Sabbath school worker and nothing else"!

Yet her Sabbath school activity also had still another interesting side to it—and this leads us to her final and most enduring contribution: "getting out gospel songs and books for Sabbath school teachers, parents, young people, and children. She had three different songbooks printed—*In His Service Songs*, *Happy Songs*, and *Sing and Praise*, the words by herself and the tunes by various well-known composers." Quite possibly, her best-loved songs were for the little ones, and her all-time greatest hit was her little composition that celebrates the Sabbath—"The Seventh Is for Jesus." Its lines are beguilingly simple: "One, two, three, four, five, six for us," repeated three times, and then the final line—"The seventh is for Jesus."[3] If there were such a thing as a Seventh-day Adventist Sabbath School Hall of Fame, Jessie would deserve election on the first ballot.

She certainly did not live the nearly 39 years following her divorce from Ellet in dreary self-pity. While she had some sad, down times, she spent the decades largely in positive and productive service. Jessie passed to a well-deserved rest in December of 1944 and was buried in the Grand View Cemetery in Los Angeles, California.

EDITH ADAMS WAGGONER[4]
1869-1945

Edith spent the remaining years of her life in Battle Creek following the death of Ellet in 1916. She continued to work as a medical librarian at the Sanitarium and logged more than 40 years in the capacity. While it is not clear what year she moved to Battle Creek, it seems best to date her arrival sometime in either late 1903 or early 1904. Thus for most of her Battle Creek years she was gainfully employed. She was apparently not a robust person physically. Pearl tells that not too long after Ellet's death Edith suffered a bout of serious illness that necessitated her hospitalization. Furthermore, Pearl suggested that she remained in somewhat frail health for the rest of her life, needing numerous treatments during the years of her widowhood. She had been ill for a year and seriously ill since March 1945 when she passed to her rest on June 10, 1945, at the age of 76. She was buried next to Ellet at the old Burlington, Michigan, cemetery, where their grave markers are still easily recognizable.

[1] Jessie F. Moser Waggoner eventually took her maiden name back after her divorce from Ellet. Thus Jessie Fremont Moser.

[2] The basic facts of this sketch come from her obituary, "Jessie F. Waggoner Moser," *Review and Herald*, Dec. 21, 1944, and a letter to H. H. Cobban, Oct. 21, 1924, which has been preserved in her sustentation file at the General Conference of Seventh-day Adventists.

[3] The song is number 22 in the classic Sabbath school kindergarten songbook entitled *Sabbath Songs for Tiny Tots—Kindergarten,* "Prepared Under the Direction of the Sabbath School Department of the General Conference" (Washington, D.C.: Review and Herald Pub. Assn., 1964; rev. 1970). Also contained in this songbook are several others by her: number 120, "Tick-tock, Tick-tock," and number 131, "Quietly, Quietly": "Quietly, quietly tiptoe along, Jesus is here, angels are near. Into the classes just where we belong, close to our teachers dear."

[4] The basic facts of this sketch derive from Edith's obituary that appeared as "Mrs. Ellet J. Wagner" in the Battle Creek *Enquirer and News,* June 12, 1945, p. 2, col. 3; and Pearl Waggoner Howard to L. E. Froom, Oct. 15, 1961, Document File 236b.

APPENDIX C

THE MYSTICAL VIEW OF THE ATONEMENT

I HAVE DRAWN THE FOLLOWING EXTRACT from L. Berkhof's *Systematic Theology** and present it in order to give the reader a fuller conceptual sense of what this version of the atonement seeks to communicate as the reason for the death of Christ. The parallels to Waggoner's thought are remarkably similar:

"The Mystical Theory.

"The mystical theory has this in common with the moral influence theory, that it conceives of the atonement exclusively as exercising influence on man and bringing about a change in him. At the same time it differs from the moral influence theory in that it conceives of the change wrought in man, not primarily as an ethical change in the conscious life of man, but as a deeper change in the subconscious life which is brought about in a mystical way. The basic principle of this theory is that, in the incarnation, the divine life entered into the life of humanity, in order to lift it to the plane of the divine. Christ possessed human nature with its inborn corruption and predisposition to moral evil; but through the influence of the Holy Spirit He was kept from manifesting this corruption in actual sin, gradually purified human nature, and in His death completely extirpated this original depravity and reunited that nature to God. He entered the life of mankind as a transforming leaven, and the resulting transformation constitutes His redemption. This is in effect, though with differences of detail, the theory of Schleiermacher [and] Edward Irving."

After his summary description, then follows Berkhof's analysis and critique:

"1. It takes no account of the guilt of man. According to Scripture the guilt of man must be removed, in order that he may be purified of his pollution; but the mystical theory, disregarding the guilt of sin, concerns itself only with the expulsion of the pollution of sin. It knows of no justification, and conceives of salvation as consisting in subjective sanctification.

"2. It rests upon false principles, where it finds in the natural order of the universe an exhaustive expression of the will and nature of God, regards sin exclusively as a power of moral evil in the world, which involves no guilt and deserves no punishment, and looks upon punishment as a mere reaction of the law of the universe against the transgressor, and not at all as a revelation of the personal wrath of God against sin.

"3. It contradicts Scripture where it makes Christ share in the pollution of sin and hereditary depravity, and deduces the necessity of His death from the sinfulness of His own nature (not all do this). By doing this, it makes it impossible to regard Him as the sinless Savior who, just because of His sinlessness, could take the place of sinners and pay the penalty for them.

"4. It has no answer to the question [of] how those who lived before the incarnation can share in the redemption of Jesus Christ. If Christ in some realistic way drove out pollution of sin during the time of His sojourn on earth, and now continues to drive it out; and if the salvation of man depends on this subjective process, how then could the Old Testament saints share in this salvation?"

* L. Berkhof, *Systematic Theology* (Grand Rapids: Wm. B. Eerdmans, 1938), pp. 389, 390.

APPENDIX D

THE SEVENTH-DAY ADVENTIST VIEW OF THE RELATIONSHIP OF JUSTIFICATION—SANCTIFICATION—THE FINAL JUDGMENT

by Hans K. LaRondelle, Th.D.

The Seventh-day Adventist view of justification, sanctification, and the final judgment is rooted in their interpretation of Israel's sanctuary services. This view is also connected with their understanding of the long-range prophecies of Daniel and Revelation. Adventism today accepts a more contextual exegesis of the particular passages of Scripture which have been used traditionally as building blocks of their unique doctrines. In the book *Seventh-day Adventists Answer Questions on Doctrines* (Washington, D.C.: Review and Herald Pub. Assn., 1957) the authors state:

"Seventh-day Adventists believe that man's understanding of God's truth is progressive. . . . In days to come we should rightly expect further unfolding of Bible truth. . . . We honor the noble line of witnesses such as Wycliffe, Luther, Tyndale, Calvin, Knox, Wesley, and other great leaders of the past, whose advance into new light led the church forward in its fuller understanding of God's will" (p. 9).

A more comprehensive statement of Adventist beliefs is offered in the book *Seventh-day Adventists Believe . . . : A Biblical Exposition of 27 Fundamental Doctrines,* Ministerial Association, General Conference of Seventh-day Adventists (Hagerstown, Md.: Review and Herald Pub. Assn., 1988). The editors declare: "We have not written this book to serve as a creed—a statement of beliefs set in theological concrete. Adventists have but one creed: 'The Bible, and the Bible alone.' . . . [This study] represents an authentic exposition of Adventist beliefs" (pp. vii, viii). A more scholarly theological exposition of Adventist beliefs by some representative scholars will soon be published as volume 12 in the Commentary Reference Series. Interestingly for our theme, in 1995 the Seventh-day Adventist Theological Seminary at Andrews University accepted the Th.D. dissertation of Gunnar Pedersen, entitled "The Soteriology of Ellen G. White Compared With the Lutheran Formula of Concord: A Study of the Adventist Doctrine of the Final Judgment of the Saints and Their Justification Before God" (Berrien Springs, Mich., November 1995).

JUSTIFICATION BY FAITH: *SOLA GRATIA—SOLA FIDE*

Basic Adventism is the gospel principle that human salvation is not through the law or by human works but solely through the saving grace of God. Representative of this core belief is a statement by Ellen G. White:

"We owe everything to grace, free grace, sovereign grace. Grace in the covenant ordained our adoption. Grace in the Savior effected our redemption, our regeneration and our adoption to heirship with Christ" (*Testimonies for the Church* [Mountain View, Calif.: Pacific Press Pub. Assn., 1948], vol. 6, p. 268).

Adventist belief accepts Christ as man's substitute and example, in this irreversible order. Faith in Christ as our substitute before God provides our justification as God's act of *declaring* the repentant believer righteous. Justification is seen as the opposite of condemnation (see Rom. 5:16; 8:1, 33, 34). The basis for the believers' justification is not their law observance, but Christ's sinless obedience (Rom. 5:18, 19). *SDAs Believe* states: "Through justification by faith in Christ, His righteousness is imputed to us. We are right with God because of Christ our Substitute [2 Cor. 5:21 quoted]" (p. 122).

AN EFFECTIVE FORENSIC JUSTIFICATION

Adventists do not believe in an exclusively forensic justification, but in an effective forensic justification. They do not compartmentalize justification and sanctification, but recognize that one and the same faith in Christ receives both the imputed righteouness and the Holy Spirit in the heart. Both are promised on the same condition by Paul. Justification is by faith without works of law (Rom. 3:28), and the gift of the Holy Spirit equally comes by faith without works of law (Gal. 3:2, 5). Paul indicates that the two gifts are inseparably joined together, so that the one cannot come without the other (Rom. 5:1, 5). Adventists agree therefore with Luther's doctrine of justification as the critical doctrine by which the church stands or falls. They would basically agree with the interpretation of Luther as presented by Paul Althaus: "Justification in the full sense of the word consists in both of these: imputation and man's transformation to a new obedience together" (*The Theology of Martin Luther* [Philadelphia: Fortress Press, 1970], p. 235).

They would also agree with Martin Greschat's evaluation of Luther's position:

"Justification and actual renewal constitute a unity, in which both—in spite of the strictly maintained logical priority of the justification of the godless—nonetheless influence each other mutually" (*Melanchthon Neben Luther: Studien zur Gestalt der Rechtfertigungslehre zwischen 1528 und 1537* [Wittenberg: Luther Verlag, 1965], p. 212; own trans.).

Adventists accept that Christ forgave or justified the repentant tax collector (Luke 18:14), but also that Christ illustrated forgiveness or justification as an act of reconciliation in His parable of the lost son. The father expressed his forgiveness by embracing and kissing his repentant son and by restoring him fully to sonship and fellowship in the father's home (Luke 15:20-24). This represented Jesus' teaching of the fuller sense of forgiveness by the heavenly Father. It is not solely an abstract declaration by the Father. It is the creative word of the Creator. In this judicial declaration occurs the miracle of reconciliation and restoration of fellowship with God. Thus righteousness by faith is also the transforming power of salvation for all believers in Christ (Rom. 1:16). Adventists have never taught the doctrine of justification as a legal abstraction but as a personal union with the living Christ, on the basis of God's imputed righteousness (see Gal. 2:15, 16, 20).

MODERN TRENDS IN PROTESTANTISM

Some Protestant scholars today admit that "the living wholeness of Luther's conception" was lost within the Protestant faith because of a compartmentalizing of justification. The Commission on Theology of the Lutheran World Federation acknowledged:

"In later Lutheranism there is an unmistakable tendency to make the doctrine of justification into a special doctrine. With the good intention of keeping the doctrine of justification pure, only its forensic aspect is stressed; and the fact is disregarded that with justification it is a question of a personal and total act. Justification is the restoration of that relationship between God and man which God wanted in the beginning" (*Justification Today*, Studies and Reports, Lutheran World [New York: National Lutheran Council. 1965], p. 16).

The contemporary trend shows, however, an opposite one-sidedness, which stresses the common mission of all churches to proclaim the gospel of grace, in which the historic doctrine of the *sola fide* becomes one doctrine among many others rather than the critical principle basic to the true understanding and proclamation of the gospel. This new stress on the doctrine of ecclesiology and the unity of the Christian church was dramatically illustrated by the decision of the former Lutheran scholar Richard John Neuhaus to become a Roman Catholic priest (in September 1990). His argument was that it was his duty to be in full communion with "the fullest and most rightly ordered reality of the church through time" (in my article "Has Rome Accepted the Gospel?" *Liberty*, January-Febuary 1992, pp. 14, 15). He maintains that the gospel is being proclaimed in the Roman Catholic Church today. This position implies that the *sola fide* doctrine should be subordinated to the concept of formal unity with the Roman Catholic Church.

A similar trend regarding the *sola fide* can be observed among the Reformed theologians today. Michael Horton asserts: "Today one can easily find theological professors at leading evangelical institutions who no longer find justification by faith alone to be true, much less necessary" (in his foreword to R. C. Sproul, *Faith Alone: The Evangelical Doctrine of Justification* [Grand Rapids: Baker Books, 1995], p. 13).

Contemporary American evangelicals are moving away from the central core of the gospel: from the Pauline message of justification by faith alone. Leading Protestants today seem to consider the *sola fide* doctrine no longer essential to the gospel of salvation, and not vital to the essence of being of a true church. Those evangelicals who in 1994 signed the document "Evangelicals and Catholics Together: The Christian Mission in the Third Millennium" (in *Evangelicals and Catholics Together: Toward a Common Mission,* ed. Charles Colson and R. J. Neuhaus [Dallas: Word Pub., 1995], pp. xxxii, xxxiii) consider the Pauline *sola fide* merely a theoretical doctrine or as "small print." The issue of justification by faith alone was effectively circumvented by the joined acceptance of the common denominator that justification is "through faith." However, both parties gave different meanings to the same formula. Here the historic view of the Reformation was eclipsed by a compromise, because Protestantism and Romanism teach fundamentally different ways of salvation. The doctrine of justification and merit remains unchanged as the watershed between two different dogmatic interpretations of the gospel.

THE ORGANIC RELATIONSHIP BETWEEN JUSTIFICATION AND SANCTIFICATION

Just as the light of the sun cannot be separated from its heat, so it is impossible to split up justification and sanctification. They remain logically distinct, but cannot be separated in experience. They form an indivisible unity, because Christ bestows both on the believer through faith in Him. Trying to divide both amounts to an effort to divide Christ Himself. On this point Calvin made a valuable contribution. This Reformer of the church offered a helpful interpretation of the "wedding garment" in Christ's parable of the wedding feast (Matt. 22:11). This garment, said Calvin, signified not exclusively the righteousness of faith, but also the renewed, sanctified life, because faith and works cannot be separated (*Commentary* on Matt. 22:11).

While Luther directed his *sola fide* doctrine mainly against the merit doctrine of Rome, Calvin's concern was the position of the Lutheran Quietists who thought that everything is settled with justification. Calvin, therefore, stressed that the Holy Spirit brings our soul into mystical union with Christ, with the total Christ (1 Cor. 1:30). Thus for Calvin, our union with Christ and justification refer to the same act of God. And this union also brings our sanctification. Calvin emphasized the thought that we receive the riches of justification not simply through Christ but *in* Christ (1 Cor. 1:5) (*Calvini Opera*, 49:310; 47:331). Tjarko Stadtland, therefore, drew the conclusion: "Calvin wants to transcend Melanchthon's juxtaposition [of justification and sanctification] by grasping both in *an organic connection*" (*Rechtfertigung und Heiligung bei Calvin* (1972), p. 131; own trans.; italics supplied). Stadtland maintains that the heart of Calvin's Reformation gospel is not the justification doctrine by itself, but the spiritual union of the soul with the living Christ through the Holy Spirit. From this union flow both gifts of grace: justification and sanctification.

We recognize that the heart of the Reformation gospel is a living heart indeed. The authentic Luther and Calvin did not restrict the gospel to a purely forensic justification doctrine. Such a restriction came only later, in the Lutheran Formula of Concord (1580), long after the Reformers had died. It seems to be construed to stress the contrast with the "Decree on Justification" of Trent (1547). The Reformers themselves, however, preached an effective justification message as the power of God for salvation. They uplifted the living Christ as the assurance of our total justification, reconciliation, and adoption as children of God and heirs of salvation. Such a faith in Christ as our personal Savior and Surety on the basis of Christ's substitutionary atoning sacrifice was a gift of God Himself.

The immediate effect of such a faith in Christ was the *indwelling* of Christ in the heart of the believer. Thus, Christ at the same time healed the sinner from his twofold evil: from his guilt and from his self-centered heart. The guilt was covered by Christ's infinite righteousness, and the selfish heart was reborn and transformed by the Holy Spirit unto willing obedience to God's revealed will. In this twofold grace of Christ the Reformers saw the imputation of God's righteousness as fundamental and conditional to the indwelling of Christ in the heart. The relationship of the Christ outside us and the Christ inside us was so intimate that they conceived this as a living or organic relationship.

ELLEN G. WHITE CONTINUES THE PROTESTANT REFORMATION

E. G. White, whose writings are regarded by the Seventh-day Adventist Church as an inspired authority, emphasized her full agreement with "the great doctrine of justification by faith, so clearly taught by Luther" (*The Great Controversy* [Mountain View, Calif. Pacific Press Pub. Assn., 1911], p. 253.) She also expressed her appreciation of John Wesley's "preaching of the great truths which he had received—justification through faith in the atoning blood of Christ, and the renewing power of the Holy Spirit upon the heart, bringing forth fruit in a life conformed to the example of Christ" (*ibid.*, p. 256).

She acknowledged that some "holiness people" went "to great extremes" on sanctification and righteousness by faith. She frankly admitted that many Seventh-day Adventists in her time had obscured the gospel of salvation: "The doctrine of justification by faith has been lost sight of by many who have professed to believe the third angel's message [see Rev. 14:6-12]" (*Review and Herald,* Aug. 13, 1889; in *Selected Messages* [Washington, D.C.: Review and Herald Pub. Assn., 1958], book 1, p. 360). She explained:

"Let the subject be made distinct and plain that it is not possible to effect anything in our standing before God or in the gift of God to us through creature merit. Should faith and works purchase the gift of salvation for anyone, then the Creator is under obligation to the creature. Here is an opportunity for falsehood to be accepted as truth. If any man can merit salvation by anything he may do, then he is in the same position as the Catholic to do penance for his sins. Salvation, then, is partly of debt, that may be earned as wages. If man cannot, by any of his good works, merit salvation, then it must be wholly of grace, received by man as a sinner because he receives and believes in Jesus. It is wholly a free gift" (manuscript 36, 1890; in *Faith and Works* [Nashville: Southern Pub. Assn., 1979], pp. 19-20).

"The righteousness by which we are justified is imputed; the righteousness by which we are sanctified is imparted. The first is our title to heaven, the second is our fitness for heaven" (*Review and Herald*, June 4, 1895).

"God's forgiveness is not merely a judicial act by which He sets us free from condemnation. It is not only forgiveness *for* sins but reclaiming *from* sin. It is the outflow of redeeming love that transforms the heart" (*Thoughts From the Mount of Blessing* [Mountain View, Calif.: Pacific Press Pub. Assn., 1956], p. 114).

She even went so far as to declare that the Seventh-day Adventists have a special calling to restore the gospel message of justification by faith:

"Several have written to me, inquiring if the message of justification by faith is the third angel's message, and I have answered, 'It is the third angel's message in verity'" (*Review and Herald,* Apr. 1, 1890; *Selected Messages,* book 1, p. 372).

IN SUMMARY

The soteriologies of Ellen White and of the Reformers are governed by the principles of grace and faith in Christ. All recognize that the grace of God in Christ is the sole meritorious ground for the believer's salvation, and that all human efforts are excluded from the basis of man's justification or forgiveness by God. Both the historic Protestant and Adventist positions maintain that saving faith consists of a personal trust in Christ, in His promises and testimony. Even faith itself is viewed as a gift of divine grace, which through the Word and the Holy Spirit initiates, restores, and increases faith manifesting itself in a response of devotion, commitment, consecration, and obedience of Christ as the ruling principle in the saints. The good works of a sanctified life are the visible signs that demonstrate and vindicate the presence of genuine faith. Both traditions also agree on the biblical definitions of justification as forgiveness of sin, based exclusively on Christ's satisfaction of the ultimate demands of the divine moral law by virtue of His righteousness and merits. Both agree that a true believer receives a full and complete salvation instantly the moment that faith is born and as long as faith perseveres.

SANCTIFICATION AND JUDGMENT

Paul can also speak of "justification" as a divine verdict in the last judgment. This eschatological aspect of Paul's theology has been ignored or denied by some Protestant theologians, yet it forms a fundamental part of the New Testament message of salvation. In continuity with the Hebrew Scriptures, Paul declares concerning the last judgment: God "will give to each person according to what he has done" (Rom. 2:6, NIV; cf. Ps. 62:12) and: "For it is not the hearers of the law who are righteous before God, but the doers of the law who will be justified" (Rom. 2:13, RSV).

The apostle is not dealing here with merely external observance, but with the internal commitment of grateful obedience, not with "works of the law" but with works or fruits of faith that are pleasing in God's sight (cf. C.E.B. Cranfield, *"A Critical and Exegetical Commentary on the Epistle to the Romans*. International Critical Commentary Series. Vol. 1, p. 155). Growth in holiness and well-doing is the Christian's sacred responsibility (see Gal. 6:9; 2 Thess. 3:13; Titus 2:11-13; 2 Peter 1:4-11; 3:11,18). The sanctified life will be taken as evidence of saving faith on the day of judgment (Rom. 2:7).

Consequently, present justification does not exempt the Christian from the final judgment. The justified believer is called to continue to "work out," that is, to actualize, his present salvation in holy fear and trembling (Phil. 2:12). Working out salvation does not mean working for salvation, but making salvation practical. Justification must be demonstrated by a sanctified life, which reveals deliverance from the bondage of sin and self. Paul's immediately following statement reveals that God generates in the believer at once the will to live right and effective power to do so: "For God is at work in you, both to will and to work for his good pleasure" (verse 13, RSV). Because God energizes the true believer constantly (Eph. 3:20), man can respond to God with moral rectitude. While the Christian's life will be "filled with the "fruits" of righteousness which come through Jesus Christ, to the glory and praise of God" (Phil. 1:11, RSV), he needs to realize that these "fruits" of good works are generated by God Himself: "he who began a good work in you will bring it to completion at the day of Jesus Christ" (verse 6, RSV; see also Eph. 2:8-10).

We may observe in the New Testament two distinct motivations for living a sanctified life: the atoning sacrifice of Christ and the apocalyptic judgment by Christ. Paul stresses for Christians the coming of the day of final reckoning: "For we must all appear before the judgment seat of Christ, so that each one may receive good or evil, according to what he has done in the body" (2 Cor. 5:10, RSV; cf. Rom. 14:10; 1 Cor. 3:15).

He warns church members more specifically: "Be sure of this, that no fornicator or impure man, or one who is covetous (that is, an idolater), has any inheritance in the kingdom of Christ and of God" (Eph. 5:5, RSV). One of the most solemn apostolic admonitions of Christian believers is:

"For if we sin deliberately after receiving the knowledge of the truth, there no longer remains a sacrifice for sins, but a fearful prospect of judgment, and a fury of fire which will consume the adversaries" (Heb. 10:26, 27, RSV). The reason for a final rejection of a professed Christian by Christ is not merely the lack of holy love and compassion (see Matt. 18:35; 25:41-46), but in particular the holding in contempt of Christ's atoning blood and insulting the grace of the Holy Spirit (Heb. 10:29).

Judgment according to works does not mean salvation on the basis of works or law observance. In the final analysis, salvation is equally by grace at the end as in the believer's first reconciliation with God. Only one new norm is applied in the final day of reckoning. Has the professed believer actually been a disciple of Christ? Has he or she appropriated the divine mercy by reflecting the Savior's love and goodness even in a small way? Can it be said of the Christian ultimately, "Well done, good and faithful servant; you have been faithful over a little . . ." (Matt. 25:23)? Because Christ's example of sinless perfection can never be fully equaled by His followers in this life and is reflected only in a small way, divine mercy is still needed in the final reckoning. Such an awareness will prompt the heart to everlasting praise, adoration, and worship of God as our Creator and Redeemer.

THE ADVENTIST DOCTRINE OF CHRIST'S HEAVENLY INTERCESSION

The distinctive tenet of Adventism is found in its sanctuary doctrine. (It is set forth in the church's statement of Fundamental Beliefs; elaborated in *Questions on Doctrine,* chaps. 29-36; and in *Seventh-day Adventist Believe,* chap. 23). A realistic encounter with Adventism must deal with this identifying core doctrine. For our present purpose we will approach the sanctuary doctrine from the perspective of salvation and the final judgment.

The Adventist view distinguishes between God's provision of salvation in the cross of Christ and its subsequent appropriation through faith by the individual believer, in harmony with Jesus' declaration in John 3:16. It further discerns in the heavenly intercession of the risen Christ two distinct phases, one prior to the final judgment, to be followed by His consummative phase during the final judgment or pre-Advent judgment.

The unique feature of Adventist soteriology is the belief that the believer's possession of salvation will be subject to an eschatological judicial act of ratification. While Adventism recognizes that Christ's intercession provides the genuine believer with the peace of a complete assurance of salvation, one's eternal destiny is still described as being legally unconfirmed prior to the final judgment of God. The fixation of one's eternal destiny still awaits its formal, judicial ratification, if the biblical revelation of a final judgment is integrated into the everlasting gospel. The recognition of a final justification of the redeemed believer in the last judgment constitutes a new theological development in Protestant theology.

The Reformation theology recognized the need for Christ's heavenly intercession, as brought to light in Romans I, Hebrews 8, and Revelation 1-3. However, Protestantism never discerned a two-phased intercession in heaven, in which the present justification must be confirmed by a formal forensic ratification in the last judgment.

Gunnar Pedersen observed striking similarity between this final judicial act of Christ and His present acts of justification of forgiveness. He states concerning E.G. White's eschatology:

"The conceptual similarities in the judicial meaning assigned to these terms [pardon and justification], both in their present and eschatological usages, including their soteriological rationale, are so striking that they cannot be ignored. In both temporal dimensions, the terms *pardon and justification* carry a forensic meaning expressive of the divine forgiveness and acceptance granted by the highest legal and judicial authority in the universe based exclusively on the provision of Christ. The conceptual similarities thus seem to create a real tension between the present existential and eschatological judicial dimensions in Adventist soteriology, but the problem, however, seems to be dissolved in the context of Ellen White's unique understanding of the mediatorial role of Christ" ("The Soteriology of Ellen G. White Compared with the Lutheran Formula of Concord" [unpublished Th.D. Diss., Andrews Univ., Berrien Springs, Mich., 1995], p. 200).

Adventists acknowledge that salvation can be received instantly through a faith relationship with the mediating Christ. It stresses at the same time the continuous intercessory ministry of Christ, even into the final judgment session. This view allows that forensic justification is seen also as a truly eschatological act, without infringing upon the gospel of Reformation theology. The function of sanctification, however, is limited to that of demonstrating the presence of genuine faith and of the believer's present salvation through the mediation of Christ. Not the degree of sanctification but the presence of discipleship is the primary issue with regard to the approval of the saints in the judgment. Sanctification has no meritorious function in humanity's salvation. This has not always been clearly stated by Adventist writers in the past.

Theologically speaking, Adventism has integrated the eschatological dimension of the final judgment in its soteriology, while Protestant theology has excluded it. Protestantism does not have a real temporal distinction between the existential reception and the final ratification of salvation, because it views both aspects basically as a present reality. Adventist theology is thus characterized by its dual temporal dimension of justification. The sanctuary doctrine includes the eschatological dimension in its soteriology, without denying the assurance of a present salvation. The ongoing mediatorial work of Christ during the last judgment resolves the seeming paradox and tension that Protestant theology experiences when it faces the twofold revelation that humanity is saved by faith as a present reality, while judged ultimately according to works as a future reality.

Both Lutheran and Reformed theologians have recognized the strained relationship between the Protestant doctrine of *sola fide* and the biblical teaching of judgment according to works, as illustrated by the ongoing debate over the seeming contradiction between Romans 3:28 and James 2:24 (see James P. Martin, *The Last Judgment in Protestant Theology From Orthodoxy to Ritschl* [Grand Rapids: Eerdmans, 1963]; Ole Modalslie, *Das Gericht nach den Werken* [Drammen, Norway: 1963]).

G. C. Berkouwer considered the Bible's insistence that all believers will come into judgment (2 Cor. 5:10) of such critical importance that he stated:

"Such reminders force us to ask ourselves whether the radical sola fide doctrine has failed to consider the whole of the multiform preaching of Scripture. For the objection is not based on a few incidental references to the eschatological judgment according to works. Judgment according to works is declared with sharp and sustained accents and we simply must listen with deep earnestness" (*Faith and Justification* [Grand Rapids: Eerdmans, 1954], p. 103).

The Adventist scholar Ivan T. Blazen has classified the various attempts to come to terms with this tension. After discussing four major approaches, he concludes that these attempts all either minimize or circumvent one of the other teaching of Scripture. Blazen sees the solution rather in a salvation-historical view that recognizes both aspects of "already" and "not yet." He explains:

"The essence of this view is that there is only one justification, and it accompanies the believer from the time of faith's inception (the 'already') all the way into the final judgment, where its reality and vitality are tested and attested by its fruits (the 'not yet'). . . . The new history God gives each believer is not over when he comes to Christ and is justified; it is just begun. At the end God asks for justification with its fruit—*not in the sense of the formula 'Faith plus works saves,'* but in the sense that justification is the source of sanctified fruit" (*"Justification and Judgment," 70 Weeks, Leviticus, Nature of Prophecy*, ed. F. B. Holbrook, Daniel and Revelation Committee Series, Biblical Research Institute, General Conference of Seventh-day Adventists [Hagerstown, Md.: Review and Herald Pub. Assn., 1986], vol. 3, p. 364.)

For Adventism justification is more than an anticipated last judgment. They believe that the New Testament relates present justification to both sanctification and the last judgment. Protestantism has formulated its Christology and soteriology apart from eschatological connections.

Adventism thus transcends the classical Protestant understanding regarding the single dimension of justification through its development of the continuous mediating work of Christ all the way into the last judgment. Gunnar Pedersen explains the contribution of Adventism in these words:

"The central Christological principle, with regard to Christ's continuous meritorious intercession prior to and during the act of judgment, apparently constitutes a new and intriguing dimension in the structure and form of Protestant soteriology, because (1) it provides a solution to the existing tension with regard to the integration of the Protestant doctrine of justification with the biblical doctrine of judgment without infringing upon its basic principles of soteriology, and (2) it seems to correlate with some of the new insights in current New Testament studies where the term *justification* is identified as an eschatological judicial concept. It is proposed in some of these New Testament studies that present justification may actually be interpreted as anticipated eschatology, or realized eschatology" ("The Soteriology of Ellen G. White," p. 207).

From an Adventist perspective the concept of a pre-Advent judgment in the heavenly sanctuary, as portrayed in Daniel 7:9-14, is not a conflict with the *sola gratia, sola fide* of the Reformation, but rather the consummation of the apostolic gospel.

INDEX

Lest We Forget . . .

"We have nothing to fear for the future, except as we shall forget the way the Lord has led us, and His teaching in our past history."—Ellen G. White.

JOSEPH BATES

The Real Founder of Seventh-day Adventism

George Knight sheds new light on the first theologian and real founder of the Adventist Church—a man who gave his estate to the Advent movement and spent the rest of his life in unpaid service to his King. 0-8280-1815-4.

3 WAYS TO SHOP

- Visit your local ABC
- Call 1-800-765-6955
- www.AdventistBookCenter.com

Prices and availability subject to change. Prices higher in Canada.

REVIEW AND HERALD®
PUBLISHING ASSOCIATION
Since 1861 | www.reviewandherald.com

Lest We Forget . . .

"We have nothing to fear for the future, except as we shall forget the way the Lord has led us, and His teaching in our past history."—Ellen G. White.

JOHN HARVEY KELLOGG

Pioneering Health Reformer

A surgeon, dietitian, inventor, administrator, religious leader, and author, Kellogg packed the accomplishments of many men into one lifetime. In this engrossing biography Richard Schwarz probes Kellogg's complicated, controversial, and unforgettable life. 0-8280-1939-8.

3 Ways to Shop

- Visit your local ABC
- Call 1-800-765-6955
- www.AdventistBookCenter.com

Prices and availability subject to change. Prices higher in Canada.

REVIEW AND HERALD® PUBLISHING ASSOCIATION
Since 1861 | www.reviewandherald.com

Lest We Forget . . .

"We have nothing to fear for the future, except as we shall forget the way the Lord has led us, and His teaching in our past history."—ELLEN G. WHITE.

W. W. PRESCOTT

Forgotten Giant of Adventism's Second Generation

Gilbert Valentine examines Prescott's impact on the church's educational system and how he helped reshape the church's theology and policies during a critical era. 0-8280-1892-8.

3 WAYS TO SHOP

- Visit your local ABC
- Call 1-800-765-6955
- www.AdventistBookCenter.com

Prices and availability subject to change. Prices higher in Canada.

REVIEW AND HERALD®
PUBLISHING ASSOCIATION
Since 1861 | www.reviewandherald.com

Lest We Forget . . .

"We have nothing to fear for the future, except as we shall forget the way the Lord has led us, and His teaching in our past history."—ELLEN G. WHITE.

JAMES WHITE

Innovator and Overcomer

Gerald Wheeler explores James White's personality, family, theology, and entrepreneurship—and reveals how personality traits and events shaped White as a man and leader.
0-8280-1719-0.

3 WAYS TO SHOP

- Visit your local ABC
- Call 1-800-765-6955
- www.AdventistBookCenter.com

Prices and availability subject to change. Prices higher in Canada.

REVIEW AND HERALD® PUBLISHING ASSOCIATION
Since 1861 | www.reviewandherald.com